THE SCOPE AND VARIETY OF U.S. DIPLOMATIC HISTORY

Volume II   Readings since 1900

Edward W. Chester
University of Texas, Arlington

PRENTICE HALL, Englewood Cliffs, NJ 07632

Library of Congress Cataloging-in-Publication Data

CHESTER, EDWARD W.
  The scope and variety of U.S. diplomatic history / Edward W. Chester.

  p. cm.
  Includes index.
  Contents: v. 1. Readings to 1913—v. 2. Readings since 1900.
  ISBN 0-13-796624-5 (v. 1).—ISBN 0-13-796632-6 (v. 2)
    1. United States—Foreign relations—Sources. I. Title.
E183.7.C464 1990
327.73—dc20   89-8722
                                                        CIP

Editorial/production supervision and
  interior design: Debbie Young and John Fleming
Cover design: Lundgren Graphics, Ltd.
Manufacturing buyer: Carol Bystrom

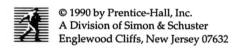 © 1990 by Prentice-Hall, Inc.
A Division of Simon & Schuster
Englewood Cliffs, New Jersey 07632

Printed in the United States of America

10 9 8 7 6 5 4 3 2 1

ISBN 0-13-796632-6

Prentice-Hall International (UK) Limited, London
Prentice-Hall of Australia Pty. Limited, Sydney
Prentice-Hall Canada Inc., Toronto
Prentice-Hall Hispanoamericana, S.A., Mexico
Prentice-Hall of India Private Limited, New Delhi
Prentice-Hall of Japan, Inc., Tokyo
Simon & Schuster Asia Pte. Ltd., Singapore
Editora Prentice-Hall do Brasil, Ltda., Rio de Janeiro

Contents

Preface   xiii

Acknowledgments   xv

---

24 Theodore Roosevelt and Latin America: Three Episodes   216

1903 President Theodore Roosevelt Discusses Events in Panama *216*
1903 The Loomis–Ehrman Correspondence at the Time
of the Panamanian Revolt Against Colombia *217*
1903 T. R.: "I Took the Canal Zone" *219*
1903 President Theodore Roosevelt Stands Up to Germany
at the Time of the Venezuelan Debt Crisis *220*
1905 A Report on Conditions in the Dominican Republic *222*
1905 The Roosevelt Corollary to the Monroe Doctrine (1904) *223*
1905 The Boston *Transcript* attacks the Roosevelt Corollary *224*

---

25 Japanese Imperialism and Japanese Immigrants   226

1905–6 President Theodore Roosevelt's Letters Criticizing
the West Coast for Its Treatment of Japanese Residents *226*
1906 The *Outlook* Takes an Unsympathetic Stance Toward the Japanese
on the Education Issue *227*
1907–8: The Gentlemen's Agreement with Japan
on the Immigration Issue *228*
1908 The Root–Takahira Agreement with Japan on the Far East *230*

26 Four Episodes in Big Stick Diplomacy   232

1904   Secretary of State John Hay and the Perdicaris
        Affair (Morocco)   232
1906   President Theodore Roosevelt and the Algeciras Conference
        on Morocco   234
1907   The America Naval Landing at the Time of the Jamaican
        Earthquake and the Reaction of Governor Swettenham   235
1907–9 The Global Tour of the U.S. Navy   237

27 Varied Interests of the Taft Administration   240

1909   Secretary of State Philander Chase Knox and the Chester
        Concession in Turkey   240
1909   The American Commission to Liberia: Instructions and Report   241
1911   The Canadian Reciprocity Issue   243
1911   The W. Morgan Shuster Financial Mission to Persia   244
1912   The Lodge Corollary to the Monroe Doctrine
        (Japan and Mexico)   246
1912   President William Howard Taft's Dollar Diplomacy   247

28 Woodrow Wilson's Mexican Policy   249

1913   Ambassador Henry Lane Wilson and the Huerta
        Government   249
1914   Admiral Frank Fletcher on the Arrest of the Crew
        of the *U.S.S. Dolphin* at Tampico   251
1916   An Eyewitness Account of Pancho Villa's Raid
        on Columbus, New Mexico   252

29 Diplomatic Episodes from the Wilson Presidency   254

1914   President Woodrow Wilson and the Repeal of the Panama
        Canal Tolls   254
1914   Theodore Roosevelt Attacks the Payment of a $25 Million
        Indemnity to Colombia   255
1915   Ambassador Henry Morgenthau, Sr.'s Account of the Turkish
        Massacre of Armenians   256
1917   The Lansing–Ishii Agreement with Japan   258
1920   Secretary of State Bainbridge Colby's Refusal Diplomatically
        to Recognize the Soviet Union   259

30 The United States as a Neutral During World War I   262

1915 The German Government's Newspaper Advertisement Warning Americans Not to Sail on the *Lusitania*   262

1916 The House–Grey Memorandum Stating that the United States Probably Would Join the War on the Side of Great Britain   263

1916 A Pro-Wilson Newspaper Advertisement from the Presidential Campaign Stressing the Peace with Honor Theme   264

1917 The Intercepted Zimmerman Telegram from Germany to Mexico   265

1917 Wilson's Cabinet and the Deteriorating Situation vis-à-vis Germany   266

31 The Declaration of War Against Germany   268

1917 Wilson's Call for a Declaration of War Against Germany   268

1917 The Louisville *Courier Journal's* "Vae Victis" Editorial Favoring the Declaration of War   269

1917 Senator Robert La Follette, Sr. Opposes U.S. Entry into World War I   271

1917 Ambassador to Great Britain Walter H. Page Evaluates Wilson's Role in World War I   272

1918 Woodrow Wilson's Fourteen Points Address to Congress   273

32 The Postwar Peace Settlement   277

1919 The War Guilt Clause (Article 231) of the Treaty of Versailles and Article 10 of the Covenant of the League of Nations   277

1919 Robert Lansing Assesses the Versailles Conference (1921)   278

1919 Herbert Hoover Discusses the Versailles Conference (1958)   279

1919 Woodrow Wilson's Final Tour Speech on Behalf of the League of Nations   280

1919 Senator Henry Cabot Lodge Explains his Reservations About the Peace Treaty (1925)   281

1920 Isolationist Senator William E. Borah's Address Critical of the League of Nations   283

1919 William Randolph Hearst Attacks the League in the New York *Evening Journal*   285

33 Major Foreign Policy Developments Under Harding, Coolidge, and Hoover   287

1921   Secretary of State Charles Evans Hughes and the Washington
        Disarmament Conference (1925)   *287*
1921   The U.S. Government and American Petroleum Interests
        in the Netherlands East Indies   *289*
1921   The Dispatching of an American Financial Mission to Persia
        Headed by Arthur Millspaugh   *290*
1925   The Bombing Raids of U.S. Flyers in Morocco   *292*
1928   The Pact of Paris (Kellogg–Briand Pact) Renouncing War
        as an Instrument of National Policy   *294*
1928   The Clark Memorandum Terminating the Roosevelt Corollary
        to the Monroe Doctrine   *295*
1930   Secretary of State Henry Stimson and the Presence of Slave
        Labor in Liberia   *297*
1932   The Stimson Doctrine: Japan and Manchuria   *298*

34 U.S. Diplomacy in the First Roosevelt Administration   300

1933   Ambassador to Cuba Sumner Welles on F.D.R.'s Promulgation
        of the Good Neighbor Policy (1944)   *300*
1933   Herbert Feis on F.D.R.'s "Sabotaging" of the London Economic
        Conference (1966)   *301*
1933   The United States and the Soviet Union Establish Diplomatic
        Relations (1966)   *303*
1935   Secretary of State Cordell Hull and the Imposition of Sanctions
        During the Italo–Ethiopian War   *305*
1936–41   Ambassador William Phillips and the Failure to Prevent War
        Between America and Italy (1952)   *307*
1936   A Retrospective Look: The Nye Committee, the Munition Makers,
        and World War I   *309*
1936   President Franklin D. Roosevelt's *I Hate War* Speech   *311*

35 The Pre-World War II Years   313

1937   The Ludlow Amendment Calling for a National Referendum
        on Declarations of War   *313*
1937   F.D.R.'s Quarantine Speech Directed Against International
        Aggressors   *314*

1937   A Representative Negative Assessment: The Chicago
Tribune   *315*

1933–37   Ambassador to Germany William E. Dodd Assesses the
Situation in Germany (1941)   *317*

1939   Ambassador to Russia Joseph Davies and the Soviet–German
Alliance (1941)   *318*

36   The United States as a Neutral, 1939–40   321

1939   The Chicago *Tribune*: "This Is Not Our War"   *321*

1939   Franklin Roosevelt Asks for the Repeal of the Arms
Embargo   *322*

1940   Prime Minister Winston Churchill's Letter to F.D.R.
vis-à-vis the Destroyers-for-Bases Deal   *323*

1940   The St. Louis *Post-Dispatch* Attacks Franklin Roosevelt
as a Dictator Who Had Committed an Act of War   *324*

1940   F.D.R. Seeks a Third Term: His Again and Again Speech   *326*

1940   The Committee to Defend America by Aiding the Allies   *327*

37   America Enters the War, 1941   330

1941   Franklin Roosevelt's Four Freedoms Message to Congress   *330*

1941   Senator Burton K. Wheeler Attacks Lend–Lease   *331*

1941   F.D.R. and Winston Churchill Draw Up the Atlantic Charter   *333*

1940   The U.S. Government Limits the Shipment of Aviation Gasoline
to Japan over Japanese Protests   *334*

1941   Ambassador Joseph Grew on the Proposed Franklin
Roosevelt–Prince Konoye Meeting (1952)   *335*

1941   Nomura and Kurusu Criticize the American Proposal to Resolve
the Differences Between the United States and Japan   *337*

1941   F.D.R. Asks Congress for a Declaration of War Against Japan
After the Attack on Pearl Harbor   *339*

38   Wartime Relations with Various Countries   341

1938–42   The Mexican Expropriation of American and British Oil
Properties   *341*

1941   Iceland Complains About the Behavior of American Military
Personnel   *343*

1942   Restrictions on U.S. Citizens in the Azores   *345*

1942–45   Ambassador Carlton J. H. Hayes and Franco's Spain   *347*
1942   Robert Murphy and the Darlan Deal vis-à-vis French North Africa   *349*
1944   The Recall of General Joseph Stilwell from China   *351*

39 The Wartime Conferences and the United Nations   354

1943   Wendell Willkie's *One World*: A Farewell to Isolationism   *354*
1943   The Casablanca Conference: Unconditional Surrender (Robert E. Sherwood, 1946)   *356*
1943   The Teheran Conference: F.D.R. and Stalin Meet (Frances Perkins, 1946)   *357*
1944   The Quebec Conference: The Morgenthau Plan for Dismantling Germany   *359*
1945   The Yalta Conference: A Defense of Roosevelt (Edward Stettinius, 1949)   *360*
1945   The Yalta Conference: The Role of Alger Hiss (James Byrnes, 1958)   *362*
1945   Senator William Langer Opposes the United Nations   *363*

40 Postwar Approaches to Foreign Policy   365

1946   Henry Wallace's Madison Square Garden Address Criticizing Harry Truman's Foreign Policy   *365*
1947   George Kennan's Anonymous *Foreign Affairs* Article on Containing Soviet Expansion   *366*
1967   Kennan Reassesses Containment Two Decades Later   *367*
1947   Former Isolationist Senator Arthur Vandenberg Endorses a Bipartisan Foreign Policy   *369*
1951   Senator Robert A. Taft and Neo-isolationism: *A Foreign Policy for Americans*   *370*
1951   Senator Joseph McCarthy and Betrayal: *America's Retreat from Victory*   *372*

41 Milestones in Containment, 1947–49   375

1947   The Truman Doctrine: Military Protection for Greece and Turkey   *375*
1947   The Chicago *Tribune* and the Truman Doctrine   *377*

1947 Under Secretary of State Will Clayton Analyzes the Marshall
Plan   *378*

1948–49 Ambassador to the Soviet Union Walter Bedell Smith Discusses
the Berlin Blockade   *380*

1949 The Point IV Program: Technical Assistance to the Underdeveloped
Nations   *382*

1949 Senator Robert A. Taft Opposes American Entry into NATO   *384*

42 Other Episodes in Truman Diplomacy — 386

1946 U.S. Oil Policy in the Postwar Era   *386*

1946 Assessing the Perón Era: The Argentine Blue Book   *388*

1947 General Douglas MacArthur on the Reconstruction of Japan   *389*

1948 President Harry Truman Recognizes the Independent State
of Israel (1956)   *391*

1945–46 General Marshall's Mission to Civil War-Torn China (1956)   *393*

1950 President Harry Truman's Statement on the Status of Taiwan   *395*

1950 Secretary of State Dean Acheson's Far Eastern Policy Excludes
South Korea from the American Defense Perimeter   *396*

43 The Korean War, 1950–53 — 398

1950 First Secretary Harold Noble Describes the Outbreak of the Korean
War (1975)   *398*

1950 The Authority of the President to Repel the North Korean
Attack   *399*

1950 General Douglas MacArthur's Letter to Representative Joseph
Martin: "There Is No Substitute for Victory"   *401*

1951 Harry Truman Recalls Douglas MacArthur (1956)   *402*

1950–53 Secretary of State Dean Acheson Views the Korean War
Retrospectively (1969)   *403*

1953 President Dwight Eisenhower's Plague-on-Both-Your-Houses
Attitude Toward Korea   *405*

1950–3 Disunity among the Allies: General James Van Fleet Views
the Korean War   *406*

44 The Diplomatic Ideology of the Eisenhower Administration — 408

1953 Secretary of State John Foster Dulles's Captive
Peoples Speech   *408*

1954   An Unwelcome Proposal: The Bricker Amendment   *409*
1956   John Foster Dulles's Policy of Brinkmanship   *411*

45 Pivotal Foreign Policy Episodes, 1953–61   413

1954   President Dwight Eisenhower Promises Continuing Aid
to South Vietnam After the French Depart   *413*
1954   Repulsing the Communist Threat to Guatemala (1957)   *414*
1955   House Joint Resolution Authorizing the President to Use
American Forces to Protect Taiwan   *416*
1956   Withdrawal of U.S. Support for the Aswan Dam in Egypt   *417*
1956   President Eisenhower Mediates on President Nasser's Seizure
of the Suez Canal   *418*
1957   The Eisenhower Doctrine for the Middle East   *420*
1958   The United States Sends Troops into Lebanon   *421*
1958   A Mob Attacks Vice President Richard Nixon's Motorcade
at Caracas, Venezuela (1962)   *423*
1959   Vice President Nixon's Confrontation with Soviet Leader Nikita
Khrushchev (1962)   *425*
1960   The U–2 Incident: The Downing of an American Spy Plane
over the Soviet Union   *427*
1960   Dwight Eisenhower Offers a Program for Africa to the United
Nations General Assembly   *429*

46 American Diplomacy Under Kennedy, Johnson, and Dean Rusk   431

1960   Senator John Kennedy's Approach to Foreign Policy:
A Twelve-point Agenda   *431*
1961   J. F. K. Establishes the Peace Corps   *433*
1961   John Kennedy Proposes an Alliance for Progress
for Latin America   *434*
1961   The *New York Times* Attacks Kennedy for Lying
About the Bay of Pigs Invasion   *437*
1962   John Kennedy Demands the Withdrawal of Soviet Offensive
Missiles from Cuba   *438*
1962   Attorney General Robert Kennedy on the Cuban
Missile Crisis (1969)   *440*
1962   Under Secretary of State George Ball on American Policy in the
Revolution-torn Congo   *442*
1963   John Kennedy's *Ich Bin Ein Berliner* Speech   *444*

1963 The Nuclear Test Ban Treaty with the Soviet Union   *445*
1964 Anti-American Riots in Panama and the Future
of the Canal (1971)   *446*
1965 American Intervention in the Dominican Republic   *448*
1967 Lyndon Johnson Meets with Aleksei Kosygin at Glassboro,
New Jersey (1971)   *450*

47 The Interminable Vietnamese Conflict   452

1961 President John Kennedy and the Neutralization of Laos   *452*
1964 The Gulf of Tonkin Resolution Authorizing American Military
Action in Southeast Asia   *453*
1964 L.B.J.'s Campaign Rhetoric on the Vietnam War   *456*
1967 The Knight Newspapers Criticize American Involvement
in Vietnam   *457*
1968 Senator Ernest Gruening Attacks South Vietnam
as a Dictatorship   *459*
1968 L.B.J. Halts the Bombing of North Vietnam (1971)   *460*
1970 President Richard Nixon's Incursion into Cambodia   *462*
1970 The McGovern–Hatfield Amendment and U.S. Withdrawal
from Vietnam   *464*
1971 The Senator Mike Gravel Edition of the Pentagon Papers   *466*
1972 National Security Advisor Henry Kissinger's Peace Negotiations
with Pham Van Dong (1982)   *468*
1975 Henry Kissinger on the Fall of the Saigon Government   *469*

48 The Foreign Policy of Nixon, Ford, and Henry Kissinger   472

1969 President Richard Nixon's Guam Doctrine and the Future
of Asia   *472*
1971 The Nixon Administration Tilts Toward Pakistan in Its War
with India (1979)   *473*
1972 Secretary of State William Rogers Endorses the Two
Chinas Policy   *475*
1972 Richard Nixon's Visit to Mainland China (1978)   *476*
1972 The Salt I Treaty with the Soviet Union   *478*
1973 Henry Kissinger on the Meaning of *Détente* (1982)   *480*
1973 Richard Nixon's Veto of the War Powers Resolution   *481*
1975 President Gerald Ford, Cambodia, and the *Mayaguez*
Crisis (1979)   *483*

49 New Diplomatic Initiatives Under Jimmy Carter   485

1976   Eastern Europe and the Ford–Carter Presidential Debates   *485*

1977   Jimmy Carter's Notre Dame Address on Foreign Policy   *486*

1977   The Two Panama Canal Treaties (1982)   *488*

1977   A Leading Critic of the Canal Treaties: Representative Daniel Flood   *490*

1978   Egypt and Israel: The Camp David Negotiations (1982)   *491*

1978   The Carter Administration Recognizes Mainland China   *493*

1979   Secretary of State Cyrus Vance and the Fall of the Somoza Regime in Nicaragua   *496*

1979–81   Deputy Secretary of State Warren Christopher Discusses the Iranian Hostage Crisis (1985)   *498*

1977–81   The Carter Foreign Policy in Retrospect: Zbigniew Brzezinski (1983)   *500*

50 Ronald Reagan and the Cold War   503

1983   Ronald Reagan on the Soviet Union as an "Evil Empire"   *503*

1983   The American Liberation of Marxist Grenada   *504*

1985   The Kissinger Commission Report on Nicaragua   *506*

1986   The American Retaliatory Attack on Libya   *508*

1987   The Inouye Committee and the Iran–Contra Affair   *510*

1987   Reagan and Gorbachev Thaw the Cold War   *511*

Proper Name and Topical Index   I-1

Geographical Index   I-11

Preface

Today, the State Department has to deal with every country on the face of the earth, some of them on a daily basis. A review of the monographs and articles published on U.S. diplomatic history since World War II reveals a similarly widening preoccupation with nations previously ignored. Unfortunately, however, both diplomatic history textbooks and books of readings have followed a more traditional path and have failed to place an appropriate emphasis on the newly independent and economically developing countries of the Third World. In focusing on treaties and diplomatic correspondence they have failed to explore adequately other important bodies of primary source material. It is the objective of this volume to remedy these shortcomings as follows:

1. The author has a special research interest in American relations with the Third World. Accordingly, he has selected several dozen items from Africa (especially Liberia), the Middle East, and the Atlantic military base islands (Iceland, the Azores, and Jamaica). His extensive research into U.S. petroleum diplomacy also has yielded a few items which appear in the section of the volume covering the years after 1900.

2. Although he has included quite a bit of diplomatic correspondence—including some unpublished documents from the National Archives—he has almost totally avoided treaties, aside from Article 231 (the war guilt clause) of the Treaty of Versailles and Article X of the Covenant of the League of Nations. In his opinion, there are few types of primary source materials which are more boring than treaties, and few less likely to engage the attention of the reader. Therefore, he instead has explored the letters, diaries, speeches, memoirs, and writings of those individuals involved in the shaping of American diplomacy, both in the legislative and executive branches. Selections from these comprise an important part of this volume.

Aside from our Presidents and Secretaries of State, there have been other individuals in the President's cabinet, members of the State Department oligarchy, and various Presidential advisors whose published works throw new light on U.S. foreign relations. These include Gideon Welles, Colonel Edward House, David Houston, Herbert Feis, Henry Morgenthau, Jr., Robert E. Sherwood, John Loftus, George W. Ball, Zbigniew Brzezinski, and Warren Christopher. Various ambassadors and diplomats also have left us their memoirs, including Nicholas

Trist, Townsend Harris, John Stevens, Henry Lane Wilson, Henry Morgenthau, Sr., Walter Hines Page, Joseph Grew, Joseph Davies, Carlton Hayes, Robert Murphy, George Kennan, Walter B. Smith, and John B. Martin.

Many members of Congress, too, have left behind a written legacy, the most important aspect of which for this book of readings is their speeches on various foreign policy issues. There were great debates in Congress on foreign policy issues at the time of the War of 1812, the Oregon controversy, the Spanish–American War, the League of Nations, and the Vietnam War, to cite only five occasions. Such prominent members of the Senate and the House as Fisher Ames, William H. Seward, Charles Sumner, Albert J. Beveridge, Robert LaFollette, Sr., William E. Borah, Arthur Vandenberg, William Langer, and Robert Taft have left to posterity memorable speeches on the vital issues of their day. Then there are various proposals introduced by members of Congress, including Abraham Lincoln's Spot Resolution, the Ludlow Amendment, and the Bricker Amendment, which remain of interest today even if they did not pass.

3. One of the greatest shortcomings of books of readings on American diplomatic history is their failure to include adequate data on Congressional, journalistic, and public attitudes toward the events and incidents which they cover. Too great an emphasis has been placed on diplomacy per se at the expense of these other important factors. Having researched the latter thoroughly, the author is in a position to preface each selection with an introduction setting forth breakdowns on foreign policy votes in Congress by party and by section, and mentioning those individuals who played a major role in the debate. In addition, he summarizes the more important journalistic reactions, where available. The result is a collection of documents set against an expanded background which will make them much more meaningful to both scholars and students.

4. In some cases, these books of readings include an entire document, when only one part of it may be genuinely interesting in retrospect. Some of these items profit from careful editing, and the author has attempted to provide this here. Moreover, if only the essential part(s) of each document is included, then there is room in the book of readings for more items and for an introduction to every document. Accordingly, it is then possible to offer a volume which truly reflects the scope and variety of American diplomatic history, and which accordingly will engage the attention of the interested reader throughout.

Hopefully the author has produced a book of readings which combines the intellect of a Leland Baldwin with the excitement of a Thomas A. Bailey—the two American historians who have most influenced his own research and writing—as he has attempted to study the past in new ways. If he has added a new dimension to the reader's understanding of American diplomatic history, then he will feel that he has succeeded in this latest undertaking of his.

Dr. Edward W. Chester
Professor of History
University of Texas at Arlington

Acknowledgments

The author wishes to thank the University of Texas at Arlington Library, especially Ms. Frances Cravens of the Photocopy Center, Ms. Lila Hedrick of the Interlibrary Loan office, and Ms. Pam Morris of Government Documents for aiding him in the compilation of the documents which make up this volume. In addition, he did research at the Library of Congress, and at other libraries in the Dallas–Fort Worth metropolitan area. He also wishes to thank Ms. Ellen Stallones for typing volume one of this manuscript, Ms. Joan Borgmeyer for typing volume two, and Ms. Pam Pezanosky for typing the permissions.

With regard to the latter, the author would like to express his deep appreciation to the following publishers and individuals for giving permission to reprint material which is under copyright. Variations from the standard phrasing are at the request of those granting permission:

- Stanley L. Falk, "Some Contemporary Views of the Monroe Doctrine," reprinted from *Américas*, bimonthly magazine published by the General Secretariat of the Organization of American States in English and Spanish.
- The Associated Press for "Excerpts from President's Speech to National Association of Evangelicals."
- Bantam Books for Jimmy Carter, *Keeping Faith*.
- Beacon Press for William Phillips, *Ventures In Diplomacy*
- "President in Chicago Says Peace Loving Lands Must Act," "Not Our War," and "Here We Go Again" copyrighted, Chicago *Tribune* Company, all rights reserved, used with permission.
- Columbia University Press for Harold Syrett, *The Papers of Alexander Hamilton*.
- Devin—Adair Publishers for Joseph McCarthy, *America's Retreat from Victory*.
- Excerpts from *Six Crises* by Richard M. Nixon. Copyright 1962 by Richard M. Nixon; John Bartlow Martin, *Overtaken by Events*. Copyright 1966 by John Bartlow Martin; *Diplomat among Warriors* by Robert Murphy. Copyright 1964 by Robert Murphy; *Roosevelt and the Russians* by Edward R. Stettinius, Jr. Copyright 1949 by Stettinius Foundation, Inc.; *A Foreign Policy for Americans*. Copyright 1951 by Robert A. Taft. These items reprinted by permission of Doubleday, a division of Bantam, Doubleday, Dell Publishing Group, Inc.
- The Emporia *Gazette* for Walter Johnson, *Selected Letters of William Allen White*.
- Exposition Press for L. C. Wright, *United States Policy towards Egypt*;

- Excerpts from *Power and Principle: Memoirs of the National Security Adviser, 1977-1981* by Zbigniew Brzezinski. Copyright 1983 by Zbigniew Brzezinski. Reprinted by permission of Farrar, Straus and Giroux, Inc.
- Reprinted by permission of the publisher from Charles Callan Tansill, *The Foreign Policy of Thomas F. Bayard, 1885-1897* (New York: Fordham University Press, 1940), pp. 141, 208. Copyright.
- Excerpts from *Ambassador Dodd's Diary*, Volume Two by William E. Dodd, Jr., and Martha Dodd, copyright 1941 by Harcourt Brace Jovanovich, Inc., and renewed 1968 by Kathryn Dodd, reprinted by permission of the publisher.
- Excerpts from *My Three Years in Moscow* by Walter Bedell Smith, copyright 1949 by Walter Bedell Smith. Excerpts from *The Time for Decision* by Sumner Welles, copyright 1944 by Sumner Welles. Excerpts from *A Time to Heal* by Gerald Ford, copyright 1979 by Gerald R. Ford. Excerpts from *Roosevelt and Hopkins*, Revised Edition by Robert E. Sherwood, copyright 1948, 1950 by Robert E. Sherwood. Excerpts from *Kennedy* by Theodore C. Sorensen, Copyright 1965 by Theodore C. Sorensen. These items reprinted by permission of Harper & Row, Publishers, Inc.
- Harper and Row Publishers, Inc. for Charles E. Hughes, *The Pathway of Peace* (1925); Ray Stannard Baker and William E. Dodd, Editors, *Woodrow Wilson* (1927); Henry Morgenthau, Jr., *Germany is Our Problem* (1945); John F. Kennedy, *The Strategy of Peace* (1960); Richard B. Morris, *John Jay* (1980); John Bassett Moore, Editor, *The Works of James Buchanan* (1908-11).
- Elting E. Morison, Editor, *Letters of Theodore Roosevelt*, copyright 1952, 1954 by the President and Fellows of Harvard College.
- D. C. Heath for Allan Nevins, *American Press Opinion*.
- From *The Vantage Point: Perspectives of the Presidency 1963-1969* by Lyndon Baines Johnson, copyright 1971 by HEC Public Affairs Foundation. Reprinted by permission of Henry Holt and Company, Inc.
- The Johns Hopkins Press for Frederick J. Dobney, Editor, *Selected Papers of Will Clayton*; W. Stull Holt, *Treaties Defeated by the Senate*; Howard K. Beale, *Theodore Roosevelt and the Rise of America to World Power*.
- From *The Turbulent Era*. Volume II by Joseph C. Grew, copyright 1952 by Joseph C. Grew. Copyright renewed 1980 by Elizabeth Lyon, Anita J. English, and Lilla Levitt. Reprinted by permission of Houghton Mifflin Company.
- Indiana University Press for Sidney Kraus, Editor, *The Great Debates*.
- Reprinted by permission from *Pulitzer Prize Editorials* by W. David Sloan. Copyright 1980 by Iowa State University Press, Ames, Iowa.
- Irvington Publishers for Young Him Kim, *East Asia's Turbulent Century*.
- Kampmann and Company for Jessie Peterson and Thelma Cox Knoles, *Pancho Villa*.
- Alfred A. Knopf for Elizabeth Brett White, *American Opinion of France*. From *The Monroe Doctrine and American Expansionism: 1843-1849* by Frederick Merk, with the collaboration of Lois Bannister Merk. Copyright 1966 by Frederick Merk. Reprinted by permission of Alfred A. Knopf, Inc.
- From *Years of Upheaval* by Henry Kissinger, copyright 1982, by Henry A. Kissinger. From *1933: Characters in Crisis* by Herbert Feis, copyright 1966 by Herbert Feis. From *White House Years* by Henry Kissinger, copyright 1979, by Henry A. Kissinger. From *Memoirs: 1925-1950* by George F. Kennan, copyright 1967, by George F. Kennan. These items reprinted by permission of Little, Brown and Company.

* Reprinted with permission of Charles Scribner's Sons, an imprint of Macmillan Publishing Company, from *The Works of Theodore Roosevelt*, Vol. XX. Copyright 1925 Charles Scribner's Sons, copyright renewed; from *The Senate and the League of Nations* by Henry Cabot Lodge, copyright 1925 Charles Scribner's Sons, copyright renewed 1953; from *United States Policy toward China* by Paul H. Clyde, copyright 1940 Duke University Press; copyright renewed 1968 Paul H. Clyde. Also a courtesy credit to MacMillan Publishing Company for Worthington Chauncey Ford, Editor, *The Writings of John Quincy Adams*.

* McGraw Hill Book Company for Herbert Hoover, *The Ordeal of Woodrow Wilson*.

* Monumenta Nipponica for Mario Cosenza, Editor, *The Complete Journal of Townsend Harris*.

* The New York *Times* for "The Right Not to Be Lied To;" "A Belated Confession;" "Excerpts from President's Speech to National Association of Evangelicals;" "Notice–Lusitania;" "You Are Working;" and "Dictator Roosevelt Commits an Act of War."

* Reprinted from *Present at the Creation, My Years in the State Department*, by Dean Acheson, copyright 1969 by Dean Acheson. Reprinted from *Thirteen Days, A Memoir of the Cuban Missile Crisis*, by Robert F. Kennedy; copyright 1971, 1969 by W. W. Norton and Company Inc.; copyright 1968 by McCall Corporation. Reprinted from *The Eisenhower Diaries*, Edited by Robert H. Ferrell. Copyright 1981 by Robert H. Ferrell. These items reprinted by permission of W. W. Norton & Company, Inc.

* Octagon Books, A Division of Hippocrene Books, Inc. for Earl Swisher, Editor, *China's Management of the American Barbarians*.

* *A Soldier Speaks: Public Papers and Speeches of General of the Army Douglas Mac-Arthur*, Major Vorin E. Whan, Jr., editor. (Frederick A. Praeger, New York, 1965.) Reprinted with permission of Praeger Publishers.

* From *Grassroots* by George McGovern, copyright 1977 by George McGovern. Reprinted by permission of Random House, Inc.

* From *The Collected Works of Abraham Lincoln* edited by Roy P. Basler. Copyright 1953 by The Abraham Lincoln Association. Reprinted by permission of Rutgers, the State University of New Jersey.

* Santa Fe *New Mexican* for "Unmasked" and "Pure Prussianism."

* St. John's University Press for Chin–tung Liang, *General Stilwell in China 1942-1944*.

* Wendell Willkie, *One World*; copyright 1943 by Wendell L. Willkie. Renewed 1970 by Philip H. Willkie. Joseph E. Davies, *Mission to Moscow*; copyright 1941 by Joseph E. Davies. Renewed 1969 by Eleanor Davies Ditzen, Rahel Davies Broun, and Emler Davies Grosjean. These items reprinted by permission of Simon and Schuster, Inc.

* Stuart Gerry Brown, Editor, *The Autobiography of James Monroe* (Syracuse: Syracuse University Press, 1959), pp. 165-66. By permission of Syracuse University Press.

* Robert W. Johannsen, Editor, *The Letters of Stephen A. Douglas*; copyright 1961 by the Board of Trustees of the University of Illinois. Reprinted by permission of the author and the University of Illinois Press.

* *The Papers of Henry Clay: 1*, edited by James F. Hopkins; copyright 1959 by the University Press of Kentucky. *The Papers of Henry Clay: 5*, edited by James F. Hopkins and Mary W. M. Hargreaves; copyright 1973 by the University Press of Kentucky.

- From *The Papers of John Marshall*, edited by William C. Stinchcombe; copyright 1979 The University of North Carolina Press. Reprinted by permission.
- Reprinted by permission of the University of Tennessee Press from Paul S. Holbo, *Tarnished Expansion: The Alaska Scandal, the Press, and Congress*; copyright 1983 by the University of Tennessee Press.
- The University of Washington Press for Raymond Esthus, *Theodore Roosevelt and Japan* and for Harold Noble, *Embassy at War*.
- Unwin Hyman Limited for R.C.F. Maugham, *The Republic of Liberia*.
- From *The Roosevelt I Knew* by Frances Perkins; copyright 1946 by Frances Perkins. Copyright renewed 1974 by Susanna W. Coggeshall. From *Henry Wallace, Harry Truman and the Cold War* by Richard Walton; copyright 1976 by Richard Walton. For these items all rights reserved. Reprinted by permission of Viking Penguin, a division of Penguin Books USA, Inc.
- Reprinted by permission of Warner Books *RN: The Memoirs of Richard Nixon*, copyright 1978 by Richard Nixon.
- *William and Mary Quarterly* for "Hamilton on the Louisiana Purchase."
- Yale University Press for Warren Christopher, *American Hostages in Iran*.
- James F. Byrnes Foundation for James F. Byrnes, *All in One Lifetime*.
- *Memoirs* by Harry S. Truman, *Years of Trial and Hope*, published by Doubleday and Co., Inc., 1956, used by permission of Margaret Truman Daniel.
- Mike Gravel for the Senator Gravel Edition of *The Pentagon Papers*.
- Grateful acknowledgment is hereby made to Dr. Henry A. Kissinger for the use of quotations from his book entitled *Years of Upheaval*, copyright 1982 by Dr. Henry A. Kissinger.
- Helen Kitchen for Helen Kitchen, Editor, *Footnotes to the Congo Story*.
- Mrs. William Tucker, Jr. and Mr. Carroll Hayes for Carlton J. H. Hayes, *Wartime Mission to Spain*.
- William A. Williams for William A. Williams, *The Shaping of American Diplomacy*.

THE SCOPE
AND VARIETY
OF U.S.
DIPLOMATIC HISTORY

Theodore Roosevelt and Latin America: 24 Three Episodes

1903 President Theodore Roosevelt Discusses Events in Panama

No aspect of the Theodore Roosevelt Presidency is as controversial as the events surrounding the revolt by means of which Panama obtained its independence from Colombia and then gave the United States permission to build an isthmian canal through the new republic. (The Colombian government had balked at approving a canal treaty.) The day before the revolt broke out in Panama, the U.S.S. Nashville had arrived there, and the American naval forces prevented Colombian troops from invading the isthmus. When Theodore Roosevelt sent a message to Congress on January 4, 1904, he took the position that the almost total absence of bloodshed on the isthmus during the revolt was due to American intervention. (It was not the first time that the U.S. military had landed there in time of crisis.) Nor, according to Roosevelt, had any American government official helped to incite the rebellion, which he claimed had the unanimous support of the Panamanian people.

SOURCE: U.S. Department of State, *Foreign Relations of the United States 1903* (Washington: Government Printing Office, 1904). See pp. 272-73.

DOCUMENT:

It thus clearly appears that the fact that there was no bloodshed on the Isthmus was directly due—and only due—to the prompt and firm enforcement by the United States of its traditional policy. During the past forty years revolutions and attempts at revolutions have succeeded one another with monotonous regularity on the Isthmus, and again and again United States sailors and marines have been landed as they were landed in this instance and under similar instructions to protect the transit. One of these revolutions resulted in three years of warfare; and the aggregate of bloodshed and misery caused by them has been incalculable.

The fact that in this last revolution not a life was lost, save that of the man killed by the shells of the Colombian gunboat, and no property destroyed, was due to the action which I have described. We, in effect, policed the Isthmus in the interest of its inhabitants and of our own national needs, and for the good of the entire civilized world. Failure to act as the Administration acted would have meant great waste of life, great suffering, great destruction of property; all of which was avoided by the firmness and prudence with which Commander Hubbard carried out his orders and prevented either party from attacking the other. Our action was for the peace both of Colombia and of Panama. It is earnestly to be hoped that there will be no unwise conduct on our part which may encourage Colombia to embark on a war which can not result in her regaining control of the Isthmus, but which may cause much bloodshed and suffering.

I hesitate to refer to the injurious insinuations which have been made of complicity by this Government in the revolutionary movement in Panama. They are as destitute of foundation as of propriety. The only excuse for my mentioning them is the fear lest unthinking persons might mistake for acquiescence the silence of mere self-respect. I think proper to say, therefore, that no one connected with this Government had any part in preparing, inciting, or encouraging the late revolution on the Isthmus of Panama, and that save from the reports of our military and naval officers, given above, no one connected with this Government had any previous knowledge of the revolution except such as was accessible to any person of ordinary intelligence who read the newspapers and kept up a current acquaintance with public affairs.

By the unanimous action of its people, without the firing of a shot—with a unanimity hardly before recorded in any similar case—the people of Panama declared themselves an independent republic. Their recognition by this Government was based upon a state of facts in no way dependent for its justification upon our action in ordinary cases. I have not denied, nor do I wish to deny, either the validity or the propriety of the general rule that a new state should not be recognized as independent till it has shown its ability to maintain its independence. This rule is derived from the principle of nonintervention, and as a corollary of that principle has generally been observed by the United States. But, like the principle from which it is deduced, the rule is subject to exceptions; and there are in my opinion clear and imperative reasons why a departure from it was justified and even required in the present instance. These reasons embrace, first, our treaty rights; second, our national interests and safety; and, third, the interests of collective civilization.

1903 The Loomis–Ehrman Correspondence at the Time of the Panamanian Revolt against Colombia

The exchange of correspondence between William Loomis, the Acting Secretary of State, and Felix Ehrman, the American Vice Consul at Panama City, gives a somewhat less neutral picture of U.S. activities at the time of the revolt than Roosevelt's public utterances. Secretary of State John Hay was then absent from Washington. One may only wonder if his reactions to the Panamanian crisis would have been the same as those of the obviously pro-Panama Loomis.

SOURCE: U.S. Congress, *Correspondence on Treaty with Colombia for Construction of Isthmian Canal*, Senate *Documents* No. 51, 58th Congress, 2nd Session, 1904. See p. 104.

DOCUMENT:

DEPARTMENT OF STATE, *Washington, November 3, 1903.*
(Sent 3.40 p.m. to the consulate-general at Panama and the consulate at Colon)

Uprising on Isthmus reported. Keep Department promptly and fully informed.

LOOMIS, *Acting.*

Mr. Ehrman to Mr. Hay. PANAMA, *November 3, 1903.* **(Received 8.15 p.m.)**

No uprising yet. Reported will be in the night. Situation is critical.

EHRMAN.

Mr. Ehrman to Mr. Hay. [Telegram.] PANAMA, *November 3, 1903.* **(Received 9.50 p.m.)**

Uprising occurred to-night, 6; no bloodshed. Army and navy officials taken prisoners. Government will be organized to-night, consisting three consuls, also cabinet. Soldiers changed. Supposed same movement will be effected in Colon. Order prevails so far. Situation serious. Four hundred soldiers landed Colon to-day [from] Barranquilla.

EHRMAN.

Mr. Loomis to Mr. Ehrman. [Telegram.] DEPARTMENT OF STATE, *Washington, November 3, 1903.* **(Sent 11.18 p.m.)**

Message sent to *Nashville* to Colon may not have been delivered. Accordingly see that following message is sent to *Nashville* immediately:
    NASHVILLE, Colon: In the interests of peace make every effort to prevent Government troops at Colon from proceeding to Panama. The transit of the Isthmus must be kept open and order maintained. Acknowledge. (Signed) DARLING, *Acting.*
    Secure special train, if necessary. Act promptly.

LOOMIS, *Acting.*

1903 T. R.: "I Took the Canal Zone"

After leaving the White House, former President Theodore Roosevelt offered a somewhat less neutral picture of his role in the Panamanian revolt against Colombia in 1903. According to the March 25, 1911 issue of the New York Times, T. R. had asserted in his Charter Day address at the University of California that he had taken the Canal Zone. Some authorities today question that he actually made such a bold statement, but there is strong evidence that he in fact did so. A mere two months after the revolt, on February 23, 1904, the Senate approved by a 66 to 14 margin the Hay–Bunau Varilla Treaty, which granted to the United States sovereign rights over a ten mile wide strip of land across Panama: the Canal Zone. Eight Southern Democrats opposed the treaty, including the pro-Nicaraguan canal route Senator John T. Morgan of Alabama.

SOURCE: "A Belated Confession," in New York *Times*, March 25, 1911. See p. 10.

DOCUMENT:

Ex-President ROOSEVELT was uncommonly frank in his address at the Charter Day exercises of the University of California. He openly, and even boastfully, admitted that the despoiling of Colombia of her most precious province, Panama, was his own personal act. We quote Mr. ROOSEVELT's language:

> I am interested in the Panama Canal because I started it. If I had followed traditional, conservative methods I would have submitted a dignified State paper of probably 200 pages to Congress and the debates on it would have been going on yet; but I took the Canal Zone and let Congress debate; and while the debate goes on the canal does also.

Quite so. "I took the Canal Zone." This is the opinion by THE TIMES when the deed was perpetrated, that Mr. ROOSEVELT took the Canal Zone. He speaks almost as though it were an act of condescension on his part to submit the matter to Congress at all. But he did "let Congress debate." This is the doctrine of the one man power, the man on horseback. POLK began the Mexican war, and he has been unsparingly denounced for it. But he made haste to let Congress assume the responsibility. We do not remember that he ever spoke of that transaction in quite the terms used by Mr. ROOSEVELT about the Canal Zone.

Doubtless Mr. ROOSEVELT's act hastened the beginning of work on the canal. He says nothing about the cost of this haste. It was very great. Leading authorities in international law have deplored this taking of the Canal Zone as an act of perfidy. In our treaty of 1846 with the Republic of New Granada, to all the covenants and benefits of which Colombia succeeded, it is declared that "the United States also guarantee in the same manner the rights of sovereignty and property which New Granada has and possesses over the said territory" of the

Isthmus. It was the guarantor himself who trod upon this guarantee, violated it, and seized as his own spoil the estate which he had assured the owner that he would protect against all spoilers, including, of course, himself. We had advance knowledge of the breaking out of the revolution in Panama. Our warships were conveniently at hand. Without our support the rebels could never have withstood the forces of the parent Government. We forbade Colombia to send her forces into the Zone to suppress the uprising. It was in that way that Mr. ROOSEVELT took the Canal Zone.

Impartial men have considered it, as we have said, an act of perfidy. It has had a lasting effect in engendering in all the South American republics a sleepless suspicion of our motives, and alarm at our policies whenever we have had occasion to make a move in their direction. They were alarmed at our attitude toward Nicaragua. There has been fresh alarm in Mexico and Central America and throughout South America because of our dispatch of troops to Texas. They fear us where it would be immensely to our advantage to have their confidence.

Mr. ROOSEVELT seems to have been aware of these considerations when in his special message to Congress of Jan. 4, 1904, he attempted a laborious defense of his policy and his acts in the Canal Zone, and of his hasty recognition of a sovereignty that could never have been created, that could never have sustained itself, without our intervention and powerful support. Quite different is the tone of his address at Berkeley. "I took the Canal Zone." The act was characteristic. So is the boast.

1903 President Theodore Roosevelt Stands Up to Germany at the Time of the Venezuelan Debt Crisis

Like Mexico during the 1860s, Venezuela was in debt to European creditors, especially the British and German, by 1900. President Theodore Roosevelt did not feel that Latin American nations should have the excuse to hide behind the Monroe Doctrine to avoid fulfilling their obligations, and dictator Cipriano Castro of Venezuela refused to let the Hague Court arbitrate the claims. In December, 1902 the British, Germans, and Italians undertook a "pacific blockade" of Venezuela, leading to the seizure of several gunboats and the sinking of two others. Venezuela agreed to arbitration, but in January, 1903 the Germans bombarded Fort San Carlos and destroyed the village. With the American press and public highly suspicious of Germany's intentions, T. R. warned its Ambassador that his country was not to seize any Venezuelan territory, and that Admiral George Dewey would proceed after ten days to the Venezuelan coast to make sure that this did not happen. Faced with this threat, Germany consented to arbitration. Thirteen years later, the President told the full story in a letter to William R. Thayer.

SOURCE: Howard K. Beale, *Theodore Roosevelt and the Rise of America to World Power* (Baltimore: Johns Hopkins University Press, 1956). See pp. 399–401.

DOCUMENT:

I speedily became convinced that Germany was the…really formidable party, in the transaction.…I became convinced that England would not back Germany in the event of a clash over the matter between Germany and the United States, but would remain neutral.…I also became convinced that Germany intended to seize some Venezuelan harbor and turn it into a strongly fortified place of arms, on the model of Kiaochow, with a view to exercising some measure of control over the future Isthmian Canal, and over South American affairs generally.…Germany declined to agree to arbitrate…and declined to say that she would not take possession of Venezuelan territory, merely saying that such possession would be "temporary"—which might mean anything. I finally decided that no useful purpose would be served by further delay, and I took action accordingly. I assembled our battle fleet, under Admiral Dewey, near Porto Rico, for "maneuvres," with instructions that the fleet should be kept in hand and in fighting trim, and should be ready to sail at an hour's notice.…

I saw the [German] Ambassador, and explained that in view of the presence of the German squadron on the Venezuelan coast I could not permit longer delay in answering my request for an arbitration, and that I could not acquiesce in any seizure of Venezuelan territory. The Ambassador responded that his Government could not agree to arbitrate, and that there was no intention to take "permanent" possession of Venezuelan territory. I answered that Kiaochow was not a "permanent" possession of Germany's—that…I did not intend to have another Kiaochow, held by similar tenure, on the approach to the Isthmian Canal. The Ambassador repeated that his Government would not agree to arbitrate. I then asked him to inform his Government that if no notification for arbitration came during the next ten days I would be obliged to order Dewey to take his fleet to the Venezuelan coast and see that the German forces did not take possession of any territory. He expressed very grave concern and asked me if I realized the serious consequences that would follow such action; consequences so serious to both countries that he dreaded to give them a name. I answered that I had thoroughly counted the cost before I decided on the step, and asked him to look at the map, as a glance would show him that there was no spot in the world where Germany in the event of conflict with the United States would be at a greater disadvantage than in the Caribbean sea.

A week later the Ambassador came to see me, talked pleasantly on several subjects, and rose to go. I asked him if he had any answer to make from his Government to my request, and when he said no, I informed him that in such event it was useless to wait as long as I had intended, and that Dewey would be ordered to sail twenty four hours in advance of the time I had set. He expressed deep apprehension, and said that his Government would not arbitrate. However, less than twenty four hours before the time I had appointed for calling the order to Dewey, the Ambassador notified me that His Imperial Majesty the German Emperor had directed him to request me to undertake arbitration myself.

1905 A Report on Conditions in the Dominican Republic

The Dominican Republic also had fallen into debt to its European creditors, and it was far less capable of defending itself than Venezuela was at that time. As a result, Theodore Roosevelt proposed that American officials take over and operate the customs houses of the Dominican Republic, and the bankrupt Dominicans acquiesced. But as John Bassett Moore pointed out in a contemporary magazine article, the island nation's problems were by no means confined to its foreign debt. Conditions in general were tumultuous in this country where Americans had invested in sugar, bananas, railroads, lumber, and petroleum.

SOURCE: John Bassett Moore, "Santo Domingo and the United States," in *Review of Reviews*, March, 1905. See pp. 294–95.

DOCUMENT:

Marauding bands roamed over the country; the capital was besieged; the house of the American diplomatic representatives was repeatedly pierced by shells; American naval vessels were fired upon, and one non-commissioned officer was killed, as the American diplomatic representative declared, deliberately; an American merchant steamer, proceeding under the escort of a naval launch to her dock, was fired upon by the Jimenez faction; the unfortified town of San Pedro de Macoris, inhabited largely by foreigners, was taken and retaken three times, and was twice bombarded; American sugar estates were preyed upon by roving partisans, and the owners daily stood in dread of the application of the torch to their cane; the American railway, running from Puerto Plata to Santiago, which had previously been exempt from attack, was seized by revolutionists, the tracks torn up, and a station burned. Since June, 1904, there has existed a nominal peace, but the enemies of the government have in places maintained a defiant position, and actually collected and used the revenues, and it is a matter of general belief that but for the restraining presence of an American man-of-war at Puerto Plata, an open revolution would have been in progress in the north since the middle of December.

That conditions so destructive and dangerous should, if possible, be abated is manifest. Nor are the interests at stake small. To say nothing of the vast concern of the Dominicans themselves in the establishment of law and order, the accumulated foreign commercial and industrial interests are so considerable that their sacrifice is not to be contemplated. The American vested interests alone are commonly valued at $20,000,000. The great sugar estates are owned chiefly by Americans and Italians. It is estimated that around San Pedro de Macoris, where in the late disturbances the estates were much damaged by roving bands, American investments in the sugar industry amount to $6,000,000. Extensive banana plantations are also owned by Americans; the United Fruit Company holds more than 18,000 acres, representing an investment of more than $500,000. There are two completed railroads, one of which is owned by British subjects, while the other, running from Puerto Plata to Santiago, was chiefly constructed and is now held and operated by the Company of the Central Dominican Railway, an American corporation. The exportation of woods is chiefly in the hands of Americans. The oil fields of Azua are being developed by an American company. The wharf privileges of the three principal ports are owned by foreigners—Americans and Italians. Four great commercial houses are owned or controlled by Germans, and one by Italians. One of the two steamship lines that regularly ply between Dominican and foreign ports is that of the American firm of W. P. Clyde & Co., while the other is French. It is sometimes suggested that, when citizens of a country go abroad and engage in business, they must be held to assume all the risks of disorder and injury in the country to which they go, and can look to the local authorities only, no matter how inefficient or malevolent they may be, for protection; but it suffices to say that no respectable government acts on any such theory.

1905 The Roosevelt Corollary to the Monroe Doctrine (1904)

In his fourth annual message to Congress in December, 1904, President Theodore Roosevelt proclaimed the Roosevelt Corollary to the Monroe Doctrine, which reserved to the United States the right to exercise international police power in the Western Hemisphere in the event of "chronic wrongdoing." A year later, in his fifth annual message to Congress on December 5, 1905, T. R. reviewed developments in the Dominican Republic during the last year, including the American collection of customs receipts there. The Senate did not approve the treaty with the Dominican Republic authorizing the latter, though, until February, 1907, and this was a modified version of the original agreement of two years earlier. On the latter occasion, partisan Southern Democrats cast twelve of the nineteen votes against the Roosevelt Corollary.

SOURCE: Richardson, *Messages and Papers of the Presidents*. See XV, 6996–97.

DOCUMENT:

Moreover, we must make it evident that we do not intend to permit the Monroe Doctrine to be used by any nation on this Continent as a shield to protect it from the consequences of its own misdeeds against foreign nations. If a republic to the south of us commits a tort against a foreign nation, such as an outrage against a citizen of that nation, then the Monroe Doctrine does not force us to interfere to prevent punishment of the tort, save to see that the punishment does not assume the form of territorial occupation in any shape. The case is more difficult when it refers to a contractual obligation. Our own Government has always refused to enforce such contractual obligations on behalf of its citizens by an appeal to arms. It is much to be wished that all foreign governments would take the same view. But they do not; and in consequence we are liable at any time to be brought face to face with disagreeable alternatives. On the one hand, this country would certainly decline to go to war to prevent a foreign government from collecting a just debt; on the other hand, it is very inadvisable to permit any foreign power to take possession, even temporarily, of the custom houses of an American Republic in order to enforce the payment of its obligations; for such temporary occupation might turn into a permanent occupation. The only escape from these alternatives may at any time be that we must ourselves undertake to bring about some arrangement by which so much as possible of a just obligation shall be paid. It is far better that this country should put through such an arrangement, rather than allow any foreign country to undertake it. To do so insures the defaulting republic from having to pay debt of an improper character under duress, while it also insures honest creditors of the republic from being passed by in the interest of dishonest or grasping creditors. Moreover, for the United States to take such a position offers the only possible way of insuring us against a clash with some foreign power. The position is, therefore, in the interest of peace as well as in the interest of justice. It is of benefit to our people; it is of benefit to foreign peoples; and most of all it is really of benefit to the people of the country concerned.

The conditions in Santo Domingo have for a number of years grown from bad to worse until a year ago all society was on the verge of dissolution. Fortunately, just at this time a ruler sprang up in Santo Domingo, who, with his colleagues, saw the dangers threatening their country and appealed to the friendship of the only great and powerful neighbor who possessed the power, and as they hoped also the will to help them. There was imminent danger of foreign intervention. The previous rulers of Santo Domingo had recklessly incurred debts, and owing to her internal disorders she had ceased to be able to provide means of paying the debts. The patience of her foreign creditors had become exhausted, and at least two foreign nations were on the point of intervention, and were only prevented from intervening by the unofficial assurance of this Government that it would itself strive to help Santo Domingo in her hour of need. In the case of one of these nations, only the actual opening of negotiations to this end by our Government prevented the seizure of territory in Santo Domingo by a European power. Of the debts incurred some were just, while some were not of a character which really renders it obligatory on or proper for Santo Domingo to pay them in full. But she could not pay any of them unless some stability was assured her Government and people.

1905 The Boston *Transcript* Attacks the Roosevelt Corollary

Most Republicans, as well as the bulk of public opinion, supported President Theodore Roosevelt's intervention in the Dominican Republic. This was also true of the country's newspapers. Exceptions included the St. Louis Globe-Democrat, the Philadelphia Press, the New York Sun, the Springfield Republican, and the New York World, which proclaimed "never was there a more grotesque, preposterous and perilous perversion of the Monroe Doctrine." A thoughtful anti-Roosevelt editorial published in the independent Republican Boston Transcript attempted to view the amended Monroe Doctrine from the standpoint of the Latin American countries, which were becoming increasingly suspicious of the United States.

SOURCE: *Current Literature*, February, 1905. See p. 108.

DOCUMENT:

There is a Latin–American side to Monroeism which ought not to be ignored, but which if disregarded may, should our policy become militant, place us in the unenviable attitude of coercing our Southern neighbors at the behest of Europe. That this is at least a possibility of our guardianship ought to be realized by everyone who is familiar with the history of Latin–American finance, a wonderful record in more senses than one. Let "The High Finance" of the Old World load itself up with these repudiated or semi-repudiated bonds at a few cents on a dollar, and receive a tip that the United States either can or may be made to intervene for a settlement or "readjustment," and there will be at once a "sharp advance," affording good profits and an embroglio on our hands. History in the last fifty years has abounded in instances of the power of "high finance." The political Latin–American side of Monroeism is found in the possible unwillingness of nations of the rank and pride of Argentina, Brazil, and Chile to accept an onerous degree of guardianship. They may insist that they prefer to do their own business in their own way and that they can best make terms without intervention or intermediary. Supposing this should be their constitution, ought we to override it, so long as the proposed settlement does not involve cession of territory? To prevent such cessions, to preserve the independence of South America against the force or machinations of the Holy Alliance, were the great ends sought by the simple Monroeism of Monroe. Since his day Monroeism has "expanded" by continued interpretations until there are signs to the southward that the public opinion in the countries affected views it with something very like distrust. It would be a strange untoward outcome of eighty years of Monroeism if a secret combination of Latin–American countries should be formed in opposition to "the overlordship of the United States."

Japanese Imperialism and Japanese Immigrants 25

1905–6 President Theodore Roosevelt's Letters Criticizing the West Coast for Its Treatment of Japanese Residents

President Theodore Roosevelt, who had helped to mediate the Russo–Japanese War of 1904–5, was faced with the additional problem of the growing hostility of West Coast whites toward the Japanese residents there. To cite one early incident, Japanese railway workers were attacked at Trenton, North Dakota, and Saco, Montana, in 1899. As of 1900, there were 20,000 Japanese immigrants in the western states, and by 1910 the figure had almost tripled. In contrast to the frequently poor Chinese, some of the Japanese were wealthy, and their purchase of land in the West offended many whites. On May 7, 1907, some Whites set up the Japanese and Korean Exclusion League in San Francisco. These developments, of course, came to the attention of T. R., who was disturbed not only by the display of bigotry but by its international ramifications. His concern is revealed in letters to Senator Henry Cabot Lodge dated June 5, 1905, and May 15, 1906.

SOURCE: Raymond A. Esthus, *Theodore Roosevelt and Japan* (Seattle: University of Washington Press, 1966). See p. 130.

DOCUMENT:

Meanwhile, I am utterly disgusted at the manifestations which have begun to appear on the Pacific slope in favor of excluding the Japanese exactly as the Chinese are excluded. The California State Legislature and various other bodies have acted in the worst possible taste and in the most offensive manner to Japan. Yet the Senators and Congressmen from these very states were lukewarm about the navy last year. It gives me a feeling of contempt and disgust to see them challenge Japanese hostility and justify by their actions any feeling the Japanese might have against us, while at the same time refusing to take steps to defend themselves against the formidable foe whom they are ready with such careless insolence to antagonize. How people can act in this way with the Russo-Japanese war going on before their eyes I cannot understand. I do all I can to counteract the effects, but I cannot accomplish everything.

* *

I hope that we can persuade our people on the one hand to act in a spirit of generous justice and genuine courtesy toward Japan, and on the other hand to keep the navy respectable in numbers and more than respectable in the efficiency of its units. If we act thus we need not fear the Japanese. But if as Brooks Adams says, we show ourselves "opulent, aggressive and unarmed," the Japanese may sometime work us an injury. In any event we can hold our own in the future, whether against Japan or Germany, whether on the Atlantic or the Pacific, only if we occupy the position of the just man armed—that is, if we do the exact reverse of what the demagogues on the one hand and the mugwumps on the other would like to have us do.

1906 The *Outlook* Takes an Unsympathetic Stance toward the Japanese on the Education Issue

In April, 1906 a great earthquake and fire devastated San Francisco. Among those who helped the victims was the Japanese Red Cross. Nevertheless, on October 11 of that year, the San Francisco Board of Education passed a resolution segregating all oriental students in a separate building. At this time, there were only ninety-three Japanese enrolled in the schools of that city. The episode caused a furor in Japan, but many Americans were not so sympathetic. A case in point was the magazine Outlook, in the opinion of which foreigners had no right to tell American schools how to operate. Its February 9, 1907 editorial bore the title, "A False Alarm."

SOURCE: "A False Alarm," in *Outlook*, February 9, 1907. See pp. 301–2.

DOCUMENT:

We advise our readers not to take too seriously the warnings of certain Washington correspondents of impending war with Japan over the school question. When correspondents cannot find news, it becomes necessary to make it; when discovery fails, invention is called into exercise. There is no danger of war with Japan on the school question. The only danger, and that we do not think is serious, certainly not imminent, is that sensational journalists in America and Japan, unconsciously co-operating, may fan race prejudices into a wholly irrational race passion. That Japan should declare war against the United States because California does not make the kind of school provision for Japanese children that Japan desires is a preposterous notion. It is no business of any other nation what provision America makes for the education of children residing within her territory. People who migrate to America must take the school provisions which they find here. A law prohibiting resident Japanese from educating their own children at their own expense Japan might resent. But what school taxes our Nation shall levy and how we shall expend them when they are collected is no concern of any other Nation. We may provide only for the education of white children, as some of the Southern States formerly did; or for education in the religion of the Episcopal Church, as England practically does; or in that of the Roman Catholic Church, as most Latin countries formerly did; or in no religion at all, as the United States does; and no other nation would have any right to complain. It is true that Japan showed great courage in her war with Russia; but no less did she show great wisdom in her diplomacy in the peace negotiations; and to attribute to her a policy of attempting to dictate to a sovereign nation how it shall conduct its public school system is to do her a dishonor that she has done nothing to deserve.

1907–8 The Gentlemen's Agreement with Japan on the Immigration Issue

President Theodore Roosevelt invited the San Francisco School Board to Washington for a conference during February, 1907. Members of that body agreed to rescind the order segregating the Japanese in the schools of that city, in return for which the American government would restrict Japanese immigration into the United States. This was accomplished through an amendment to the Immigration Act of 1907, and also through an understanding between the two countries known as the Gentlemen's Agreement. (Since this did not take the form of a treaty, there was no Senatorial vote on it.) The main objective of the Gentlemen's Agreement—set forth in an interchange of documents between the Japanese Foreign Office and the U.S. Department of State—was to withhold passports from Japanese laborers intending to migrate to the United States. A few students and tourists from Japan continued to visit this country, while "picture brides" of Japanese laborers already in the United States were permitted to emigrate to the mainland until 1920. Then, in 1924 Congress passed a Japanese Exclusion Act, again with the same western and southern backing which the Chinese Exclusion Act of 1882 had enjoyed.

SOURCE: Kim, *East Asia's Turbulent Century.* See pp. 260–62.

DOCUMENT:

Memorandum of the Japanese Foreign Office to the Department of State, December 31, 1907

1. The Imperial Government are determined to continue their announced policy of issuing no passports good for the American mainland to either skilled or unskilled Japanese laborers, except to those who have previously resided in the United States, or the parents, wives or children of Japanese residents.

2. They intend, however, to continue to grant passports to settle agriculturists. As was known to the predecessor of His Excellency the Ambassador on the 26th of May last the Japanese Government have exercised with reference to those persons very careful and rigorous supervision and restriction. The privilege has only been granted to *bona fide* agriculturists intending to settle in certain specified localities. In order to avoid all possible subterfuge, the central administration will continue rigidly to apply the precautionary measures set forth in the explanatory memorandum of May 26th.

3. The Imperial Government have formulated instructions to local Governors that in every case of application for a passport to the United States by a student, merchant, tourist or the like, thorough investigation must be made to determine whether the applicant is not likely to become a laborer after reaching the United States. A material and indispensable part of this investigation relates to the financial status of the applicant. If he is not rich enough in his own right to assure the permanence of his status as a student, merchant or tourist, surety will be required of his family or special patron in the case of a student, or of his firm or company in the case of a merchant or mercantile employee, guaranteeing the payment of expenses and a monthly allowance of say 40 yen; and, in the case of tourists, the payment of sufficient travelling expenses. The passport applied for will only be issued after this surety has been given. As a further precaution in the case of students no such passports will be issued except to students who have passed through the middle schools.

4. So far as concerns the Hawaiian Islands, which it is proposed to set aside from the scope of the questions under consideration, it is the present intention of the Imperial Government experimentally to stop all emigration to those Islands for some time to come, except in isolated cases of returning emigrants and of the parents, wives and children, of those already resident in the Islands.

5. The Imperial Government intend to take measures regarding the emigration of Japanese laborers to foreign territory adjacent to the United States, which in their opinion will effectually remove all cause for complaint on that account.

The Department of State to the Japanese Foreign Office,
January 23, 1908

1st. Passports should be exact and specific and issued with the greatest care to prevent forgery and false personation.

2nd. The issuance of passports to laborers who have formerly been in American territory or to the parents, wives, or children of laborers already there, should be carefully safeguarded and limited, otherwise abuses are, it is feared, certain.

3rd. With reference to settled agriculturists, the gist of the precautionary measures to be taken is noted and it is understood that a settled agriculturist is a small farmer capitalist and not merely a farm laborer paid under contract out of the produce of his agricultural work, and that with this criterion a reasonable number of passports only will be issued to persons of such economic status. It is to be observed that unless the alleged character of farmer is accompanied by actual title to land it is quite likely to be merely a cover for a violation of our contract labor laws and this should be specifically guarded against.

4th. It is quite important also that the Japanese Government's definition of laborer be conformable to our own....For illustration, from December 27 to January 10 there arrived at Pacific posts 118 Japanese who were laborers according to our rules but who had obtained passports otherwise than as laborers. During that period only four arrived with passports as laborers.

We cannot believe that the Imperial Japanese Government will find serious difficulty in devising some quite unobjectionable system of registration or of certificates, or other evidence by which may be identified those engaged in manual labor in American territory lawfully and without violation of their passports.

1908 The Root–Takahira Agreement with Japan on the Far East

Later in 1908, Japanese Ambassador Takahira and Secretary of State Elihu Root reached an understanding on the Far Eastern situation known as the Root–Takahira Agreement. Again there was no Senatorial roll-call vote on this document. It dealt with such topics as Pacific Ocean commerce, the preservation of the existing status quo in the region, and the Open Door in China. The United States thereby recognized Japan's special position in Southern Manchuria, from which American and European bankers proved unable to dislodge her with the assistance of the Chinese.

SOURCE: U.S. Department of State, *Foreign Relations of the United States 1908* (Washington: Government Printing Office, 1912). See pp. 511–12.

DOCUMENT:

The Secretary of State to the Japanese Ambassador.

DEPARTMENT OF STATE.
Washington, November 30, 1908.

EXCELLENCY: I have the honor to acknowledge the receipt of your note of to-day setting forth the result of the exchange of views between us in our recent interviews defining the understanding of the two Governments in regard to their policy in the region of the Pacific Ocean.

It is a pleasure to inform you that this expression of mutual understanding is welcome to the Government of the United States as appropriate to the happy relations of the two countries and as the occasion for a concise mutual affirmation of that accordant policy respecting the Far East which the two Governments have so frequently declared in the past.

I am happy to be able to confirm to your excellency, on behalf of the United States, the declaration of the two Governments embodied in the following words:

1. It is the wish of the two Governments to encourage the free and peaceful development of their commerce on the Pacific Ocean.

2. The policy of both Governments, uninfluenced by any aggressive tendencies, is directed to the maintenance of the existing status quo in the region above mentioned, and to the defense of the principle of equal opportunity for commerce and industry in China.

3. They are accordingly firmly resolved reciprocally to respect the territorial possessions belonging to each other in said region.

4. They are also determined to preserve the common interests of all powers in China by supporting by all pacific means at their disposal the independence and integrity of China and the principle of equal opportunity for commerce and industry of all nations in that Empire.

5. Should any event occur threatening the status quo as above described or the principle of equal opportunity as above defined, it remains for the two Governments to communicate with each other in order to arrive at an understanding as to what measures they may consider it useful to take.

Accept, Excellency, the renewed assurance of my highest consideration.

Four Episodes in Big Stick Diplomacy 26

1904 Secretary of State John Hay and the Perdicaris Affair (Morocco)

The seizure of American nationals living or traveling abroad is by no means a new practice, although the activities of international terrorists in recent years have focused continuing attention on it. In 1904, the Moroccan native chieftain Raisuli kidnapped Ion Perdicaris, a Greek subject who allegedly held American naturalization papers. With the Republican National Convention then going on, Secretary of State John Hay demanded "Perdicaris alive or Raisuli dead," but privately warned against the use of force without specific instructions. The Moorish court eventually put up most of the ransom for Perdicaris's release. As for Raisuli, he sarcastically commented on the U.S. naval presence in the Mediterranean: "I hear America has many strong fish in the sea, but I have seen none of them come up on the beach."

SOURCE: U.S. Department of State, *Foreign Relations of the United States 1904* (Washington: Government Printing Office, 1905). See pp. 496, 498–99, 501, 503–4.

DOCUMENT:

Mr. Gummeré to Mr. Hay, American Consulate-General, Tangier, May 19, 1904 (Mr. Gummeré reports that on the night of the 18th of May, about 8:30 o'clock, a band of natives headed by a bandit named Raisuli, who kidnapped Mr. Walter Harris the year previous, broke into the country house of Mr. Perdicaris, a prominent American citizen, and carried away Mr. Perdicaris and his stepson, Mr. Varley, a British subject. Mr. Perdicaris' house is situated about 3 miles from Tangier.

The consul-general and the British minister have informed the Sultan's deputy that the Moorish authorities are to be held personally responsible, and in order to secure the release of the captives they have insisted that any terms demanded by Raisuli be immediately granted. They are also dispatching a special courier to the court to have the Sultan's deputy instructed to comply with such requests as they may make.

The consul-general regards the situation as serious, and asks that a man-of-war be sent to enforce the demands.)

Mr. Hay to Mr. Gummeré, Department of State, Washington, June 9, 1904 (Mr. Hay informs Mr. Gummeré that while the President desires everything possible to be done to secure the release of Mr. Perdicaris, the United States is not to be put in the position of guaranteeing any concessions made by the Sultan to the bandits. It should be clearly understood that if Mr. Perdicaris should be murdered, the life of the murderer will be demanded, and in no case will the United States be a party to any promise of immunity for his crime. Anything which may be regarded as an encouragement to brigandage or blackmail should be avoided in the negotiations.)

Mr. Gummeré to Mr. Hay, American Consulate-General, Tangier, June 15, 1901 (In view of the Department's intimation that the Moorish Government will be held responsible for the lives of the murderers, the absolute impotency of the Moorish Government and its inability to inflict punishment must be understood. The brigand utterly disregards the idea of punishment by the Moorish Government. The whole army of the Sultan consists of less than 2,000 men, and this number is daily diminishing. Having awaited the result of the negotiations for one month, the consul-general is now firmly convinced that the time has arrived when the brigand and his supporters should be plainly warned that they will be punished by the great Powers to whom the captives belong if they are injured or are not immediately released, and adds that their lives may in this way be preserved; but that in order not to jeopardize the lives of all Christians in Morocco it would be necessary that such a threat of punishment should be fulfilled to the letter.)

Mr. Gummeré to Mr. Hay, American Consulate-General, Tangier, June 17, 1904 (Mr. Gummeré reports that the brigand's negotiator returned last night and announces that the terms having been accepted, the Moorish prisoners were released today, and the $50,000 in Spanish notes and $20,000 gold must be delivered to the bandit at Tarrasdant, where he is now, when Messrs. Perdicaris and Varley would be released. To this earnest objection was made by the British minister and Mr. Gummeré on the ground that the bandit, once having the money and prisoners, would not without further demand give up the captives. Finally it was proposed that $20,000 silver, and the remainder in notes (gold coin having been waived), together with the prisoners, should be taken by Muley Ahmed, one of the Wazan Shereefs, and the brigand's negotiator, to the village of Zellal in the Beni Msur, a friendly tribe about six hours from Tangier, to be met there by Muley Ali, the other Wazan Shereef, with the captives, in charge of the brigand, and the exchange effected.

Mr. Hay to Mr. Gummeré, Department of State, Washington, June 22, 1904 (Mr. Hay states that this Government "wants Perdicaris alive or Raisuli dead." Further than this, least possible complications with Morocco or other powers is desired. Mr. Gummeré is instructed not to arrange for landing marines or seizing custom-house without the Department's specific directions.)

Mr. Gummeré to Mr. Hay, American Consulate-General, Tangier, June 24, 1904 (Mr. Gummeré reports the arrival of the captives at their home shortly after midnight, and states that they are well, but have been fatigued with the long journey.)

1906 President Theodore Roosevelt and the Algeciras Conference on Morocco

Two years after the Perdicaris episode, Franco–German rivalry over independent Morocco led to the holding of a multinational conference at Algeciras, Spain. In view of the fact that the United States had ratified treaties with Morocco in 1786, 1836, 1865, and 1880, it is not surprising that the American government sent a delegation there. Led by Henry White, the U.S. group played an important role. The General Act of Algeciras gave the French and the Spanish a privileged position vis-à-vis the native police force, but also maintained an open door for Germany and other foreign powers in Morocco. The anti-German American press was enthusiastic, but the U.S. Senate only ratified this document with the qualification that it was doing so "without purpose to depart from the traditional American foreign policy." Many Democrats were disturbed by the Moroccan negotiations. As for President Theodore Roosevelt, he took a hard line toward Germany on Morocco, just as he had done three years earlier at the time of the Venezuelan debt controversy. T. R.'s private views were revealed in a letter which he wrote to Whitelaw Reid, the expansionist editor of the New York Tribune, on June 27, 1906.

SOURCE: Elting E. Morison, Editor, *Letters of Theodore Roosevelt*, 8 Volumes (Cambridge: Harvard University Press, 1951–54). See V, 318–19.

DOCUMENT:

To Whitelaw Reid—Confidential, Washington, June 27, 1906

I like the Kaiser and the Germans. I wish to keep on good terms with them. I agree with you in thinking it even more important that we should keep on good terms or better terms with the English; but of course when the English are such fools as to keep a man like Durand here while the Germans have a man like Speck, it increases the difficulty of my task.

In this Algeciras matter you will notice that while I was most suave and pleasant with the Emperor yet when it became necessary at the end I stood him on his head with great decision. Of course the vital feature of what I did was the verbal statement to Sternberg that in case the Emperor declined to submit to what was reasonable I should have to make public all of our correspondence in order to justify my position in entering into the negotiations. This last statement will in all probability never be made public.

As for the Germans, I really treat them much more cavalierly than I do the English, and I am immensely amused at the European theory (which cannot, however, be the theory of the French Government) that I am taken in by the Kaiser. I am very polite with him, but I am ready at an instant's notice to hold my own.

1907 The American Naval Landing at the Time of the Jamaican Earthquake and the Reaction of Governor Swettenham

Surveys of American diplomatic history, as well as the more chronologically and topically restricted monographs, rarely comment on American relations with Jamaica, although the former British colony is an important Caribbean island. On occasion, though, significant developments involving Jamaica have taken place, as was the case when the Governor of the island, Sir Alexander Swettenham, overreacted to the landing of American naval personnel under the command of Rear Admiral C. H. Davis. On January 16, 1907, the American consul telegraphed the State Department: "Fearful earthquake followed by fire; Kingston destroyed; hundreds of lives lost; food sadly wanted. Consulate partially destroyed; fireproof safe." In the resulting furor over the challenged American landing, Swettenham eventually resigned. A contemporary pro-Swettenham account of events appeared in the Nineteenth Century that Summer.

SOURCE: Ian Malcolm, "The 'White Flag' in Jamaica," in *Nineteenth Century*, June 1907. See pp. 909–11.

DOCUMENT:

The publication of the White Paper (or, as it should be called, the 'White Flag') which is said to deal with 'Correspondence relating to the resignation of Sir. A. Swettenham of his office as Governor of Jamaica,' has an importance that is of Imperial gravity. The fact that it was issued in the late days of April, and that it is therefore now six weeks old, must not preclude the British public from giving its most serious attention to the manner in which the colonial Office has seen fit to treat one of the oldest and most faithful of British public servants.

I cannot help believing that a full comprehension of even a few of the circumstances carefully eliminated from the White Paper will show Sir A. Swettenham to have been a far better guardian of British honour than the slightly hysterical and very official individual who has caused the retirement of the Governor. For convenience sake I will tabulate the events as they occurred, with such notes as seem desirable to elucidate the position.

The 14th of January. The earthquake at Kingston; ruin of the city and deplorable loss of life. The Governor wired to Santiago de Cuba to purchase bandages, &c.

The 15th of January. Parts of Kingston in flames; news probably reached Havana.

The 16th of January. At midnight two United States battleships and a cruiser, under command of Rear-Admiral Davis, arrived in Kingston harbour. The officers went immediately on board the *Port Kingston,* escorted thither by the Governor himself, who made it plain that he desired no salute.

The 17th of January. The United States ships fired a salute; the Admiral landed fifty armed men and working parties; the United States flag was hoisted in a field on British territory and an American hospital was installed.

This done the Admiral writes to the Governor explaining that the visiting navy let off its guns by mistake, and then proceeds to 'propose' and 'judge' and 'direct' concerning the situation, as though there were no such person as a British Governor within a thousand miles.

I landed working parties from both ships to-day [he writes]. I propose to land parties to-morrow unless you expressly desire me not to do so....I judge the police surveillance of the city is not adequate....I shall direct the medical officers of my squadron....I trust that you will justify me in the matter....

Later in the day the Admiral wires to his Chief-in-Command at Havana to the effect that

Sir A. Swettenham is a man of great power; declined my offer to land working parties to assist in hospital, to police streets, clear away debris and bury the dead....Later by request [Query—by whose request?] I landed fifty men under arms to prevent a mutiny in the penitentiary.

There was no mutiny; both inside and outside the penitentiary the populace preserved an attitude of admirable composure under the circumstances, so these troops were withdrawn by request of the Governor, who had never authorised their landing,

as he has assured me [continues the Admiral] he is capable of controlling the situation. He has West Indian Regiment 1,000 strong, and two companies of artillery besides insular constabulary....I consider it my duty to remain for the present at least. Situation is too confusing, and conflicting stories, reports, complaints, and rumours too contradictory to enable me at present to form a clear judgment of actual situation.

From this unique document it will be seen that Governor Swettenham's assurances that he was quite able to look after Kingston impressed the Admiral very little; and that the latter was quite prepared to take yet another island in the Caribbean Sea under the sheltering wing of the American eagle. He felt, however, that he would require justification for his action, and therefore he asked for it in his letter to the Governor. From a communication supplied later by Admiral Evans to the Navy Department we learn that on this date (the 17th of January) Admiral Davis *received a reply of thanks* from the Governor, 'who thinks that he has the situation well in hand.'

> *The 18th of January.* Lord Elgin telegraphs that he does not desire to fetter the Governor's discretion, &c.

> President Roosevelt offers official assistance.
> Admiral Davis cables for more dressings for the wounded.
> Sir A. Swettenham replies to Admiral Davis's letter.

It must be remembered that the Governor had already courteously thanked the Admiral on the previous day for his assistance, even though he had not invoked it. He also knew that the Admiral entirely mistrusted his reading of the situation, and was becoming a difficult problem in a situation already sufficiently complicated. He never doubted the *bona fides* of the sentence in the Admiral's letter: 'I shall land troops to-morrow *unless you expressly desire me not to do so,*' any more than he questioned the humanity and kindliness of the Admiral's intentions. But he had to get rid of these armed parties of American soldiers, whose presence among negroes was both profoundly unpopular and also a serious danger; moreover he had to prove to a questioning world that Britain can still manage Jamaica without outside help. And so, trying to combine frankness with some jocularity, he wrote the private letter beginning 'Dear Admiral Davis.' I am not concerned to defend the epistolary style of Sir A. Swettenham; possibly his humour was less suited to the occasion than the directness of his request that a foreign force should leave the island. But the public is anxious to know how it is that an obviously private letter found its way into the public Press, and then became incorporated in a Parliamentary paper.

1907–9 The Global Tour of the U.S. Navy

At the time of the Spanish–American War, Theodore Roosevelt was Secretary of the Navy. Nine years later he was President, and he sent the American Navy around the world on a grand tour. In his Autobiography, T. R. stated that his major objective in doing so was to impress the American people, but it would appear that he also was delivering a message to the Japanese. Roosevelt, moreover, boldly proclaimed that he had made the decision to dispatch the Navy without consulting with his Cabinet. The jingo press of the United States (especially the Hearst newspapers) talked of war, but our most bellicose President ended his tenure in the White House on a note of peace.

SOURCE: Theodore Roosevelt, *Works.* See XX, 535–37.

DOCUMENT:

In my own judgment the most important service that I rendered to peace was the voyage of the battle fleet round the world. I had become convinced that for many reasons it was essential that we should have it clearly understood, by our own people especially, but also by other peoples, that the Pacific was as much our home waters as the Atlantic, and that our fleet could and would at will pass from one to the other of the two great oceans. It seemed to me evident that such a voyage would greatly benefit the navy itself; would arouse popular interest in and enthusiasm for the navy; and would make foreign nations accept as a matter of course that our fleet should from time to time be gathered in the Pacific, just as from time to time it was gathered in the Atlantic, and that its presence in one ocean was no more to be accepted as a mark of hostility to any Asiatic power than its presence in the Atlantic was to be accepted as a mark of hostility to any European power. I determined on the move without consulting the Cabinet, precisely as I took Panama without consulting the Cabinet. A council of war never fights, and in a crisis the duty of a leader is to lead and not to take refuge behind the generally timid wisdom of a multitude of councillors. At that time, as I happen to know, neither the English nor the German authorities believed it possible to take a fleet of great battleships around the world. They did not believe that their own fleets could perform the feat, and still less did they believe that the American fleet could. I made up my mind that it was time to have a show-down in the matter; because if it was really true that our fleet could not get from the Atlantic to the Pacific, it was much better to know it and be able to shape our policy in view of the knowledge. Many persons publicly and privately protested against the move on the ground that Japan would accept it as a threat. To this I answered nothing in public. In private I said that I did not believe Japan would so regard it because Japan knew my sincere friendship and admiration for her and realized that we could not as a nation have any intention of attacking her; and that if there were any such feeling on the part of Japan as was alleged that very fact rendered it imperative that that fleet should go. When in the spring of 1910 I was in Europe I was interested to find that high naval authorities in both Germany and Italy had expected that war would come at the time of the voyage. They asked me if I had not been afraid of it, and if I had not expected that hostilities would begin at least by the time that the fleet reached the Straits of Magellan. I answered that I did not expect it; that I believed that Japan would feel as friendly in the matter as we did; but that if my expectations had proved mistaken, it would have been proof positive that we were going to be attacked anyhow, and that in such event it would have been an enormous gain to have had the three months' preliminary preparation which enabled the fleet to start perfectly equipped. In a personal interview before they left I had explained to the officers in command that I believed the trip would be one of absolute peace, but that they were to take exactly the same precautions against sudden attack of any kind as if we were at war with all the nations of the earth; and that no excuse of any kind would be accepted if there were a sudden attack of any kind and we were taken unawares.

My prime purpose was to impress the American people; and this purpose was fully achieved. The cruise did make a very deep impression abroad; boasting about what we have done does not impress foreign nations at all, except unfavorably, but positive achievement does; and the two American achievements that really impressed foreign peoples during the first dozen years of this century were the digging of the Panama Canal and the cruise of the battle fleet round the world. But the impression made on our own people was of far greater consequence. No single thing in the history of the new United States navy has done as much to stimulate popular interest and belief in it as the world cruise.

Varied Interests
of the Taft Administration 27

1909 Secretary of State Philander Chase Knox and the
Chester Concession in Turkey

Aside from Egypt, American interest in the Middle East was not as great during the nine-teenth century as it was in Africa. U.S. activity in the Middle East, however, began to esca-late after 1900, in part because of the massive petroleum deposits of the region. A case in point was the abortive Chester concession of 1908, which the German interests opposed, and which the Turkish Parliament debated without approving. (An attempt to revive it in 1923 also proved unsuccessful.) In exchange for building most of the public works of Tur-key, particularly the railroads, Admiral Colby M. Chester obtained the right to exploit the Arghana copper mine and certain Turkish oil fields. (Turkey at that time spread over more of the Middle East than it does today.) As for the U.S. government, it was in favor of equal investing opportunities as well as equal trading privileges for American nationals overseas, but Secretary of State Philander Chase Knox admitted to Ambassador to Turkey Oscar Straus that "applicants claiming to represent American interests are often irresponsible." In this November 1, 1909 letter Knox also pointed out that the basic determination of the legit-imacy of the U.S. entrepreneurs rested with the on-the-scene Ambassador rather than the geographically far removed State Department.

SOURCE: U.S. Department of State, *Foreign Relations of the United States 1909* (Washington: Govern-ment Printing Office, 1914). See pp. 595–96.

DOCUMENT:

The Secretary of State to Ambassador Straus.

DEPARTMENT OF STATE,
Washington, November 1, 1909.
SIR: The department has received your No. 2, of September 23, regarding the demands made upon the embassy by American citizens seeking concessions in Turkey and the limits or the scope of the official assistance to be given by the embassy in such matters.

You strongly urge the continuance of the rule which, in accordance with an understanding with the department, you adopted during your ministership at Constantinople, in the past—that in applications for concessions on matters of a financial nature should, in the first instance, be made direct to the department, so that the department would not only be advised but might also give such instructions as to it appeared in accordance with the policy and interests of the Government, and that the action of the embassy be limited to securing for such claimants to concessions who seem to be deserving of it an introduction to the respective departmental chiefs having charge of such matters, and then to leave such persons to depend upon their own efforts, without having any right further to claim or rely upon the embassy's assistance in conducting their negotiations.

As you are aware, the general policy of the department has been to seek to have the same opportunity and facilities for submitting proposals, tendering bids, and obtaining contracts as are enjoyed by concerns of any other foreign country afforded to reputable representatives of American concerns, without espousing the claim of any particular individual or firm to the exclusion of others.

The department could not undertake to investigate the financial responsibility of applicants or to ascertain whether they are entitled to the support of the embassy, and thus make the ambassador a bare agent to state and carry into effect the department's conclusions.

It might be possible, however, and expedient for the department to receive and act upon such applications in the first instance in a routine and *pro forma* way, in order to have a record here and to initiate action by the ambassador, upon whom must rest the real responsibility for determining by the usual method at his place of residence the credit and standing of applicants.

It appears from your dispatch that you are sufficiently aware that applicants claiming to represent American interests are often irresponsible, and your judgment and experience are such as to enable you to give due weight to the standing of the firms who seek your assistance. You need, therefore, no instructions either to support, as far as possible, all proper American efforts to undertake the development of railway projects and obtain public contracts or to guard against any support of unworthy people.

The department would be pleased to receive a further expression of your opinion as to the most desirable manner of treating cases of this character, with a view to avoiding delay by forwarding to Washington the applications in Turkey of those who are known to be responsible or to be acting as representatives of reputable concerns.

1909 The American Commission to Liberia: Instructions and Report

At the turn of the twentieth century, Liberia not only faced continuing territorial encroachments by both Great Britain and France along its borders, but also the possibility of the

Germans establishing a protectorate over the entire country. Liberia further complicated matters by granting an exclusive mining concession to an English syndicate in 1900, which offended German entrepreneurs. Obviously concerned about the fate of their country, a group of Liberian commissioners suggested on June 1, 1908 that the United States should guarantee the territorial integrity of their nation and further assist them by sending expert personnel there. Just before leaving office, President Theodore Roosevelt sent a fact-finding commission to Liberia composed of Roland Falkner, George Sale, and Emmett Scott. Their report dated October 6, 1909 was highly critical of both the British and the French, and suggested that the United States make available financial aid, police training, and scientific research to Liberia. Limited assistance was extended to the African republic, but no treaty or convention was signed, due to Senatorial reluctance and likely British opposition.

SOURCE: U.S. Congress, *Report of the Commission of the United States to the Republic of Liberia*, Senate Document No. 457, 61st Congress, 2nd Session, 1910. See pp. 10–11.

DOCUMENT:

The hinterland of Liberia is practically an unknown region. It is unsettled except for the native tribes, mostly evil disposed toward Liberia, and by occasional French or British stragglers. Administrative and police protection in those regions is practically beyond the power of the Government at Monrovia, while, on the other hand, Great Britain and France are alike insistent upon holding Liberia responsible for the safety of their nationals.

In view of these conditions Great Britain constrained Liberia to conclude an arrangement by which the frontier police of Liberia should be officered by British subjects; on the other hand, France claims the right to establish posts for the protection of the French settlers in Liberian territory when the local power is insufficient.

Of course a boundary of indefinite character thus overpassed becomes no boundary, and the claim of the other party elastically moves inward to keep pace with its stragglers.

The report of the Liberian Commission, herewith submitted, goes very fully into the present questions with Great Britain.

Naturally the importance of this phase of the Liberian situation has led the commissioners to give it the leading place in their report, and to base upon it the first of their recommendations, namely, that the United States extend its aid to Liberia in the prompt settlement of pending boundary disputes. It is the conclusion of the commission that Liberia alone is helpless to obtain a definitive fixation of her boundaries, and that while in the past her negotiations have not been unskillful, she has at every turn been forced to yield to each new aggression. The commission believe that a form of action can be found which is consonant with diplomatic usage and which will enable the United States to appear as attorney or next friend of Liberia and bring to the negotiations of Liberia the ability and prestige of the United States.

The report of the commission deals extensively with the question of the financial situation of Liberia. The debt, both domestic and foreign, is analyzed. It has been for the most part incurred under disadvantageous circumstances, and yet, considering the limited resources and impoverished condition of the national exchequer of Liberia, the total sum, internal and external, is comparatively small—less than one and a half million dollars in all. The recommendation of the commission looks to the establishment of some system of collection and control of the revenues of the country for the benefit alike of the Government and the creditors, modeled in some respect upon the plan which has been of such practical success in Santo Domingo, and that as a part of this plan the existing debt be refunded.

The further recommendation is made that the agencies intrusted with this financial control should also take part in the reform of the internal finances of the Republic.

Both of these suggestions are eminently practical.

The fourth recommendation is that the United States lend its aid to Liberia in organizing and drilling an adequate constabulary or frontier police force.

The importance of this recommendation can hardly be overestimated. It is a vital concomitant of any effective settlement of the boundary questions with Liberia's powerful neighbors to the north and east. As already said, the vague and uncertain character of the boundary, in itself a sufficiently grave evil, is made worse by the virtual inability of Liberia to police any boundary whatever.

The fifth recommendation of the commission is that the United States establish and maintain a research station in Liberia to aid in the development of the agricultural and natural wealth of the country, and to inaugurate the improvements in the line of hygiene and sanitation, so necessary in a tropical and insalubrious climate, and which the experience gained in Cuba, Panama, and the Philippines especially qualifies the United States to devise and execute.

The sixth and last recommendation is that the United States establish a naval coaling station in Liberia.

The advantage and, indeed, the necessity of doing this, if the United States is to undertake the friendly offices outlined in the other recommendations, is obvious.

The report of the commission and its recommendations have received most attentive study on the part of the Department of State and the conclusion is reached that action in the suggested lines is not only expedient but in the nature of a duty to a community which owes its existence to the United States and is the nation's ward.

1911 The Canadian Reciprocity Issue

In 1909 Congress passed the Payne–Aldrich Tariff, a protective measure which threatened commerce between the United States and Canada. Representatives of the two nations thereupon concluded a reciprocity agreement on January 26, 1911 which, among other things, lowered the American tariff on Canadian agricultural products and reduced the Canadian tariff on American manufactured goods. The reciprocity bill passed the House of

Representatives on April 21 by a vote of 268 to 89, and the Senate on July 22 by a vote of 53 to 27, with the Middle West and Great Plains states casting two-thirds of the nay votes. Democratic Speaker of the House Champ Clark of Missouri spoke on behalf of this measure proposed by the Republican Taft Administration on February 4, 1911, and even went so far as to endorse the annexation of Canada. Less enthusiastic were the agricultural interests of the Great Plains. But in the final analysis it was the antireciprocity conservatives who doomed reciprocity by winning the Canadian national election of 1911, unlike the outcome in the Canadian national election of 1988.

SOURCE: *Congressional Record*, February 14, 1911. See p. 2520.

DOCUMENT:

Mr. CLARK of Missouri. The chief thing that this country needs in its business is a wider market, and I am in favor of this reciprocity bill because it gives wider markets to American products. That will be one great point gained. Considered as a whole our exports are large, but our per capita exports are smaller than those of any other great commercial nation on earth, which is not a healthy condition. As much as any other living man I desire to see them increased. Therefore I am for this bill, because it will increase our exports. I am in favor of this bill because it establishes closer trade relations with one of our nearest neighbors, and the closer trade relations you have with your neighbors the better off you are. When Thomas Jefferson delivered his first inaugural on the 4th day of March, 1801, he enunciated the principles upon which this Government should be conducted, and one of the principles was: "Peace, commerce, and honest friendship with all nations; entangling alliances with none." That has been the mainspring of our policy ever since, or should have been. We have spent or will spend somewhere in the neighborhood of $500,000,000 to build the Panama Canal. Therefore I am in favor of the reciprocity treaty to promote our trade relations. That is what we spent that money for. We are not spending that vast sum because we are altruists, but as a business matter. I am for it, because I hope to see the day when the American flag will float over every square foot of the British-North American possessions clear to the North Pole. They are people of our blood. They speak our language. Their institutions are much like ours. They are trained in the difficult art of self-government. My judgment is that if the treaty of 1854 had never been abrogated the chances of a consolidation of these two countries would have been much greater than they are now.

1911 The W. Morgan Shuster Financial Mission to Persia

Not only were American investors active in the Middle East after 1900 (the Chester concession was only one example of many), but U.S. advisors also were offering their services to governments there. In 1907 a revolution took place in Persia, and this led to the overthrow of the existing absolutist system of government and its replacement by a constitu-

tional regime. During the same year, the Anglo–Russian convention established a Russian sphere of interest in the northern part of the country and a British one in the South. Since Persian finances were then in a rather chaotic state, the Persians sought outside assistance in straightening them out, and American lawyer W. Morgan Shuster came to the rescue. As the Treasurer General of Persia, he technically was an employee of its government, and thus did not officially represent the United States there. Facing opposition from corrupt politicians, the Russians, and the British, he left Teheran at the end of 1911. The diplomatic correspondence of the period reflects some of the problems which Shuster faced in Persia.

SOURCE: U.S. Department of State, *Foreign Relations of the United States 1911* (Washington: Government Printing Office, 1918). See pp. 684–86.

DOCUMENT:

The American Minister to the Secretary of State

AMERICAN LEGATION, *Teheran, November 30, 1911.*

In reference to my contract with Persian Government on file Department of State, I have faithfully performed same, executing duties of treasurer general under greatest difficulties to the satisfaction of Persian Legislature, Government, and people. At noon yesterday Russia presented 48-hour ultimatum to Persia demanding my dismissal and that my assistants should be subjected to the approval of Russia and England. Six other Americans serving here with contracts similar to mine and eight others en route to sign contracts, all authorized by Persian Legislature. Russia evidently intends making it impossible for Americans to serve Persian Government. Russian semiofficial press has long been waging campaign of abuse against me, calling me Jew. Apparently no prospect of Persian Parliament revoking my contract. Request prompt information as to protection to which American citizens having contracts made with friendly sovereign nation are entitled under these peculiar circumstances. I am personally indifferent to result, but feel heavy responsibility for 14 other Americans brought here largely through my influence. It is probable that the failure of Parliament to revoke my contract will be followed by actual interference by Russia with my duties, powers, and rights thereunder. I am asking this information not as Persian official but as American citizen.

The American Ambassador to Russia to the Secretary of State.

AMERICAN EMBASSY, *St. Petersburg, December 15, 1911.*

SIR: I have the honor to report that I called to-day upon M. Sazonoff, the minister of foreign affairs.

In connection with Persian matters he confirmed the statement telegraphed to you on December 8, 1911, to the effect that complete personal protection would be given to Mr. Shuster, including, if necessary, an armed escort out of Persia.

He added that Mr. Shuster's selection was particularly disagreeable to Russia, not only on account of his action, but because he is a Jew. I ventured to say that in this at least I thought he was mistaken, but he insisted upon it with great emphasis and ascribed Shuster's interests to this alleged fact. Nevertheless he assured me that Shuster's personal protection by Russia could be absolutely relied upon.

The American Minister to the Secretary of State.

AMERICAN LEGATION, *Teheran, December 28, 1911.*

The Cabinet notified Shuster in writing that the Cabinet and the commission mentioned in my telegram of December 22, 6 p.m., yielding to the ultimatum were compelled to recall him from the Persian service, employing expression similar to language of the ultimatum. He answered acquiescing and expressing willingness to turn over to successor who might be designated. Polite oral messages accompanied the Cabinet communication and Shuster's response. He hopes to depart from Teheran within a week or two. Date not fixed yet. His party will consist only wife, two small daughters, nurse, secretary, and one or two American men.

1912 The Lodge Corollary to the Monroe Doctrine (Japan and Mexico)

Unlike the original Monroe Doctrine, the Lodge Corollary was passed by the Senate as Senate Resolution No. 371 on August 2, 1912. Here the threat to the United States came not from a Spain intent on reconquering Latin America or a Russia desirous of expanding down the Pacific Coast, but rather from a group of Japanese investors who wished to purchase a large site near Magdalena Bay in Baja California, Mexico. This particular area had great potential as a naval base. State Department protests caused the Japanese to withdraw, but Republican Senator Henry Cabot Lodge of Massachusetts nevertheless prevailed on the Senate to pass a resolution embodying the abstract principle involved in the Magdalena Bay episode. The vote was a curious one. Although the resolution passed by an overwhelming 51 to 4 vote, two-fifths of the Senators abstained from voting on the resolution.

SOURCE: U.S. Senate, *Journal*, 62nd Congress, 2nd Session, August 2, 1912. See p. 511.

DOCUMENT:

RESOLVED: That when any harbor or other place in the American continents is so situated that the occupation thereof for naval or military purposes might threaten the communications or the safety of the United States, the Government of the United States could not see, without grave concern, the possession of such harbor or other place by any corporation or association which has such a relation to another Government, not American, as to give that Government practical power of control for naval or military purposes.

1912 President William Howard Taft's Dollar Diplomacy

Rather than adopt a Big Stick approach to foreign policy as had Theodore Roosevelt, President William Howard Taft instead took a somewhat different approach: Dollar Diplomacy. American capitalists would exert partial control over foreign countries, especially those in Latin America and the Far East, through trade and investment rather than through military intervention. Dollar Diplomacy was to be implemented by Secretary of State Philander Chase Knox, who had been a corporate lawyer; Knox once commented on how the American dollar could aid suffering humanity. In his annual message to Congress dated December 3, 1912, President Taft stressed the importance of a merchant marine and a foreign service, as well as of U.S. bankers and newspapers being active overseas. Instead of passively watching developments there, American diplomatic officials should actively cooperate with U.S. businessmen to achieve the optimum economic results.

SOURCE: Richardson, *A Compilation of the Messages and Papers of the Presidents.* See XVI, 7789–90.

DOCUMENT:

It is not possible to make to the Congress a communication upon the present foreign relations of the United States so detailed as to convey an adequate impression of the enormous increase in the importance and activities of those relations. If this Government is really to preserve to the American people that free opportunity in foreign markets which will soon be indispensable to our prosperity, even greater efforts must be made. Otherwise the American merchant, manufacturer, and exporter will find many a field in which American trade should logically predominate preempted through the more energetic efforts of other governments and other commercial nations.

There are many ways in which through hearty cooperation the legislative and executive branches of this Government can do much. The absolute essential is the spirit of united effort and singleness of purpose. I will allude only to a very few specific examples of action which ought then to result. America can not take its proper place in the most important fields for its commercial activity and enterprise unless we have a merchant marine. American commerce and enterprise can not be effectively fostered in those fields unless we have good American banks in the countries referred to. We need American newspapers in those countries and proper means for public information about them. We need to assure the permanency of a trained foreign service. We need legislation enabling the members of the foreign service to be systematically brought in direct contact with the industrial, manufacturing, and exporting interests of this country in order that American business men may enter the foreign field with a clear perception of the exact conditions to be dealt with and the officers themselves may prosecute their work with a clear idea of what American industrial and manufacturing interests require.

1913 Ambassador Henry Lane Wilson and the Huerta Government

There was a revolution in Mexico during 1911, culminating in the exile of the long-term dictator Porfirio Diaz, and ushering in the modern era of Mexican history. The new President, Francisco Madero, lasted less than two years before Victoriano Huerta deposed this impractical idealist. Madero was then imprisoned and murdered, possibly on the orders of Huerta. Outgoing President William Howard Taft adopted a hands-off approach to these developments, but incoming President Woodrow Wilson inaugurated an era of Moral Diplomacy by refusing to recognize Huerta. Despite Wilson's rebuff, Huerta was probably no worse than most heads of state who obtain power by toppling the existing government, and he defended his actions in an interview with the American Ambassador to Mexico, Henry Lane Wilson. Here Huerta refers to the various unresolved issues between the two nations.

SOURCE: Henry Lane Wilson, *Diplomatic Episodes in Mexico, Belgium, and Chile* (New York: Doubleday, Page and Company, 1927). See p. 301.

DOCUMENT:

Mexico, May 7, 1913.

I saw the President to-day at his request. He said that he had been wanting to have a consultation with me for some time relative to the delayed recognition of this government by the government of the United States. I replied that believing the interests of our own country as well as those of Mexico were involved in the early recognition of the latter by the former, I had made repeated representations to Washington urging the resumption of full and cordial official relations, but that neither the Department of State nor the President had given expression to any views and that I was without any guidance as to our attitude, save by conjecture. I said to him that possibly immediate recognition might be brought about by the prompt and unreserved settlement of all of the questions pending between the two governments which formed the basis of my letter of February 24, 1913, to him. I added that I could only surmise that this might be the reason for withholding recognition and that my government might, in deference to a certain section of public opinion, be delaying its action so as to follow other nations in making official recognition; that perhaps the question of recognition might be influenced by the complete reestablishment of peace in Mexico.

The President then asked me if he might talk to me unreservedly as a friend of Mexico and as his personal friend. I consented to this with the reservations that I could have no secrets from my government concerning political matters. He then went on to say, speaking with much earnestness, eloquence, and some bitterness, "that the Mexican nation was solvent and independent and that his administration, though not elected, had been as legally constituted as any government could possibly be and had entered upon the task of reestablishing peace with a bankrupt treasury left by the Madero administration, which had plundered the nation, and with no army; that by careful administration and skillful direction of public funds a new army had been built up and equipped and was about to take the field for active operations against the rebels"; this recruiting he said was now going on at the rate of eight hundred soldiers a day; that peace was being rapidly established throughout the republic, except in certain districts on or near the border and in the state of Morelos; all other outbreaks he said were pure brigandage; that by the end of June he expected to have peace reestablished throughout the republic. He stated that the loan which the government had been negotiating for some time was about to be closed and that the governments of Germany, France, and Italy would soon follow England and Spain in recognizing this republic.

In view of these facts the President said he felt that 'the attitude of the government of the United States in refusing to accord recognition to this government was unwise, unfriendly and, in the event that it should fail to sustain itself, the opinion of the world was certain to place the responsibility for whatever disasters might follow upon the administration at Washington.' In view of this situation he said 'that his government did not feel that it would be justified, in the face of a hostile public opinion and because of the undignified position in which it would be placed by so doing, in concluding the questions at present pending between the two governments; that is to say, the Chamizal, the Colorado River case, the special claims cases, and the general claims.' He added 'that the Washington government's views in these cases, together with the Tlalhualilo case, which had been entirely concluded, had been accepted in principle by this government and that if the government of the United States would place his government in the position of discussing the questions as matters between two friendly and sovereign, if not equally powerful, states, their prompt settlement could be expected, but not before.

1914 Admiral Frank Fletcher on the Arrest of the Crew of the *U.S.S. Dolphin* at Tampico

Relations between the United States and Mexico continued to deteriorate in the months ahead, with the Wilson administration lifting its embargo on arms shipments to the Mexican rebels in February. On April 9, 1914 Mexican authorities arrested the crew of the whale-boat U.S.S. Dolphin, who had gone ashore for gasoline, and marched its members through the streets of the city. The release of the prisoners and a Mexican claim that the incident was the fault of a subordinate did not satisfy Admiral Henry Mayo, the Commander of the American fleet at Tampico, who demanded both a formal apology and a twenty-one-gun salute from Mexican General Morelos Zaragoza. Zaragoza expressed his regrets in writing, and Huerta deplored the episode, but there was no twenty-one-gun salute. Another American Admiral, Frank Fletcher, telegraphed his version of the Tampico incident to Secretary of the Navy Josephus Daniels.

SOURCE: U.S. Department of State, *Foreign Relations of the United States 1914* (Washington: Government Printing Office, 1922). See pp. 451–52.

DOCUMENT:

April 11, 1914, 2 p.m.

Written reports of arrest of boat's crew just received from Mayo and all details are in agreement with the cable dispatch of April 9, 5 p.m. He states that at twelve o'clock a German came on board and reported that the crew of the *Dolphin's* whaleboat and paymaster in charge, who had gone ashore for gasoline, had been arrested by a squad of Federal soldiers. Lieutenant Commander Earle was at once dispatched officially to demand release of these men from General Zaragoza and to ask for explanation. The boat's crew and paymaster were released about 1.30 and returned to the ship. Upon hearing the report of Lieutenant Commander Earle, a letter was sent to Zaragoza by Captain Moffett, in uniform and sidearms. Written reports by Earle, Paymaster Copp, Commander Moffett, German from whom gasoline was purchased, and members of boat's crew, were received, and all agree upon details. Earle reports he was accompanied by Consul Miller and the man from whom the gasoline was purchased. The General, as soon as he learned the facts, immediately dispatched orders to have the paymaster and the men released, and stated that he was sincerely sorry for the occurrence: that the officer in command was ignorant of the first laws of war and was carrying out his instructions to allow no boats whatever at that warehouse dock. Earle told the General that we had no means of knowing there was any objection to going to that dock, which was inside the Federal lines. The General again apologized, and upon returning Earle found that the whaleboat and crew had already been released.

Earle further states in substance that the crew were loading the boat with gasoline and had about eight cases left. Two men were in the boat. An officer in charge of a squad of ten soldiers, all well armed, arrived on the scene and told the paymaster he and the men were under arrest and to come with him. The officer ordered the men in the boat to come out. The men did not come out of the boat and the soldiers then started towards the boat with determined gestures and they again directed the men to leave the boat. Seeing this the paymaster ordered the men to come out. At this time the United States colors were flying from the staff in the bow and the stern of the whaleboat. The soldiers formed in a squad around the men and the paymaster and marched them about five minutes walk, crossing a railroad track which apparently marked the Federal line of defense. At this point an officer of high rank was met and after questioning the lieutenant he seemed angry and directed all hands to return to the boat, where they were told to complete the loading. The boat was not allowed to leave, however, until another officer came up, who shook hands with the paymaster and apologized profusely and allowed the boat to go. The time between the arrest and release was about one hour. The paymaster states his protests and explanations as to his identity and rights were unheeded by the officer [and adds] "On our return, after being allowed to finish loading, we were not allowed to return [to the ship] until the arrival of an officer with the following message:"

> The General sends his excuses and informs you that he has been misinformed and that you can return to your ship.

> *Admiral Mayo states in his report:*

> The arrest of this officer and these men, some of whom were taken from a United States boat flying the United States flag, and the marching of these men through the streets publicly, under armed guard, was, I consider, such a humiliating and gross insult to them and to the flag of the United States that such public apology and reparation as I ask for in my letter to General Zaragoza should be insisted upon.

I am of the opinion that there is ample justification for the demands made by Mayo and that the taking of men from a naval boat flying the American flag is an hostile act which can not be excused by a plea of ignorance on the part of a commissioned Mexican officer. Undue delay in complying with demand to salute American flag only intensifies situation, and retaliatory measures, even to the seizing of a Mexican gunboat, would not be excessive under the circumstances.

1916 An Eyewitness Account of Pancho Villa's Raid on Columbus, New Mexico

In July, 1914, three months after the Tampico incident, President Victoriano Huerta fled to Spain. The American government did not recognize his successor, General Venustiano Carranza, until October, 1915, partly because of the Carranza's attacks on the Catholic church. But Carranza did not enjoy total control over Mexico. His one-time chief lieutenant,

Francisco "Pancho" Villa, launched a revolt against Carranza in the North. Eager to incite a war between Mexico and the United States, Villa raided the town of Columbus, New Mexico on March 9, 1916, leaving behind seventeen American corpses. Cattle inspector Daniel J. "Buck" Chadborn wrote a firsthand account of the surprise attack. Both the American press and Congress were enraged by the incident, and President Wilson ordered General John J. Pershing to invade Mexico with a force of 12,000 men, in an ultimately futile search for Villa that the Carranza regime grudgingly permitted.

SOURCE: Jessie Peterson and Thelma Cox Knoles, *Pancho Villa: Intimate Recollections by People Who Knew Him* (New York: Hastings House, 1977). See pp. 205–6.

DOCUMENT:

I was awakened about 4 a.m. on that morning by the sound of shots. My ranch home was on the eastern outskirts of town. Jack Thomas, another deputy sheriff, was working for me on my ranch and staying at the house. We both jumped up, grabbing our clothes and our guns. At first we thought the commotion was just some cowboys celebrating. By the time we were dressed we knew it was more serious than cowboys shooting into the air to let off steam. There were more shots and quite a bit of yelling going on right in the center of town.

Jack and I took my wife and the three children to a sort of storm cellar near the house. Our neighbors, the John Moores and their two children got to the cellar about that time. The women and kids were plenty scared, but we figured that with the entrance to the dugout hidden by brush they'd be safe down there.

By the time we got into town there were several buildings burning. Bullets were flying everywhere. In the light from the fires we could see a milling mob of Mexicans wearing the big sombreros and crossed gunbelts of Pancho Villa's followers. There were bands of them, shooting and yelling 'Viva Villa!' and 'Viva Mexico!' The Commercial Hotel was blazing. I remember a couple of Customs men, Jolly Garner, nephew of John Nance Garner, and Ben Aguirre, saving a woman from the second floor of the hotel. They got her out and down to the ground by lowering her with sheets tied together. The hotel burned clear to the ground.

The raiders were plundering and looting the burning stores of everything they could carry out. Many of them were just kids. I found one dead boy about fourteen holding a pair of woman's black patent slippers. Another dead boy had his hands full of candy. I saw Steve Birchfield, a rancher, who'd escaped from the hotel. He was still shaking from his experience. The bandits had caught him in his hotel room and demanded his money. In desperation Steve gave them his checkbook. Then, while they were fighting over it, he slipped out and ran. It was a plain miracle that he wasn't killed, because several men in the hotel were shot down. At daylight, all of a sudden it seemed, things got quiet. The Villistas pulled out and hit south for the border.

Diplomatic Episodes from the Wilson Presidency 29

1914 President Woodrow Wilson and the Repeal of the Panama Canal Tolls

During the Taft Administration (1912), Congress passed a measure exempting American coastwise shipping (such as that traveling between San Francisco and New York) from paying any tolls when passing through the yet uncompleted Panama Canal. The measure was directed against transcontinental railroads in the United States, but foreign shippers found it offensive, since the Hay–Pauncefote Treaty of 1901 stipulated that all nations would pay the same rates. Reversing his earlier stance, President Wilson called for the repeal of the tolls exemption in a message to Congress on March 5, 1914. This greatly pleased the British, but greatly offended the Hearst press. Repeal easily cleared the House, but only won by a 50 to 35 margin in the Senate, where Republicans and Westerners led the opposition.

SOURCE: *Congressional Record*, March 5, 1914. See p. 4313.

DOCUMENT:

The PRESIDENT, Mr. Speaker, Mr. President, gentlemen of the Congress, I have come to you upon an errand which can be very briefly performed, but I beg that you will not measure its importance by the number of sentences in which I state it. No communication I have addressed to the Congress carried with it graver or more far-reaching implications as to the interest of the country, and I come now to speak upon a matter with regard to which I am charged in a peculiar degree, by the Constitution itself, with personal responsibility.

I have come to ask you for the repeal of that provision of the Panama Canal Act of August 24, 1912, which exempts vessels engaged in the coastwise trade of the United States from payment of tolls, and to urge upon you the justice, the wisdom, and the large policy of such a repeal with the utmost earnestness of which I am capable.

In my own judgment, very fully considered and maturely formed, that exemption constitutes a mistaken economic policy from every point of view, and is, moreover, in plain contravention of the treaty with Great Britain concerning the canal concluded on November 18, 1901. But I have not come to urge upon you my personal views. I have come to state to you a fact and a situation. Whatever may be our own differences of opinion concerning this much debated measure, its meaning is not debated outside the United States. Everywhere else the language of the treaty is given but one interpretation, and that interpretation precludes the exemption I am asking you to repeal. We consented to the treaty; its language we accepted, if we did not originate; and we are too big, too powerful, too self-respecting a Nation to interpret with too strained or refined a reading the words of our own promises just because we have power enough to give us leave to read them as we please. The large thing to do is the only thing that we can afford to do, a voluntary withdrawal from a position everywhere questioned and misunderstood. We ought to reverse our action without raising the question whether we were right or wrong, and so once more deserve our reputation for generosity and for the redemption of every obligation without quibble or hesitation.

I ask this of you in support of the foreign policy of the administration. I shall not know how to deal with other matters of even greater delicacy and nearer consequence if you do not grant it to me in ungrudging measure.

1914 Theodore Roosevelt Attacks the Payment of a $25 Million Indemnity to Colombia

Another example of the Wilson Administration trying—this time unsuccessfully—to reverse the policy of an earlier President was its 1914 treaty with Colombia. In this document, the American government expressed "sincere regret" that the United States acquired the Canal Zone through the Panamanian revolution, and agreed to pay Colombia an indemnity of $25 million. As expected, Theodore Roosevelt erupted in protest. He sent a scathing letter to the Chairman of the Senate Foreign Relations Committee, and the Senate blocked passage of the treaty for the time being. But Theodore Roosevelt died in 1919, and the presence of oil in Colombia weakened opposition to the treaty in the United States. When the Senate finally approved the treaty in 1921, after a seven-year delay, by an overwhelming majority of 69 to 19, most of the opposition came from pro-Roosevelt Middle Westerners and Westerners.

SOURCE: Morison, Editor, *Letters of Theodore Roosevelt*, VII, 777–79.

DOCUMENT:

Sir: If there is any intention of your Committee to act favorably on the proposed Treaty with Colombia by which we are to pay Colombia twenty-five million dollars and to express regret for the action taken in the past, I respectfully request to be heard thereon.

I was President throughout the time of the negotiations, first with Colombia and then with Panama, by which we acquired the right to build the Panama Canal. Every act of this Government in connection with these negotiations and the other proceedings for taking possession of the Canal Zone and beginning the building of the Canal was taken by my express direction or else in carrying out the course of conduct I had laid down. I had full knowledge of everything of any importance that was done in connection with the transaction by any agent of the Government and I am solely responsible for what was done. The then Secretary of State, John Hay, had almost as complete a firsthand knowledge of what occurred, but no man living, except myself, has this firsthand knowledge; and no man, living or dead, shared the responsibility for the action with me, save in a wholly minor degree.

I ask for this hearing because I regard the proposed Treaty as a crime against the United States, an attack upon the honor of the United States, which, if true, would convict the United States of infamy, and a serious menace to the future well-being of our people. Either there is warrant for paying this enormous sum and for making the apology, or there is not. If there is no warrant for it, then the payment is simply the payment of belated blackmail. If there is warrant for it, then we have no business to be on the Isthmus at all. The payment can only be justified upon the ground that this nation has played the part either of a thief or of the receiver of stolen goods. In such case the only proper course is to restore everything to the original owner. In such case it is a crime to remain on the Isthmus and it will be much worse than an absurdity for the President, the Secretary of State, and other officials of the Government to take part in opening the Canal....

As a matter of fact every action we took was not only open but was absolutely straight and was rendered absolutely necessary by the misconduct of Colombia and the dignity of the United States and the interests not only of the United States but of the world in having the Canal built. Every action we took was in accordance with the highest principles of public and private morality.

1915 Ambassador Henry Morgenthau, Sr.'s Account of the Turkish Massacre of Armenians

The mistreatment of minorities by majorities has been an all-too-frequent occurrence in Middle Eastern history. At the same time that Americans were debating the relative merits of silver and gold during the Election of 1896, they also were sympathizing with those Armenians whom the Turks were persecuting. Two decades later, with World War I raging in Europe, the Turks renewed their assault. The American Ambassador to Turkey, Henry Morgenthau, Sr., wrote a rather graphic description of the persecution in a letter to Secretary of State Robert Lansing dated July 10, 1915.

SOURCE: U.S. Department of State, *Foreign Relations of the United States 1915 Supplement* (Washington: Government Printing Office, 1928). See pp. 982–84.

DOCUMENT:

The Ambassador in Turkey (Morgenthau) to the Secretary of State

Constantinople, July 10, 1915, 9 a.m.

Persecution of Armenians assuming unprecedented proportions. Reports from widely scattered districts indicate systematic attempt to uproot peaceful Armenian populations and through arbitrary arrests, terrible tortures, wholesale expulsions and deportations from one end of the Empire to the other accompanied by frequent instances of rape, pillage, and murder, turning into massacre, to bring destruction and destitution on them. These measures are not in response to popular or fanatical demand, but are purely arbitrary and directed from Constantinople in the name of military necessity, often in districts where no military operations are likely to take place. The Moslem and Armenian populations have been living in harmony, but because Armenian volunteers, many of them Russian subjects, have joined Russian Army in the Caucasus and because some have been implicated in armed revolutionary movements and others have been helpful to Russians in their invasion of Van district, terrible vengeance is being taken. Most of the sufferers are innocent and have been loyal to Ottoman Government. Nearly all are old men [and] women. All the men from 20 to 45 are in Turkish army. The victims find themselves dispossessed of their homes and sent on foot to be dispersed in districts where they are unknown, and no provisions have been made to lodge or to feed them. We have in several places been refused permission to relieve their misery or to have access to them. In some few instances where they opposed these measures and took refuge in the mountains and some arms or bombs were found, it provoked the authorities to further cruelties which they attempt to justify by the opposition. Untold misery, disease, starvation, and loss of life will go on unchecked. Consul Davis of Harput reports:

> Professors American College have been tortured. Some others have died under torture or lost mind. Many hundred young Armenian men originally taken as soldiers, some of whom were students American College, have been sent away without food, clothing, or money. Night of June 23 several hundred other Armenians recently arrested, including professors, American College, were sent away in the middle of the night without food, clothing, or money. Many deaths are reported en route in both lots of prisoners. Preparations are being made apparently to send away many more. I was informed confidentially to-day that an enormous sum of money is now being demanded of the local Armenians. There seems to be a systematic plan to crush the Armenian race. All things make us apprehend permanent closing of American schools.

That only refers to one place. Many Armenians are becoming Moslems to avoid persecution. In addition to humanitarian considerations we have a real interest through the fact that certain objectionable Armenians involved in these forced dispossessions and deportations are naturalized citizens of the United States and that the charitable and educational work of the American Board will suffer considerably and in many places will cease altogether.

The only embassy here which might assist in lessening these atrocities is the German, but I believe it will simply content itself with giving advice and a formal protest probably intended for record and to cover itself from future responsibility. German Ambassador is about to leave on a six weeks' vacation. Have impressed on him that he and his Government will have considerable share in the odium. Immediately upon arrival of his substitute I shall make herculean efforts to enlist his sympathies. Austrian Ambassador has promised me to try to influence Minister of the Interior.

I have repeatedly spoken to the Grand Vizier and pleaded earnestly with Minister of the Interior and Minister of War to stop this persecution. My arguments were unavailing except as to Constantinople. The men in authority are revolutionists and displaced the Hamidian Government with the cooperations of some Armenian revolutionists who know their method and are feared by them as a possible nucleus of a [counterrevolution?] against the present authorities. They admit that they will resort to any and every means to prevent their losing control of Government. They state that it is the Union and Progress committee's nationalistic policy which they refused to modify even when Russia, France, and Great Britain threatened Ottoman Cabinet Ministers with personal responsibility. Turkish authorities desire to avail themselves of present conditions when three of the great powers are at war with them, Italy in strained relations, and the two others are their allies and therefore will not interfere when they are successfully defending the formidable attack at the Dardanelles.

I have conferred with various American missionaries now here [from] Tajmarsovan [Marsovan?], Beirut, Bardizag, and Constantinople, and all agree that present crisis is worse than 1895 and 1896 massacres, but none of them could suggest any further steps than those I have already taken. They fear that the matter will have to run its course. Turkish authorities have definitely informed me that I have no right to interfere with their internal affairs. Still I desire to ask whether you have any suggestions.

1917 The Lansing–Ishii Agreement with Japan

During World War I, Japan, which had an alliance with Great Britain, fought on the same side as the United States. But the American government was quite disturbed by Japanese expansionist tendencies in the Far East, as exemplified by the Twenty-One Demands which Japan presented to China in January, 1915. To Americans, the Twenty-One Demands appeared to challenge the political and territorial integrity of China, and to threaten the Open Door. Shortly after the United States had entered the war, Viscount Ishii journeyed to America to confer with Secretary of State Robert Lansing. The resulting agreement which they reached on November 2 partially undermined the Open Door by conceding that Japan had special interests in China, but it also may have kept Japan in the war on the Allied side.

SOURCE: U.S. Department of State, *Foreign Relations of the United States 1917* (Washington: Government Printing Office, 1926). See p. 264.

DOCUMENT:

Department of State
Washington, November 2, 1917.

Excellency: I have the honor to communicate herein my understanding of the agreement reached by us in our recent conversations touching the questions of mutual interest to our Governments relating to the Republic of China.

In order to silence mischievous reports that have from time to time been circulated, it is believed by us that a public announcement once more of the desires and intentions shared by our two Governments with regard to China is advisable.

The Governments of the United States and Japan recognize that territorial propinquity creates special relations between countries and consequently the Government of the United States recognizes that Japan has special interests in China, particularly in the part to which her possessions are contiguous.

The territorial sovereignty of China, nevertheless, remains unimpaired, and the Government of the United States has every confidence in the repeated assurances of the Imperial Japanese Government that while geographical position gives Japan such special interests they have no desire to discriminate against the trade of other nations or to disregard the commercial rights heretofore granted by China in treaties with other powers.

The Governments of the United States and Japan deny that they have any purpose to infringe in any way the independence or territorial integrity of China, and they declare, furthermore, that they always adhere to the principle of the so-called "open door" or equal opportunity for commerce and industry in China.

Moreover, they mutually declare that they are opposed to the acquisition by any government of any special rights or privileges that would affect the independence or territorial integrity of China, or that would deny to the subjects or citizens of any country the full enjoyment of equal opportunity in the commerce and industry of China.

1920 Secretary of State Bainbridge Colby's Refusal Diplomatically to Recognize the Soviet Union

The Wilson Administration, which refused to recognize the Huerta regime in Mexico, likewise refused to recognize the new Marxist government of the Soviet Union. A "Great Red Scare" spread over the United States during 1919, with its targets including not only Communists, but also Socialists, anarchists, and syndicalists. Some radicals were even deported. Given this climate of opinion, it is not surprising that Robert Lansing's successor as Secretary of State, Bainbridge Colby, would reassert the Wilson Administration's official refusal to recognize the Soviet Union. In one of his most noted state papers, Colby wrote to Italian Ambassador Avezzana on August 20, 1920. Here Colby expressed his faith in the Russian people, but not in the Marxist regime currently in power there.

SOURCE: U.S. Department of State, *Foreign Relations of the United States 1920, Volume III* (Washington: Government Printing Office, 1936). See pp. 465–66.

DOCUMENT:

The United States maintains unimpaired its faith in the Russian people, in their high character and their future. That they will overcome the existing anarchy, suffering and destitution we do not entertain the slightest doubt. The distressing character of Russia's transition has many historical parallels, and the United States is confident that restored, free and united Russia will again take a leading place in the world, joining with the other free nations in upholding peace and orderly justice.

Until that time shall arrive the United States feels that friendship and honor require that Russia's interests must be generously protected, and that, as far as possible, all decisions of vital importance to it, and especially those concerning its sovereignty over the territory of the former Russian Empire, be held in abeyance. By this feeling of friendship and honorable obligation to the great nation whose brave and heroic self-sacrifice contributed so much to the successful termination of the war, the Government of the United States was guided in its reply to the Lithuanian National Council on October 15, 1919, and in its persistent refusal to recognize the Baltic States as separate nations independent of Russia. The same spirit was manifested in the note of this Government, of March 24, 1920, in which it was stated, with reference to certain proposed settlements in the Near East, that "no final decision should or can be made without the consent of Russia."

In line with these important declarations of policy, the United States withheld its approval from the decision of the Supreme Council at Paris recognizing the independence of the socalled republics of Georgia and Azerbaijan, and so instructed its representative in Southern Russia, Rear-Admiral Newton A. McCully. Finally, while gladly giving recognition to the independence of Armenia, the Government of the United States has taken the position that the final determination of its boundaries must not be made without Russia's cooperation and agreement. Not only is Russia concerned because a considerable part of the territory of the new State of Armenia, when it shall be defined, formerly belonged to the Russian Empire: equally important is the fact that Armenia must have the good will and the protective friendship of Russia if it is to remain independent and free.

These illustrations show with what consistency the Government of the United States has been guided in its foreign policy by a loyal friendship for Russia. We are unwilling that while it is helpless in the grip of a non-representative government, whose only sanction is brutal force, Russia shall be weakened still further by a policy of dismemberment, conceived in other than Russian interests.

In the view of this Government, there cannot be any common ground upon which it can stand with a Power whose conceptions of international relations are so entirely alien to its own, so utterly repugnant to its moral sense. There can be no mutual confidence or trust, no respect even, if pledges are to be given and agreements made with a cynical repudiation of their obligations already in the mind of one of the parties. We cannot recognize, hold official relations with, or give friendly reception to the agents of a government which is determined and bound to conspire against our institutions; whose diplomats will be the agitators of dangerous revolt; whose spokesmen say that they sign agreements with no intention of keeping them.

The United States as a Neutral during World War I

30

1915 The German Government's Newspaper Advertisement Warning Americans Not to Sail on the *Lusitania*

Once World War I had broken out in Europe, the British declared the North Sea to be a military area, and placed a large number of mines there. The Germans retaliated by declaring a submarine war zone around the British Isles on February 4, 1915. Despite the fact that both American and British ships were attacked during the days ahead, the flow of travelers from the United States to the British Isles did not stop. On May 1, 1915, the German government placed a proceed-at-your-own-risk advertisement in the New York Times. *Later that day, the* Lusitania *sailed from New York City, with nearly 200 Americans on the passenger list, along with 4,200 cases of small-arms cartridges and other military contraband. Six days later, on May 7, a German submarine torpedoed the* Lusitania *off the Irish coast, with the resulting 1,198 deaths including 128 Americans. Quite naturally, this incident generated a gigantic wave of anti-German sentiment across this country, but at this time there was as yet little editorial sentiment in favor of the United States declaring war on Germany.*

SOURCE: "Notice!" in New York *Times,* May 1, 1915. See p. 19.

DOCUMENT:

NOTICE!

TRAVELLERS intending to embark on the Atlantic voyage are reminded that a state of war exists between Germany and her allies and Great Britain and her allies; that the zone of war includes the waters adjacent to the British Isles; that, in accordance with formal notice given by the Imperial German Government, vessels flying the flag of Great Britain, or of any of her allies, are liable to destruction in those waters and that travellers sailing in the war zone on ships of Great Britain or her allies do so at their own risk.

IMPERIAL GERMAN EMBASSY
WASHINGTON, D.C., APRIL 22, 1915

1916 The House–Grey Memorandum Stating that the United States Probably Would Join the War on the Side of Great Britain

Considering the fact that the American bankers lent a great deal of money to Great Britain (and to France) prior to the U.S. entry into World War I, it is hardly surprising that the American government opted to fight on the British side. Public opinion in this nation also was more pro-British than pro-German, in part because Great Britain was our mother country, in part because of real and alleged German atrocities in Belgium and elsewhere. Early in 1916 Colonel Edward House, representing the Wilson Administration, met with Sir Edward Grey, representing the British government. In Grey's memorandum dated February 22, he revealed that Wilson was in favor of a conference of belligerents for the purpose of ending the war, and that if Germany would not cooperate, the United States would probably enter the war on the Allied side.

SOURCE: Charles Seymour, *The Intimate Papers of Colonel House,* 4 Volumes (Boston: Houghton Mifflin Company, 1926–28).

DOCUMENT:

Colonel House told me that President Wilson was ready, on hearing from France and England that the moment was opportune, to propose that a Conference should be summoned to put an end to the war. Should the Allies accept this proposal, and should Germany refuse it, the United States would probably enter the war against Germany.

Colonel House expressed the opinion that, if such a Conference met, it would secure peace on terms not unfavourable to the Allies; and, if it failed to secure peace, the United States would [probably] leave the Conference as a belligerent on the side of the Allies, if Germany was unreasonable. Colonel House expressed an opinion decidedly favourable to the restoration of Belgium, the transfer of Alsace and Lorraine to France, and the acquisition by Russia of an outlet to the sea, though he thought that the loss of territory incurred by Germany in one place would have to be compensated to her by concessions to her in other places outside Europe. If the Allies delayed accepting the offer of President Wilson, and if, later on, the course of the war was so unfavourable to them that the intervention of the United States would not be effective, the United States would probably disinterest themselves in Europe and look to their own protection in their own way.

I said that I felt the statement, coming from the President of the United States, to be a matter of such importance that I must inform the Prime Minister and my colleagues; but that I could say nothing until it had received their consideration. The British Government could, under no circumstances, accept or make any proposal except in consultation and agreement with the Allies. I thought that the Cabinet would probably feel that the present situation would not justify them

in approaching their Allies on this subject at the present moment; but, as Colonel House had had an intimate conversation with M. Briand and M. Jules Cambon in Paris, I should think it right to tell M. Briand privately, through the French Ambassador in London, what Colonel House had said to us; and I should, of course, whenever there was an opportunity, be ready to talk the matter over with M. Briand, if he desired it.
Foreign Office
22 February 1916

1916 A Pro-Wilson Newspaper Advertisement from the Presidential Campaign Stressing the Peace with Honor Theme

Promoting Woodrow Wilson for reelection in 1916, the Democrats employed the slogan, "He kept us out of war." Unquestionably, Wilson's noninterventionist stance endeared him to both the German–Americans and the Irish–Americans, while Theodore Roosevelt's belligerent stance may have caused some antiwar voters not to cast their ballot for the Republican nominee, Charles Evans Hughes. A typical Democratic newspaper advertisement concluded, "If you want war, vote for Hughes! If you want peace with honor vote for Wilson!" It began as follows.

SOURCE: Political advertisement in New York *Times*, November 4, 1916. See p. 6.

DOCUMENT:

> YOU ARE WORKING;—Not Fighting!
> ALIVE AND HAPPY;—Not Cannon Fodder!
> WILSON AND PEACE WITH HONOR:
> or
> HUGHES WITH ROOSEVELT AND WAR?

Roosevelt says we should hang our heads in shame because we are not at war with Germany in behalf of Belgium!

Roosevelt says that following the sinking of the *Lusitania* he would have foregone diplomacy and seized every ship in our ports flying the German Flag. That would have meant war!

Hughes Says He and Roosevelt are in Complete Accord!

Senator Fall, who has vast interests in Mexico and is Candidate Hughes' advisor as to Mexican Affairs declares "a Hughes war would be preferable to a Wilson peace."

Read the published list of Heavy Subscribers to the Republican campaign fund, then look up the list of Americans with enormous interests in Mexico and learn why those who place the almighty dollar ahead of human life would not hesitate to plunge this country into an ignoble war of conquest—would not stop at sacrificing thousands and thousands of American lives in their greed for oil and gold.

The Lesson Is Plain:

IF YOU WANT WAR, VOTE FOR HUGHES

IF YOU WANT PEACE WITH HONOR

VOTE *FOR* WILSON!

1917 The Intercepted Zimmermann Telegram from Germany to Mexico

Early in 1917, the German Foreign Minister, Arthur Zimmermann, sent a message to the German Minister to Mexico via Count Bernstorff, the German Ambassador to the United States. The British intercepted this communication, and gave a copy of it to the American government. The Zimmermann telegram proposed nothing less than a German–Mexican alliance, although the Germans hardly were in a position to extend considerable financial assistance to Mexico, and the Mexicans hardly were in a position to reconquer the southwestern United States. The Mexican army, though, could have kept its American counterpart tied down along their common border, and thus not available for fighting on the Western front in Europe.

SOURCE: U.S. Department of State, *Foreign Relations of the United States 1917* (Washington: Government Printing Office, 1931). See p. 147.

DOCUMENT:

We intend to begin on the 1st of February unrestricted submarine warfare. We shall endeavor in spite of this to keep the United States of America neutral. In the event of this not succeeding, we make Mexico a proposal of alliance on the following basis: make war together, make peace together, generous financial support and an understanding on our part that Mexico is to reconquer the lost territory in Texas, New Mexico, and Arizona. The settlement in detail is left to you. You will inform the President of the above most secretly as soon as the outbreak of war with the United States of America is certain and add the suggestion that he should, on his own initiative, invite Japan to immediate adherence and at the same time mediate between Japan and ourselves. Please call the President's attention to the fact that the ruthless employment of our submarines now offers the prospect of compelling England in a few months to make peace. Signed, Zimmermann.

1917 Wilson's Cabinet and the Deteriorating Situation vis-à-vis Germany

In mid-March, 1917, German submarines sank four unarmed American merchant ships, with a heavy loss of life. On March 19, 1917, Secretary of State Robert Lansing wrote President Woodrow Wilson that war between the United States and Germany was bound to come. The next day, on March 20, there was a Cabinet meeting at which Wilson brought up the matter of declaring war on Germany. Those present included Secretary of the Treasury William G. McAdoo, Secretary of War Newton Baker, Secretary of the Navy Josephus Daniels, Secretary of the Interior Franklin Lane, Postmaster General Albert S. Burleson, Attorney General Thomas Gregory, Secretary of Agriculture David H. Houston, Secretary of Commerce William Redfield, and Secretary of Labor William Wilson. After discussing the matter, the Cabinet opted for war with Germany. Houston wrote an account of this meeting in his Cabinet memoirs.

SOURCE: David H. Houston, *Eight Years with Wilson's Cabinet 1913 to 1920*, 2 Volumes (Garden City: Doubleday, Page and Company, 1926). See I, 243–44.

DOCUMENT:

Baker said he thought that immediate steps should be taken, or that the country would demand that immediate steps be taken, to raise a great army and that universal training be inaugurated. I added that I was in favour of both, but that in the meantime other things could be done. I suggested that Congressional sanction would be required for the things I thought should be done. It should first of all recognize that a state of war existed. Even if that step was not to be taken, it was desirable to have the Legislative branch in thorough understanding and accord with the Executive. We were drifting. Why delay two weeks? Call Congress and ask it to declare that a state of war existed, to pass the necessary legislation, and to vote the needed appropriations or authorizations. There could be no halfway measures. War could not be waged mildly.

McAdoo spoke to the same effect, indicating many domestic matters which would need immediate attention. Lansing said little or nothing, as usual. Wilson, Secretary of Labour, said that he had reluctantly made up his mind that action had to be taken. We were at war. Congress should be called to declare that it existed. Gregory and Baker and Redfield expressed the same opinion. Lane said nothing. Burleson and Daniels had not spoken.

The President said: "Burleson, you and Daniels have said nothing."

Burleson replied quietly: "We are at war. I am in favour of calling Congress at the earliest moment."

Daniels gave us the views of the naval experts.

The President said that the principal things which had occurred since he had last addressed Congress which differed, except in degree, from what had been discussed, were the Russian Revolution, the talk of more liberal institutions in Germany, and the continued reluctance of our ships to sail. If our entering the war would hasten and fix the movements in Russia and Germany, it would be a marked gain to the world and would tend to give additional justification for the whole struggle, but he could not assign these things as reasons for calling Congress at an earlier date. The justification would have to rest on the conduct of Germany, the clear need of protecting our rights, of getting ready, and of safeguarding civilization against the domination of Prussian militarism.

I remarked that he would not have to determine the details of his address or his exact recommendations till a few days later, but that what he had said was sufficient. The entire Cabinet was definitely in favour of going to the mat with Germany and of going immediately and with all the nation's power.

The Declaration of War Against Germany 31

1917 Wilson's Call for a Declaration of War Against Germany

On April 2, 1917, Woodrow Wilson addressed Congress. In his speech he asked for a declaration of war against the "Prussian autocracy," while also proclaiming that this nation remained "the sincere friends of the German people." Like James Madison's war message in 1812, Wilson's address 105 years later stressed the violation of American rights as a neutral, but it also decried the general ruthlessness of the German submarine commanders. (This was a variation on the Teutonic Menace Hypothesis that Germany was barbaric, militaristic, and expansionistic.) Rather than start a war, war instead had been thrust on the United States.

SOURCE: *Congressional Record*, April 2, 1917. See pp. 102–3.

DOCUMENT:

On the third of February last I officially laid before you the extraordinary announcement of the Imperial German Government that on and after the first day of February it was its purpose to put aside all restraints of law or of humanity and its submarines to sink every vessel that sought to approach either the ports of Great Britain and Ireland or the western coasts of Europe or any of the ports controlled by the enemies of Germany within the Mediterranean. The new policy has swept every restriction aside. Vessels of every kind, whatever their flag, their character, their cargo, their destination, their errand, have been ruthlessly sent to the bottom without warning and without thought of help or mercy for those on board, the vessels of friendly neutrals along with those of belligerents. Even hospital ships and ships carrying relief to the sorely bereaved and stricken people of Belgium, though the latter were provided with safe conduct through the proscribed areas by the German Government itself and were distinguished by unmistakable marks of identity, have been sunk with the same reckless lack of compassion or of principle.

I was for a little while unable to believe that such things would in fact be done by any government that had hitherto subscribed to the humane practices of civilized nations. International law had its origin in the attempt to set up some law which would be respected and observed upon the seas, where no nation had right of dominion and where lay the free highways of the world. By painful stage after stage has that law been built up, with meager enough results, indeed, after all was accomplished that could be accomplished, but always with a clear view, at least, of what the heart and conscience of mankind demanded. This minimum of right the German Government has swept aside under the plea of retaliation and necessity and because it had no weapons which it could use at sea except these which it is impossible to employ as it is employing them without throwing to the winds all scruples of humanity or of respect for the understandings that were supposed to underlie the intercourse of the world. I am not now thinking of the loss of property involved, immense and serious as that is, but only of the wanton and wholesale destruction of the lives of non-combatants, men, women, and children, engaged in pursuits which have always, even in the darkest periods of modern history, been deemed innocent and legitimate. Property can be paid for; the lives of peaceful and innocent people cannot be. The present German submarine warfare against commerce is a warfare against mankind.

It is a war against all nations. American ships have been sunk, American lives taken, in ways which it has stirred us very deeply to learn of, but the ships and people of other neutral and friendly nations have been sunk and overwhelmed in the waters in the same way. There has been no discrimination. The challenge is to all mankind. Each nation must decide for itself how it will meet it.

1917 The Louisville *Courier Journal's* "Vae Victis" Editorial Favoring the Declaration of War

The editor of the Louisville Courier Journal *during World War I was Henry Watterson. A bitter critic of William Jennings Bryan as Secretary of State, his contempt for Germany and the Central Powers was shown by his motto: "To Hell with the Hohenzollerns and the Hapsburgs." Watterson's anti-German editorial, "Vae Victis," which appeared in the April 7, 1917 issue of the* Courier Journal *just after Congress had declared war on Germany, won him a Pulitzer Prize in 1918.*

SOURCE: W. David Sloan, *Pulitzer Prize Editorials: America's Best Editorial Writing, 1917–1979* (Ames: Iowa State University Press, 1980). See pp. 7–9.

DOCUMENT:

Rally round the flag, boys"—Uncle Sam's Battle song;
"Sound the bold anthem! War dogs are howling;
Proud bird of Liberty screams through the air!—*The Hunters of Kentucky*

It is with solemnity, and a touch of sadness, that we write the familiar words of the old refrain beneath the invocation to the starry banner, the breezy call of hero-breeding bombast quite gone out of them; and the glad shout of battle; the carrion note of defiance; because to us, not as to Nick of the Woods, and his homely co-mates of the forest, but rather as to the men of '61, comes this present call to arms.

We may feel with the woman's heart of Rankin of Montana, yet repudiate with manly disdain the sentimental scruples of Kitchin of North Carolina.

There are times when feeling must be sent to the rear; when duty must toe the line; when the aversion brave men have for fighting must yield to the adjuration, "Give me liberty, or give me death!" That time is now upon us.

Unless Patrick Henry was wrong—unless Washington and the men of the Revolution were wrong, that time is upon us. It is a lie to pretend that the world is better than it was; that men are truer, wiser; that war is escapable; that peace may be had for the planning and the asking. The situation which without any act of ours rises before us is as exigent as that which rose before the Colonists in America when a mad English King, claiming to rule without accountability, asserted the right of Kings and sent an army to enforce it. A mad German Emperor, claiming partnership with God, again elevates the standard of right divine and bids the world to worship, or die.

Like a bolt out of the blue flashed the war signal from the very heart of Europe. Across the Atlantic its reverberations rolled to find us divided, neutral, and unprepared. For fifteen years a body of German reservists disguised as citizens have been marching and counter-marching. They grew at length bold enough to rally to the support of a pan-German scheme of conquest and a pro-German propaganda of "kultur," basing its effrontery in the German-American vote, which began its agitation by threatening us with civil war if we dared to go to war with Germany. There followed the assassin sea monsters and the airship campaign of murder.

All the while we looked on with either simpering idiocy or dazed apathy. Serbia? It was no affair of ours. Belgium? Why should we worry? Foodstuffs soaring—war stuffs roaring—everybody making money—the mercenary, the poor of heart, the mean of spirit, the bleak and barren of soul, could still plead the Hypocrisy of Uplift and chortle: "I did not raise my boy to be a soldier." Even the *Lusitania* did not awaken us to a sense of danger and arouse us from the stupefaction of ignorant and ignoble self-complacency.

First of all on bended knee we should Pray to God to forgive us. Then erect as men, Christian men, soldierly men, to the flag and the fray wherever they lead us—over the ocean—through France to Flanders—across the Low Countries to Koln, Bonn and Koblenz—tumbling the fortress of Ehrenbreitstein into the Rhine as we pass and damming the mouth of the Moselle with the debris of the ruin we make of it—then on, on to Berlin, the Black Horse Cavalry sweeping the Wilhelmstrasse like lava down the mountain side, the Junker and the saber rattler flying before us, the tunes being "Dixie" and "Yankee Doodle," the cry being

"Hail the French Republic—Hail the Republic of Russia—welcome the Commonwealth of the Vaterland—no peace with the Kaiser—no parley with Autocracy, Absolutism and the divine right of Kings—to Hell with the Hapsburg and the Hohenzollern!"

1917 Senator Robert La Follette, Sr. Opposes U.S. Entry into World War I

Woodrow Wilson did not receive unanimous Congressional approval for a declaration of war from Congress. The war resolution passed the Senate by a vote of 82 to 6 on April 4, and the House of Representatives by a vote of 372 to 50 two days later. Middle Westerners cast the bulk of the antiwar ballots in the House of Representatives, while future Presidential candidate Robert La Follette, Sr. of Wisconsin spoke out against the war resolution in the Senate. Not only was the Middle West geographically isolated from the more internationalist Atlantic and Pacific Coasts, there were also quite a few settlers of German descent there. In a lengthy speech delivered in the Senate on April 4, 1917, La Follette attacked Great Britain for violating our neutral rights on the Atlantic Ocean and for mining the North Sea in alleged retaliation against Germany.

SOURCE: *Congressional Record*, April 4, 1917. See pp. 231–32.

DOCUMENT:

It is not my purpose to go into detail into the violations of our neutrality by any of the belligerents. While Germany has again and again yielded to our protests, I do not recall a single instance in which a protest we have made to Great Britain has won for us the slightest consideration, except for a short time in the case of cotton. I will not stop to dwell upon the multitude of minor violations of the neutral flag, seizing and appropriating our goods without the least warning or authority in law, and impressing, seizing, and taking possession of our vessels and putting them into her own service. I have constituents, American citizens, who organized a company and invested large sums of money in the purchase of ships to engage in foreign carrying. Several of their vessels plying between the United States and South America were captured almost in our own territorial waters, taken possession of by the British Government, practically confiscated, and put into her service or the service of her admiralty. They are there to-day, and that company is helpless. When they appealed to our Department of State they were advised that they might "file" their papers. And were given the further suggestion that they could hire an attorney and prosecute their case in the English prize court. The company did hire an attorney and sent him to England, and he is there now, and has been there for almost a year, trying to get some redress, some relief, some adjustment of those rights.

But those are individual cases. There are many others. All these violations have come from Great Britain and her allies, and are in perfect harmony with Britain's traditional policy as absolute master of the seas.

I come now, however, to one other event in the naval policy of Great Britain during this war, which to my mind is absolutely controlling upon the action we should take upon the question under consideration.

On the 2d of November, 1914, only three months after the beginning of the war, England issued a proclamation, the most ruthless and sweeping in its violation of neutral rights that up to that time had ever emanated from a civilized government engaged in prosecuting a war, announcing that on three days' notice all of the North Sea, free under international law to the trade of the world, would be entered by our merchant ships at their peril. She based her action upon an assertion that the German Government had been scattering mines in waters open to the world's commerce.

The North Sea, a great stretch of the Atlantic Ocean, extending from Scotland to Iceland, was barred to the commerce of the world, the neutral commerce, that had the same right there that you have to walk down Pennsylvania Avenue.

Before considering the piratical character of this document as a whole it will be noted that while it proposes to use every effort to warn neutral shipping it allows just three days for the warning.

Do you observe that the country with whom we are about to yoke ourselves issued this proclamation, unheard of before in the history of the world, mining a great area of the Atlantic Ocean with deadly contact mines, and gave to the neutral nations only three days' notice? It issued its declaration on the 2d of November, and it went into effect of the 5th day of November.

Of the preliminary allegations in the note concerning the scattering of mines by Germany in the open sea around the British Isles, no proof of it has ever been furnished, so far as I am aware; and, even if it were true, certainly would not have remedied the condition to mine a much larger portion of the sea upon which neutral ships must travel. I say this because of the highsounding but obviously false and hypocritical assertion contained in the proclamation that Britain is taking this action in order to maintain trade between neutral countries within the limits of international law. She was, in fact, by her action absolutely destroying trade between neutral countries, and the penalties for disobeying her orders, and which operate automatically and inexorably, was the destruction by mines of all ships and passengers venturing into the prohibited portion of the sea.

1917 Ambassador to Great Britain Walter H. Page Evaluates Wilson's Role in World War I

The American Ambassador to Great Britain, Walter Hines Page, a literary man with no previous diplomatic experience, developed a great fondness for the British. On the eve of Wilson's war message, Page wrote a memorandum for his own records highly critical of

Wilson. According to the Ambassador, the President had been far too tolerant of Germany, and too enamored of his role as a peacemaker. Failing to lead, Wilson had not acted decisively.

SOURCE: Burton J. Hendrick, *The Life and Letters of Walter H. Page,* 2 Volumes (Garden City: Doubleday, Page and Company, 1922). See II, 222–23.

DOCUMENT:

Embassy of the United States of America, April 1, 1917

In these last days, before the United States is forced into war—by the people's insistence—the preceding course of events becomes even clearer than it was before; and it has been as clear all the time as the nose on a man's face.

The President began by refusing to understand the meaning of the war. To him it seemed a quarrel to settle economic rivalries between Germany and England. He said to me last September that there were many causes why Germany went to war. He showed a great degree of toleration for Germany; and he was, during the whole morning that I talked with him, complaining of England. The controversies we had with England were, of course, mere by-products of the conflict. But to him they seemed as important as the controversy we had with Germany. In the beginning he had made—as far as it was possible—neutrality a positive quality of mind. He would not move from that position.

That was his first error of judgment. And by insisting on this he soothed the people—sat them down in comfortable chairs and said, "Now stay there." He really suppressed speech and thought.

The second error he made was in thinking that he could play a great part as peacemaker—come and give a blessing to these erring children. This was strong in his hopes and ambitions. There was a condescension in this attitude that was offensive.

He shut himself up with these two ideas and engaged in what he called "thought." The air currents of the world never ventilated his mind.

This inactive position he has kept as long as public sentiment permitted. He seems no longer to regard himself not to speak as a leader—only as the mouthpiece of public opinion after opinion has run over him.

He has not breathed a spirit into the people: he has encouraged them to supineness. He is *not* a leader, but rather a stubborn phrasemaker.

And now events and the aroused people seem to have brought the President to the necessary point of action; and even now he may act timidly.

1918 Woodrow Wilson's Fourteen Points Address to Congress

No foreign policy statement which Woodrow Wilson made as President exceeds in importance his Fourteen Points address, which he delivered to Congress on January 8, 1918. The fourteen points included general principles applicable to the entire world ("open cove-

nants of peace openly arrived at"), and specific demands restricted to a single nation (the restoration of Belgium). Far from winning universal acceptance, these fourteen points were quite controversial, especially the one concerning Russia. Critics observed that Moses had only ten commandments, while former President Theodore Roosevelt only gave his full-fledged support to several of the points. Nevertheless, they had an impact on the post-World War I peace settlement, even though they did not win complete acceptance from the other Allied powers.

SOURCE: *Congressional Record,* January 8, 1918. See p. 691.

DOCUMENT:

We entered this war because violations of right had occurred which touched us to the quick and made the life of our own people impossible unless they were corrected and the world secured once for all against their recurrence. What we demand in this war, therefore, is nothing peculiar to ourselves. It is that the world be made fit and safe to live in; and particularly that it be made safe for every peace-loving nation which, like our own, wishes to live its own life, determine its own institutions, be assured of justice and fair dealing by the other peoples of the world as against force and selfish aggression. All the peoples of the world are in effect partners in this interest, and for our own part we see very clearly that unless justice be done to others it will not be done to us. The programme of the world's peace, therefore, is our programme; and that programme, the only possible programme, as we see it, is this:

I.   Open covenants of peace, openly arrived at, after which there shall be no private international understandings of any kind but diplomacy shall proceed always frankly and in the public view.

II.   Absolute freedom of navigation upon the seas, outside territorial waters, alike in peace and in war, except as the seas may be closed in whole or in part by international action for the enforcement of international covenants.

III.   The removal, so far as possible, of all economic barriers and the establishment of an equality of trade conditions among all the nations consenting to the peace and associating themselves for its maintenance.

IV.   Adequate guarantees given and taken that national armaments will be reduced to the lowest point consistent with domestic safety.

V.   A free open-minded, and absolutely impartial adjustment of all colonial claims, based upon a strict observance of the principle that in determining all such questions of sovereignty the interests of the populations concerned must have equal weight with the equitable claims of the Government whose title is to be determined.

VI.   The evacuation of all Russian territory and such a settlement of all questions affecting Russia as will secure the best and freest cooperation of the other nations of the world in obtaining for her an unhampered and unembarrassed opportunity for the independent determination of her own political development and national policy and assure her of a sincere welcome into the society of free nations under institutions of her own choosing; and, more than a welcome, assistance also of every kind that she may need and may herself desire. The treatment accorded Russia by her sister nations in the months to come will be the acid test of their good will, of their comprehension of her needs as distinguished from their own interests, and of their intelligent and unselfish sympathy.

VII. Belgium, the whole world will agree, must be evacuated and restored, without any attempt to limit the sovereignty which she enjoys in common with all other free nations. No other single act will serve as this will serve to restore confidence among the nations in the laws which they have themselves set and determined for the government of their relations with one another. Without this healing act the whole structure and validity of international law is forever impaired.

VIII. All French territory should be freed and the invaded portions restored, and the wrong done to France by Prussia in 1871 in the matter of Alsace–Lorraine, which has unsettled the peace of the world for nearly fifty years, should be righted, in order that peace may once more be made secure in the interest of all.

IX. A readjustment of the frontiers of Italy should be effected along clearly recognizable lines of nationality.

X. The peoples of Austria–Hungary, whose place among the nations we wish to see safeguarded and assured, should be accorded the freest opportunity of autonomous development.

XI. Rumania, Serbia, and Montenegro should be evacuated; occupied territories restored; Serbia accorded free and secure access to the sea; and the relations of the several Balkan states to one another determined by friendly counsel along historically established lines of allegiance and nationality; and international guarantees of the political and economic independence and territorial integrity of the several Balkan states should be entered into.

XII. The Turkish portions of the present Ottoman Empire should be assured a secure sovereignty, but the other nationalities which are now under Turkish rule should be assured an undoubted security of life and an absolutely unmolested opportunity of autonomous development, and the Dardanelles should be permanently opened as a free passage to the ships and commerce of all nations under international guarantees.

XIII. An independent Polish state should be erected which should include the territories inhabited by indisputably Polish populations, which should be assured a free and secure access to the sea, and whose political and economic independence and territorial integrity should be guaranteed by international covenant.

XIV. A general association of nations must be formed under specific covenants for the purpose of affording mutual guarantees of political independence and territorial integrity to great and small states alike.

In regard to these essential rectifications of wrong and assertions of right we feel ourselves to be intimate partners of all the governments and peoples associated together against the Imperialists. We cannot separate in interest or divide in purpose. We stand together until the end.

The Postwar Peace Settlement 32

1919 The War Guilt Clause (Article 231) of the Treaty of Versailles and Article 10 of the Covenant of the League of Nations

> *Germany did not start World War I in the sense that Adolf Hitler attacked Poland on September 1, 1939 to start World War II. Nevertheless, at Versailles the Big Four opted to blame the war on the Germans (who were quite naturally resentful) as a prelude to demanding reparations from them. This condemnation is to be found in Article 231, the so-called war guilt clause. An equally controversial aspect of the Treaty of Versailles was the Covenant of the League of Nations, Article 10 of which committed the other members of that body to come to the aid of any member threatened by external aggression. Isolationists were of the opinion that this might well involve the U.S. in a war not directly affecting its vital interests.*

SOURCE: C. F. Redmond, Compiler, *U.S. Treaties, Conventions, Protocols and Agreements 1910–1923*, (Washington: Government Printing Office, 1923). See pp. 3339 and 3419.

DOCUMENT:

Article 10.

The Members of the League undertake to respect and preserve as against external aggression the territorial integrity and existing political independence of all Members of the League. In case of any such aggression or in case of any threat or danger of such aggression the Council shall advise upon the means by which this obligation shall be fulfilled.

Article 231.

The Allied and Associated Governments affirm and Germany accepts the responsibility of Germany and her allies for causing all the loss and damage to which the Allied and Associated Governments and their nationals have been subjected as a consequence of the war imposed upon them by the aggression of Germany and her allies.

1919 Robert Lansing Assesses the Versailles Conference (1921)

Secretary of State Robert Lansing was a member of the American peace commission at the Versailles Conference after World War I, along with Wilson, Colonel Edward House, General Tasker H. Bliss, and career diplomat Henry White. When Wilson returned to the United States for one month early in 1919, Lansing and House made various concessions which Wilson found objectionable. Lansing later testified on behalf of the Treaty of Versailles before the Senate Committee on Foreign Relations, after negotiators had finalized this document. Nevertheless, Lansing was by no means fully satisfied with what Wilson had accomplished at Paris, as is evidenced by numerous criticisms of the President which he set forth in his diplomatic memoirs.

SOURCE: Robert Lansing, *The Big Four and Others at the Peace Conference* (Boston: Houghton Mifflin Company, 1921). See pp. 71–73.

DOCUMENT:

The President, as we review his career as a peace commissioner at Paris, stands forth as one of the great dominating figures of the Conference, who reached the zenith of his power over the public mind of Europe, over the delegates and over the negotiations at the first plenary session of the Conference. The reasons for his decline in power, a fact which can hardly be questioned, may be one or more of many. First, the loss of his superior position by intimate personal intercourse with the European statesmen, which could have been avoided if he had remained in the United States or if he had declined to sit as a delegate at Paris. Second, his evident lack of experience as a negotiator and his failure to systematize the work of the American Commission and to formulate a programme. Third, his seclusiveness and apparent determination to conduct personally almost every phase of the negotiations and to decide every question alone and independently. Fourth, his willingness to arrange all settlements behind closed doors with the three other heads of states present at the Conference. Fifth, his unavoidable lack of knowledge of the details of some of the simple as well as the intricate problems to be solved. Sixth, his insistence on the adoption of the covenant of the League of Nations, as drafted, and the overcoming of opposition by concessions to national aspirations, the justice of which was at least disputable. Seventh, his loss of the initiative in the formulation of the provisions of the treaties. Eighth, his apparent abandonment of the smaller nations and his tacit denial of the equality of nations by consenting to the creation of an oligarchy of the Great Powers at the Conference and in a modified form in the covenant. And, ninth, the impression, which greatly increased after his return from the United States in March, that the American people were not a unit in support of his aims as to a league of nations, as those aims were disclosed by the report made to the Peace Conference.

This list might be extended, but the reasons stated are sufficient to explain much that occurred at Paris and also many of the features of the treaty of peace with Germany which have been the subject of debate, censure, and denunciation.

1919 Herbert Hoover Discusses the Versailles Conference (1958)

Although Herbert Hoover was elected President as a Republican in 1928, he first came to widespread public attention while a member of the Wilson Administration, in which he served as the U.S. Food Administrator. Hoover later attended the Versailles Conference, where he engaged in an informal conference with General Jan C. Smuts of South Africa and noted British economist John Maynard Keynes. Despite Hoover's later opposition to the Keynesian-inspired deficit spending of the New Deal, Hoover and Keynes were in agreement at Versailles that the peace treaty being drawn up there was likely to have negative economic consequences.

SOURCE: Herbert Hoover, *The Ordeal of Woodrow Wilson* (New York: McGraw Hill Book Company, 1958). See pp. 234–35.

DOCUMENT:

I certainly had no admiration for the conduct of the German militarists. But if the world was to have peace, it had, in my mind to choose one of two alternatives: to reduce Germany to such poverty and political degradation that initiative and genius would be extinguished; or to give her terms that would permit the new representative government under President Ebert to live with the hope that free government might develop the nation as a peaceful member of the family of mankind. If this were not done, there would come either a return of the sullen militarists or the already infectious Communists—both with aggression in their souls.

I was convinced that the terms set up in this draft of the Treaty would degrade all Europe and that peace for the long run could not be built on these foundations. I believed the Treaty contained the seeds of another war. It seemed to me that the economic provisions alone would pull down the whole Continent and, in the end, injure the United States.

I arose at early daylight and went for a walk in the deserted streets. Within a few blocks I met General Smuts and John Maynard Keynes of the British Delegation. We seemed to have come together by some sort of telepathy. It flashed into all our minds why each was walking about at that time of morning. Each was greatly disturbed. We agreed that the consequences of many parts of the proposed Treaty would ultimately bring destruction. We also agreed that we would do what we could among our own nationals to point out the dangers.

General Smuts had full knowledge of Old World diplomacy, an independent mind and often real statesmanship. Keynes was the economist for the British Delegation. Lloyd George apparently did not like him and referred to him as the "Puck of Economics." He had a brilliant mind, powerful in analysis, and the gift of expression. Like most intellectuals, he was usually groping for new shapes and forms for the world, rather than for wisdom in what to do next. That sort of mind has a high place in the world, although it sometimes gets on the nerves of the fellow who must keep the machinery of civilization operating in the meantime. However, Keynes and I agreed fully on the economic consequences of the Treaty.

1919 Woodrow Wilson's Final Tour Speech on Behalf of the League of Nations

By the Fall of 1919 it was becoming apparent that the Treaty of Versailles was encountering increased opposition in the Senate. With radio not yet in wide use, President Wilson decided to take his case to the American people by means of a 9,500 mile train tour. Given the somewhat precarious state of his health, this was a risky gamble, but he did receive a rather enthusiastic welcome on the Pacific Coast and in the Rocky Mountains. The President, however, experienced a physical collapse after speaking at Pueblo, Colorado, after which he returned to Washington where he suffered a stroke. Among the more interesting features of his speech at Pueblo were an endorsement of an international charter for the rights of labor, and an attack on hyphenated Americans. Many German-Americans and Irish-Americans had been opposed to the United States entering the war on the side of Great Britain.

SOURCE: Ray Stannard Baker and William E. Dodd, Editors, *Woodrow Wilson, War and Peace: Presidential Messages, Addresses, and Public Papers (1917–1924),* 2 Volumes (New York: Harper and Brothers, 1927). See II, 400–401.

DOCUMENT:

There is an organized propaganda against the League of Nations and against the treaty proceeding from exactly the same sources that the organized propaganda proceeded from which threatened this country here and there with disloyalty, and I want to say—I cannot say too often—any man who carries a hyphen about with him carries a dagger that he is ready to plunge into the vitals of this Republic whenever he gets ready. If I can catch any man with a hyphen in this great contest I will know that I have got an enemy of the Republic. My fellow citizens, it is only certain bodies of foreign sympathies, certain bodies of sympathy with foreign nations that are organized against this great document which the American representatives have brought back from Paris. Therefore, in order to clear away the mists, in order to remove the impressions, in order to check the falsehoods that have clustered around this great subject, I want to tell you a few very simple things about the treaty and the Covenant.

Do not think of this treaty of peace as merely a settlement with Germany. It is that. It is a very severe settlement with Germany, but there is not anything in it that she did not earn. Indeed, she earned more than she can ever be able to pay for, and the punishment exacted of her is not a punishment greater than she can bear, and it is absolutely necessary in order that no other nation may ever plot such a thing against humanity and civilization. But the treaty is so much more than that. It is not merely a settlement with Germany; it is a readjustment of those great injustices which underlie the whole structure of European and Asiatic society. This is only the first of several treaties. They are all constructed upon the same plan. The Austrian treaty follows the same lines. The treaty with Hungary follows the same lines. The treaty with Bulgaria follows the same lines. The treaty with Turkey, when it is formulated, will follow the same lines. What are those lines? They are based upon the purpose to see that every government dealt with in this great settlement is put in the hands of the people and taken out of the hands of coteries and of sovereigns who had no right to rule over the people. It is a people's treaty, that accomplishes by a great sweep of practical justice the liberation of men who never could have liberated themselves, and the power of the most powerful nations has been devoted not to the aggrandizement but to the liberation of people whom they could have put under their control if they had chosen to do so. Not one foot of territory is demanded by the conquerors, not one single item of submission to their authority is demanded by them. The men who sat around that table in Paris knew that the time had come when the people were no longer going to consent to live under masters, but were going to live the lives that they chose themselves, to live under such governments as they chose themselves to erect. That is the fundamental principle of this great settlement.

And we did not stop with that. We added a great international charter for the rights of labor. Reject this treaty, impair it, and this is the consequence to the laboring men of the world, that there is no international tribunal which can bring the moral judgments of the world to bear upon the great labor questions of the day. What we need to do with regard to the labor questions of the day, my fellow countrymen, is to lift them into the light, is to lift them out of the haze and distraction of passion, of hostility, not into the calm spaces where men look at things without passion. The more men you get into a great discussion the more you exclude passion. Just so soon as the calm judgment of the world is directed upon the question of justice to labor, labor is going to have a forum such as it never was supplied with before, and men everywhere are going to see that the problem of labor is nothing more nor less than the problem of the elevation of humanity.

1919 Senator Henry Cabot Lodge Explains His Reservations About the Peace Treaty (1925)

Republican Senator Henry Cabot Lodge of Massachusetts and Democratic President Woodrow Wilson were rival scholars in politics, and eventually developed a strong personal dislike for each other. Whereas Lodge had long been associated with the Mahan–

Roosevelt imperialist stance on foreign policy, Wilson was a global idealist committed to his Fourteen Points and the League of Nations. Contrary to a widespread popular misconception, Lodge was not an Irreconcilable toward the Treaty of Versailles (as Senators Hiram Johnson and William E. Borah were), but rather a Reservationist willing to accept an amended treaty. In addition, one must remember that had Lodge edged too close to Wilson's position, his fellow Republicans might have deposed him as the Chairman of the Senate Foreign Relations Committee. Lodge wrote an account of the struggle over the League in his The Senate and the League of Nations *(1925), which quite understandably is highly critical of Wilson.*

SOURCE: Henry Cabot Lodge, *The Senate and the League of Nations* (New York: Charles Scribners Sons, 1925). See pp. 224–26.

DOCUMENT:

Mr. Wilson was a master of the rhetorical use of idealism. He spoke the language very well and he convinced many people who were content with words that he was a man of vision and one ready to sacrifice all to his ideals. He had a selection of phrases which he used very skillfully. I might say, for instance, that "breaking the heart of the world" was one and "making the world safe for democracy" was another, while "vision," "uplift" and "forward-looking" were seldom absent. These are fair examples of his successful use of this form of popular appeal. But no one who ever studied Mr. Wilson's acts, whether as an opponent or as a supporter, if at all clear-sighted, could fail to perceive that in dealing with political or international questions, whether great or small, Mr. Wilson was extremely practical and always had in view some material and definite purposes which would result, if successful, possibly in benefit to the world, certainly in benefit to himself. Anyone who attempted to deal with Mr. Wilson, therefore, in opposition or in support, who proceeded on the theory that he was a "visionary" and an "idealist" was certain to meet with disappointment. M. Clemenceau is reported to have said, and the saying had wide currency, that "Mr. Wilson talked like Jesus Christ and acted like Lloyd George." It was a rough gibe but, like many another, it had a strong foundation in truth, and M. Clemenceau knew Mr. Wilson very well and had come into very sharp contact and conflict with him. If President Wilson had been a true idealist, in regard to the covenant of the League of Nations, for example, he would have saved his covenant and secured its adoption by the Senate of the United States by accepting some modification of its terms, since the man who really seeks the establishment of an ideal will never sacrifice it because he cannot secure everything he wants at once, and always estimates the principle as more important than its details and qualifications. If it had been a real ideal with Mr. Wilson and tinged with no thought of self, he would have succeeded in large measure, just as Lincoln did when he put aside for the time the emancipation of the slaves, on which his heart was set, in order to preserve the Union, which to him was the highest ideal and the dominant purpose at the moment.

In support of my opinion I might make a long list of men who suffered extinction, who were simply dropped down the *oubliette*, so far as can be discerned, because their advice had not been agreeable to Mr. Wilson. Their honest opinions had in some degree differed from his and they had ventured to tell him the whole truth as they understood and believed it. I think I may say that if I needed any outside support of my estimate of Mr. Wilson, who to me was simply an element to be calmly and cooly considered in a great problem of international politics, I could find it in some of those utterances of his close friends to which I have referred. But I am content to leave it where it stands and can only say that the theory which I adopted as to the motives for Mr. Wilson's actions and which therefore would enable me to forecast his coming attitude on any question were never misleading or inaccurate. As the strenuous days which were filled by the contest over the League of Nations passed by, almost every one bringing its difficult and its crucial question, I made no mistake in my estimate of what President Wilson would do under certain conditions. He, of course, was not only a leading element in my problem, but because he had been thrown into the Presidency by the lottery of presidential nominations he was of necessity a chief figure in the composition of the scene which I have attempted to depict.

There are those still extant who speak of Mr. Wilson as a "very great man." An able man in certain ways, an ambitious man in all ways he certainly was; by no means a commonplace man. But "very great men" are extremely rare. Mr. Wilson was not one of them. He was given the greatest opportunity ever given to any public man in modern times which we may date from the Revival of Learning in Europe. Having this opportunity he tried to use it and failed. The failure necessarily equalled the opportunity in magnitude and the failure was complete and was all his own. No one could have destroyed such a vast opportunity except the man to whom it was given, and in this work of destruction unaided and alone Mr. Wilson was entirely successful. Difficult as such an achievement in the face of such an opportunity was, it does not warrant describing the man who wrought the destruction in any sense as a "very great man."

1920 Isolationist Senator William E. Borah's Address Critical of the League of Nations

Republican Senator William E. Borah of Idaho, who died in 1940, was one of the leading isolationists between the two world wars. Like Hiram Johnson, he opposed American entry into both the World Court and the League of Nations. During the debate in the Senate over American membership in the League, Borah unleashed a blistering indictment of Great Britain and France, whom he accused of large-scale land grabbing. Later that year the pro-League Democrats lost the Presidential election to the Republicans in a landslide.

SOURCE: *Congressional Record*, March 3, 1920. See pp. 3800–1.

DOCUMENT:

Mr. Borah.   There never was such land-grabbing in the history of Europe as we are proposing to underwrite. It is larger than the original thirteen Colonies, larger than the Louisiana Purchase, larger than that vast territory which I have named lying west of the great Mississippi River.

Senators, when you have ratified the treaty and proceeded to your homes you will be called upon to explain to the people of the United States whether you are willing for your boys and their boys to underwrite this unconscionable and indefensible seizure of territory. You will be called upon to say to them, "We propose that you shall hold Egypt in subjection, that you shall hold Mesopotamia in subjection, that you shall hold Persia in subjection. Bear in mind to-day, my friends, that there is not a foot of this 1,607,000 square miles of territory but what is in open objection to the reign of the British Empire. Persia is objecting, Egypt is objecting, even old India is in insurrection, and from one end of this vast empire to the other this new territory is now in open protest against land-grabbing which has been going on.

Take Persia, which has an area of 607,200 square miles. I did not include that in the other estimate. If you include Persia you have got something like 2,000,000 square miles of territory which you have turned over to the British Empire as a result of the peace conference at Versailles. Not strange that Lord Curzon should say:

> Great Britain has gained in this war all and indeed more than she set out to win. Our navy remains at the end of the war intact and unassailed. The principle of the freedom of the seas, which is the basis of our national existence, stands unimpaired and unimpugned. The British protectorate over Egypt is provided for in one of the clauses of the treaty, and our new possessions are made safe under our command.

Col. Hilder in the House of Commons said:

> The outstanding feature of the peace treaty is that it puts the British Empire at the highest point that it has ever reached in regard to territorial and world influence. Largely by force of circumstances and the leading part which our navy and army took in either the breaking down or destroying of the enemy we have been left with far greater territory and power than at any other period in the history of our race.

So far as I am individually concerned I do not care—except for the people who are held in subjection—anything about the possessions of the British Empire. I am not complaining if she can take these subject peoples and satisfy them and make them believe that they are better off under her rule and reign than they are without it; I do not care to what extent the British Empire legitimately spreads its influence over the world. I am not envious of her power nor jealous of her extended holdings. What I object to, my friends, is that we are becoming responsible for this condition of affairs; that we are proposing to underwrite and guarantee it; and we shall be under just the same obligation to see that Egypt remains a part of the British Empire as we shall be to see that Canada remains a part of the British Empire. When you say that Europe has changed, that there are different standards and different principles and different policies, consider the question of the freedom of the seas, of the conscription of armies, of secret diplomacy, of broken pledges, of land grabbing, and that is what we are asked to enter into and become a part of.

Now, let me read again what the President said the other day:

> But if substantial agreement on what is just and reasonable is not to determine international issues, * * * then the time is not yet come when this Government can enter a concert of powers the very existence of which must depend upon a new spirit and a new order of affairs.

But Great Britain is not the only nation which has been grabbing land and whose activities we propose to underwrite. France has taken possession of Syria in contravention of every principle upon which we went into the conference at Versailles, and in opposition to the wishes of the people and inhabitants of the territory. France is holding Syria to-day by force of arms. Blood is being shed there over the title which France claims, and it is one of the things which is stirring the very soul of the great Moslem peoples, the most deadly when aroused to war that have ever inhabited the face of the earth. Countless millions of Mussulmans from India and Egypt and China and all parts of the earth where they inhabit are now stirred to their depths by reason of the action of Great Britain in Egypt and in Persia and of France in Syria. It is this condition of affairs, this "new spirit" and "new order," into which we are asked to enter. Has Europe changed? Where is the "new spirit"? Where is the "new order"?

1919 William Randolph Hearst Attacks the League in the New York *Evening Journal*

The newspaper publisher William Randolph Hearst, who had played a major role in pushing the United States into the Spanish–American War, afterward became a prominent isolationist. In the opinion of Hearst, American membership in the League of Nations might well lead to the abandonment of the Monroe Doctrine, and would be less likely to guarantee peace than an isolationist United States flaunting its naval power. A representative example of his thinking is an editorial which appeared in the New York Evening Journal during 1919 (specific date not available).

SOURCE: Mrs. Fremont Older, *William Randolph Hearst: American* (Freeport: Books for Libraries Press, 1972). See pp. 424–25.

DOCUMENT:

A League of Nations is of no real value....There was a League of Nations after the Napoleonic wars, and the object of that League was to end war forever. But within a very few years the very nations that composed the League were at each other's throats.

There were two Leagues of Nations before the war—the Entente and the Triple Alliance. The war between these nations was precipitated by the disposition of these two Leagues to meddle in Balkan difficulties. The League of Nations will not establish peace. In fact, the real danger is that it will drag the United States into war that it would otherwise have no connection with.

Nothing that I know of will establish world peace at present. The abolition of war is like the abolition of slavery, a matter of education and civilization. But peace for our own country can be secured if we retire behind the greatest navy in the world and attend to our own business. The object of the League is good. The intention of the framers is good, but I am seriously afraid that the League will develop complications which would be a distinct injury to our country, and which will lead us to depart from the very wise principles of the founders of this Republic who warned us against mingling in and meddling in European complications and conflicts.

The League of Nations means that we together with other members of the League would be compelled to take an interest in, and to a certain extent, to take part in the various quarrels of minor European nations and even major European nations. This we ought not to do.

The League of Nations also means that European nations constituting a majority of the League will proceed to interfere in matters affecting this Western Hemisphere of ours. This means an abandonment of the Monroe Doctrine, the submission of our inter-American questions to a court, the majority of which will be disposed to decide matters against the interests of the United States. I cannot see how the Democratic Party can be willing to abandon the Monroe Doctrine, a doctrine which has proved to be of such great advantage to this country and to the whole Western Hemisphere.

Major Foreign Policy Developments under Harding, Coolidge, and Hoover 33

1921 Secretary of States Charles Evans Hughes and the Washington Disarmament Conference (1925)

The leading diplomatic achievement of the Harding administration was the treaties resulting from the Washington Disarmament Conference of 1921–22. This meeting was the brainchild of Senator William E. Borah of Idaho, who obtained widespread public support for his plan. Under one of the agreements the United States, Great Britain, and Japan were to accept a 5–5–3 ratio in capital ships, while under another agreement (the Four Power Treaty) these three countries and France were to respect each others' rights in the Pacific Basin. Still another understanding, the Nine Power Treaty, bound the signatories to honor "the sovereignty, the independence, and the territorial and administrative integrity of China." It was the Four Power Treaty which encountered the most opposition in the Senate, where it drew the opposition of twenty-seven Senators, twenty-three of them Democrats and fourteen from the South. In his discussion of the treaty before the American Historical Association on December 29, 1922, Secretary of State Charles Evans Hughes focused his attention on such topics as the Open Door and spheres of influence.

SOURCE: Charles E. Hughes, *The Pathway of Peace* (New York: Harper and Brothers, 1925). See pp. 50–53.

DOCUMENT:

Pacific and Far Eastern Questions. The indirect result of the Conference in the Shantung settlement was, as I have said, of controlling importance. The Four-Power Treaty in the simplest manner solved a great problem while pledging nothing contrary to our traditions. It created the atmosphere of peace and confidence in friendly relations, and at the same time provided for the immediate termination of the Anglo-Japanese Alliance, thus disposing of one of the most difficult questions relating to the Far East.

The Chinese Treaties give China a Magna Charta. We could not provide stability for China but we did provide assurances of respect for her sovereignty, independence and territorial and administrative integrity, and the full and most unembarrassed opportunity to develop and maintain for herself an efficient and stable government. We have done all that we can do for China short of the interference which she resents and we condemn.

For the first time the principle of the Open Door, or equality of commercial opportunity, in its application to China, has the sanction of a precise definition in appropriate treaty provisions. We were not content with general statement of principles; we proceeded to particulars.

It was the opinion of all the delegates at the Conference that the time had arrived for a definite and succinct statement and the added assurance of a binding obligation. Accordingly, in the Treaty setting forth the principles and policies to be applied in relation to China, the contracting Powers other than China agree that they will not seek nor support their respective nationals in seeking "**(a)** any arrangement which might purport to establish in favor of their interests any general superiority of rights with respect to commercial or economic development in any designated region of China; **(b)** any such monopoly or preference as would deprive the nationals of any other Power of the right of undertaking any legitimate trade or industry in China, or of participating with the Chinese government, or with any local authority, in any category of public enterprise, or which by reason of its scope, duration or geographical extent is calculated to frustrate the practical application of the principle of equal opportunity."

And, further, they agree "not to support any agreements by their respective nationals with each other designed to create Spheres of Influence or to provide for the enjoyment of mutually exclusive opportunities in designated parts of Chinese territory."

Spheres of influence are no longer sanctioned. As Mr. Balfour stated in the Conference the phraseology adopted in the resolution which later became the provision of the Treaty quoted above "admirably expressed the view that that custom had not only gone but had gone forever and was now explicitly condemned."

The Open Door policy is not limited to China. Recently we have had occasion to apply it to mandated territories. It voices, whenever and wherever there may be occasion, the American principle of fair treatment and freedom from unjust and injurious discrimination. The more specific statement in the Chinese Treaty of what this policy connotes cannot fail to be of great value as a precedent in dealing with similar questions elsewhere.

The Washington Conference, if its work continues to enjoy the same support in public sentiment which was so emphatically expressed at the time, will not only afford a better assurance of peace and the continuance of friendly relations, but will serve to illustrate the method of effective international co-operation which fully accords with the genius of American institutions.

1921 The U.S. Government and American Petroleum Interests in the Netherlands East Indies

By the end of World War I, the Netherlands East Indies had become one of the important focal points of global petroleum activity. American oilmen wished to have access to Netherlands East Indies (NEI) oil, but the Dutch government was highly protective of its mineral riches there, and it sometimes favored foreign entrepreneurs who were not Americans. The United States now began to use Dutch interest in American oil properties as a bargaining chip in its diplomatic negotiations, as Minister to the Netherlands William Phillips stressed in an April 25, 1921 communication to Secretary of State Charles Evans Hughes. This letter reasserted the traditional American principle of equal commercial opportunity. It was not until 1928, however, that Jersey Standard obtained a large amount of additional petroleum acreage in the Netherlands East Indies.

SOURCE: U.S. Department of State, *Foreign Relations of the United States 1921, Volume II* (Washington: Government Printing Office, 1936). See pp. 536–38.

DOCUMENT:

The Minister in the Netherlands (Phillips) to the Secretary of State

The Hague, April 25, 1921

Following is text of note handed to Minister for Foreign Affairs April 19th:

Excellency, during the last twelve months I have, on several occasions, presented to Your Excellency the very great interest of my Government in the participation by American capital in the development of the mineral oil deposits of the Netherlands East Indies. With your approval I have also had frequent interviews with the Minister of the Colonies on this same subject.

On every occasion I have sought to impress upon the Government of the Netherlands that the real interest of the Government of the United States in these matters lies in the recognition of the principle of mutual or reciprocal accessibility to vital and natural resources by the nationals of the United States and by those of foreign countries, and the belief that the recognition of the principle of equal opportunity is the solution of the future oil problems throughout the world. I have pointed out that the United States has for years carried a burden of supplying a large part of the petroleum consumed by other countries, that Dutch capital has had free access to American oil deposits, and that the petroleum resources of no other country have been so heavily drawn upon to meet foreign needs as the petroleum resources of the United States. I have pointed out that in the future ample supplies of petroleum have become indispensable to the life and prosperity of my country as a whole, because of the fact that the United States is an industrial nation in which distance renders transportation difficult and agriculture depends largely on labor-saving devices using petroleum products.

In these circumstances, my Government finds no alternative than the adoption of the principle of equally good opportunity with the proviso that no foreign capital may operate in public lands unless its government accords similar or like privileges to American citizens; and furthermore I have submitted that in the light of the future needs of the United States such very limited and purely defensive provisions as the above might become inadequate should the principle of equality of opportunity not be recognized in foreign countries.

It is perhaps needless to say that my Government is fully aware of the laws and regulations in the Indies which prohibit foreign companies as such from entering the Colonies for the development of mineral oils. On the other hand, my Government is very greatly concerned when it becomes apparent that the monopoly of such far-reaching importance in the development of oil is about to be bestowed upon a company in which foreign capital other than American is so largely interested.

In this connection, I desire most earnestly to divert [sic] to Your Excellency's attention the fact that American capital stands ready to assist in the development of the Djambi fields and other oil deposits in the Netherlands Indies.

In conclusion, I venture to say once more that my Government attaches the highest importance to the recognition of the principles of reciprocity and equal opportunity in the solution of the oil problem, as well as the extension to American capital organized under Dutch law of the same privileges and benefits which are granted to other foreign capital similarly organized under the laws of the Netherlands.

1921 The Dispatching of an American Financial Mission to Persia Headed by Arthur Millspaugh

After World War I, Persia (now Iran) remained in need of financial advice, but W. Morgan Shuster was unwilling to return there. The State Department then recommended Arthur C. Millspaugh, an economic specialist, but stipulated that Millspaugh would be acting in the capacity of a private citizen. Millspaugh remained in Persia for five years (1922–27) as the Director General of Persian Finances. He introduced a number of reforms, which he summarized in the following statement to the press on September 17, 1927. By this time, Millspaugh had encountered growing opposition from both bureaucrats and aristocrats in Persia; the Shah himself had begun to turn against Millspaugh. Millspaugh accordingly resigned his position and returned to the United States.

SOURCE: U.S. Department of State, *Foreign Relations of the United States 1921, Volume III* (Washington: Government Printing Office, 1936). See pp. 564–66.

DOCUMENT:

Dr. A.C. Millspaugh, Administrator General of the Finances of Persia has arrived in Washington after terminating five years of work in that country as head of the American Financial Mission.

Dr. Millspaugh left America in the Fall of 1922 with eleven assistants, having entered into a contract with the Persian Government which gave him complete charge of the finances, including the control of the personnel of the financial administration and an absolute power of veto over expenditures and financial obligations. The contracts of several members of the Mission having expired, the Majless (Persian Parliament) in 1925 authorized the employment of twelve additional Americans for the finances, including an agricultural expert, bringing the total of the Mission to sixteen. Soon after, an American director of highways, Mr. A. F. Morris, was engaged; and, following the decision of the Government and Majless to construct a railroad, Mr. W. B. Poland was appointed director of railroad construction and was provided with a staff of eleven American engineers. More recently, Mr. F. C. Clapp of New York has been engaged to study and report on the petroleum resources of the country. The Majless also authorized the establishment of a National Bank and the engagement of an American as Director.

At the time of the departure of Dr. Millspaugh from Persia in August of this year, there were fourteen Americans in the Ministry of Finance and thirteen in the Ministry of Public Works.

Dr. Millspaugh said:

At the time of the arrival of the American Mission in Persia in November, 1922, the civil administrations of the country, particularly the Ministry of Finance, were in a state of demoralization, corruption and chaos. The Persian people, while ancient in their history and traditions, were young in the experience of popular government, and, with rudimentary standards of public honesty and duty, were unable to separate finance and administration from the wasting and corrupting influences of internal and foreign politics.

Huge sums in taxes remained uncollected and arrears of salaries and claims against the Government had accumulated to an amount of over fifteen million dollars. In the fiscal year 1922–23 the deficit was over $2,500,00[0] in a budget of approximately twenty million. The funds applied to productive purposes were negligible and judicial, educational, and sanitary institutions were practically non-existent. The hopeful factors in the situation were: the achievements of Reza Khan Pahlevi in establishing order and security; the decision of the Government and Majless to obtain the effective assistance of foreign experts; the universal genuine desire in the country for reform and progress; the general sentiment of sound nationalism; and the characteristics of the people—quick, intelligent, adaptable, and industrious.

During its almost five years of work, the American Mission made encouraging progress in reorganizing the tax system; revenues increased from twenty million to thirty-one million dollars; expenditures were placed on a budgetary basis and accounting was established in all departments except the Ministry of War; the budget was balanced and in the last two fiscal years a substantial surplus was created; the funded debt was reduced and the payment of claims begun; $1,500,000 was being devoted annually to the construction and maintenance of highways; a fund of over ten million dollars, increasing at the rate of six million dollars a year, was established for railroad construction; appropriations for agricultural development were increased; telegraph lines were extended, wireless stations were erected and are working, commercial air transport is in operation over three main routes; mail transport has been largely motorized; steps were taken to encourage domestic industry and to promote exports, the Government adopted a program of curtailing opium cultivation, which is now being discussed at Geneva, sufficient revenues were allocated to public instruction to render possible the establishment in a few years of universal elementary education; sanitation facilities were extended. Just before my leaving, the Majless passed a law for a national bank and I had proposed appropriations for irrigation works, for the settlement of the tribes on the land, and for the encouragement of the rug industry.

There was convincing evidence at the time of my departure that a large majority of all the influential classes of the people, such as the merchants, clericals, landed proprietors, and office-holders, a majority of the deputies of the Parliament, a majority of the ex-prime ministers and ex-ministers who had held office during the period of our work, even a majority of the Council of Ministers at the time of my departure, were in favor of the renewal of my contract without essential change. The Government proposed, however, that any dispute in the future between the Minister of Finance and myself should be decided according to the nature of the dispute, by the Council of Ministers, by an *ex-officio* commission of high Persian officials, or by the Majless. My counter-proposal that disputes over the interpretation of my contract should be decided by the Majless was not accepted by the Government. My feeling was, that the Government proposal, if accepted by me, would have deprived me of all effective control over expenditures and would have prevented the Mission from continuing to serve the real needs of the Persian people.

One must view with keen regret the decision of the Shah which may interrupt an undertaking which had become internationally known as a unique and useful service by a devoted group of Americans to an ancient and awakened, but still undeveloped, Oriental nation.

1925 The Bombing Raids of U.S. Flyers in Morocco

By the end of 1924, Abd-el-Krim, a native leader, had terrorized the Spanish Zone of Morocco and had pushed on toward the border of the French Zone. In most countries, including the United States, Abd-el-Krim was something of a hero. Nevertheless, a group of private American flyers entered the war on the French side and bombed Riff villages from the air. Their exploits received a generally hostile reaction in the United States, as is attested to by the following summary of press coverage. The State Department informed the American flyers that they were violating certain laws prohibiting citizens of this country from entering the military service of foreign nations, although the French were not unexpectedly appreciative of their efforts. That November, during the rainy season, the flyers went on what turned out to be a permanent furlough.

SOURCE: "American Bombers and Riff Babies," in *Literary Digest*, October 31, 1925. See pp. 29–30.

DOCUMENT:

Some Americans will rejoice at the news that the American aviators who have been bombing the Riffs are to be on furlough through the rainy season, beginning November 14—a furlough which some correspondents believe will become permanent. Tho they especially disclaim that they have bombed villages filled with women and children and other non-combatants, dispatches have reached this country from time to time that the American flyers had scored many "sure hits" in dropping bombs on Riff villages. As was told in *The Literary Digest* of October 3, the Consul-General at Tangier was notified by the State Department that the American flyers were apparently violating the laws of the United States in giving military service against a people with which the United States is not at war. But there are reasons against this military service higher than any which depend on legal technicalities, in the opinion of some American observers. The Pittsburgh *Post* prints this dispatch: "What was once a tiny hamlet with a few houses huddled together…is to-night a ruin testifying to American accuracy in air-bombing," and comments: "And what were once loving mothers and bright, beautiful, prattling babies, and feeble, harmless old men and women, the dispatch might have added, but doesn't, are to-night mangled corpses." Saying that these aviators do not represent America, *The Post* asks:

> Why are they fighting the Riffians in the first place? The United States has no quarrel with these Berber tribesmen, whose only offense against the French and Spanish is that they are trying to expel the foreign usurpers from their land. Probably the Riffians in the long run will be better off under European rule than as an independent nation. They are a semi-barbarous people with customs and practises of which civilization disapproves. Still they may point to the killing of their women and children by the airmen as an example of barbarism on the part of so-called civilized people. The American nation traditionally has always felt sympathetic toward a country striving to throw off a foreign yoke. The American aviators would have been acting more in keeping with the spirit of their native land if they had volunteered to fight for the Riffians, instead of against them. There would have been something gallant and chivalrous in going to the aid of these brave mountaineers fighting for liberty against overwhelming odds.
>   But there is nothing gallant or chivalrous in raining bombs on defenseless villages. It is unspeakably dirty business.

No matter what well-reasoned theses may be developed over the Moroccan situation, observes the New York *Sun*, "it is felt by the average American that the Riffs are a valorous and liberty-loving people." As *The Sun* looks at it further,

> They may be wrong in their present revolt, which is nominally against the Sultan of Morocco, but actually against the foreign overlordship of France and Spain. But, right or wrong, liberty and independence are their watchwords, and to many American imaginations it is strange that men who should have imbibed a love for liberty in their infancy should interfere in such a quarrel and in such a way.

Bitter criticism of the American aviators comes from *The Christian Century* (Undenominational). It notes the "gusto" appearing in some of the dispatches telling how the American flyers have bombed whole villages off the map, and recalls:

> When Germans blew up French villages or dropt bombs on London districts these same American newspapers boiled with indignation. That was a part of war—always cruel and savage—but fought by nationals who at least had the excuse of patriotism. In the case of these American soldiers of fortune there is no excuse except the joy of the man-hunt. It is royal sport, and the fact that women and children who have the misfortune to have been born in these Riffian villages are victims means no more than the death of rabbits when one hunts big game.

On the other hand, the American aviators in the Moroccan service assert that their conduct is perfectly proper, both from a legal and a moral view-point. According to an interview with a correspondent of the New York *Herald Tribune*, Lieut.-Col. Charles Kerwood, second in command of the American air squadron, says the Americans are volunteers in the guard of the Sultan of Morocco, and the officer asserts that the members of the squadron have never received official news or even official intimation that their activities were against the policy of the American Government. On the contrary, Colonel Kerwood says that they have received constant assurances that their participation in the Moroccan campaign was being well received by the people at home. He recites that Ambassador Herrick had sent the Americans a message, saying that if he were only young enough he would be delighted to join them in the work they were doing.

1928 The Pact of Paris (Kellogg–Briand Pact) Renouncing War as an Instrument of National Policy

Idealism in American foreign relations reached its peak with the signing and ratification of the agreement outlawing war as an instrument of national policy. In its original form this had taken the form of a two country pact between the United States and France, with Secretary of State Frank Kellogg and Foreign Minister Aristide Briand respectively, handling the negotiations. Eventually, a total of fifteen nations agreed to the final version (which did permit defensive war) on August 27, 1928. When it came before the Senate for a vote in January 1929, the Kellogg-Briand Pact was ratified by the overwhelming margin of 85 to 1. Whatever the pact's merits may have been, within a decade Europe was again at war.

SOURCE: Edward J. Trenwith, Compiler, *U.S. Treaties, Conventions, Protocols and Agreements 1923–1937* (Washington: Government Printing Office, 1938). See pp. 5130–4.

DOCUMENT:

The President of the German Reich, the President of the United States of America, His Majesty the King of the Belgians, the President of the French Republic, His

Majesty the King of Great Britain, Ireland and the British Dominions beyond the Seas, Emperor of India, His Majesty the King of Italy, His Majesty the Emperor of Japan, the President of the Republic of Poland, the President of the Czechoslovak Republic,

Deeply sensible of their solemn duty to promote the welfare of mankind;

Persuaded that the time has come when a frank renunciation of war as an instrument of national policy should be made to the end that the peaceful and friendly relations now existing between their peoples may be perpetuated;

Convinced that all changes in their relations with one another should be sought only by pacific means and be the result of a peaceful and orderly process, and that any signatory Power which shall hereafter seek to promote its national interests by resort to war should be denied the benefits furnished by this Treaty;

Hopeful that, encouraged by their example, all the other nations of the world will join in this humane endeavor and by adhering to the present Treaty as soon as it comes into force bring their peoples within the scope of its beneficent provisions, thus uniting the civilized nations of the world in a common renunciation of war as an instrument of their national policy;

Have decided to conclude a Treaty and for that purpose have appointed as their respective Plenipotentiaries:

Who, having communicated to one another their full powers found in good and due form have agreed upon the following articles:

Article I. The High Contracting Parties solemnly declare in the names of their respective peoples that they condemn recourse to war for the solution of international controversies, and renounce it as an instrument of national policy in their relations with one another.

Article II. The High Contracting Parties agree that the settlement or solution of all disputes or conflicts of whatever nature or of whatever origin they may be, which may arise among them, shall never be sought except by pacific means.

Article III. The present Treaty shall be ratified by the High Contracting Parties named in the Preamble in accordance with their respective constitutional requirements, and shall take effect as between them as soon as all their several instruments of ratification shall have been deposited at Washington.

1928 The Clark Memorandum Terminating the Roosevelt Corollary to the Monroe Doctrine

By the time of the Coolidge administration, the American government was beginning to retreat from its policy, begun by Theodore Roosevelt, of intervening in Latin America. Accordingly, Under Secretary of State J. Reuben Clark drew up a scholarly 236 page memorandum in 1928, which Frank Kellogg's successor as Secretary of State, Henry Stim-

son, had published in 1930. In the introduction to this document, Clark stated that the Monroe Doctrine affirmed the dichotomy between America and Europe, not between the United States and Latin America. Certain interventions by the American government in the affairs of Cuba, the Dominican Republic, Haiti, and Nicaragua might therefore be justified on grounds of security and self-preservation, but not under the Monroe Doctrine itself.

SOURCE: J. Reuben Clark, *Memorandum on the Monroe Doctrine,* Senate *Documents* No. 114, 71st Congress, 2nd Session, 1930. See pp. xix–xx.

DOCUMENT:

It is of first importance to have in mind that Monroe's declaration in its terms, relates solely to the relationships between European states on the one side, and, on the other side, the American continents, the Western Hemisphere, and the Latin American Governments which on December 2, 1823, had declared and maintained their independence which we had acknowledged.

It is of equal importance to note, on the other hand, that the declaration does not apply to purely inter-American relations.

Nor does the declaration purport to lay down any principles that are to govern the interrelationship of the states of this Western Hemisphere as among themselves.

The Doctrine states a case of United States vs. Europe, not of United States vs. Latin America.

Such arrangements as the United States has made, for example, with Cuba, Santo Domingo, Haiti, and Nicaragua, are not within the Doctrine as it was announced by Monroe. They may be accounted for as the expression of a national policy which, like the Doctrine itself, originates in the necessities of security or self-preservation—a policy which was foreshadowed by Buchanan (1860) and by Salisbury (1895), and was outlined in what is known as the "Roosevelt corollary" to the Monroe Doctrine (1905) in connection with the Dominican debt protocol of 1904; but such arrangements are not covered by the terms of the Doctrine itself.

Should it become necessary to apply a sanction for a violation of the Doctrine as declared by Monroe, that sanction would run against the European power offending the policy, and not against the Latin American country which was the object of the European aggression, unless a conspiracy existed between the European and the American states involved.

In the normal case, the Latin American state against which aggression was aimed by a European power, would be the beneficiary of the Doctrine not its victim. This has been the history of its application. The Doctrine makes the United States a guarantor, in effect, of the independence of Latin American states, though without the obligations of a guarantor to those states, for the United States itself determines by its sovereign will when, where, and concerning what aggressions it will invoke the Doctrine, and by what measures, if any, it will apply a sanction. In none of these things has any other state any voice whatever.

1930 Secretary of State Henry Stimson and the Presence of Slave Labor in Liberia

During 1930, the League of Nations received a critical report from a three-man committee it had appointed to survey conditions in Liberia, one of whose members was the Negro American Dr. Charles Johnson. The State Department then proposed that the Liberian government implement various reforms, but Liberia's slowness in carrying out these reforms led the State Department to complain to the Liberian Consul General at Baltimore on November 17, 1930. Partly as a result of this pressure, the Liberian legislature in the following months passed acts prohibiting the export of contract labor overseas, providing for the reorganization of the hinterland, forbidding pawning, establishing a public health and sanitary service, and permitting unrestricted trade with the interior. Another of the members of the three-man commission, the prominent Liberian Arthur Barclay, then became the President of his country.

SOURCE: U.S. Department of State, *Foreign Relations of the United States 1930, Volume III* (Washington: Government Printing Office, 1945). See pp. 369–70.

DOCUMENT:

The Department of State to the Liberian Consulate General at Baltimore

Memorandum. The establishment of the International Commission of Inquiry into the Existence of Slavery and Forced Labor was agreed upon with extreme reluctance by the Liberian Government. The Liberian Government consistently denied, both before and during the investigation, that either slavery or forced labor existed in the Republic. The Commission, comprising one American member, one member nominated by the League of Nations, and one member appointed by Liberia, began its work in April of this year. It submitted its unanimous report to the Liberian Government on September 8, 1930. The American member delivered a signed copy to the Department of State on October 21, 1930.

This report is a shocking indictment of the Liberian Government's policy of suppression of the natives,—permitted, if not actually indulged in, by nearly all the high officials of Liberia, including the Vice President of the Republic. The conclusions are drawn from over two hundred and sixty depositions. Many suspicious criminal practices and even torture are cited.

While direct criminal participation in the shipment of forced labor to the Spanish colony of Fernando Po, under conditions characterized by the report as "scarcely distinguishable from slave raiding and slave trading," is established against Vice President Yancy, several district commissioners, county superintendents and many other officials, the President of Liberia and members of his cabinet were aware of these and other abuses, having received recorded complaints from the natives. High officials of the Liberian Government made use on their private farms of forced labor, often brutally and ruthlessly impressed under the guise of Government work. The report establishes the existence of domestic and tribal slavery, as well as "pawning" of natives.

Since the submission of the report on September 8, 1930, the Government of Liberia has made numerous promises of reform, but, in so far as the American Government is aware, the Government of Liberia has failed to submit definite plans for their execution. The Department of State is informed that a Cabinet committee was appointed to examine the report, but that its recommendations comprised a series of only partial reforms, without measures for carrying them out. Subsequently, two Executive Proclamations were issued—one forbidding the further exportation of Laborers, and the other declaring domestic servitude and "pawning" illegal. Neither carried adequate sanctions. With respect to the latter, the American Government points out that slavery has always been "illegal" in Liberia, having been expressly forbidden by the Constitution of 1847.

On September 30, 1930, the President of Liberia informed the American Government that the Liberian Government "accepted the recommendations of the International Commission" and agreed to carry them out.

1932 The Stimson Doctrine: Japan and Manchuria

Japanese expansionism in the Far East reasserted itself in 1931. On September 18 of that year, an explosion (which the Japanese themselves might have detonated) did a slight amount of damage to the Japanese-controlled South Manchurian railroad. Japanese troops now quickly invaded South Manchuria and occupied various key positions, in obvious violation of the Kellogg–Briand Pact, the Nine Power Pact, and the Covenant of the League of Nations. But the League of Nations did not stop the Japanese, and President Herbert Hoover did not want to involve the United States in a Far Eastern conflict. Secretary of State Henry Stimson, though, addressed a protest to the Japanese and Chinese governments early in 1932, and elaborated on his ideas in a letter to Senator William E. Borah dated February 23, which he regarded as perhaps the most significant state paper he had ever composed. His opposition to the Japanese invasion of Manchuria became known as the Stimson Doctrine.

SOURCE: U.S. Department of State, *Foreign Relations of the United States: Japan, 1931–1941, Volume I* (Washington: Government Printing Office, 1943). See pp. 83–87.

DOCUMENT:

You have asked my opinion whether, as has been sometimes recently suggested, present conditions in China have in any way indicated that the so-called Nine Power Treaty has become inapplicable or ineffective or rightly in need of modification, and if so, what I considered should be the policy of this Government.

Six years later the policy of self-denial against aggression by a stronger against a weaker power, upon which the Nine Power Treaty had been based, received a powerful reinforcement by the execution by substantially all the nations of the world of the Pact of Paris, the so-called Kellogg–Briand Pact.

The recent events which have taken place in China, especially the hostilities which having been begun in Manchuria have lately been extended to Shanghai, far from indicating the advisability of any modification of the treaties we have been discussing, have tended to bring home the vital importance of the faithful observance of the covenants therein to all of the nations interested in the Far East. It is not necessary in that connection to inquire into the causes of the controversy or attempt to apportion the blame between the two nations which are unhappily involved; for regardless of cause or responsibility, it is clear beyond peradventure that a situation has developed which cannot, under any circumstances, be reconciled with the obligations of the covenants of these two treaties, and that if the treaties had been faithfully observed such a situation could not have arisen. The signatories of the Nine Power Treaty and of the Kellogg–Briand Pact who are not parties to that conflict are not likely to see any reason for modifying the terms of those treaties. To them the real value of the faithful performance of the treaties has been brought sharply home by the perils and losses to which their nationals have been subjected in Shanghai.

That is the view of this Government. We see no reason for abandoning the enlightened principles which are embodied in these treaties. We believe that this situation would have been avoided had these covenants been faithfully observed, and no evidence has come to us to indicate that a due compliance with them would have interfered with the adequate protection of the legitimate rights in China of the signatories of those treaties and their nationals.

On January 7th last, upon the instruction of the President, this Government formally notified Japan and China that it would not recognize any situation, treaty or agreement entered into by those governments in violation of the covenants of these treaties, which affected the rights of our Government or its citizens in China. If a similar decision should be reached and a similar position taken by the other governments of the world, a *caveat* will be placed upon such action which, we believe, will effectively bar the legality hereafter of any title or right sought to be obtained by pressure or treaty violation, and which, as has been shown by history in the past, will eventually lead to the restoration to China of rights and titles of which she may have been deprived.

In the past our Government, as one of the leading powers on the Pacific Ocean, has rested its policy upon an abiding faith in the future of the people of China and upon the ultimate success in dealing with them of the principles of fair play, patience, and mutual goodwill. We appreciate the immensity of the task which lies before her statesmen in the development of her country and its government. The delays in her progress, the instability of her attempts to secure a responsible government, were foreseen by Messrs. Hay and Hughes and their contemporaries and were the very obstacles which the policy of the Open Door was designed to meet. We concur with those statesmen, representing all the nations in the Washington Conference who decided that China was entitled to the time necessary to accomplish her development. We are prepared to make that our policy for the future.

U.S. Diplomacy in the First Roosevelt Administration

1933 Ambassador to Cuba Sumner Welles on F.D.R.'s Promulgation of the Good Neighbor Policy (1944)

Unlike Secretary of State Cordell Hull, who had been a Democratic Senator from Tennessee before becoming Secretary of State, Ambassador to Cuba (and later Under Secretary of State) Sumner Welles was a specialist in Latin American affairs. Welles found that President Franklin Roosevelt was similarly interested in this part of the world, which he had visited on a number of occasions. But when F.D.R. pledged the United States to follow a Good Neighbor policy in his first inaugural address, he did not specifically refer to Latin America. Nor was he the first President to implement such a policy, as the Hoover Administration had taken steps in that direction. Nevertheless, it is Franklin Roosevelt who is widely credited with establishing the Good Neighbor Policy toward Latin America.

SOURCE: Sumner Welles, *The Time for Decision* (New York: Harper and Brothers, 1944). See pp. 191–93.

DOCUMENT:

When Franklin Roosevelt became President he had for a long time taken a deep and constructive interest in inter-American affairs. He believed that in its own interest this country should put its relations with its American neighbors upon a new and completely different foundation. He believed primarily that it must abandon its long-standing policy of interference, and above all of military intervention. He was convinced that the juridical equality of all the American nations must be recognized in practice as well as in words. Furthermore, he was persuaded of the necessity for inter-American consultation whenever trouble within one republic threatened to become a source of danger to the others. This would ensure that mediation or any protective measure would be undertaken only by concerted action.

Moreover, President Roosevelt, unlike all of his predecessors, had been long familiar with the nations of Central and South America, from both personal knowledge and experience. He had, long before he assumed office, visited Venezuela and Colombia. During his eight years as Assistant Secretary of the Navy, he had had occasion to visit Panama and Cuba, and he had not only visited, but voyaged extensively through, the Dominican Republic and Haiti, for whose peoples he had developed a peculiar regard. Finally, while not fluent in the Spanish language, he could understand it and read it with ease. All this facilitated his grasp of the underlying problems of inter-American relations and made it easier for him to determine the most effective methods of remedying the mistakes of the past.

He was constantly anxious to obtain the fullest possible information on developments in the Western Hemisphere, and to learn every aspect of the problems, both political and economic, which were affecting the welfare of the other American peoples. He was particularly interested in finding markets in the United States for new exports from the countries to the south as the most practical way to relieve their growing economic distress. During the months prior to his inauguration, inter-American relations formed an important part of his study of national problems. As one of the basic objectives in his foreign policy, he set the creation of hemispheric unity.

This new inter-American policy came to be known as the "good neighbor policy" more by chance than by deliberate intent. In his first inaugural message, President Roosevelt announced that the United States would pursue in its dealings with all the nations of the world the policy of the good neighbor. The phrase was not intended to apply solely to the other American republics. But in an address on Pan-American Day, the first April 14 after he took office, the President laid special emphasis upon this aspect of his foreign policy as the course which his government would follow in its dealings with the peoples of the New World. Inasmuch as his words were immediately backed by practical action in this hemisphere, it was not many months before the people of Central and South America, and subsequently of the United States, seized upon the "good neighbor" phrase as particularly applicable to the policy pursued by this government in its dealings with the twenty other republics. It has now so definitely become associated with inter-American relations that its broader meaning, as used in the President's first inaugural message, has been lost.

1933 Herbert Feis on F.D.R.'s "Sabotaging" of the London Economic Conference (1966)

During the early years of the Roosevelt Presidency, Herbert Feis was an economic advisor to the State Department. After leaving government service, he wrote a number of books examining American foreign policy during the age of F.D.R. In one of these volumes, he analyzed the developments surrounding Roosevelt's decision to scuttle the June, 1933 London Economic Conference, and its gold bloc currency stabilization program. Roosevelt chose to treat the global depression as basically an American phenomenon, and the New Deal accordingly evolved in a nationalist rather than an internationalist direction in the months which followed.

SOURCE: Herbert Feis, *1933: Characters in Crisis* (Boston: Little, Brown and Company, 1966). See pp. 220 and 223–24. Also see footnotes on pp. 219–20.

DOCUMENT:

The text of the declaration which Roosevelt had before him when he wrote his reply began by recording that the signatory governments agreed that "stability in the international monetary field be attained as quickly as possible" and that "Gold exchange be re-established as the international measure of exchange value, it being recognized that the parity and time at which each of the countries now off gold undertake to stabilize must be decided by the respective governments concerned."

The governments whose currencies were on the gold standard reasserted their determination to maintain that standard at the parities which existed at that time.

The governments not on the gold standard reaffirmed that their ultimate objective was to restore, under proper conditions, their international monetary standard based on gold.

That evening the President and Mrs. Roosevelt, Morgenthau and Howe sat around and talked for several hours about foreign exchange, gold and world exports. Morgenthau brought out charts based on relationships between the three which Professor George Warren of Cornell had developed. He also summarized for the President an article in the *Saturday Evening Post* by Garet Garrett, a talented but tricky journalist. Its oversimplified contentions may be indicated by two brief excerpts. "Does foreign trade promote prosperity, or is it the prosperity of individual nations that produce foreign trade? If it is the latter way—if it is the prosperity of individual nations that produces foreign trade—then obviously the first problem in a state of world-wide depression is not how to reinflate foreign trade; the first problem is that of mending the internal economy of nations, each one to find out how it shall balance its own budget, re-employ its own people, restore its own solvency." And, "the war of currencies…is not a competitive debasement of money in the world of foreign trade; it is a money war among nations, carried on by governments." Roosevelt listened attentively.

Before he went to bed late that night the President wrote his reply, addressing it to Hull. He flatly rejected the joint declaration. After some dubious and jumbled comments on some of its details—indicating haste in composition—Roosevelt said that he could not assent to any accord that might morally obligate our government now or later to approve the export of gold from the United States.

In the main paragraphs concluding the message the President in effect dismissed the whole effort to reach even a quickly terminable accord about the relative value of the dollar and other currencies—an effort which he had allowed to proceed so far.

At this time, any fixed formula of stabilization by agreement must necessarily be artificial and speculative. It would be particularly unwise from political and psychological standpoints to permit limitation of our action to be imposed by any other nation than our own. A sufficient interval should be allowed the United States to permit in addition to the plan [play] of economic forces a demonstration of the value of price lifting efforts which we have well in hand. These successful forces will be beneficial to other nations if they join with us toward the same end.

It would be well to reiterate the fact that England left the gold standard nearly two years ago and only now is seeking stabilization. Also that France did not stabilize for three years or more. If France seeks to break up the Conference just because we decline to accept her dictum we should take the sound position that the Economic Conference was initiated and called to discuss and agree on permanent solutions of world economics and not to discuss the domestic economic policy of one nation out of the 66 present. When the Conference was called, its necessity was obvious although the problem of stabilization of the American dollar was not even in existence.

1933 The United States and the Soviet Union Establish Diplomatic Relations (1966)

It was the Wilson administration which decided not to recognize the new Communist regime in the Soviet Union. The three Republican Presidents of the 1920s continued this policy. The Bolsheviks in turn repudiated the Czarist debts, ignored the claims of American citizens, and attempted to export revolution to the capitalistic nations. But by the time of the Great Depression, conditions had changed throughout the world. A number of other countries had defaulted on their debt payments to the United States, and unfriendly regimes were emerging in Japan and Germany. The innovative F.D.R. thus decided to take a bold new step—to recognize the now firmly entrenched Communist regime in the Soviet Union. A survey of 1,100 newspapers across the United States revealed that 63 percent were in favor of this step. Herbert Feis here analyzes the culmination of the diplomatic negotiations.

SOURCE: Feis, *1933: Characters in Crisis.* See pp. 318 and 321–25.

DOCUMENT:

The endeavors of the American negotiators centered on achieving five purposes: (1) a pledge that the Soviet government and all organizations under its control would refrain from activities aimed at injuring the United States or subverting its government; (2) a settlement of the loans which the American government had made to the provisional government of Alexander Kerensky in 1917; (3) a promise to compensate private American holders of Russian government bonds and Americans whose property had been confiscated; (4) a pledge that American nationals in Russia would be accorded religious freedom, and (5) assurances that any American nationals who might be placed under arrest by the Russian authorities would have good treatment and legal protection.

Litvinov gave reasons for denying, or qualifying, or countering each of these stipulations.

During the following five days—from November 12 to 16—Litvinov became a little more yielding on almost all points discussed. The American negotiators on their part whittled down their stipulations. During these days neither the White House nor the State Department issued any bulletins about the progress of the talks. And I cannot illuminate their silence.

On the evening of November 16, the President gave his annual dinner to the cabinet, followed by a musicale. After the guests left, the President invited Phillips, Morgenthau (who had just been made Acting Secretary of the Treasury) and Bullitt to join Litvinov and him in his study. On the desk were the several sets of letters in which the understandings reached were set forth. The President read them aloud. Litvinov objected to the use in several of the documents of the phrase "The Government of the United States expects" as being in the nature of an ultimatum. The Americans insisted it be kept in, and Litvinov gave way when the President agreed to change the phrasing to "will expect." The President and Litvinov took up their pens and scratched their signatures at the same time. Then they exchanged the letters. Roosevelt seemed to be in high good humor at the outcome of this venturesome negotiation. Litvinov was more repressed but also clearly pleased. The group quaffed only beer in celebration. No ceremonial champagne was served.

By the foremost pair of letters the resumption of diplomatic relations was effectuated.

In his letter Roosevelt said that he was happy to inform Litvinov that the American government had decided to establish normal diplomatic relations with the government of the Union of Soviet Socialist Republics, trusting that the future relations between the two countries would "forever remain normal and friendly." Litvinov in his acknowledgement stated that the Soviet government was glad to establish normal diplomatic relations with the United States and affirmed that he shared the President's hopes.

This pair of letters was supplemented by four other sets. In one set the Soviet government averred that it would be its fixed policy not to interfere in any manner in the internal affairs of the United States, and "to refrain, and to restrain all persons in government service and all organizations of the Government or under its direct or indirect control, including the organizations in receipt of any financial assistance from it, from any act overt or covert liable in any way whatsoever to injure the tranquillity, prosperity, order, or security of the whole or any part of the United States..." and also "not to permit the formation or residence on its territory of any organization or group...or of representatives or officials of any organization or group which has as an aim the overthrow or the preparation for the overthrow of, or the bringing about by force of a change in the political or social order of the whole or any part of the United States..."

In another set of letters Roosevelt expressed the deep wish that American nationals in Russia would be able to exercise liberty of conscience in religious worship without suffering in any way therefrom. He enumerated those religious activities which American nationals were to be allowed to carry on without annoyance or molestation of any kind. Litvinov answered by citing various provisions of Soviet law which could be deemed to guarantee the requested rights and privileges.

In a third set of letters the Soviet government promised to conclude at once a consular convention which would grant American nationals in the Soviet Union the right to the same legal protection enjoyed by nationals of any other foreign country. Litvinov also, in a separate statement dealing with the particular question of prosecution for "economic espionage," gave assurances that the Soviet government would not interfere with efforts to obtain such economic information as was procured by legitimate means, and which was not regarded as secret, or the dissemination of which was not forbidden by regulations.

In still another set of the communications exchanged, the Soviet government waived its claim for damages because of the participation of American military forces in the expedition to Siberia during the years 1918 to 1921. Litvinov agreed to relinquish any such claims after being shown documentary evidence that the American purpose had been to counteract Japanese activities in Russian territory.

It was arranged that Litvinov should remain in Washington for a few days after the end of the formal negotiations to review more thoroughly this complicated field of claims and counterclaims. But the ensuing talks did not disentangle them. He left this country with the understanding that negotiations would commence once more after the American ambassador took up his post in Moscow. No agreement, it may be noted, was ever reached and no payment was ever made on these obligations. The American government ignored them when it included the Soviet Union among the recipients of lend-lease after Germany had hauled it into the Second World War.

Similarly, the subsequent effort to formulate a favorable basis for Soviet–American trade—now that the two countries were again in diplomatic relations with each other—got nowhere for a long time.

1935 Secretary of State Cordell Hull and the Imposition of Sanctions During the Italo–Ethiopian War

Italy had been seeking revenge against Ethiopia ever since Ethiopia had defeated Italy at Adowa in 1896—like Dienbienphu a half-century later, one of the rare instances of a colonial power suffering a military defeat at the hands of a non-European people. In 1934–35, the Italian dictator Benito Mussolini attempted to expand the boundaries of the Italian Empire in Africa by attacking Ethiopia. Emperor Haile Selassie appealed to the League of Nations, which branded Italy as the aggressor in this conflict. Here in the United States, many Italian–Americans opposed the U.S. taking drastic action against Mussolini. The Roosevelt administration did embargo the shipment of arms and implements of war to both belligerents, but it did not agree to impose economic sanctions on Italy. Nor did the League of Nations move to restrict the one key Italian import (oil), whose curtailment would have made a difference in halting Mussolini's African caper.

SOURCE: U.S. Department of State, *Foreign Relations of the United States 1935, Volume I* (Washington: Government Printing Office, 1953). See pp. 836–37.

DOCUMENT:

The Ambassador in Italy (Breckenridge Long) to the Secretary of State

Rome, September 18, 1935—1 p.m.

If sanctions are invoked at Geneva I sincerely hope the American Government will not associate itself with them. There would be many unfortunate grave repercussions at home and unnecessary complications here.

The Congress passed at its recent session directory legislation governing the relations between the American Government and belligerents. In my opinion the American Government ought to act under that legislation and without reference to the program of any other government or group of governments and should so time its acts and so phrase its declarations on the subject that it will exclude the assumption that it is acting in concert with other powers.

Please pardon my presumption but the implications in the telegram under reference indicate the possibility of some thought of action in concert which I would consider a serious political and international error.

The Secretary of State to the Chargé in the United Kingdom (Ray Atherton)

Washington, September 20, 1935—11 a.m.

With reference to the possibilities of a desire at some future time for information with regard to the attitude of this Government with respect to collective measures which might be adopted by the League in connection with this controversy, I shall endeavor to give you some of our thoughts in that regard.

This Government and the American people are deeply interested in the maintenance of peace, in the settlement of international disputes by peaceable methods and in avoiding being involved in war. The recent Joint Resolution of Congress, providing for certain steps to be taken by this country upon the outbreak or during the progress of war provides among other things for an embargo against the shipment of arms and implements of war to belligerent nations. This provision is mandatory upon the President in the event of an outbreak or during the progress of war. The President is given authority in this Joint Resolution to define the items to be prohibited shipment.

This Government would not join in the imposition of sanctions upon any nation involved in the pending controversy between Italy and Ethiopia. As far as concerns any action to be taken by this Government in connection with measures which might be adopted by collective action under the League with reference to the Italo–Ethiopian controversy, it would of course be obviously impossible for this Government to arrive at any conclusion with regard thereto before it was placed in full possession of the reasons and bases upon which such collective action by the League were founded and a complete description of the specific measures to be put into effect. You can, I am sure, quite well understand that no advantage could be gained from any premature discussion of hypothetical possibilities in this regard.

1936 Ambassador William Phillips and the Failure to Prevent War Between America and Italy (1952)

Although they were later partners in the Axis, Adolf Hitler of Germany and Benito Mussolini of Italy did not agree on every issue, and there was some personal rivalry between the two. Even after the Italian triumph in its war with Ethiopia, the American government was hopeful that it might keep Italy neutral during the impending European conflict. This dream was shattered when Italy attacked France in June, 1940. The U.S. Ambassador to Italy during the late 1930s was William Phillips. In his diplomatic memoirs, Phillips described Mussolini as an extraordinary personality who might have been a great Italian leader and statesman, had he not succumbed to military displays and territorial annexations.

SOURCE: William Phillips, *Ventures in Diplomacy* (Boston: The Beacon Press, 1952). See pp. 326–27.

DOCUMENT:

Presumably it was the Italian victory in Ethiopia that started Mussolini on his downward path, for it convinced him that Italy's destiny lay in military prowess. He had been angered by the imposition of sanctions against Italy by the League of Nations. The British sanctions hurt him particularly for rightly or wrongly he, and indeed a large section of the Italian people, thought that Italy's need for territorial expansion to ease her over-population had been tacitly recognized by the British. Often Italians, even liberal Italians, spoke of the devious ways in which the vast British and French colonial empires had been created and they bitterly resented the hostile attitude of the League to what they regarded as Italy's natural rights.

A warning of possible sanctions came too late. By then Mussolini's prestige was involved; he could not retreat merely upon the orders of foreign states from a position publicly taken. So he pursued the adventure to its inglorious conclusion, and this easy military success turned his head. Had he not defied the League and the United States? The new title of Emperor of Ethiopia was given to the King to show the world that Italy was now to be reckoned a great power, and that he, Mussolini was at the height of his prestige. The dangerous fact that all power was centered in him did not then seem to disturb the people unduly. They appreciated his interest in their welfare, his success in promoting their self respect, the grandiose spectacles he staged for their pleasure. There was pride in an Italian resurgence under Mussolini's dramatic leadership. But in 1938 it became evident that Ethiopia had not satisfied the Duce's territorial ambitions. He became obsessed with the vision of himself as a modern Caesar, restoring Italy to her former greatness under the ancient Roman Empire. "The Mediterranean must become once more an Italian lake with a window opening on the Atlantic." All the while his vanity was being assiduously fanned by Hitler, for Italy had a definite role to play in Hitler's grand design for world conquest. The Italian navy must dominate the Mediterranean and thereby immobilize a substantial portion of the British fleet in that region, while Germany proceeded to conquer Europe and Great Britain.

Roosevelt understood the German strategy and the importance of preserving Italy's neutrality. For while Italy remained inactive, British supply lines through the Mediterranean to the Middle East would not be molested. That he did everything in his power to induce Mussolini to preserve his independence is now a matter of record. While at first he certainly hoped that his influence and the growing military power of the United States might effectively counteract Hitler's hold on Mussolini, his later appeals to the Duce were, in my opinion, written merely for the sake of the record.

The first three and a half years of my mission to Italy had been hopeful and happy years. But with the departure of the Allied Embassies from Rome in 1940, our relations with the Italian Government declined steadily. Whether it was worthwhile or even desirable after Mussolini's June 10 declaration for me to continue at my post was certainly debatable, for a Chargé d'Affaires was all that was really necessary to preserve the contacts.

My mission failed. Italy entered the war, against the western Allies and against the United States. However, my sympathy for the Italians, helplessly bound as they were to the ambitions of two remorseless dictators was profound. My liking for them and my admiration for their many great qualities were never diminished by the war; it is a satisfaction to see the courage and hard work with which the Italian people have lifted their country to a position of renewed respect among the democratic nations of the world.

1936 A Retrospective Look: The Nye Committee, the Munition Makers, and World War I

Rural, agricultural, and isolated, North Dakota arguably has been the most isolationist state, sending such antiglobalists to the Senate as Gerald Nye and William Langer, who cast one of the two nay votes against the United Nations Charter. Nye, who had once been the editor of a county seat weekly, came to see that his youthful enthusiasm for the League of Nations would be a handicap for anyone seeking political office in this heavily German and Scandinavian state. When he conducted an investigation of the munitions traffic as a United States Senator in the mid-1930s, he attracted a great deal of attention, but he failed to prove that it had been the munition makers who had led the United States into World War I. Far more important factors had been German submarine warfare, real and alleged German atrocities, the Teutonic Menace Hypothesis, the superiority of British propaganda, and massive American loans to Great Britain and France.

SOURCE: U.S. Senate, *Munitions Industry*, Report No. 944, Part 3, 74th Congress, 2nd Session, February 24 (calendar day, April 20), 1936. See pp. 1–4, 7–8.

DOCUMENT:

Earlier reports (74th Cong. Rept. 577) and a bill, H.R. 5529, as amended by the committee, represent the committee's contribution to the task of taking the profits out of war. This bill was unanimously recommended to Congress by the committee, and it is hoped that its early passage will serve as effective warning to all concerned that there will be no more profiteering in the unhappy eventuality that this Nation should again be engaged in war.

The committee has been in remarkable agreement on the need for neutrality legislation, following its studies of the adequacy of existing legislation upon which the Senate asked it to report. Its members have taken a most active part in securing the passage of new neutrality legislation, both in 1935 and in 1936, and believe that this legislation represents a great and wholesome advance in the interests of keeping this Nation out of foreign wars. While in its present form it is still temporary, it is hoped by all the members of the committee that the legislation will be strengthened even further and made a permanent part of the Nation's law.

The committee feels that if it had done nothing else at all, its work on the bill to take the profits out of war and to create a public understanding for the need of that bill and for the need of a bill to strengthen our neutrality laws would amply warrant the time and energy spent by the members of the committee.

The present report covers the activities and character of the munitions companies investigated and proposes certain methods of control. The committee, which has been unanimous in its findings throughout, is unanimously agreed on the need for strict controls, but finds itself in disagreement on the recommended methods by which such control can best be exercised.

I. THE NATURE OF THE MUNITIONS COMPANIES. The committee finds, under the head of "the nature of the industrial and commercial organizations engaged in the manufacture or of traffic in arms, ammunitions, or other implements of war" that almost none of the munitions companies in this country confine themselves exclusively to the manufacture of military materials. Great numbers of the largest suppliers to the Army and Navy (Westinghouse, General Electric, du Pont, General Motors, Babcock and Wilcox, etc.) are predominantly manufacturers of materials for civilian life.

II. THE SALES METHODS OF THE MUNITIONS COMPANIES. The committee finds, under the head of sales methods of the munitions companies, that almost without exception, the American munitions companies investigated have at times resorted to such unusual approaches, questionable favors and commissions, and methods of "doing the needful" as to constitute, in effect, a form of bribery of foreign governmental officials or of their close friends in order to secure business.

III. THEIR ACTIVITIES CONCERNING PEACE EFFORTS. The committee finds, under this head, that there is no record of any munitions company aiding any proposals for limitation of armaments, but that, on the contrary, there is a record of their active opposition by some to almost all such proposals, of resentment toward them, of contempt for those responsible for them, and of violation of such controls whenever established, and of rich profiting whenever such proposals failed.

IV. THE EFFECT OF ARMAMENTS ON PEACE. The committee finds, under the head of the effect of armaments on peace, that some of the munitions companies have occasionally had opportunities to intensify the fears of people for their neighbors and have used them to their own profit.

The committee finds, further, that the very quality which in civilian life tends to lead toward progressive civilization, namely the improvements of machinery, has been used by the munitions makers to scare nations into a continued frantic expenditure for the latest improvements in devices of warfare. The constant message of the traveling salesman of the munitions companies to the rest of the world has been that they now had available for sale something new, more dangerous and more deadly than ever before and that the potential enemy was or would be buying it.

While the evidence before this committee does not show that wars have been started solely because of the activities of munitions makers and their agents, it is also true that wars rarely have one single cause, and the committee finds it to be against the peace of the world for selfishly interested organizations to be left free to goad and frighten nations into military activity.

The committee finds, further, that munitions companies engaged in bribery find themselves involved the civil and military politics of other nations, and that this is an unwarranted form of intrusion into the affairs of other nations and undesirable representation of the character and methods of the people of the United States.

1936 President Franklin D. Roosevelt's *I Hate War* Speech

During the dozen years when he served as President, Franklin Roosevelt delivered a number of memorable speeches. Among those which came back to haunt him later was the address which he gave at Chautauqua, New York on August 14, 1936. In this speech, F.D.R. talked about the Good Neighbor Policy, and then shifted his attention to the remainder of the world. Midway through his address, Roosevelt made the famous remark: "I have seen war. I hate war." He then entered into a discussion of some of the causes of war: ancient hatreds, unsettled frontiers, newborn fanaticisms, different religions, conflicting economic and political systems, racial tensions. F.D.R. closed his speech with an examination of the neutrality legislation which Congress had recently begun to pass.

SOURCE: Samuel I. Rosenman, Compiler, *The Public Papers and Addresses of Franklin D. Roosevelt*, 13 Volumes (New York: Random House, 1938–50). See V, 288–899.

DOCUMENT:

Of necessity, we are deeply concerned about tendencies of recent years among many of the Nations of other continents. It is a bitter experience to us when the spirit of agreements to which we are a party is not lived up to. It is an even more bitter experience for the whole company of Nations to witness not only the spirit but the letter of international agreements violated with impunity and without regard to the simple principles of honor. Permanent friendships between Nations as between men can be sustained only by scrupulous respect for the pledged word.

In spite of all this we have sought steadfastly to assist international movements to prevent war. We cooperated to the bitter end—and it was a bitter end—in the work of the General Disarmament Conference. When it failed we sought a separate treaty to deal with the manufacture of arms and the international traffic in arms. That proposal also came to nothing. We participated—again to the bitter end—in a conference to continue naval limitations, and when it became evident that no general treaty could be signed because of the objections of other Nations, we concluded with Great Britain and France a conditional treaty of qualitative limitation which, much to my regret, already shows signs of ineffectiveness.

We shun political commitments which might entangle us in foreign wars; we avoid connection with the political activities of the League of Nations; but I am glad to say that we have cooperated whole-heartedly in the social and humanitarian work at Geneva. Thus we are a part of the world effort to control traffic in narcotics, to improve international health, to help child welfare, to eliminate double taxation and to better working conditions and laboring hours throughout the world.

We are not isolationists except in so far as we seek to isolate ourselves completely from war. Yet we must remember that so long as war exists on earth there will be some danger that even the Nation which most ardently desires peace may be drawn into war.

I have seen war. I have seen war on land and sea. I have seen blood running from the wounded. I have seen men coughing out their gassed lungs. I have seen the dead in the mud. I have seen cities destroyed. I have seen two hundred limping, exhausted men come out of line—the survivors of a regiment of one thousand that went forward forty-eight hours before. I have seen children starving. I have seen the agony of mothers and wives. I hate war.

I have passed unnumbered hours, I shall pass unnumbered hours, thinking and planning how war may be kept from this Nation.

I wish I could keep war from all Nations; but that is beyond my power. I can at least make certain that no act of the United States helps to produce or to promote war. I can at least make clear that the conscience of America revolts against war and that any Nation which provokes war forfeits the sympathy of the people of the United States.

The Pre-World War II Years 35

The Ludlow Amendment Calling for a National
Referendum on Declarations of War

Under the Constitution of the United States, the individual states ratify amendments to the Constitution. There are no national referenda, however, on such issues as declaring war, despite the fact that a number of state constitutions allow for the submission of referenda to the voters. On January 14, 1935, Democratic Representative Louis Ludlow of Indiana introduced a resolution into the House calling for a Constitutional amendment providing for a nationwide referendum on declarations of war, except in the case of invasion. The Roosevelt administration opposed this resolution, despite the fact that one national poll conducted in 1937 registered 73 percent approval. It was not until early 1938 that the House voted on whether or not to discharge the Committee on the Judiciary and the Committee on Rules from consideration of the Ludlow Amendment. The motion failed, 188 to 209, with the Republicans and most Democrats from West of the Mississippi voting in favor. Southern Democratic opposition was due in part to Ludlow's unsuccessful sponsorship of an antilynching bill.

SOURCE: "History of the Ludlow Resolution," in *Congressional Digest*, February, 1938. See p. 41.

DOCUMENT:

Following is the text of the Ludlow War Resolution (H.J. Res. 199), as originally introduced and as voted on by the House:

> Section 1. Except in case of attack by armed forces, actual or immediately threatened, upon the United States or its territorial possessions, or by any non-American nation against any country in the Western Hemisphere, the people shall have the sole power by a national referendum to declare war or to engage in warfare overseas. Congress, when it deems a national crisis to exist in conformance with this article, shall by concurrent resolution refer the question to the people.
>
> Sec. 2. Congress shall by law provide for the enforcement of this section.
>
> Sec. 3. This article shall become operative when ratified as an amendment to the Constitution by convention in the several States, as provided in the Constitution.

When the Ludlow Resolution was called up in the House on January 10, Speaker William B. Bankhead took the floor and read the following letter from President Roosevelt:

The White House
Washington, January 6, 1938

My Dear Mr. Speaker: In response to your request for an expression of my views respecting the proposed resolution calling for a referendum vote as a prerequisite for a declaration of war, I must frankly state that I consider that the proposed amendment would be impracticable in its application and incompatible with our representative form of government.

Our Government is conducted by the people through representatives of their own choosing. It was with singular unanimity that the founders of the Republic agreed upon such free and representative form of government as the only practical means of government by the people.

Such an amendment to the Constitution as that proposed would cripple any President in his conduct of our foreign relations; and it would encourage other nations to believe that they could violate American rights with impunity.

I fully realize that the sponsors of this proposal sincerely believe that it would be helpful in keeping the United States out of war. I am convinced it would have the opposite effect.

1937 F.D.R.'s Quarantine Speech Directed Against International Aggressors

The world moved closer to war in 1937, when the Japanese invaded China. A year earlier, the Germans had reoccupied the Rhineland. Despite the fact that he continued to sign the neutrality legislation passed by Congress, Franklin Roosevelt was becoming increasingly concerned about the deteriorating global situation. In his boldest foreign policy declaration prior to Pearl Harbor, F.D.R. asserted in a speech at Chicago on October 5, 1937, that law-abiding nations should quarantine the aggressors. Those Americans favoring collective security were highly enthusiastic, but so great was isolationist sentiment in the United States that the President decided to announce that he really had not said what many people were reading into his speech.

SOURCE: Rosenman, Compiler, *The Public Papers and Addresses of Franklin D. Roosevelt*. See VI, 409–10.

DOCUMENT:

The overwhelming majority of the peoples and nations of the world today want to live in peace. They seek the removal of barriers against trade. They want to exert themselves in industry, in agriculture and in business, that they may increase their wealth through the production of wealth-producing goods rather than striving to produce military planes and bombs and machine guns and cannon for the destruction of human lives and useful property.

In those nations of the world which seem to be piling armament on armament for purposes of aggression, and those other nations which fear acts of aggression against them and their security, a very high proportion of their national income is being spent directly for armaments. It runs from thirty to as high as fifty percent. We are fortunate. The proportion that we in the United States spend is far less—eleven or twelve percent.

How happy we are that the circumstances of the moment permit us to put our money into bridges and boulevards, dams and reforestation, the conservation of our soil and many other kinds of useful works rather than into huge standing armies and vast supplies of implements of war.

I am compelled and you are compelled, nevertheless, to look ahead. The peace, the freedom and the security of ninety percent of the population of the world is being jeopardized by the remaining ten percent who are threatening a breakdown of all international order and law. Surely the ninety percent who want to live in peace under law and in accordance with moral standards that have received almost universal acceptance through the centuries, can and must find some way to make their will prevail.

The situation is definitely of universal concern. The questions involved relate not merely to violations of specific provisions of particular treaties; they are questions of war and of peace, of international law and especially of principles of humanity. It is true that they involve definite violations of agreements, and especially of the Covenant of the League of Nations, the Briand-Kellogg Pact and the Nine Power Treaty. But they also involve problems of world economy, world security and world humanity.

It is true that the moral consciousness of the world must recognize the importance of removing injustices and well-founded grievances; but at the same time it must be aroused to the cardinal necessity of honoring sanctity of treaties, of respecting the rights and liberties of others and of putting an end to acts of international aggression.

It seems to be unfortunately true that the epidemic of world lawlessness is spreading.

When an epidemic of physical disease starts to spread, the community approves and joins in a quarantine of the patients in order to protect the health of the community against the spread of the disease.

1937 A Representative Negative Assessment: the Chicago *Tribune*

F.D.R. delivered his Quarantine Speech in the heart of the isolationist Middle West, the home of Colonel Robert R. McCormick's isolationist, anti-Roosevelt Chicago Tribune. *The* Tribune *was predictably critical, as was the equally isolationist Hearst press. Even the* Wall

Street Journal *advised the Roosevelt administration to "Stop Foreign Meddling: America Wants Peace." Among the few newspapers that encouraged the President to adopt policies implementing his Quarantine Speech were the San Francisco* Chronicle, *the Los Angeles* Times, *the Milwaukee* Journal, *and the* Christian Science Monitor *of Boston. There was no Congressional vote of approval on the Quarantine Speech.*

SOURCE: Parke Brown, "President in Chicago Says Peace Loving Lands Must Act," in Chicago *Tribune*, October 6, 1937. See p. 1.

DOCUMENT:

Those Chicagoans who went yesterday to see a bridge dedicated, those who gathered at the curbstones to see a President pass in a shower of ticker tape, and those who sat at their radios to hear some words on peace, these and many more found themselves last night the center of a world-hurricane of war fright! President Roosevelt came to Chicago to bless the bridge that spans two delightful and peaceful park systems.

He talked war.

When some eight or ten thousand spectators of the bridge dedication turned to their homes concern was written on most of their faces. It would be improper to say that in their faces were reflected the ghastly recollections of just twenty years ago. But if the market crash, if the hurried and startled cables from London and Geneva and Berlin and Rome and Paris, if the echoes from every city in America were correctly estimated the President did not talk peace.

It was of war. And the talk in the crowd that slowly trickled away was of leagues of nations and of marching troops and the nation back in the training camps.

The President clearly suggested that the United States might be compelled to enter alliances with peace loving nations to curb more warlike peoples.

To the citizens who heard the President the event of the day was the linking up of thirty miles of boulevard. Many of his hearers, as he read on in a calm, dispassionate voice, had the impression that before the end of the talk he would set forth some specific proposal for leaguing the peace loving against the warlike nations, with the United States sitting in with the former group. There was no such proposal, and Mr. Roosevelt boarded his train for Hyde Park, N.Y., without making his meanings more definite.

Even so, the speech was looked on as the most important by far of the President's western trip, during which he made thirty public appearances. He said that he had deliberately chosen the center of the mid-west for a discussion of war and peace, and his manner, as well as the careful wording of his message, indicated he was intensely serious and had given his subject much thought.

1933–37 Ambassador to Germany William E. Dodd Assesses the Situation in Germany (1941)

Like Claude Bowers (Chile) and Carlton J. H. Hayes (Spain) during World War II, William E. Dodd was a historian turned diplomat. As a recognized authority on the American South, Dodd was quite familiar with one group asserting its superiority over another, whether it be whites and blacks, or Nazis and Jews. His assessment of the deteriorating European situation during the first Roosevelt administration is critical of the Germans, whom he regarded as "by nature more democratic than any other great race in Europe." But Dodd by no means exclusively lambasted Germany and its allies to the degree that Ambassador to Germany James Gerard had done three decades earlier in his diplomatic memoirs. Instead, Dodd also placed considerable blame on the great business and industrial groups throughout the world who had raised trade barriers and undercut disarmament conferences between the two world wars.

SOURCE: William E. Dodd, Jr. and Martha Dodd, Editors, *Ambassador Dodd's Diary 1933–1938* (New York: Harcourt, Brace and Company, 1941). See pp. 446–47.

DOCUMENT:

I have been four and a half years in Europe with the hope of serving my country. How much one could do is an open question. The present-day world has learned nothing from the World War. Instead of keeping the treaties of 1919–23, nearly all peoples have violated them. Twice as much money is being spent now each year in preparation for another war as was spent in 1913, in spite of the fact that nearly all peoples were bearing the greatest debts known to history. Shall we be confronted by another world war? And would isolation be possible for any great industrial country?

With war preparations and the raising of trade barriers beyond anything known to modern history, another method of government has been adopted in Rome, Berlin and Tokyo. Over that vast area freedom of religion has ceased to exist and universities no longer govern themselves. In a single country 1,600 professors and teachers in high schools have been dismissed. Leaders in several countries have undertaken to dismiss, expel, imprison or kill Jews. There is no doubt that they have at times profiteered, but what other class or people has been free of such members? Anyone who knows the facts of 1914–20 cannot forget that Jews fought bravely on both sides of the terrible war, and some outstanding members of this people gave millions of dollars to save the helpless, even starving, Germans in 1918–20.

In a vast region where religious freedom is denied, where intellectual initiative and discovery are not allowed, and where race hatreds are cultivated daily, what can a representative of the United States do? Democratic peoples must maintain their faiths at home; their representatives must try to improve international co-operation; and on proper occasions they must remind men of the importance of world peace, easier commercial relations, and the significance of democratic civilization for which peoples have struggled since the sixteenth century. With these ideals in mind, I felt that I must represent my country the best I could while dwelling among the Germans, who are by nature more democratic than any other great race in Europe.

Could one be successful? I made addresses on suitable occasions and described our international difficulties, never criticizing the government to which I had been sent. When invitations to partisan affairs were sent to me, I maintained the attitude which our country has maintained since the Presidency of George Washington. Was it the duty of representatives of democratic countries to attend conferences where democracy was ridiculed and attacked? I cannot think so.

The logical outcome of vast war preparations is another war, and what would another war leave of modern civilization? There are curious misunderstandings. Great business and industrial groups failed to recognize the necessity of international co-operation after 1920. Some of their chiefs defeated world peace efforts at Geneva more than once because they thought the sale of arms and war materials more important than world peace. Other groups insisted in 1923 and 1930 on trade barriers which made debt payments impossible. So many influential men have failed to see that inventions, industrial revolution, and financial relations have brought mankind to a point where co-operation and peace are the first conditions of prosperity for the masses of men everywhere.

1939 Ambassador to Russia Joseph Davies and the Soviet–German Alliance (1941)

On August 23, 1939, the Communist Soviet Union and Nazi Germany unexpectedly signed a nonaggression pact. A week later, on September 1, Adolf Hitler attacked Poland, thus starting World War II. The individual who had represented the United States as its Ambassador to the Soviet Union in the years immediately preceding this event (1936–38) was Joseph E. Davies. In his diplomatic memoirs, Davies pointed out how Soviet relations with the West had begun to deteriorate after Munich, and that Stalin had become suspicious that Great Britain and France expected for him to fight Hitler alone. In the foreword to his volume, Davies, a self-described capitalist and individualist, observed that "all believers in Christ and Christ's teachings are theoretical communists, to the degree that they are 'for' the brotherhood of man."

SOURCE: Joseph E. Davies, *Mission to Moscow* (New York: Simon and Schuster, 1941). See pp. xviii, 454–56.

DOCUMENT:

An old French philosopher said, "When you know a man you cannot hate him." Leaders of the Union of Soviet Socialist Republics I came to know. They are a group of able, strong men. I disagree with them in many respects; but I accord to them, that which I assume unto myself, namely, credit for honest convictions and integrity of purposes. In my opinion, these men believe that they are doing right. There can be little doubt, in the face of the record, but that, consistent with their own security, they are devoted to the cause of peace for both ideological and practical reasons. I came to have a deep respect and affection for the Russian people. They have great qualities of imagination and idealism which they have reflected in their literature, in their music, and in their art. They have equally great spiritual qualities which they have translated into aspirations to better the conditions of life of common men, and which they have heroically demonstrated in their capacity to make the supreme sacrifice of life itself, for the cause in which they believe.

During the Litvinov tenure in the Foreign Office, there was to be sure a very strong moral impulse of hostility toward Germany and the aggressor powers beginning with the accession of Hitler to power. During that period the Soviet regime, in my opinion, diligently and vigorously tried to maintain a vigorous common front against the aggressors and were sincere advocates of the "indivisibility of peace."

Litvinov's able battle for peace and democratic ideas at the League of Nations and the vigorous attitude of the Soviet government in being prepared to fight for Czechoslovakia were indications of real sincerity of purpose and a marked degree of high-mindedness.

Beginning with Munich, and even before, however, there has been an accumulation of events which gradually broke down this attitude on the part of the Soviet government.

During my tenure in Moscow I was much impressed with the fact that the Russians were undoubtedly severely irked by what appeared to be a policy of "pinpricking" and an attitude of superiority and "talking down" which diplomatic missions of the Western powers assumed toward the Soviet government. The Soviets are proud and resented this deeply.

Then followed a series of developments which aggravated the relationships between the Soviet government and the Western democracies.

The Soviets were "humiliated" and "deeply hurt" by being excluded from Munich.

Out of "appeasement" there grew still greater distrust, so far as the Soviet government was concerned, in either the capacity, the intention, or even the "pledged word" of the Chamberlain government or the Daladier government.

The Soviet proposals for a "realistic alliance" to stop Hitler were rejected, by the Chamberlain government, out of consideration for the feelings of the Poles and the Baltic states.

During the Soviet–British–French negotiations, including the sessions of the Strang mission and Military Missions to Moscow, this distrust was intensified by the fact that these authorities were not clothed with power to close a final, definite realistic alliance.

The suspicion continued to grow that Britain and France were playing a diplomatic game to place the Soviets in the position where Russia would have to fight Germany alone.

Then there came the Hudson proposals for economic rehabilitation of Germany which again smacked of "appeasement" from the point of view of the Soviets. This was followed by the adjournment of Parliament by the Chamberlain government, without the conclusion of any definite agreement with Russia and the discovery by the Soviet leaders that a British Economic Mission had been sent to Denmark, allegedly with Chamberlain's blessing, to study economic appeasement, along the line of policy which has been initiated by Hudson.

Added to this France and England had persisted in a refusal to enter into an unequivocal agreement to support Russia in the protection of Russia's vital interest, in preventing the absorption through internal aggression of the Baltic states, whereas Russia had offered unequivocal support to Britain and France to come to their aid if their vital interests were affected by a German attack upon Belgium or Holland, regardless of the character of the aggression.

These events served to feed suspicion and arouse the dissatisfaction of the realistic Soviet leaders, including Stalin. Apparently they got "fed up" with attempting to stop the aggressors by participation in European affairs, and characteristically boldly reversed their attitude and decided to secure their own position by making a pact of nonaggression with Germany, which would assure peace for Russia, at least for a time, regardless of any possibility of war in Europe.

The foregoing is a theory as to what induced this situation, from such facts and impressions as I have gathered and obtained.

The dominant motive of the Soviets is and always has been "self-interest." For a time they were ardent advocates of active militant hostility against aggressors, in order to preserve peace. This was not only because of love of peace *per se* but also because it was to their interest.

The United States as a Neutral, 1939–40 36

1939 The Chicago *Tribune:* "This Is Not Our War"

It hardly came as a surprise when the isolationist Chicago Tribune *proclaimed on September 2, 1939—the day after the Germans attacked Poland—that "This is not our war." Most Americans were probably opposed at this point in time to sending U.S. troops to Europe. After Great Britain and France had declared war on Germany, the United States affirmed its neutrality. Yet President Roosevelt felt compelled to observe that: "This nation will remain a neutral nation, but I cannot ask that every American remain neutral in thought as well."*

SOURCE: "Not Our War," in Chicago *Tribune*, September 2, 1939. See p. 10.

DOCUMENT:

This is not our war. We did not create the Danzig situation. We did not sign the treaty of Versailles. The peace America made with Germany did not contain another war. The United States did not take spoils. It did not divide up colonies. It had nothing to do with the remaking of Europe which sowed war on nearly every frontier of the new map.

This is not our war because we refrained from doing the things which would cause it. France and Great Britain are not weak nations. They are great empires. Their pooled resources are enormous. They have allies which joined them in self-interest. They can draw on the man power of Africa and Asia. Their combined fleets control the seas. They are not amateurs in war. They attained their world position by fighting.

They have adopted policies which brought them into conflict with Germany, Italy, and Japan. Their statesmen are intelligent. They could count the costs and weigh the risks. It would not be a new experience for these empires to fight for what they have. Their histories are full of this.

America could not influence their decisions or control their policies. America is not responsible for the consequences. The duty of the United States government is to the people of the United States. Europe has had crises before and will have them again. This is not our war. We should not make it ours. We should keep out of it.

We may think their side is the better side. But it is their war. They are competent to fight it. Great pressure will be brought to bear on the United States. Americans will be told that this is their fight. That is not true. The frontiers of American democracy are not in Europe, Asia or Africa.

1939 Franklin Roosevelt Asks for the Repeal of the Arms Embargo

Beginning in 1935, Congress began to pass a series of neutrality acts designed to keep the United States out of another world war. After the German attack on Poland, however, F.D.R. asked that the arms embargo provision be repealed, so that the United States legally might sell munitions to Great Britain and France. Such isolationist Senators as Arthur Vandenberg of Michigan fought repeal, but Congress approved the arms embargo termination by clear-cut majorities in both houses. American ships, though, still were prohibited from entering the war zone around the British isles that was proclaimed on November 4, 1939.

SOURCE: *Congressional Record*, September 21, 1939. See pp. 10–11.

DOCUMENT:

Beginning with the foundation of our constitutional government in the year 1789, the American policy in respect to belligerent nations, with one notable exception, has been based on international law. Be it remembered that what we call international law has had as its primary objectives the avoidance of war and the prevention of the extension of war.

The single exception was the policy adopted by this Nation during the Napoleonic wars, when, seeking to avoid involvement, we acted for some years under the so-called Embargo and Nonintercourse Acts. That policy turned out to be a disastrous failure, first, because it brought our own Nation close to ruin; and, second, because it was the major cause of bringing us into active participation in European wars in our own War of 1812. It is merely reciting history to recall to you that one of the results of the policy of embargo and nonintercourse was the burning in 1814 of part of this Capitol in which we are assembled.

Our next deviation by statute from the sound principles of neutrality and peace through international law did not come for 130 years. It was the so-called Neutrality Act of 1935—only 4 years ago—an act continued in force by the joint resolution of May 1, 1937, despite grave doubts expressed as to its wisdom by many Senators and Representatives and by officials charged with the conduct of our foreign relations, including myself. I regret that the Congress passed that act. I regret equally that I signed that act.

On July 14 of this year I asked the Congress, in the cause of peace and in the interest of real American neutrality and security, to take action to change that act.

I now ask again that such action be taken in respect to that part of the act which is wholly inconsistent with ancient precepts of the law of nations—the embargo provisions. I ask it because they are, in my opinion, most vitally dangerous to American neutrality, American security, and American peace.

These embargo provisions, as they exist today, prevent the sale to a belligerent by an American factory of any completed implements of war, but they allow the sale of many types of uncompleted implements of war, as well as all kinds of general material and supplies. They, furthermore, allow such products of industry and agriculture to be taken in American-flag ships to belligerent nations. There in itself—under the present law—lies definite danger to our neutrality and our peace.

1940 Prime Minister Winston Churchill's Letter to F.D.R. vis-à-vis the Destroyers-for-Bases Deal

One of the most important developments in American foreign policy prior to Pearl Harbor was the destroyers-for-bases deal with Great Britain. This took the form of an executive agreement rather than a treaty. American expansionists had been interested in acquiring the British island possessions of the New World since the latter part of the nineteenth century, and after World War I they unsuccessfully proposed swapping some of these for the cancellation of the war debt which the British owed the United States. Two decades later, on September 3, 1940, Franklin Roosevelt (who had firsthand knowledge of the British island possessions of the Atlantic) acquired sites for American military bases in Newfoundland and Bermuda as outright gifts. He also obtained rent-free bases for ninety-nine years in the Bahamas, Jamaica, Antigua, St. Lucia, Trinidad, and British Guiana. Then, in a separate but simultaneous transaction, the United States transferred fifty overage destroyers to Great Britain. Ambassador Joseph Kennedy revealed Winston Churchill's thinking on this matter in a letter to the President dated August 22, 1940.

SOURCE: U.S. Department of State, *Foreign Relations of the United States 1940, Volume III* (Washington: Government Printing Office, 1958). See pp. 68–69.

DOCUMENT:

The Ambassador in the United Kingdom (Kennedy) to the Secretary of State

London, August 22, 1940—5 p.m.

2856. Secret and personal for the President from Former Naval Person.

I am most grateful for all you are doing on our behalf. I had not contemplated anything in the nature of a contract, bargain or sale between us. It is the fact that we had decided in Cabinet to offer you naval and air facilities off the Atlantic coast quite independently of destroyers or any other aid. Our view is that we are two friends in danger helping each other as far as we can. We should therefore like to give you the facilities mentioned without stipulating for any return and even if tomorrow you found it too difficult to transfer the destroyers, et cetera, our offer still remains open because we think it is in the general good.

I see difficulties and even risks in the exchange of letters now suggested or in admitting in any way that the munitions which you send us are a payment for the facilities. Once this idea is accepted people will contrast on each side what is given and received. The money value of the armaments would be computed and set against the facilities and some would think one thing about it and some another.

Moreover Mr. President as you well know each island or location is a case by itself. If for instance there were only one harbor or site how is it to be divided and its advantages shared. In such a case we should like to make you an offer of what we think is best for both rather than to embark upon a close cut argument as to what ought to be delivered in return for value received.

What we want is that you shall feel safe on your Atlantic seaboard so far as any facilities in possessions of ours can make you safe and naturally if you put in money and make large developments you must have the effective security of a long lease.

1940 The St. Louis *Post Dispatch* Attacks Franklin Roosevelt as a Dictator Who Had Committed an Act of War

While Franklin Roosevelt was comparing the destroyers-for-bases deal with the Louisiana Purchase, public opinion polls were revealing that six Americans out of ten were favorably disposed to the transaction. A story about the deal appeared in Newsweek *titled: "Swap of Destroyers for Bases Makes U.S. Dream Come True: Nation's Eastern Flank Thus Made Almost Impregnable." The majority of the American press mirrored the sentiments of* Newsweek, *but the St. Louis* Post Dispatch *was displeased to the point that it not only published an editorial bitterly attacking the transaction, but also had it reprinted as an advertisement in the New York* Times *on the following day.*

SOURCE: "Dictator Roosevelt Commits An Act of War," in New York *Times*, September 4, 1940. See p. 19.

DOCUMENT:

Mr. Roosevelt today committed an act of war.

He also became America's first dictator.

Secretly, his Secretary of State, Mr. Hull, entered into an agreement with the British Ambassador that amounts to a military and naval alliance with Great Britain. This secretly negotiated agreement was consummated yesterday, Sept. 2.

Today Congress is *informed* of the agreement. Note well the word "informed." Although the President referred to his under-cover deal as ranking in importance with the Louisiana Purchase, he is not asking Congress—the elected representatives of the people—to ratify this deal. He is *telling* them, it already has been ratified by him—America's dictator.

The President has passed down an edict that compares with the edicts forced down the throats of Germans, Italians and Russians by Hitler, Mussolini and Stalin.

He hands down an edict that may eventually result in the shedding of the blood of millions of Americans; that may result in transforming the United States into a goose-stepping, regimented slave state.

Under our Constitution, treaties with foreign powers are not legal without the advice and consent of the Senate. This treaty, which history may define as the most momentous one ever made in our history, was put over without asking the Senate either for its advice or its consent.

The authority which the President quotes for his fatal and secret deal is an opinion from the Attorney-General. Whatever legal trickery this yes-man may conjure up, the fact is that the transfer of the destroyers is not only in violation of American law, but is also in violation of the Hague Covenant of 1907, solemnly ratified by the United States Senate in 1908. It is an outright act of war.

Undeterred by law or the most primitive form of common sense, the President is turning over to a warring power a goodly portion of the United States Navy, against the repeated statements of Senators, Navy Department officials and officers of the Navy that the ships are needed for our own defense.

But that is only one phrase of this insane performance. We get in exchange leases on British possessions in this Hemisphere—but only leases. What good will these leases be if Hitler should acquire title to these islands by right of conquest? There is even the possibility that, in the course of a negotiated peace, Great Britain might be forced to cede these islands to Hitler.

What, then, will become of Roosevelt's leases? Obviously, to avoid all sorts of possible complications, we should have full sovereignty over our own naval and air bases.

Of all sucker real estate deals in history, this is the worst, and the President of the United States is the sucker.

Thomas Jefferson did not lease Louisiana from Napoleon Bonaparte. He acquired it outright, to have and to hold forever.

Woodrow Wilson didn't lease the Virgin Islands from Denmark, with *the advice and consent of the United States Senate,* he bought them.

In the case of Newfoundland and Bermuda, Mr. Roosevelt tells us that the right to bases "are gifts—generously given and gladly received." In other words, the great and rich United States is taking largess from a nation that owes us more than five and a half billion dollars! We are accepting a tip, according to the President.

For at least ten years this newspaper has repeatedly called attention to the urgent desirability of acquiring Caribbean islands owned by Britain and France for our own defense purposes. In that belief, we are ardently in agreement with Mr. Roosevelt.

No move was made to this end by Roosevelt or his predecessors, despite the fact that we had a trading argument in the billions of war debts owed to us by France and Britain.

No, Roosevelt saw France go down without negotiating for the islands in exchange for the debts, and only now, with Britain in the throes of a desperate war, does the President move to protect our shores.

But, in doing so, he commits an act of war. He strips our navy of fifty valuable ships and he enters into leases which might not be worth the paper they are written upon in a month's time.

And all this is done in utmost contempt of democratic processes and of the Constitution of the United States.

If this secretly negotiated deal goes through, the fat is in the fire and we all may as well get ready for a full-dress participation in the European war.

If Roosevelt gets away with this, we may as well say good-by to our liberties and make up our mind that henceforth we live under a dictatorship.

If Congress and the people do not rise in solemn wrath to stop Roosevelt now—at this moment—then the country deserves the stupendous tragedy that looms right around the corner.

1940 F.D.R. Seeks a Third Term: His Again and Again Speech

Several days before the 1940 Presidential election, Franklin Roosevelt gave one of his most controversial speeches, at Boston. After talking about how he had strengthened the Army and the Navy, F.D.R. told the fathers and mothers of America "again and again and again" that he was not going to send their sons abroad to fight. That November, Roosevelt won a third term, and thirteen months later the Japanese attacked Pearl Harbor, in the process bringing the United States into World War II.

SOURCE: Rosenman, Compiler, *The Public Papers and Addresses of Franklin D. Roosevelt.* See IX, 516–17.

DOCUMENT:

Our objective is to keep any potential attacker as far from our continental shores as we possibly can.

That is the record of the growth of our Navy. In 1933 a weak Navy; in 1940 a strong Navy. Side-line critics may carp in a political campaign. But Americans are mighty proud of that record and Americans will put their country first and partisanship second.

Speaking of partisanship, I remind you—when the naval Expansion Bill came up in 1938 the vast majority of Republican members of the Congress voted against building any more battleships.

What kind of political shenanigans are these?

Can we trust those people with national defense?

Next, take up the Army: Under normal conditions we have no need for a vast Army in this country. But you and I know that unprecedented dangers require unprecedented action to guard the peace of America against unprecedented threats.

Since that day, a little over a year ago, when Poland was invaded, we have more than doubled the size of our regular Army. Adding to this, the Federalized National Guardsmen, our armed land forces now equal more than 436,000 enlisted men. And yet there are armies overseas that run four and five and six million men.

The officers and men of our Army and National Guard are the finest in the world.

They will be, as you know, the nucleus for the training of the young men who are being called under the Selective Service Act, 800,000 of them in the course of this year out of nearly 17,000,000 registered—in other words, a little less than 5 percent of the total registration.

General Marshall said to me the other day that the task of training those young men is, for the Army, a "profound privilege."

Campaign orators seek to tear down the morale of the American people when they make false statements about the Army's equipment. I say to you that we are supplying our Army with the best fighting equipment in all the world.

And while I am talking to you mothers and fathers, I give you one more assurance.

I have said this before, but I shall say it again and again and again:

Your boys are not going to be sent into any foreign wars.

They are going into training to form a force so strong that, by its very existence, it will keep the threat of war far away from our shores.

The purpose of our defense is defense.

1940 The Committee to Defend America by Aiding the Allies

As the likelihood of American involvement in the spreading global conflict increased, rival organizations were set up in the United States. One was the isolationist America First, and the other was the Committee to Defend America by Aiding the Allies. The latter's first head was the noted Kansas journalist William Allen White, who along with Elihu Root, Henry Stimson, and Nicholas Murray Butler was one of the few prominent internationalists in the isolationist-dominated Republican Party. On December 20, 1940, White sent a letter to fellow newspaperman Roy Howard, in which he set forth the limits of American involvement in World War II: "The Yanks Are Not Coming." When the committee began to move in a more interventionist direction, White resigned.

SOURCE: Walter Johnson, Editor, *Selected Letters of William Allen White 1899–1943* (New York: Henry Holt and Company, 1947). See pp. 416–17.

DOCUMENT:

To Roy Howard, Scripps–Howard Newspapers, December 20, 1940

Dear Roy: Look now, Roy, you and I have been buddies more or less, and I hope I have deserved the honor of your friendship these twenty years and more, and why I am sending this is on account that a friend in Washington says you are preparing to strafe our outfit and particularly me because we are heading HB for war. All right, only this:

The only reason in God's world I am in this organization is to keep this country out of war. I don't go an inch further or faster than Wendell Willkie or the American Legion or the American Federation or the National Grange; nor an inch further or faster than you went this month in the Filipino magazine on the Eastern question. I am abreast of you and no further, and I haven't changed since we talked in Chicago last July. The story is floating around that I and our outfit are in favor of sending convoys with British ships or our own ships, a silly thing, for convoys, unless you shoot, are confetti and it's not time to shoot now or ever. Another thing: The America First crowd keeps insisting that we are in favor of repealing the Johnson Act [law forbidding the United States to lend money to nations that defaulted on their war debts], a stupid thing to do because it would not help Great Britain and there are half a dozen other good legal ways to get aid to Great Britain. The President is following his own way. But the Johnson Act should not be repealed and we are not for it. Still one more charge: it is not true even remotely that we favor repealing [the Neutrality Law] to carry contraband of war into the war zone. That would be leading us to war and our organization and I personally are deeply opposed to it. If I was making a motto for the Committee to Defend America by Aiding the Allies, it would be "The Yanks Are Not Coming." We could not equip them and feed them if they went. We have less than two hundred thousand ready, and we need them worse at home on the assembly belt than we need them in Europe. War would defeat the end for which our committee is organized to defend America by aiding Great Britain and would bring on a thirty-year conflict. The Yanks are not going because if they went to war they would lose our cause. That is my firm unshakable belief. And to strafe me because some members of our organization, who are not officially representing us, are martial-minded is as foolish and unfair as it would be to call the Knights of Columbus appeasers because Joe Kennedy [Joseph Kennedy, who resigned as ambassador to England] gave Roosevelt the Judas kiss. Not one official utterance of our organization has anything remotely suggestive that we feel the only alternative for American defense through aid to Great Britain is war. Moreover, I have sat in all executive councils, all policy-making committees, and I have never heard war seriously discussed in any official group of our organization at any time. I hope you know that I am not a liar, and I hope you feel I am not a sucker, and I trust you will believe what I am writing.

America Enters the War, 1941 37

1941 Franklin Roosevelt's Four Freedoms Message to Congress

On January 6, 1941, Franklin Roosevelt delivered his Ninth Annual Message to Congress. Toward the end, he enumerated the four freedoms which he would like to see established throughout the world. There was freedom of speech, freedom of religion—both guaranteed by the U.S. Constitution—freedom from want, and freedom from fear. F.D.R.'s Four Freedoms theme was the World War II counterpart of Woodrow Wilson's hope that World War I would make the world safe for democracy.

SOURCE: Rosenman, Compiler, *The Public Papers and Addresses of Franklin D. Roosevelt*. See IX, 672.

DOCUMENT:

In the future days, which we seek to make secure, we look forward to a world founded upon four essential human freedoms.

The first is freedom of speech and expression—everywhere in the world.

The second is freedom of every person to worship God in his own way—everywhere in the world.

The third is freedom from want—which, translated into world terms, means economic understandings which will secure to every nation a healthy peacetime life for its inhabitants—everywhere in the world.

The fourth is freedom from fear—which, translated into world terms, means a world-wide reduction of armaments to such a point and in such a thorough fashion that no nation will be in a position to commit an act of physical aggression against any neighbor—anywhere in the world.

That is no vision of a distant millennium. It is a definite basis for a kind of world attainable in our own time and generation. That kind of world is the very antithesis of the so-called new order of tyranny which the dictators seek to create with the crash of a bomb.

To that new order we oppose the greater conception—the moral order. A good society is able to face schemes of world domination and foreign revolutions alike without fear.

Since the beginning of our American history, we have been engaged in change—in a perpetual peaceful revolution—a revolution which goes on steadily, quietly adjusting itself to changing conditions—without the concentration camp or the quick-lime in the ditch. The world order which we seek is the cooperation of free countries, working together in a friendly, civilized society.

This nation has placed its destiny in the hands and head and hearts of its millions of free men and women; and its faith in freedom under the guidance of God. Freedom means the supremacy of human rights everywhere. Our support goes to those who struggle to gain those rights or keep them. Our strength is our unity of purpose.

To that high concept there can be no end save victory.

1941 Senator Burton K. Wheeler Attacks Lend–Lease

Franklin Roosevelt's Four Freedoms address to Congress also included a recommendation that lend–lease be made available to the Allies. On March 8, 1941, lend–lease legislation passed the Senate 60 to 31, while on March 11 it cleared the House 317 to 71; the initial appropriation was for 7 billion dollars. Most Senators and Representatives from the Middle West were strongly opposed to lend–lease, and the Chicago Tribune *greeted the enactment of this measure with the headline "Senate Passes Dictator Bill." Almost all of the Southern members of Congress favored lend–lease, but the Far West was sharply divided. Highly critical was isolationist Democratic Senator Burton K. Wheeler of Montana, who regarded the scheme as one which would "plow under every fourth American boy."*

SOURCE: *Congressional Record*, Appendix, January 12, 1941. See pp. 178–79.

DOCUMENT:

The lend–lease policy, translated into legislative form, stunned a Congress and a nation wholly sympathetic to the cause of Great Britain. The Kaiser's blank check to Austria–Hungary in the first World War was a piker compared to the Roosevelt blank check of World War II. It warranted my worst fears for the future of America, and it definitely stamps the President as war-minded.

The lend–lease–give program is the New Deal's triple A foreign policy; it will plow under every fourth American boy.

Never before have the American people been asked or compelled to give so bounteously and so completely of their tax dollars to any foreign nation. Never before has the Congress of the United States been asked by any President to violate international law. Never before has this Nation resorted to duplicity in the conduct of its foreign affairs. Never before has the United States given to one man the power to strip this Nation of its defenses. Never before has a Congress coldly and flatly been asked to abdicate.

If the American people want a dictatorship—if they want a totalitarian form of government and if they want war—this bill should be steam-rollered through Congress, as is the wont of President Roosevelt.

Approval of this legislation means war, open and complete warfare. I, therefore, ask the American people before they supinely accept it, Was the last World War worth while?

If it were, then we should lend and lease war materials. If it were, then we should lend and lease American boys. President Roosevelt has said we would be repaid by England. We will be. We will be repaid, just as England repaid her war debts of the first World War—repaid those dollars wrung from the sweat of labor and the toil of farmers with cries of "Uncle Shylock." Our boys will be returned—returned in caskets, maybe; returned with bodies maimed; returned with minds warped and twisted by sights of horrors and the scream and shriek of high-powered shells.

Considered on its merits and stripped of its emotional appeal to our sympathies, the lend–lease–give bill is both ruinous and ridiculous. Why should we Americans pay for war materials for Great Britain who still has $7,000,000,000 in credit or collateral in the United States? Thus far England has fully maintained rather than depleted her credits in the United States. The cost of the lend–lease–give program is high in terms of American tax dollars, but it is even higher in terms of our national defense. Now it gives to the President the unlimited power to completely strip our air forces of its every bomber, of its every fighting plane.

It gives to one man—responsible to no one—power to denude our shores of every warship. It gives to one individual the dictatorial power to strip the American Army of our every tank, cannon, rifle, or antiaircraft gun. No one would deny that the lend–lease–give bill contains provisions that would enable one man to render the United States defenseless, but they will tell you, "The President would never do it." To this I say, "Why does he ask the power if he does not intend to use it?" Why not, I say, place some check on American donations to a foreign nation?

Is it possible that the farmers of America are willing to sell their birthright for a mess of pottage?

Is it possible that American labor is to be sold down the river in return for a place upon the Defense Commission, or because your labor leaders are entertained at pink teas?

Is it possible that the American people are so gullible that they will permit their representatives in Congress to sit supinely by while an American President demands totalitarian power—in the name of saving democracy?

I say in the kind of language used by the President—shame on those who ask the powers—and shame on those who would grant them.

1941 F.D.R. and Winston Churchill Draw Up the Atlantic Charter

During August, 1941, President Franklin Roosevelt met Prime Minister Winston Churchill at sea off the coast of Newfoundland. Although the two leaders conferred for the purpose of discussing such pressing issues as lend–lease, common defense, and Japanese aggression, they also drew up an eight-point program for the postwar world that came to be known as the Atlantic Charter. This document reflected a number of Woodrow Wilson's Fourteen Points a quarter of a century earlier, as well as F.D.R.'s more recent Four Freedoms. By its attack on "the Hitlerite government of Germany," the Atlantic Charter moved the United States away from a somewhat isolationist stance toward a more interventionist position, and quite naturally irritated the America Firsters convinced that the United States had entered into a tacit alliance with Great Britain.

SOURCE: U.S. Department of State *Bulletin*, August 16, 1941. See pp. 125–26.

DOCUMENT:

The President of the United States and the Prime Minister, Mr. Churchill, representing His Majesty's Government in the United Kingdom, have met at sea.

They have been accompanied by officials of their two Governments, including high-ranking officers of their Military, Naval, and Air Services.

The whole problem of the supply of munitions of war, as provided by the Lease–Lend Act, for the armed forces of the United States and for those countries actively engaged in resisting aggression has been further examined.

Lord Beaverbrook, the Minister of Supply of the British Government, has joined in these conferences. He is going to proceed to Washington to discuss further details with appropriate officials of the United States Government. These conferences will also cover the supply problems of the Soviet Union.

The President and the Prime Minister have had several conferences. They have considered the dangers to world civilization arising from the policies of military domination by conquest upon which the Hitlerite government of Germany and other governments associated therewith have embarked, and have made clear the stress which their countries are respectively taking for their safety in the face of these dangers.

They have agreed upon the following joint declaration:

Joint declaration of the President of the United States of America and the Prime Minister, Mr. Churchill, representing His Majesty's Government in the United Kingdom, being met together, deem it right to make known certain common principles in the national policies of their respective countries on which they base their hopes for a better future for the world.

First, their countries seek no aggrandizement, territorial or other;

Second, they desire to see no territorial changes that do not accord with the freely expressed wishes of the peoples concerned;

Third, they respect the right of all peoples to choose the form of government under which they will live; and they wish to see sovereign rights and self-government restored to those who have been forcibly deprived of them;

Fourth, they will endeavor, with due respect for their existing obligations, to further the enjoyment by all States, great or small, victor or vanquished, of access, on equal terms, to the trade and to the raw materials of the world which are needed for their economic prosperity;

Fifth, they desire to bring about the fullest collaboration between all nations in the economic field with the object of securing, for all, improved labor standards, economic advancement, and social security;

Sixth, after the final destruction of the Nazi tyranny, they hope to see established a peace which will afford to all nations the means of dwelling in safety within their own boundaries, and which will afford assurance that all the men in all the lands may live out their lives in freedom from fear and want;

Seventh, such a peace should enable all men to traverse the high seas and oceans without hindrance;

Eighth, they believe that all of the nations of the world, for realistic as well as spiritual reasons, must come to the abandonment of the use of force. Since no future peace can be maintained if land, sea, or air armaments continue to be employed by nations which threaten, or may threaten, aggression outside of their frontiers, they believe, pending the establishment of a wider and permanent system of general security, that the disarmament of such nations is essential. They will likewise aid and encourage all other practicable measures which will lighten for peace-loving peoples the crushing burden of armaments.

1940 The U.S. Government Limits the Shipment of Aviation Gasoline to Japan over Japanese Protests

American interest in Far Eastern petroleum began to intensify after World War II had broken out. Japanese access to the extensive petroleum output of the Netherlands East Indies became a critical issue; if the United States refused to supply Japan with oil, Japan might move against the Dutch colony. American petroleum exports to the Japanese significantly increased during 1940, but Secretary of War Henry Stimson and Secretary of the Treasury Henry Morgenthau believed that an oil embargo would force the Japanese to show greater restraint. They eventually succeeded in persuading F.D.R. to interdict the shipment of aviation gasoline outside the Western Hemisphere on July 31, over the objections of the State Department. The Japanese protested this action as discriminatory on August 3, but did not occupy the Netherlands East Indies until February 1942—two months after they had attacked Pearl Harbor.

SOURCE: U.S. Department of State, *Foreign Relations of the United States Japan 1931–1941, Volume II* (Washington: Government Printing Office, 1943). See pp. 218–19.

DOCUMENT:

The Japanese Embassy to the Department of State

The Japanese Government has taken note of the Proclamation, dated July 26, 1940, by the President of the United States of America, for the administration of section 6 of the Act of Congress approved July 2, 1940, entitled "An Act to expedite the strengthening of the national defense," and the Regulations, dated July 26, 1940, governing the exportation of articles and materials designated in the President's Proclamation of July 2, 1940, and the announcement of July 31 recommended by Colonel R.L. Maxwell, Administrator of Export Control.

The announcement of July 31, the introduction to which stated that it was issued with the approval of the President, is as follows:

> In the interests of the National Defense the export of aviation gasoline is being limited to nations of the Western Hemisphere, except where such gasoline is required elsewhere for the operations of American owned companies.

It is the understanding of the Japanese Government that the announcement expresses the policy to be followed by the Government of the United States in applying the above mentioned Proclamations and Regulations to the export of aviation gasoline and that that policy, by limiting the export destinations, is tantamount to an embargo on aviation gasoline so far as countries outside the Western Hemisphere are concerned. As a country whose import of American aviation gasoline is of immense volume, Japan would bear the brunt of the virtual embargo. The resultant impression would be that Japan had been singled out for and subjected to discriminatory treatment.

While reserving all rights of further action, the Government of Japan wishes to protest against the policy of the Government of the United States set forth in the announcement under review.

[Washington,] August 3, 1940.

1941 Ambassador Joseph Grew on the Proposed Franklin Roosevelt–Prince Konoye Meeting (1952)

The entry of the United States into the war against Japan in December, 1941 is still a matter of controversy, especially with regard to whether or not the American government knew in advance that the Japanese were going to bomb Hawaii. Another unresolved issue is whether Franklin Roosevelt could have prevented the attack on Pearl Harbor by meeting with the Japanese Prime Minister, Prince Konoye, at some location in the Pacific during the fall of 1941. F.D.R. scuttled the proposed conference by demanding concessions in advance from Konoye; in October 1941, the Konoye ministry fell, and the Japan-

ese militarists took over. Among those who regarded the proposed meeting with Konoye as a missed opportunity for the United States was the American Ambassador to Japan, Joseph Grew.

SOURCE: Joseph C. Grew, *Turbulent Era: A Diplomatic Record of Forty Years 1904–1945,* 2 Volumes (Boston: Houghton Mifflin Company, 1952). See II, 1373–74.

DOCUMENT:

It was held by our Government in its consideration of the wisdom of the proposed meeting, and it has been advanced by commentators since, that Prince Konoye's record was bad and that in the light of that record he could not be trusted. Konoye was responsible, as Prime Minister, for the invasion of China in 1937 and for joining the Axis in 1940. At all times he was under terrific pressure. In such matters one has to be guided by impressions. Certainly no one who was present at that three-hour meeting on the evening of September 6, 1941, could have doubted the sincerity of his determination to reach an agreement with the United States. He frankly admitted his responsibility for allowing his country to move into its then predicament but he said with equal frankness that he was the only statesman in Japan capable of reversing the engine. He knew that Japan could not afford to go to war with the United States. He knew beyond peradventure the only basis on which an agreement could be reached, namely the withdrawal of Japanese forces from Indochina and China. He knew that only on the general basis of Mr. Hull's four points could such an agreement be had. These things he admitted to me and said he was prepared and able to carry them out. Whether he could have done so is a question which can probably never be answered with entire satisfaction, but he himself at that time expressed to me complete confidence that he could—and that he was the only person who could.

From the records it is a simple matter to prove that Prince Konoye, in his assurances to me, had his tongue in his cheek. In such cases the impressions of the moment are not controlling but they cannot be brushed off. Mr. Dooman and I were convinced at that moment that he meant what he said. I still believe he did.

As for the records, Konoye's position at that time was one of the most difficult ever encountered by a statesman. In the Imperial Conference of September 6, 1941, he assured the War Minister that if President Roosevelt failed in the Juneau meeting to "understand" Japan's policy, he would turn around and come home. Unless Konoye could get the leaders of the armed forces to play along, he knew very well that his proposed meeting with the President would be futile and that there would be no purpose in going to meet Roosevelt at all. If Konoye was capable of deliberately misleading the American Ambassador, he was equally capable of misleading his own military leaders on the ground that the end justified the means. Is it beyond the bounds of reason to believe that what Konoye hoped to accomplish was to obtain from Roosevelt an agreement of so dramatic a character in the best interests of the future welfare of his country, even though it might put a stop to further aggression, to the southern advance and to the conquest of China, that the Japanese people would be swept off their feet and, with the support of the Emperor and of the many influential "moderates" in Japan who were tired of the years of war and fighting could have blocked the path even of the military extremists? Even in Japan, public opinion could be a powerful weapon. This is approximately what Konoye told me he expected to do.

1941 Nomuru and Kurusu Criticize the American Proposal to Resolve the Differences Between the United States and Japan

Early in November 1941 the Japanese government sent Saburo Kurusu as a special envoy to the United States. Kurusu had an American wife. On November 26 he and Japanese Ambassador Kichisaburo Nomura met with Secretary of State Cordell Hull. By this time a compromise settlement between the two sides was no longer a realistic possibility. The Japanese were willing to make concessions vis-à-vis French Indo-China, but would not withdraw their troops from the Chinese mainland, which was a major American objective. On December 1 the Japanese government decided to make war on the United States, but also agreed to continue negotiations so as to lull the Americans into a false sense of security. Joseph W. Ballantine of the Division of Far Eastern Affairs took notes at the fateful November 26 conference between Hull and the two Japanese diplomats, and it was he who authored the "Memorandum of a Conversation" which stands as the official record of what transpired there.

SOURCE: U.S. Department of State, *Japan 1931–1941, Volume II.* See pp. 764–65.

DOCUMENT:

Memorandum of a Conversation

[Washington] November 26, 1941

The Japanese Ambassador and Mr. Kurusu called by appointment at the Department. The Secretary handed each of the Japanese copies of an outline of a proposed basis of an agreement between the United States and Japan and an explanatory oral statement.

After the Japanese had read the documents, Mr. Kurusu asked whether this was our reply to their proposal for a *modus vivendi*. The Secretary replied that we had to treat the proposal as we did, as there was so much turmoil and confusion among the public both in the United States and in Japan. He reminded the Japanese that in the United States we have a political situation to deal with just as does the Japanese Government, and he referred to the fire-eating statements which have been recently coming out of Tokyo, which he said had been causing a natural reaction among the public in this country. He said that our proposed agreement would render possible practical measures of financial cooperation, which, however, were not referred to in the outline for fear that this might give rise to misunderstanding. He also referred to the fact that he had earlier in the conversations acquainted the Ambassador of the ambition that had been his of settling the immigration question but that the situation had so far prevented him from realizing that ambition.

Mr. Kurusu offered various depreciatory comments in regard to the proposed agreement. He noted that in our statement of principles there was a reiteration of the Stimson doctrine. He objected to the proposal for multilateral non-aggression pacts and referred to Japan's bitter experience of international organizations, citing the case of the award against Japan by the Hague in the Perpetual Leases matter. He went on to say that the Washington Conference Treaties had given a wrong idea to China, that China had taken advantage of them to flaunt Japan's rights. He said he did not see how his Government could consider paragraphs (3) and (4) of the proposed agreement and that if the United States should expect that Japan was to take off its hat to Chiang Kai-shek and propose to recognize him Japan could not agree. He said that if this was the idea of the American Government he did not see how any agreement was possible.

The Secretary asked whether this matter could not be worked out.

Mr. Kurusu said that when they reported our answer to their Government it would be likely to throw up its hands. He noted that this was a tentative proposal without commitment, and suggested that it might be better if they did not refer it to their Government before discussing its contents further informally here.

The Secretary then referred to the oil question. He said that public feeling was so acute on that question that he might almost be lynched if he permitted oil to go freely to Japan. He pointed out that if Japan should fill Indochina with troops our people would not know what lies ahead in the way of a menace to the countries to the south and west. He reminded the Japanese that they did not know what tremendous injury they were doing to us by keeping immobilized so many forces in countries neighboring Indochina. He explained that we are primarily out for our permanent futures, and the question of Japanese troops in Indochina affects our direct interests.

Mr. Kurusu reverted to the difficulty of Japan's renouncing its support of Wang Ching-wei. The Secretary pointed out that Chiang Kai-shek had made an outstanding contribution in bringing out national spirit in China and expressed the view that the Nanking regime had not asserted itself in a way that would impress the world. Mr. Kurusu agreed with what the Secretary had said about Chiang, but observed that the question of the standing of the Nanking regime was a matter of opinion. His arguments on this as well as on various other points were specious, and unconvincing.

1941 F.D.R. Asks Congress for a Declaration of War Against Japan After the Attack on Pearl Harbor

On December 7, 1941, the Japanese launched their surprise attack on Pearl Harbor, which severely damaged both the U.S. air-force and fleet there. On the next day, Franklin Roosevelt delivered his A Date Which Will Live in Infamy Speech to Congress, in which he asked for a declaration of war. The only nay vote in either House was cast by Republican Representative Jeannette Rankin of Montana, who also had opposed American entry into World War I a quarter of a century earlier. Three days later, Germany and Italy declared war on the United States, thus preventing a possibly acrimonious debate in Congress as to whether this country should also declare war on the other Axis powers.

SOURCE: Rosenman, Compiler, *The Public Papers and Addresses of Franklin D. Roosevelt.* See X, 514–15.

DOCUMENT:

Mr. Vice President, and Mr. Speaker, and Members of the Senate and House of Representatives:

Yesterday, December 7, 1941—a date which will live in infamy—the United States of America was suddenly and deliberately attacked by naval and air forces of the Empire of Japan.

The United States was at peace with that Nation and, at the solicitation of Japan, was still in conversation with its Government and its Emperor looking toward the maintenance of peace in the Pacific. Indeed, one hour after Japanese air squadrons had commenced bombing in the American Island of Oahu, the Japanese Ambassador to the United States and his colleague delivered to our Secretary of State a formal reply to a recent American message. And while this reply stated that it seemed useless to continue the existing diplomatic negotiations, it contained no threat or hint of war or of armed attack.

It will be recorded that the distance of Hawaii from Japan makes it obvious that the attack was deliberately planned many days or even weeks ago. During the intervening time the Japanese Government has deliberately sought to deceive the United States by false statements and expressions of hope for continued peace.

The attack yesterday on the Hawaiian Islands has caused severe damage to American naval and military forces. I regret to tell you that very many American lives have been lost. In addition American ships have been reported torpedoed on the high seas between San Francisco and Honolulu.

Yesterday the Japanese Government also launched an attack against Malaya.

Last night Japanese forces attacked Hong Kong.

Last night Japanese forces attacked Guam.

Last night Japanese forces attacked the Philippine Islands.

Last night the Japanese attacked Wake Island.

And this morning the Japanese attacked Midway Island.

Japan has, therefore, undertaken a surprise offensive extending throughout the Pacific area. The facts of yesterday and today speak for themselves. The people of the United States have already formed their opinions and well understand the implications to the very life and safety of our Nation.

As Commander in Chief of the Army and Navy I have directed that all measures be taken for our defense.

But always will our whole Nation remember the character of the onslaught against us.

No matter how long it may take us to overcome this premeditated invasion, the American people in their righteous might will win through to absolute victory.

I believe that I interpret the will of the Congress and of the people when I assert that we will not only defend ourselves to the uttermost but will make it very certain that this form of treachery shall never again endanger us.

Hostilities exist. There is no blinking at the fact that our people, our territory, and our interests are in grave danger.

With confidence in our armed forces—with the unbounding determination of our people—we will gain the inevitable triumph—so help us God.

I ask that the Congress declare that since the unprovoked and dastardly attack by Japan on Sunday, December 7, 1941, a state of war has existed between the United States and the Japanese Empire.

Wartime Relations with Various Countries 38

1938–42 The Mexican Expropriation of American and British Oil Properties

In 1917, the new Mexican constitution had reserved subsoil petroleum rights to the government of that nation rather than to the foreign oil firms. There ensued two decades of controversy, culminating in the expropriation of certain American and British petroleum holdings by President Lázaro Cárdenas following a labor dispute. The United States government recognized the right of Mexico to do this, provided that the foreign oil firms were compensated; this raised the highly debatable issue of just how much the seized oil properties were worth. At an earlier date, moreover, the Mexican government also had begun to take over American agrarian holdings there, as Secretary of State Cordell Hull frequently pointed out in his diplomatic correspondence with Mexican authorities during this period. The Japanese attack on Pearl Harbor on December 7, 1941 led the United States to settle the expropriation dispute on April 17, 1942 by means of the Cooke–Zevada agreement, under which the American oil firms received far less than they initially had demanded for their seized holdings.

SOURCE: U.S. Department of State *Bulletin*, April 13, 1940. See p. 380.

DOCUMENT:

Following is the text of a note from the Secretary of State to the Ambassador of Mexico, Señor Dr. Don Francisco Castillo Nájera:

April 3, 1940.

Excellency: During the course of the past years there have arisen between the Government of the United States and the Government of Mexico many questions for which no friendly and fair solution, satisfactory to both Governments, has been found. Certain of these problems are of outstanding importance and their equitable solution would redound to the immediate benefit of the peoples of both of our countries.

Animated by the desire to find such an adjustment of all of these pending matters, this Government proposed some two years ago an immediate and comprehensive study by representatives of the Government of the United States and of the Government of Mexico, for the purpose of preparing the way for an expeditious settlement of these controversial questions, the just solution of which would undoubtedly do much to cement the friendly relations between our neighboring peoples.

At that very moment the Government of Mexico by an executive decree expropriated large holdings of oil properties, amounting in value to many millions of dollars and belonging to American nationals, for which no payment has been made and for which there is no present prospect of payment. At various times the Government of Mexico has indicated its ability and readiness to pay. But the fact remains that no payments have been made.

The Government of the United States readily recognizes the right of a sovereign state to expropriate property for public purposes. This view has been stated in a number of communications addressed to your Government during the past two years and in conversations had with you during that same period regarding the expropriation by your Government of property belonging to American nationals. On each occasion, however, it has been stated with equal emphasis that the right to expropriate property is coupled with and conditioned on the obligation to make adequate, effective and prompt compensation. The legality of an expropriation is in fact dependent upon the observance of this requirement.

During the last twenty-five years, one American interest in Mexico after another has suffered at the hands of the Mexican Government. It is recognized that the Mexican Government is making payments on the Special Claims which have to do solely with damages caused by revolutionary disturbances between 1910 and 1920, and has started payments for farm lands expropriated since August 30, 1927. But the Mexican Government has made no compensation for the large number of General Claims of long standing which include an extensive group of claims for the expropriation of farm lands prior to August 30, 1927. It has made no adjustment either of the foreign debt or of the railroad debt both long in default and in both of which American citizens hold important investments. Moreover, the question of the railroad debt was further complicated by the expropriation of the Mexican National Railways on June 23, 1937. Finally, on March 18, 1938, the Mexican Government took over American-owned petroleum property to the value of many millions of dollars, and although two years have elapsed, not one cent of compensation has been paid.

This treatment of American citizens, wholly unjustifiable under any principle of equity or international law, is a matter of grave concern to this Government. These long-standing matters must of necessity be adjusted if the relations between our two countries are to be conducted on a sound and mutually cooperative basis of respect and helpfulness.

As an important step towards placing relations between the two countries on this basis, I suggest resorting to the appropriate, fair and honorable procedure of arbitration. Accordingly, I suggest that the two Governments agree (1) to submit to impartial arbitration all the questions involved in the oil controversy and to clothe a tribunal with authority not only to determine the amount to be paid to American nationals who have been deprived of their properties, but also the means by which its decision shall be executed to make certain that adequate and effective compensation shall promptly be paid, and (2) either to submit to an umpire, as contemplated by the General Claims Protocol of 1934, the un-adjudicated claims falling under the Convention of 1923, or proceed immediately to the negotiation of an en bloc settlement in accordance with that Protocol.

1941 Iceland Complains About the Behavior of American Military Personnel

The United States militarily occupied both Greenland and Iceland during 1941. Unlike sparsely inhabited, geographically enormous, and culturally primitive Greenland, Iceland is more densely settled, more geographically compact, and much more literate. Icelanders long have been hostile to foreign domination; they won complete domestic autonomy from Denmark in 1903, and became a sovereign kingdom under the Danish crown in 1918. During World War II, the British occupied Iceland (in 1940) in order to prevent a possible German invasion, and American troops joined them a year later at the invitation of the Icelandic government. Unfortunately, relations between the military personnel of both the United States and Great Britain and the citizens of this island–state were troublesome at times, as certain documents in the files of the National Archives reveal.

SOURCE: "Memorandum of Conversation," October 3, 1941, Record Group 59, decimal file 859A 20/127, National Archives, Washington, D.C. See pp. 1–3.

DOCUMENT:

1. American soldiers, particularly sailors and the regular army enlisted men, are much too belligerent with the Icelanders. Our men seem to want to fight and begin swinging on Icelanders simply for the fun of it. Attacks are usually without provocation and seemingly without motive. The men seem quite sober and not at all under the influence of liquor. Very often the men trail Icelanders for several blocks endeavoring all the while to pick a fight.

2. There have been several recorded instances where taxis have been hired by soldiers for protracted periods of time. The men have not paid for the cab, and have simply walked off telling the chauffeur that they had no money with which to pay. The police have tried to run down some of these parties, and actually have gotten one or two, whereupon the men have paid immediately. The police intimate that if liberty parties could travel in army vehicles rather than taxis, there would be no trouble. It is very difficult to control such instances because there is no way of holding the men.

3. There have been some occasions where soldiers have taken private automobiles and driven off with them, damaging them, and then have left them beside the road.

4. The British soldiers have a very profound disrespect for the Icelandic police, and for Icelanders, which has been fostered by their officers. Soldiers should not be encouraged by their officers to adopt an overbearing or condescending attitude towards Icelanders, for they are a very proud people and do not like to be placed in a position of inferiority.

5. The Icelandic police believe that it is dangerous to have the soldiers carry arms while in the city. There have been numerous cases of shooting by British soldiers since the occupation began, very often while the men were under the influence of liquor, and much damage has been done.

6. Soldiers, particularly the British, have done considerable damage to property while on liberty in the city. This has consisted in smashing furniture and crockery in cafes and restaurants, damaging installations, and very often breaking windows.

7. The police state that one of the worst evils in the city of Reykjavik is the isolated Nissen hut one finds here and there on private property. This is one of the means whereby girls, particularly the younger ones, have been seduced, and there is a very large file in the police office dealing with this problem. The Police Chief tells me that many Icelanders, including very distinguished members of the community, have been in his office time after time broken and sobbing when apprised of the comings and goings of daughters of the family. British officers seem to condone invitations to small parties given by the enlisted men in these isolated Nissen huts. The Chief of Police feels that if these Nissen huts can be removed from the city, it would be a solution to the problem.

8. The road intersection defenses and the pill boxes are a source of great annoyance to the people of Reykjavik. They serve no useful purpose from a military point of view, and could very well be liquidated. They are a road hazard, principally because they form blind corners at important road crossings.

9. Since alcohol is the more fruitful source of trouble among the troops, the police recommend that nothing but beer be authorized for the troops, and that it be consumed on the premises of the military canteens only.

10. The question of how to deal with girls under eighteen is one which is of the greatest concern to the Icelandic Government. I told the Police Chief that I had recommended to General Bonesteel that some effort be made to keep the younger girls from the dance halls and public gatherings. General Bonesteel has assured me that there will be no dances on the military reservations. General Marston has agreed that there will be no dances on the military reservations where the Marines are quartered. The Icelandic police recommend that Icelandic and American military police be present together at any public dances or gatherings to keep the younger girls out. If the Icelandic police should be present alone, it might cause hostility, whereas if accompanied by American military police it would work out much more satisfactorily; the Icelanders would know the girls personally, and the military police could oblige the soldiers to give up their partners if too young.

11. One very sore point among Icelanders is the shouting and yelling by soldiers on the streets. The Marines are not given to this and are much more quiet. However, since the arrival of the army, the enlisted men are very noisy on Reykjavik streets, shouting, whistling and yelling. There is universal anger against this on the part of the Icelanders. There have been instances where Icelanders, particularly the older men, have objected and have asked the soldiers to make less noise, and have been attacked and knocked down. The number of such old men attacked is large enough to be regrettable.

1942 Restrictions on U.S. Citizens in the Azores

Like Eire, Switzerland, Sweden, Turkey, and Spain, Portugal remained neutral during World War II. During World War I, the United States had acquired a temporary military base at Ponta Delgada in the Azores, a group of nine islands in the mid-Atlantic under Portuguese control. Official U.S. interest in the islands between the two world wars, however, was minimal. Then after the Americans had entered World War II in 1942, the civil governor of Ponta Delgada caused a sensation by demanding that all foreigners living outside that city move there, and that once in the city they had to assemble at a local football field when the signal was given. This is one of the more extreme examples of the problems which American citizens living in neutral countries faced during World War II. The U.S. government eventually pressured officials in Lisbon to cancel the second part of this order, and in November, 1944 the United States signed an agreement for the construction of an airbase on Santa Maria. Clearly, the latter was an unneutral act on the part of the Portuguese, who no longer had to fear a German invasion.

SOURCE: U.S. Department of State, *Foreign Relations of the United States, Volume III* (Washington: Government Printing Office, 1942). See pp. 232–33 and 238–39.

DOCUMENT:

The Consul at Ponta Delgada, Azores (Dawson)
to the Secretary of State

Ponta Delgada, March 29, 1942, 5 p.m.

I have received a circular letter dated March 28 from the Civil Governor of Ponta Delgada transmitting an order of the military command of the Azores of which the following is translation of the text:

1. All foreigners without exception are required to concentrate themselves on the football field of the local high school following any rifle firing or signal of 3 shots fired by artillery or the firing of three mortars.

2. All foreigners including consular officers found outside the concentration field 1 hour after the beginning of the concentration will be considered spies and will be executed without trial of any kind.

3. Any foreigner who by reason of exceptional conditions is unable to present himself in the concentration camp shall communicate at once with the General Headquarters of the Military Command and must at once consider himself a prisoner in the place where he is.

This action is probably the result of recent flights by unidentified planes over this island too high to be recognized but one heard by me about 6 a.m. March 27 sounded like a German motor. Compliance with this order would leave no time for the destruction of codes, confidential correspondence, passport blanks, et cetera. I pointed out to the Governor that in case of emergency I am instructed by my Government to remain in the Consulate. I respectfully request instructions. The Legation has been informed. Please acknowledge the receipt of this telegram as I am in doubt whether it will be transmitted.

The Consul at Ponta Delgada, Azores (Dawson) to the Secretary of State

Ponta Delgada, March 31, 1942—11 a.m.

The local Government has ordered that all foreigners without exception whatsoever residing on this island outside the city of Ponta Delgada must establish their place of residence within the area of the city not later than April 4 under penalty of imprisonment or deportation. The Acting Civil Governor has informed me verbally that this measure applies to all those persons registered as American citizens. In the island of São Miguel alone there are 94 such persons and hundreds of others born in the United States who may claim citizenship. There are few citizens of other nations so this order will affect primarily American citizens. The order apparently was issued at the request of the military authorities due to fear of fifth column activities in the event of an invasion attempt.

The Minister in Portugal (Fish) to the Secretary of State

Lisbon, April 21, 1942—10 p.m.

Last night Dr. Costa Carneiro assured the Legation that while the authorities in Azores were compelled to take precautions the absurd order issued at Ponta Delgada requiring all foreigners including Consuls to proceed to a football field following a signal was a mistake and was being dealt with. He explained that the precautions taken by the insular authorities were aimed at coping with fifth column activities and had of necessity to be addressed to all foreign Consuls. He suggested that it might be in the interest of the United States that these precautionary measures were taken since they applied to our enemies. The Legation has been informed by the Consul in Ponta Delgada that situation is calmer since arrival of General Passos e Sousa who appears to have been sent for an investigation. Military Attaché informs me [that] he has heard that the General's predecessor who was responsible for the above mentioned order will be recalled and it had even been suggested that he is mentally unbalanced.

The Minister in Portugal (Fish) to the Secretary of State

Lisbon, May 5, 1942—5 p.m.

Last night the Director General of Political Affairs referred to the canceling of certain orders to which we had strongly objected regarding our Consuls in the Azores. He said, however, that the military insisting that the order that all foreigners in São Miguel must move into Ponta Delgada could not be canceled. He assured the Legation, however, that the insular authorities have been cautioned to cause as little hardship as possible and that the order would be carried out "with moderation."

The Legation pointed out that most of the Americans in the island were poor people of Portuguese origin who could not afford to move from their farms into town. In reply, the Foreign Office official repeated the argument previously reported that it was in our interest that these precautionary measures were taken since they applied equally to our enemies and that the military authorities had flatly refused to cancel these restrictions.

1942–45 Ambassador Carlton J. H. Hayes and Franco's Spain

Another World War II neutral, Spain, had been more openly identified with Germany and Italy, especially since the time of the Spanish Civil War. Clearly, Francisco Franco had much in common with both fellow dictators Adolf Hitler and Benito Mussolini, but he did not join the Axis. The American government supplied the Spanish with petroleum and other vital items during World War II, and assured Franco that it had no intention of attacking Spanish territory. At the same time, though, the United States began to pressure the Spanish into selling wolfram to the Allies rather than to Hitler. Columbia University historian Carlton J. H. Hayes, the American Ambassador to Spain, described in his diplomatic memoirs how Franco moved from pro-Axis nonbelligerency to pro-Allies neutrality as the war progressed.

SOURCE: Carlton J. H. Hayes, *Wartime Mission to Spain 1942–1945* (New York: The Macmillan Company, 1946). See pp. 298–300.

DOCUMENT:

So long as Axis victory seemed to him inevitable, so long as almost the whole continent of Europe was at the mercy of Germany, with German armies massed near the Pyrenees and German submarines infesting the seas adjacent to Spain, General Franco let Hitler and indeed the world believe that he was pro-Axis. Nevertheless, whatever may have been his inmost thoughts and personal fears in the matter, the fact remains that at least from the date of his dismissal of Serrano Suner from the Foreign Office and the leadership of the Falange, in September, 1942, General Franco guided or backed the responsible officials of his Government in approximating Spain's official position to the pro-Allied position of the large majority of the Spanish people.

From September, 1942, to June, 1943, while the Spanish Government was still ostensibly "non-belligerent" and hence technically "unneutral," it not only placed no obstacle in the way of our landings and military operations in North Africa and southern Italy but gave us significant facilities, such as *de facto* recognition of the French committee of National Liberation at Algiers and of its official representatives in Spain; free transit through Spain of over 25,000 volunteers (chiefly French) for active service with our armed forces in North Africa; non-internment of several hundreds of our forced-landed military airmen and their evacuation through Gibraltar; immediate delivery to us, quite uncompromised, of secret equipment on forced-landed planes; and freedom and full opportunity to carry on economic warfare with the Axis on Spanish territory by means of pre-emptive buying of wolfram, mercury, fluorspar, skins, woolen goods, etc., and blacklisting of Spanish firms doing business with the Axis.

From July, 1943, to May, 1944, the Spanish Government shifted its declared position from "non-belligerency" to "neutrality," and gradually increased the facilities it was according us to the detriment of the Axis. It not only curbed the discrimination against us in the Falangist-controlled press of the country, withdrew the Blue Division and Blue Air Squadron from the Eastern front, and replaced pro-Axis with pro-Allied diplomatic representatives in countries of Europe and Latin America, but it permitted the commercial sale of American propaganda magazines, granted us control of all passenger traffic, by Spanish airplanes as well by ships, between Spain and Spanish Morocco, and withheld recognition of Mussolini's "Social Republican" Government in North Italy.

Moreover, it speeded up the evacuation of Allied refugees and forced-landed airmen, arranged for the escape to Spain of a considerable number of Jews from Hungary, Germany, and the Low Countries, and tolerated, even to the point of abetting, the very important clandestine activities of our secret espionage services directed toward obtaining from across the Pyrenees invaluable military information about German troop movements and dispositions in France. Finally, as the result of a series of negotiations, pressed by us and vehemently opposed by Germany, Spain embargoed all exports of wolfram to the Axis from February to May and agreed to allow thereafter only token shipments (which stopped altogether after our landing in France in June, 1944). Simultaneously, the Spanish Government agreed to submit to arbitration the question of the internment of Italian warships which had been held for several months in the Balearic Islands, to close the German Consulate at Tangier, and to expel its staff and other Axis agents suspected of espionage or sabotage against us.

From July, 1944, the Spanish Government repeatedly indicated, by word and likewise by deed, that its policy toward us was one of "benevolent neutrality." It authorized our use of Barcelona as a free port of entry for supplies for France and other "liberated" areas. It expelled or interned several hundred German agents. It assured us it would not harbor persons adjudged by competent Allied tribunals to be "war criminals." It rescinded practically all censorship restrictions on American journalists in Spain and arranged with the United Press to utilize this American news service for the Spanish press.

It was the first foreign government to make a general air agreement with ours, and under this, we obtained transit and landing rights in Spain for three different American air lines and also for our army planes. It finally put into effect between Madrid and New York the direct radio–telegraphic circuit which had been the object of protracted and fruitless negotiations by us with the Spanish Monarchy prior to 1931 and with the Spanish Republic prior to the Civil War. On the eve of my departure from Spain, in January, the Foreign Minister notified me that his Government had released the interned Italian warships. Already the outstanding, and long-standing, difficulties between the Spanish Government and the American owned Telephone Company were the subject of amicable negotiations which issued, just after I left, in a mutually satisfactory agreement. Moreover, the Foreign Minister had already agreed to stop the carrying of any merchandise by the German airline between Barcelona and Stuttgart (the only means left to Germany of getting goods from or to Spain), and had expressed a desire to discontinue this German line altogether if only we would consent to the maintenance of some sort of communication between Spain and Switzerland. This also was accomplished shortly after I left Spain. Furthermore, both the Foreign Minister and General Franco himself repeatedly made clear, not only in conversation with me, but by inspired articles in the Spanish press, their hostility to Japan and their intention, in due course, of breaking diplomatic relations with it. This, too, they did soon after I left.

1942 Robert Murphy and the Darlan Deal vis-à-vis French North Africa

When France surrendered to Germany in 1940, Germany occupied only the Northern and Western parts of the defeated nation. The remainder of France—along with its overseas empire—was placed under the control of a pro-German regime at Vichy. The United States continued to maintain diplomatic relations with Vichy France, but in November, 1942 it launched a large-scale invasion of French North Africa. At this time, Admiral Jean-François Darlan, the Vice Premier of Vichy France, was in Algiers. This highly controversial figure now threw his support to the Allies, and was of considerable assistance prior to his assassination on Christmas Eve, 1942. Like F.D.R., Darlan's son was a victim of polio, and he sought treatment for him in the United States. Career diplomat Robert Murphy, then Franklin Roosevelt's own personal representative in North Africa, committed to writing his impressions of the Vichy leader.

SOURCE: Robert Murphy, *Diplomat Among Warriors* (Garden City: Doubleday and Company, 1964). See pp. 140–42.

DOCUMENT:

I was indeed close to the enigmatic little French admiral during the next six weeks, until he was assassinated in Algiers on Christmas Eve. Probably I got to know him better than any other American ever did and, strangely, I grew to like him. I was particularly impressed by how cleverly Darlan safeguarded French national interests. Although he was leading from weakness, knowing the hostility toward him in Britain and the United States, no negotiator could have obtained more Allied concessions for the benefit of France. While discussions in Algiers were still in critical stage, Roosevelt was induced to make a statement describing arrangements with Darlan as a "temporary expedient," justified solely by the stress of battle. The Roosevelt statement was interpreted by some French commanders as a partial repudiation of assurances already given, and Darlan had to move fast to hold his subordinates in line. The agreement signed on November 23 provided guarantees of French sovereignty in the African empire, and left unimpaired French imperial controls over African populations. Moreover, Darlan exacted from Americans even more lavish pledges to reconstruct French armed forces than Clark had offered to Mast at Cherchell.

Out of the military clauses in the Clark–Darlan agreement emerged the massive American military aid program for France while World War II was in progress. Under that program the United States fully equipped and trained eight French divisions in North Africa, partially outfitted and trained three more in France, supplied equipment for nineteen air squadrons, and also extensively re-equipped the French Navy. Under this wartime program the United States supplied the French with fourteen hundred aircraft, thirty thousand machine guns, three thousand artillery guns, five thousand tanks and self-propelled weapons, and fifty-one million rounds of ammunition. Whatever Darlan's apparent failings during his Vichy period, he proved during his last weeks that he was a French patriot.

While thus protecting the interests of France, Darlan also contributed more to the Allied cause than most people knew at the time. He invited me to listen on extension telephones to several of his conversations with French commanders during the first critical days of the invasion, and to read some of his messages before he sent them. No one but Darlan, I am sure, could at that time have induced Nogues to end resistance in Morocco so quickly, or have persuaded General Pierre Boisson, Governor General of French West Africa, to deliver that great territory and the port of Dakar without the firing of a shot.

Several times Darlan said to me, "Please tell your President that any time he decides I am more of a liability than an asset to him, I will gladly step down." He even offered to leave with us a signed resignation, undated, which could be put into effect whenever we desired. "All I ask," he said, "is the privilege of visas and transportation to the United States for myself and my wife."

The reason Darlan wanted to go with his wife to the United States was because their son Alain was at Warm Springs, Georgia, undergoing treatment at the infantile paralysis clinic made famous by Roosevelt. Infantile paralysis, in fact, figured rather importantly in the "Darlan deal." It was responsible for Darlan's presence in Algiers at the time of the invasion, and it influenced the emotions of both the French Admiral and the American President. When I informed Leahy by cablegram two days before the landings that Darlan had arrived in Algiers because of his son's paralysis, Leahy promptly informed Roosevelt. Describing this incident in his memoirs, Leahy wrote: "The first thing that impressed Roosevelt was the nature of the boy's illness. Roosevelt remembered his own illness and proposed that we send a letter to Darlan. I replied I thought it would be a very nice thing to do. Later Roosevelt sent Darlan's son to Warm Springs and kept him there for a considerable time. Darlan was most grateful, and it is my belief that this thoughtfulness on the part of the President helped us in the critical situation that was developing." After Darlan's assassination, his widow visited her son as a guest of the American Government.

1944 The Recall of General Joseph Stilwell from China

China was on the side of the Allies during World War II, but it played a largely defensive role due to the presence of Japanese troops on Chinese soil and the instability of the alliance between the Chinese Nationalists and the Chinese Communists. Still another complicating factor was the mutual hostility between Generalissimo Chiang Kai-shek and the Theater Commander, American General Joseph W. "Vinegar Joe" Stilwell. During 1944, Major General Patrick J. Hurley was sent to China as a special Presidential envoy. On October 9, 1944, Chiang made a blistering written attack on Stilwell to F.D.R. through Hurley, accompanied by the following aide-mémoire. Ten days later, the War Department notified Stilwell that he had been recalled. In all fairness to Chiang, it should be noted that Stilwell had become contemptuous of the Chinese leader, whom he privately described as "the Peanut."

SOURCE: Chin-tung Liang, *General Stilwell in China 1942–1944: The Full Story* (New York: St. John's University Press, 1972). See pp. 267–69.

DOCUMENT:

Both the President and the War Department are dependent on General Stilwell for information concerning the military situation in China. Thus the President may not be aware that I not only have no confidence in General Stilwell, but also lack confidence in his military judgment. I believe the record sustains my opinion and I shall summarize it briefly.

General Stilwell and I have never agreed about the Burma campaign. I have naturally been anxious for a campaign in Burma which would reopen land communications with China. At the same time, in view of the enemy's superior communications in that area and the difficult terrain, I have always insisted that the only strategically sound campaign in Burma was one which included amphibious operations in South Burma to insure rapid collapse of the enemy's resistance. From the first, I have repeatedly warned General Stilwell that a limited offensive in North Burma would be more costly than could be justified by the results and might even prove exceedingly dangerous. I gave my opinion to the President when we met in Cairo.

At the Cairo Conference, commitments were finally made by the representatives of the United States and Great Britain which appeared to ensure the kind of Burma campaign where I could approve. Unhappily, those commitments were abandoned shortly after I left Cairo. General Stilwell then came to me and announced that he proposed to proceed with a limited offensive in North Burma. I again warned him of the consequences, stating specifically that I feared the project would be difficult and costly, and would engage all of China's limited resources which were then most urgently needed in China. He treated my warning lightly, and intimated that if I maintained my attitude, China would be suspected of wishing to withhold any real contribution to the Allied cause. At length I consented to his employing the Ramgarh troops which were entirely American-trained and equipped and with the clear understanding that these forces were all that would be forthcoming.

It was not long before my warning was substantiated. The moment obstacles were encountered in Burma, General Stilwell began to use every sort of pressure to induce me to commit additional forces. I shall not enter into details. It is enough to say that by the beginning of May, the Burma campaign had drained off most of the properly trained and equipped reserves in China. At the same time, it had greatly reduced the incoming supply tonnage so that during the ensuing critical months, it was impossible to strengthen the military position in any area within China. It was not until June that the Hump tonnage, exclusive of the B-29 project, again reached the January level.

As I had feared, the Japanese took advantage of the opportunity thus offered to launch an offensive within China, attacking first in Honan and then in Hunan. The forces brought to bear by the Japanese in their offensive in east China were six times as great as those confronting General Stilwell in North Burma, and the consequences of defeat were certain to outweigh in China all results of victory in the North Burma campaign. Yet General Stilwell exhibited complete indifference to the outcome in east China; so much so that in the critical days of the east China operations, he consistently refused to release lend–lease munitions already available in Yunnan for use in the east China fighting. Prior to June 1944, with the exception of the Yunnan Expeditionary Force, the entire Chinese Army did not receive a single rifle or piece of artillery from American Lend–Lease. It was not until the first week of June 1944, that General Stilwell at last visited Chungking to discuss the east China situation with me. When the enemy's offensive was already on the way to its objectives, General Stilwell finally consented to give a small quantity of equipment to the Chinese armies in east China, and to facilitate more air support. In all, excepting the Yunnan Expeditionary Force, the Chinese armies have received 50 mountain guns, 320 anti-tank rifles and 506 bazookas.

In short, we have taken Myitkyina but we have lost almost all of east China, and in this General Stilwell cannot be absolved of grave responsibility. Even now he appears to be unaware of the implications of this fact and the grave damage to prestige and morale of the Chinese Army. It is possible that this fact, fundamentally important as it is, had not been pointed out to the President. Whatever my opinion of General Stilwell as a man may be, I might bring myself to appoint him to command in China if I thought well of him as a military leader. However, with all the facts before me I have come to the conclusion that he is not competent to envisage or to deal with problems of such range and complexity as now confront us.

Wartime Conferences and the United Nations 39

1943 Wendell Willkie's *One World:* A Farewell to Isolationism

In 1940, Wendell Willkie was the Republican Presidential candidate, and like F.D.R. he promised aid to the Allies. Far removed from the Borah–Johnson isolationist wing of his party, Willkie undertook a global trip during World War II on the Gulliver; *this airplane made stops in Latin America, Africa, the Middle East, China, and the Soviet Union. Upon his return, Willkie penned that* Bible *of internationalism,* One World. *Proclaiming himself a Wilsonian and a believer in the League of Nations, Willkie pointed out that world peace had economic as well as political roots. Despite his party's conversion to internationalism, Willkie failed to obtain the Republican Presidential nomination in 1944 and was dead by the end of the year.*

SOURCE: Wendell Willkie, *One World* (New York: Simon and Schuster, 1943). See pp. 196–98.

DOCUMENT:

It was only a short time ago—less than a quarter of a century—that the allied nations gained an outstanding victory over the forces of conquest and aggression then led by imperial Germany.

But the peace that should have followed that war failed primarily because no joint objectives upon which it could be based had been arrived at in the minds of the people, and therefore no world peace was possible. The League of Nations was created full-blown; and men and women, having developed no joint purpose, except to defeat a common enemy, fell into capricious arguments about its structural form. Likewise, it failed because it was primarily an Anglo–French–American solution, retaining the old colonial imperialisms under new and fancy terms. It took inadequate account of the pressing needs of the Far East, nor did it sufficiently seek solution of the economic problems of the world. Its attempts to solve the world's problems were primarily political. But political internationalism without economic internationalism is a house built upon sand. For no nation can reach its fullest development alone.

Our own history furnishes, I believe, another clue to our failure. One of our most obvious weaknesses, in the light of what is going on today, is the lack of any continuity in our foreign policy. Neither major party can claim to have pursued a stable or consistent program of international cooperation even during the relatively brief period of the last forty-five years. Each has had its season of world outlook—sometimes an imperialistic one—and each its season of strict isolationism, the Congressional leadership of the party out of power usually, according to accepted American political practice, opposing the program of the party in power, whatever it might be.

For years many in both parties have recognized that if peace, economic prosperity, and liberty itself were to continue in this world, the nations of the world must find a method of economic stabilization and co-operative effort.

These aspirations at the end of the First World War, under the presidency of Woodrow Wilson, produced a program of international co-operation intended to safeguard all nations against military aggression, to protect racial minorities, and to give the oncoming generation some confidence that it could go about its affairs without a return of the disrupting and blighting scourge of war. Whatever we may think about the details of that program, it was definite, affirmative action for world peace. We cannot state positively just how effective it might have proved had the United States extended to it support, influence, and active participation.

But we do know that we tried the opposite course and found it altogether futile. We entered into an era of strictest detachment from world affairs. Many of our public leaders, Democratic and Republican, went about the country proclaiming that we had been tricked into the last war, that our ideals had been betrayed, that never again should we allow ourselves to become entangled in world politics which would inevitably bring about another armed outbreak. We were blessed with natural barriers, they maintained, and need not concern ourselves with the complicated and unsavory affairs of an old world beyond our borders.

We shut ourselves away from world trade by excessive tariff barriers. We washed our hands of the continent of Europe and displayed no interest in its fate while Germany rearmed. We torpedoed the London Economic Conference when the European democracies, with France lagging in the rear, were just beginning to recover from the economic depression that had sapped their vitality, and when the instability of foreign exchange remained the principal obstacle to full revival. And in so doing, we sacrificed a magnificent opportunity for leadership in strengthening and rehabilitating the democratic nations, in fortifying them against assault by the forces of aggression which at that very moment were beginning to gather.

The responsibility for this does not attach solely to any political party. For neither major party stood consistently and conclusively before the American public as either the party of world outlook or the party of isolation. If we were to say that Republican leadership destroyed the League of Nations in 1920, we must add that it was Democratic leadership that broke up the London Economic Conference in 1933.

1943 The Casablanca Conference: Unconditional Surrender (Robert E. Sherwood, 1946)

The Newfoundland meeting which culminated in the Atlantic Charter was only the first of several important conferences between Franklin Roosevelt and Winston Churchill, some with other Allied leaders present. One of the most important of these took place at Casablanca, French Morocco, in June, 1943. Here, the Americans, the British, and the French agreed to invade Sicily and Italy, and also to open a second front elsewhere. Perhaps the most controversial decision to come out of this conference was the call for the Axis to surrender unconditionally. The American people proudly applauded this decision, but it nevertheless was to cause some major problems, including the total collapse of the German and Japanese governments at the end of the war. In a detailed study, Presidential advisor Robert E. Sherwood pointed out that F.D.R. apparently conceived the idea of unconditional surrender on his own, without first consulting Winston Churchill. During World War II, Pulitzer Prize-winning playwright Sherwood served as the Director of the Overseas Branch of the Office of War Information.

SOURCE: Robert E. Sherwood, *Roosevelt and Hopkins: An Intimate History* (New York: Harper and Brothers, 1950). See pp. 695–97.

DOCUMENT:

I wrote Winston Churchill asking him if he had discussed the unconditional surrender statement with Roosevelt before the press conference at Casablanca, and his reply was as follows:

> I heard the words "Unconditional Surrender" for the first time from the President's lips at the Conference. It must be remembered that at that moment no one had a right to proclaim that Victory was assured. Therefore, Defiance was the note. I would not myself have used these words, but I immediately stood by the President and have frequently defended the decision. It is false to suggest that it prolonged the war. Negotiation with Hitler was impossible. He was a maniac with supreme power to play his hand out to the end, which he did; and so did we.

Roosevelt himself absolved Churchill from all responsibility for the statement. Indeed, he suggested that it was an unpremeditated one on his own part. He said, "We had so much trouble getting those two French generals together that I thought to myself that this was as difficult as arranging the meeting of Grant and Lee—and then suddenly the press conference was on, and Winston and I had had no time to prepare for it, and the thought popped into my mind that they had called Grant 'Old Unconditional Surrender' and the next thing I knew, I had said it."

Roosevelt, for some reason, often liked to picture himself as a rather frivolous fellow who did not give sufficient attention to the consequences of chance remarks. In this explanation, indicating a spur-of-the-moment slip of the tongue, he certainly did considerably less than justice to himself. For this announcement of unconditional surrender was very deeply deliberated. Whether it was wise or foolish, whether it prolonged the war or shortened it—or even if it had no effect whatsoever on the duration (which seems possible)—it was a true statement of Roosevelt's considered policy and he refused all suggestions that he retract the statement or soften it and continued refusal to the day of his death. In fact, he re-stated it a great many times.

What Roosevelt was saying was that there would be no negotiated peace, no compromise with Nazism and Fascism, no "escape clauses" provided by another Fourteen Points which could lead to another Hitler. (The ghost of Woodrow Wilson was again at his shoulder.) Roosevelt wanted this uncompromising purpose to be brought home to the American people and the Russians and the Chinese, and to the people of France and other occupied nations, and he wanted it brought home to the Germans—that neither by continuance of force nor by contrivance of a new spirit of sweet reasonableness could their present leaders gain for them a soft peace. He wanted to ensure that when the war was won it would stay won.

Undoubtedly his timing of the statement at Casablanca was attributable to the uproar over Darlan and Peyrouton and the liberal fears that this might indicate a willingness to make similar deals with a Goering in Germany or a Matsuoka in Japan.

It is a matter of record that the Italians and the Japanese were ready to accept unconditional surrender as soon as effective force was applied to their homelands. Whether they might have done so sooner, or whether the Germans might ever have done so, under any circumstances whatsoever, are matters for eternal speculation. One thing about Roosevelt's famous statement is certain, however—he had his eyes wide open when he made it.

1943 The Teheran Conference: F.D.R. and Stalin Meet (Frances Perkins, 1946)

Master politician Franklin Roosevelt had few equals in turning on the charm, but in Russian dictator Joseph Stalin he was confronting something more than a rival political boss. Boasting about "Uncle Joe" that "I can handle that old buzzard," F.D.R. met Stalin for the first time at Teheran between November 28 and December 1, 1943. (The Russians long had coveted the Northern part of oil-rich Iran.) It was agreed here that the Western democracies would invade France in the spring of 1944, while the Soviets would attack Germany from the East. Secretary of Labor Frances Perkins described in her political memoirs how

Roosevelt attempted to win over the Russian leader by poking fun at Churchill. This may have warmed up Stalin, but it hardly altered his long-term, hard line goals and objectives. Stalin also kept secret the fact that he had some knowledge of the English language, and thus did not have to rely totally on his translator.

SOURCE: Frances Perkins, *The Roosevelt I Knew* (New York: Viking Press, 1946) See pp. 83–85.

DOCUMENT:

The Russians interested and intrigued him. He couldn't get the servants around the house to talk to him. They rendered efficient service, smiled broadly and charmingly, but said nothing. And although he was accustomed to a gay exchange of personal greetings and ideas with people in other countries, he liked them.

He had gone prepared to like Stalin and determined to make himself liked. He told me the story of his encounter with Stalin while I was trying to talk with him about a particular piece of legislation then in the Congress:

> You know, the Russians are interesting people. For the first three days I made absolutely no progress. I couldn't get any personal connection with Stalin, although I had done everything he asked me to do. I had stayed at his Embassy, gone to his dinners, been introduced to his ministers and generals. He was correct, stiff, solemn, not smiling, nothing human to get hold of. I felt pretty discouraged. If it was all going to be official paper work, there was no sense in my having made this long journey which the Russians had wanted. They couldn't come to America or any place in Europe for it. I had come there to accommodate Stalin. I felt pretty discouraged because I thought I was making no personal headway. What we were doing could have been done by the foreign ministers.
>
> I thought it over all night and made up my mind I had to do something desperate. I couldn't stay in Teheran forever. I had to cut through this icy surface so that later I could talk by telephone or letter in a personal way. I had scarcely seen Churchill alone during the conference. I had a feeling that the Russians did not feel right about seeing us conferring together in a language which we understood and they didn't.
>
> On my way to the conference room that morning we caught up with Winston and I had just a moment to say to him, "Winston, I hope you won't be sore at me for what I am going to do."
>
> Winston just shifted his cigar and grunted. I must say he behaved very decently afterward.
>
> I began almost as soon as we got into the conference room. I talked privately with Stalin. I didn't say anything that I hadn't said before, but it appeared quite chummy and confidential, enough so that the other Russians joined us to listen. Still no smile.
>
> Then I said, lifting my hand up to cover a whisper (which of course had to be interpreted) 'Winston is cranky this morning, he got up on the wrong side of the bed.'
>
> A vague smile passed over Stalin's eyes, and I decided I was on the right track. As soon as I sat down at the conference table, I began to tease Churchill about his Britishness, about John Bull, about his cigars, about his habits. It began to register with Stalin. Winston got red and scowled, and the more he did so, the more Stalin

smiled. Finally Stalin broke out into a deep, hearty guffaw, and for the first time in three days I saw light. I kept it up until Stalin was laughing with me, and it was then that I called him "Uncle Joe." He would have thought me fresh the day before, but that day he laughed and came over and shook my hand.

From that time on our relations were personal, and Stalin himself indulged in an occasional witticism. The ice was broken and we talked like men and brothers.

1944 The Quebec Conference: The Morgenthau Plan for Dismantling Germany

There were two Quebec Conferences involving F.D.R. and Winston Churchill, the first in August, 1943 and the second in September, 1944. At the second meeting, the two Allied leaders agreed on the location of the American and British zones of occupation in the Western half of postwar Germany. By far the most controversial item on the agenda here was the so-called Morgenthau Plan of Secretary of the Treasury Henry Morgenthau, Jr. Morgenthau wanted totally to demilitarize Germany, to shrink its boundaries, to set up two German states, and to deindustrialize the Ruhr. Morgenthau wished to transform Germany into an agrarian society. Franklin Roosevelt temporarily adopted this radical scheme— which complemented unconditional surrender—but later withdrew his support for it.

SOURCE: Henry Morgenthau, Jr., *Germany Is Our Problem* (New York: Harper and Brothers, 1945). See. p. 1 of four-page insert preceding the Table of Contents.

DOCUMENT:

Top Secret: Program to Prevent Germany from starting a World War III

1. *Demilitarization of Germany*
   It should be the aim of the Allied Forces to accomplish the complete demilitarization of Germany in the shortest possible period of time after surrender. This means completely disarming the German Army and people (including the removal or destruction of all war material), the total destruction of the whole German armament industry, and the removal or destruction of other key industries which are basic to military strength.
2. *New Boundaries of Germany*
   (a) Poland should get that part of East Prussia which doesn't go to the U.S.S.R. and the southern portion of Silesia.
   (b) France should get the Saar and the adjacent territories bounded by the Rhine and the Moselle Rivers.
   (c) As indicated in 4 below an International Zone should be created containing the Ruhr and the surrounding industrial areas.
3. *Partitioning of New Germany*
   The remaining portion of Germany should be divided into two autonomous, independent states, (1) a South German state comprising Bavaria, Wuerttemberg, Baden and some smaller areas and (2) a North German state comprising a large part of the old state of Prussia, Saxony, Thuringia and several smaller states.
   There shall be a custom union between the new South German state and Austria, which will be restored to her pre-1938 political borders.

4. *The Ruhr Area.* (The Ruhr, surrounding industrial areas, as shown on the map, including the Rhineland, the Keil Canal, and all German territory north of the Keil Canal.) Here lies the heart of German industrial power. This area should not only be stripped of all presently existing industries but so weakened and controlled that it can not in the foreseeable future become an industrial area. The following steps will accomplish this:

   (a) Within a short period, if possible not longer than 6 months after the cessation of hostilities, all industrial plants and equipment not destroyed by military action shall be completely dismantled and transported to Allied Nations as restitution. All equipment shall be removed from the mines and the mines closed.

   (b) The area should be made an international zone to be governed by an international security organization to be established by the United Nations. In governing the area the international organization should be guided by policies designed to further the above stated objective.

1945 The Yalta Conference: A Defense of Roosevelt (Edward Stettinius, 1949)

Roosevelt, Churchill, and Stalin met for the last time as a group during February, 1945 in the Soviet Union at Yalta, a resort town on the Crimean Peninsula. The Big Three dealt with a galaxy of issues here, among them the four-way occupation of defeated Germany, three votes for the Soviet Union in the General Assembly of the United Nations, free elections in the nations of Central and Eastern Europe, shifting the boundaries of Poland, and eventual Russian participation in the Far Eastern conflict. Did the dying Roosevelt surrender too much to Stalin? The Republicans claimed so in the years ahead. One of the strongest defenders of F.D.R. was the diplomatically inexperienced Secretary of State Edward Stettinius, who had replaced Cordell Hull late in 1944 and was only to hold office for seven months before the new President, Harry Truman, replaced him with James Byrnes.

SOURCE: Edward R. Stettinius, Jr, *Roosevelt and the Russians: The Yalta Conference*, Edited by Walter Johnson (Garden City: Doubleday and Company, 1949). See pp. 303–6.

DOCUMENT:

What did the Soviet Union gain in eastern Europe which she did not already have as the result of the smashing victories of the Red Army? Great Britain and the United States secured pledges at Yalta, unfortunately not honored, which did promise free elections and democratic governments.

    What, too, with the possible exception of the Kuriles, did the Soviet Union receive at Yalta which she might not have taken without any agreement? If there had been no agreement, the Soviet Union could have swept into North China, and the United States and the Chinese would have been in no real position to prevent it. It must never be forgotten that, while the Crimea Conference was taking place, President Roosevelt had just been told by his military advisers that the surrender of Japan might not occur until 1947, and some predicted even later.

The President was told that without Russia it might cost the United States a million casualties to conquer Japan. It must be remembered, too, that at the time of the Yalta Conference it was still uncertain whether the atomic bomb could be perfected and that, since the Battle of the Bulge had set us back in Europe, it was uncertain how long it might take for Germany to crack. There had been immense optimism in the autumn of 1944, as Allied troops raced through France, that the war was nearly over. Then came the Battle of the Bulge, which was more than a military reversal. It cast a deep gloom over the confident expectation that the German war would end soon. In Washington, for instance, the procurement agencies of the armed services immediately began placing new orders on the basis of a longer war in Europe than had been estimated.

With hindsight, it can be said that the widespread pessimism was unwarranted. The significant fact is not, however, this hindsight but the effect of this thinking of the strategy and agreements made in the Crimea. It was important to bring the Soviet Union into the united sphere of action. Russian co-operation in the Japanese war ran parallel to their co-operation in the world organization and to united action in Europe. Furthermore, critics of the Far Eastern agreement have tended to overlook the fact that in the agreement the Soviet Union pledged that China was to retain "full sovereignty in Manchuria" and that the Soviet Union would conclude a pact of friendship with the Chinese Nationalist Government. It is my understanding that the American military leaders felt that the war had to be concluded as soon as possible. There was the fear that heavy casualties in Japan or the possible lack of continuous victories would have an unfortunate effect on the attitude of the American people.

President Roosevelt had great faith in his Army and Navy staffs, and he relied wholeheartedly upon them. Their insistent advice was that the Soviet Union had to be brought into the Far Eastern war soon after Germany's collapse. The President, therefore, in signing the Far Eastern agreement, acted upon the advice of his military advisers. He did not approve the agreement from any desire to appease Stalin and the Soviet Union.

It is apparently the belief of some critics of the Yalta Conference that it would have been better to have made no agreements with the Soviet Union. Yet if we had made no agreements at Yalta, the Russians still would have been in full possession of the territory in Europe that President Roosevelt is alleged to have given them. The failure to agree would have been a serious blow to the morale of the Allied world, already suffering from five years of war; it would have meant the prolongation of the German and Japanese wars; it would have prevented the establishment of the United Nations; and it would probably have led to other consequences incalculable in their tragedy for the world.

President Roosevelt did not "surrender" anything significant at Yalta which it was within his power to withhold. The agreements, on the other hand, speeded up the end of the war and greatly reduced American casualties. The Yalta Conference, also, made it possible to create the United Nations.

1945 The Yalta Conference: The Role of Alger Hiss (James Byrnes, 1958)

Like Edward Stettinius, James Byrnes had been present at Yalta. Also representing the United States there was another State Department official, Alger Hiss, who later gained widespread notoriety when Whittaker Chambers accused him of passing secrets to the Russians. (Hiss was eventually convicted in the second of two trials in November, 1949, but for perjury rather than treason.) Just how important a role did Hiss play at Yalta as one of Stettinius's three special aides? To Republican critics of Democratic foreign policy in the years ahead, it was a major one. According to Byrnes, though, if Hiss did have an influence, it was not decisive. Certainly Stettinius and Sir Anthony Eden, the British Foreign Minister, played a much larger role in shaping Allied policy at Yalta than did Hiss.

SOURCE: James F. Byrnes, *All in One Lifetime* (New York: Harper and Brothers, 1958). See pp. 259–60.

DOCUMENT:

A more controversial figure was also present. The day following our arrival, the President handed me a paper prepared by the State Department containing proposals for a European High Commission to control liberated areas, and requested me to give an opinion on it after talking to the department representative in charge of this question. Alger Hiss was then brought to my room by Hopkins. He was one of Mr. Stettinius' three special aides and had already participated in the departmental discussions at Marrakech in North Africa and at Naples on matters to be considered at the conference. This was my first meeting with him at Yalta. He told me several members of the Department had contributed to the document which the President had given me. Some of its provisions did not accord with my thinking, and when I conveyed my objections to the President there were some revisions made before he presented the proposal at a plenary session.

Mr. Hiss has been frequently pictured as exercising a dominating and detrimental influence upon the President at Yalta. My opinion is that, if he did, it was indirect. For example, the evidence indicates that before our party ever arrived in the Crimea, the State Department group had decided to recommend to the President that he try to bring about agreement on the desirability of securing the maximum degree of unity between the Chinese Communists and the Nationalist government. According to Stettinius, he stressed this point of view in talking to Mr. Eden at Malta, and Eden had agreed and said he hoped that the Soviets could be persuaded to do what they could to further it. Later this was to be described as an instance of Mr. Roosevelt's willingness to "surrender" to the Communists, but it was a British–American policy agreed upon by Eden and Stettinius before reaching Yalta.

It is plain that Hiss had easy access, for good or evil, to Stettinius and Hopkins, who were, of course, trusted advisers of the President. Hiss did not sit at the conference table, as has often been stated. He attended the third plenary meeting, at which the Dumbarton Oaks proposals for a world security organization were under discussion; then I believed him to be present because of his employment in the relevant division of the State Department. He sat in the rear of the room and was frequently consulted by Mr. Hopkins and Mr. Stettinius. The record shows that while he did not sit at the conference table, he did subsequently attend all other sessions, as well as the meetings held by the Foreign Ministers throughout the conference.

1945 Senator William Langer Opposes the United Nations

Unlike the Treaty of Versailles a quarter of a century earlier, the Charter of the United Nations easily passed the Senate on July 28, 1945 by a vote of 89 to 2. The only two nay votes were those of William Langer and Henrik Shipstead; the dying Hiram Johnson was in the hospital, but if present he would have cast a third vote against the Charter. Another longtime isolationist, Burton K. Wheeler, voted aye, but nevertheless asserted that the Charter was "a declaration of pious intentions." As for Republican Langer, he represented heavily rural and predominantly isolationist North Dakota in the Senate. In his anti-UN speech, Langer claimed that the adoption of the Charter would perpetuate war, would enslave millions of people, and would lead to an ongoing draft at home.

SOURCE: *Congressional Record*, July 28, 1945. See pp. 8188–89.

DOCUMENT:

Mr. President, during my service in the Senate in behalf of the common people, I have never sold the truth to serve the hour. I have no quarrel with the vote of any honest Senator upon this floor. Each one took the same oath that I took, namely, to defend and uphold the Constitution of the United States of America.

Practically all Members of this body have indicated that they will vote for the charter. Under my oath, Mr. President, and under my conscience, I cannot so vote. If I did I would feel that I was betraying the hundreds of thousands who have died in this war for the United States, and the hundreds of thousands who have sacrificed their loved ones and their treasure. I would be willing to vote for the appropriation of the last dollar in the United States Treasury, and the last dollar that we could borrow if, by spending that money, we could eliminate war, which we all abhor and hate. I would unhesitatingly vote for the Charter if I felt that it offered even the tiniest hope of a permanent peace. But, in spite of that, Mr. President, I feel from the bottom of my heart that the adoption of the Charter—and, make sure, we are going to implement it—will mean perpetuating war. I feel that it will mean the enslavement of millions of people from Poland to India, from Korea to Java, as well as people in many other places on this earth.

Mr. President, I feel that the adoption of the Charter will be one step more toward compulsory and military conscription, and all that which goes with war.

In my opinion, the charter is not at all similar to the Constitution of the United States which was adopted by the Original Colonies. I may say at this point that I agree with what the distinguished Senator from New Hampshire [Mr. Bridges] said earlier in the day, when he stated:

> Most important of all, the American Constitution went to great length to guarantee genuine equality to States entering into the Union. Neither Ben Franklin nor the other members of the Constitutional Convention would have tolerated a constitution by which two or three or more of the States were given a veto power over all of the rest.

Mr. President, I say to you and to the other Members of the Senate that, in my judgment, if the Charter had been in effect when the American Revolution took place, France and all other countries who came to help us would not have been able to come, and today we would still be a colony under the rule of England.

Mr. President, in my campaign for the senatorship 5 years ago I pledged to the fathers and mothers of North Dakota that I would never vote to send our boys away to be slaughtered upon the battlefields of Europe. I kept that pledge on this floor. I promised in that campaign to vote in the Senate to expend the last dollar, if necessary, in order to defend the Western Hemisphere. Again I say, Mr. President, that I kept that pledge to the people of North Dakota.

Having so pledged myself, and having been elected to my senatorship upon such pledge, and not having been elected to create an organization to which we would give a promise, either express or implied, that it would have authority to send our boys all over the earth, I cannot support the Charter. I believe it is fraught with danger to the American people, and to American institutions. I further believe that when a candidate for office pledges himself by specific promises, these promises should be honored, regardless of the political consequences which may follow to the candidate who made them.

Furthermore, Mr. President, I reiterate that we ought not to vote on this Charter in the absence of our 11,000,000 fighting men and women. They are now away, and we do not know what their attitude will be upon their return, after having been to the four corners of the earth and after having fought upon the seven seas. We sit here, Mr. President, in our fine offices and upon this senatorial floor, blissfully ignorant of what those 11,000,000 veterans may be thinking. After all, they constitute the backbone of the common people of America. Certainly there is no reason for such a hurry to pass this Charter that some steps could not have been taken to have referred the matter to the people of the country, including the men and women in the armed forces, before the final vote was taken upon it. As their representative here in the Senate, I cannot, I will not, God helping me, vote for a measure which I believe to be unlawful under our Constitution, a measure which, in my opinion, betrays the very people who sent us to the Senate as their representatives.

Postwar Approaches to Foreign Policy 40

1946 Henry Wallace's Madison Square Garden Address Criticizing Harry Truman's Foreign Policy

President Harry Truman's hardening line against the Soviet Union became increasingly evident during his first year in office. But not everyone in government and politics approved of his Cold War diplomacy. A case in point was former Vice President and present Secretary of Commerce Henry Wallace. On September 12, 1946, Wallace gave a speech, "The Way to Peace," at Madison Square Garden in New York City. In this, the most famous and controversial speech of his career, Wallace pointed out that other nations had periodically invaded Russia over the years, and that it was not the concern of the United States if the Soviet Union assumed a dominant position in Eastern Europe. By the end of the month, Truman had asked Wallace for his resignation.

SOURCE: Richard J. Walton, *Henry Wallace, Harry Truman, and the Cold War* (New York: The Viking Press, 1976). See pp. 102–4.

DOCUMENT:

To achieve lasting peace, we must study in detail just how the Russian character was formed—by invasions of Tatars, Mongols, Germans, Poles, Swedes, and French; by the czarist rule based on ignorance, fear, and force; by the intervention of the British, French, and Americans in Russian affairs from 1919 to 1921; by the geography of the huge Russian land mass situated strategically between Europe and Asia; and by the vitality derived from the rich Russian soil and the strenuous Russian climate. Add to all this the tremendous emotional power which Marxism and Leninism gives to the Russian leaders—and then we can realize that we are reckoning with a force which cannot be handled successfully by a "Get tough with Russia" policy. "Getting tough" never bought anything real and lasting— whether for schoolyard bullies or businessmen or world powers. The tougher we get, the tougher the Russians will get.

Throughout the world there are numerous reactionary elements which had hoped for an Axis victory—and now profess great friendship for the United States. Yet, these enemies of yesterday and false friends of today continually try to provoke war between the United States and Russia. They only long for the day when the United States and Russia will destroy each other.

We must not let our Russian policy be guided or influenced by those inside or outside the United States who want war with Russia. This does not mean appeasement.

We most earnestly want peace with Russia—but we want to be met halfway. We want cooperation. And I believe that we can get cooperation once Russia understands that our primary objective is neither saving the British Empire nor purchasing oil in the Near East with the lives of American soldiers. We cannot allow national oil rivalries to force us into war. All of the nations producing oil, whether inside or outside of their own boundaries, must fulfill the provisions of the United Nations Charter and encourage the development of world petroleum reserves so as to make the maximum amount of oil available to all nations of the world on an equitable, peaceful basis—and not on the basis of fighting the next war.

For her part, Russia can retain our respect by cooperating with the United Nations in a spirit of open-minded and flexible give-and-take.

The real peace treaty we now need is between the United States and Russia. On our part, we should recognize that we have no more business in the *political* affairs of Eastern Europe than Russia has in the *political* affairs of Latin America, Western Europe, and the United States. We may not like what Russia does in eastern Europe. Her type of land reform, industrial expropriation, and suppression of basic liberties offends the great majority of the United States.

But whether we like it or not the Russians will try to socialize their sphere of influence just as we try to democratize our sphere of influence.

1947 George Kennan's Anonymous *Foreign Affairs* Article on Containing Soviet Expansion

In July, 1947, State Department official George Kennan anonymously published an article in Foreign Affairs *on "The Sources of Soviet Conduct." This proved to be the most famous exposition of the containment doctrine vis-à-vis the Soviet Union. Containment was a long-term policy which emphasized that the American response to the Soviet challenge should vary in intensity depending on the circumstances. If the Soviets expelled an American diplomat, the United States in return would ask a Soviet diplomat to leave rather than launch World War III. The majority of the American people went along with containment, but only so long as it did not involve the United States in a no-win foreign war such as Korea or Vietnam. Despite the threat which the Russians posed, Kennan made it clear in his article that the Soviets were not attempting to impose Communism on the world overnight.*

SOURCE: George Kennan, "The Sources of Soviet Conduct," in *Foreign Affairs*, July 1947, pp. 374–75.

DOCUMENT:

The Kremlin is under no ideological compulsion to accomplish its purposes in a hurry. Like the Church, it is dealing in ideological concepts which are of long-term validity, and it can afford to be patient. It has no right to risk the existing achievements of the revolution for the sake of vain baubles of the future. The very teachings of Lenin himself require great caution and flexibility in the pursuit of Communist purposes. Again, these precepts are fortified by the lessons of Russian history: of centuries of obscure battles between nomadic forces over the stretches of a vast unfortified plain. Here caution, circumspection, flexibility and deception are the valuable qualities; and their value finds natural appreciation in the Russian or the oriental mind. Thus the Kremlin has no compunction about retreating in the face of superior force. And being under the compulsion of no timetable, it does not get panicky under the necessity for such retreat. Its political action is a fluid stream which moves constantly, wherever it is permitted to move, toward a given goal. Its main concern is to make sure that it has filled every nook and cranny available to it in the basin of world power. But if it finds unassailable barriers in its path, it accepts these philosophically and accommodates itself to them. The main thing is that there should always be pressure, increasing constant pressure, toward the desired goal. There is no trace of any feeling in Soviet psychology that that goal must be reached at any given time.

These considerations make Soviet diplomacy at once easier and more difficult to deal with than the diplomacy of individual aggressive leaders like Napoleon and Hitler. On the one hand it is more sensitive to contrary force, more ready to yield on individual sectors of the diplomatic front when that force is felt to be too strong, and thus more rational in the logic and rhetoric of power. On the other hand it cannot be easily defeated or discouraged by a single victory on the part of its opponents. And the patient persistence by which it is animated means that it can be effectively countered not by sporadic acts which represent the momentary whims of democratic opinion but only be intelligent long-range policies on the part of Russia's adversaries—policies no less steady in their purpose, and no less variegated and resourceful in their application, than those of the Soviet Union itself.

In these circumstances it is clear that the main element of any United States policy toward the Soviet Union must be that of a long-term, patient but firm and vigilant containment of Russian expansive tendencies.

1967 Kennan Reassesses Containment Two Decades Later

The world changed in the two decades after George Kennan first set forth his theories on containment, and Kennan's thinking similarly evolved. In 1947, the Communists had not yet taken over China, while in Eastern Europe Marshal Tito of Yugoslavia had yet to break with the Soviet Union. By 1967, Kennan had come to admit that his anonymous Foreign Affairs *article suffered from various deficiencies: a failure to put more stress on Eastern Europe, a failure to emphasize political rather than military containment, and a failure to point out that certain parts of the globe were more vital than others. Not on Kennan's list were Greece and Turkey, which President Harry Truman placed under a protective American umbrella in 1947, the same year that Kennan's article came out.*

SOURCE: George F. Kennan, *Memoirs 1925–1950* (Boston: Little, Brown and Company, 1967). See pp. 357–59.

DOCUMENT:

A serious deficiency of the article was the failure to mention the satellite area of Eastern Europe—the failure to discuss Soviet power, that is, *in terms of* its involvement in this area. Anyone reading the article would have thought—and would have had every reason to think—that I was talking only about Russia proper; that the weaknesses of the Soviet system to which I was drawing attention were ones that had their existence only within the national boundaries of the Soviet state; that the geographic extension that had been given to the power of the Soviet leaders, by virtue of the recent advances of Soviet armies into Eastern Europe and the political exploitation of those advances for Communist purposes, were irrelevant to the weaknesses of which I was speaking. Obviously, in mentioning the uncertainties of the Soviet situation—such things as the weariness and poor morale among the population, the fragility of the constitutional arrangements within the party, etc.—I would have had a far stronger case had I added the characteristic embarrassments of imperialism which the Soviet leaders had now taken upon themselves with their conquest of Eastern Europe, and the unlikelihood that Moscow would be permanently successful in holding this great area in subjection.

A second serious deficiency of the X-Article—perhaps the most serious of all—was the failure to make clear that what I was talking about when I mentioned the containment of Soviet power was not the containment by military means of a military threat, but the political containment of a political threat. Certain of the language used—such as "a long-term, patient but firm and vigilant containment of Russian expansive tendencies" or "the adroit and vigilant application of counterforce at a series of constantly shifting geographical and political points"—was at best ambiguous, and lent itself to misinterpretation in this respect.

A third great deficiency, intimately connected with the one just mentioned, was the failure to distinguish between various geographic areas, and to make clear that the "containment" of which I was speaking was not something that I thought we could, necessarily, do everywhere successfully, or even needed to do everywhere successfully, in order to serve the purpose I had in mind. Actually, as noted in connection with the Truman Doctrine above, I distinguished clearly in my own mind between areas that I thought vital to our security and ones that did not seem to me to fall into this category. My objection to the Truman Doctrine message revolved largely around its failure to draw this distinction. Repeatedly, at that time and in ensuing years, I expressed in talks and lectures the view that there were only five regions of the world—the United States, the United Kingdom, the Rhine valley with adjacent industrial areas, the Soviet Union, and Japan—where the sinews of modern military strength could be produced in quantity; I pointed out that only one of these was under Communist control; and I defined the main task of containment, accordingly, as one of seeing to it that none of the remaining ones fell under such control. Why this was not made clear in the X-Article is, again, a mystery. I suppose I thought that such considerations were subsumed under the reference to the need for confronting the Russians with unalterable counterforce *"at every point where they show signs of encroaching upon the interests of a peaceful world."*

1947 Former Isolationist Senator Arthur Vandenberg Endorses a Bipartisan Foreign Policy

Republican Senator Arthur Vandenberg of Michigan was a pre-World War II isolationist who embraced the United Nations and internationalism following World War II. He was one of the leading architects of a bipartisan foreign policy during the Truman Presidency. But as Kennan's containment policy was frequently misinterpreted in the years ahead, so was Vandenberg's bipartisanship, which did not guarantee advance Republican support for any and every diplomatic initiative of the Truman administration. As Vandenberg pointed out in a speech in the Senate on March 18, 1947, bipartisanship only applied to the United Nations and the European peace treaties, not to China or to Latin America, or even to Greece and Turkey.

SOURCE: *Congressional Record*, March 18, 1947. See p. 2167.

DOCUMENT:

I regret the necessity of making this statement at this critical moment when partisan politics should be totally removed from foreign-policy consideration. But I am unable to ignore the unfortunate implications in the letter and statement released last night by the executive director of the Democratic National Committee calling upon the chairman of the Republican National Committee to join in a party statement endorsing the so-called Truman policy in Greece and Turkey. The Democratic chairman repeatedly used my name in his letter and statement. Of course, this was without my knowledge. It is unavoidable that I should speak plainly as a result.

   Mr. President, when bipartisan foreign policy gets into the rival hands of partisan national committees it is in grave danger of losing its precious character. No matter how worthy the announced intentions, it can put foreign policy squarely into politics which, under such circumstances, are no longer calculated to stop at the water's edge. However unwittingly, this is precisely what Mr. Sullivan invites. I hope Mr. Reece will not accept the invitation. He has faithfully kept his party out of foreign-policy politics. I am sure he will continue to do so.

Bipartisan foreign policy is not the result of political coercion but of nonpolitical conviction. I never have even pretended to speak for my party in my foreign-policy activities. I have relied upon the validity of my actions to command whatever support they may deserve. I have never made any semblance of a partisan demand for support and I never shall. What I decline to do myself I cannot permit the executive director of the Democratic National Committee to attempt in my name.

It also is necessary, now, to get the record straight. This bipartisan foreign policy has been confined within relatively narrow limits. It has applied to the United Nations. It has applied to peace treaties in Europe. It has applied to nothing else. I have had nothing to do, for example, with China policies or pan-American policies except within the United Nations, and at times I have been satisfied with neither. The first I ever heard of the Greco–Turkish policy was when the President disclosed his thoughts 10 days ago at the White House. I do not complain. But I do not propose to be misunderstood.

I have said that we have no safe alternative but to uphold the President's hands at this dangerous hour. But I have also said that total information must be made available to Congress and the country, and that Congress must completely explore and approve the means by which the President's policy is to be implemented.

I expect every Republican, like every Democrat, to respond to his own conscience. I expect all of them to act not as partisans but as Americans. I expect none of them to yield their judgments, at such an hour, to the political dictates of any party managers. On the latter basis, bipartisan foreign policy would die in revolt. I hope we may avoid that tragedy. The quicker last night's appeal, no matter how nobly meditated, is forgotten the better it will be for the United States.

1951 Senator Robert A. Taft and Neo-isolationism: *A Foreign Policy for Americans*

Vandenberg's fellow pre-World War II isolationist, Senator Robert Taft of Ohio, embraced internationalism much more cautiously than the Michigander. In 1951, just prior to launching his unsuccessful bid for the Republican Presidential nomination the next year, Taft published a short book expressing his neo-isolationist views: A Foreign Policy for Americans. *Lamenting Soviet advances under the Truman administration, Taft also blasted the United Nations, which had failed to maintain the peace. In his opinion, peace was preservable only through an international tribunal which enforced the rule of law and justice among nations with the consent of the participating countries.*

SOURCE: Robert A. Taft, *A Foreign Policy for Americans* (Garden City: Doubleday and Company, 1951). See pp. 6, 8, 11–13.

DOCUMENT:

Power without foresight leads to disaster. Our international relations have been conducted with so little foresight since 1941 that six years after vast military victories in Europe and Asia we face a more dangerous threat than any that has menaced us before. Our soldiers, sailors, marines, and airmen have not failed us. Our political leaders have. By 1941 anyone who was not bamboozled by Soviet psychological warfare knew that the Soviet Government was a predatory totalitarian tyranny intent on establishing Communist dictatorship throughout the world. But our leaders failed to foresee that the Soviet Union would turn against us after the defeat of Germany and Japan. They made no attempt to insure our future against that eventuality. They brought forth no positive policy for the creation of a free and united Europe or for the preservation of the independence of China. They preferred wishful thinking to facts, and convinced themselves that Stalin would cooperate with them to create a free world of permanent peace. So at Teheran, Yalta, and Potsdam they handed Stalin the freedom of eastern Europe and Manchuria, and prepared our present peril.

In 1941 Stalin ruled 180 million subjects and was not sure that he or his empire would survive. In 1951 Stalin directs 800 million people. Unless our foreign policy is conducted more competently than it has been during the past ten years, our very survival is in doubt. There may be infinite arguments as to the wisdom of many steps in our foreign policy since 1943. But there can be little argument as to its results.

Fundamentally, I believe the ultimate purpose of our foreign policy must be to protect the liberty of the people of the United States. The American Revolution was fought to establish a nation "conceived in liberty." That liberty has been defended in many wars since that day. That liberty has enabled our people to increase steadily their material welfare and their spiritual freedom. To achieve that liberty we have gone to war, and to protect it we would go to war again.

Only second to liberty is the maintenance of peace. The results of war may be almost as bad as the destruction of liberty and, in fact, may lead, even if the war is won, to something very close to the destruction of liberty at home. War not only produces pitiful human suffering and utter destruction of many things worthwhile, but it is almost as disastrous for the victor as for the vanquished. From our experience in the last two world wars, it actually promotes dictatorship and totalitarian government throughout the world. Much of the glamour has gone from it, and war today is murder by machine. World War II killed millions of innocent civilians as well as those in uniform and in many countries wiped out the product of hundreds of years of civilization.

We have now taken the lead in establishing the United Nations. The purpose is to establish a rule of law throughout the world and protect the people of the United States by punishing aggression the moment it starts and deterring future aggression through joint action of the members of such an organization.

I think we must recognize that this involves the theory of a preventive war, a dangerous undertaking at any time. If, therefore, we are going to join in such an organization it is essential that it be effective. It must be a joint enterprise. Our Korean adventure shows the tremendous danger, if the new organization is badly organized or improperly supported by its members and by the public opinion of the people of the world.

The United Nations has failed to protect our peace, I believe, because it was organized on an unsound basis with a veto power in five nations and is based, in fact, on the joint power of such nations, effectively only so long as they agree. I believe the concept can only be successful if based on a rule of law and justice between nations and willingness on the part of all nations to abide by the decisions of an impartial tribunal.

The fact that the present organization has largely failed in its purpose has forced us to use other means to meet the present emergency, but there is no reason to abandon the concept of collective security which, by discouraging and preventing the use of war as national policy, can ultimately protect the liberty of the people of the United States and enforce peace.

1951 Senator Joseph McCarthy and Betrayal: *America's Retreat from Victory*

Perhaps no modern American political figure has been as notorious and controversial as Republican Senator Joseph McCarthy of Wisconsin, whose wideranging attacks on alleged Communists inside and outside the U.S. government led to the coining of a new term: McCarthyism. Early in 1950, McCarthy charged in a speech at Wheeling, West Virginia that there were 57 or 81 or 205 Communists in the State Department. Then in 1951, he brought out a book entitled America's Retreat from Victory, *which openly blamed the loss of mainland China to the Communists on General George C. Marshall, Secretary of State Dean Acheson, and other high-ranking Truman administration officials. For several years, McCarthy was a powerful figure in American politics, but his support had begun to crumble by the time of the McCarthy–Army hearings, held in the spring and summer of 1954. Censured by the U.S. Senate in November of that year, McCarthy died three years later, broken in spirit and body. But he is still remembered today as one of the great Red-baiters in American history, and the flaming rhetoric of his 1951 attack on Marshall is vintage McCarthy.*

SOURCE: Joseph R. McCarthy, *America's Retreat from Victory: The Story of George Catlett Marshall* (New York: Devin–Adair Company, 1951). See pp. 170–72.

DOCUMENT:

It was Marshall who sent Deane to Moscow to collaborate with Harriman in drafting the terms of the wholly unnecessary bribe paid to Stalin at Yalta. It was Marshall who ignored the contrary advice of his senior, Admiral Leahy, of MacArthur and Nimitz; manipulated intelligence reports, brushed aside the potentials of the A-bomb, and finally induced Roosevelt to reinstate Russia in its pre-1904, imperialistic position in Manchuria; an act which, in effect, signed the death warrant of the Republic of China.

It was Marshall, with Acheson and Vincent assisting, who created the China policy which, destroying China, robbed us of a great and friendly ally, a buffer against the Soviet imperialism with which we are at war.

It was Marshall who went to China to execute the criminal folly of the disastrous Marshall mission.

It was Marshall who, upon returning from a diplomatic defeat for the United States at Moscow, besought the reinstatement of forty millions in lend-lease for Russia.

It was Marshall who for two years suppressed General Wedemeyer's report, which is a direct and comprehensive repudiation of the Marshall policy.

It was Marshall who, disregarding Wedemeyer's advices on the urgent need for military supplies, the likelihood of China's defeat without ammunition and equipment, and our "moral obligation" to furnish them, proposed instead a relief bill bare of military support.

It was the State Department under Marshall, with the wholehearted support of Michael Lee and Remington in the Commerce Department, that sabotaged the $125,000,000 military-aid bill to China in 1948.

It was Marshall who fixed the dividing line for Korea along the thirty-eighth parallel, a line historically chosen by Russia to mark its sphere of interest in Korea.

It was Marshall's strategy for Korea which turned that war into a pointless slaughter, reversing the dictum of Von Clausewitz and every military theorist after him that the object of a war is not merely to kill but to impose your will on the enemy.

It was Marshall–Acheson strategy for Europe to build the defense of Europe around the Atlantic Pact nations, excluding the two great wells of anti-Communist manpower in Western Germany and Spain and spurning the organized armies of Greece and Turkey—another case of following the Lattimore advice of "let them fall but don't let it appear that we pushed them."

It was Marshall who, advocating timidity as a policy so as not to annoy the forces of Soviet imperialism in Asia, admittedly put a brake on the preparations to fight, rationalizing his reluctance on the ground that the people are fickle and, if war does not come, will hold him to account for excessive zeal.

If Marshall were merely stupid, the laws of probability would have dictated that at least some of his decisions would have served this country's interest. Even if Marshall had been innocent of guilty intention, how could he have been trusted to guide the defense of this country further? We have declined so precipitously in relation to the Soviet Union in the last six years, how much swifter may be our fall into disaster with Marshall's policies continuing to guide us? Where will all this stop? This is not a rhetorical question; ours is not a rhetorical danger. Where next will Marshall's policies, continued by Acheson, carry us?

What is the objective of the conspiracy? I think it is clear from what has occurred and is now occurring: to diminish the United States in world affairs, to weaken us militarily, to confuse our spirit with talk of surrender in the Far East and to impair our will to resist evil. To what end? To the end that we shall be contained and frustrated and finally fall victim to Soviet intrigue from within and Russian military might from without. Is that farfetched? There have been many examples in history of rich and powerful states which have been corrupted from within, enfeebled and deceived until they were unable to resist aggression.

1947 The Truman Doctrine: Military Protection for Greece and Turkey

At the close of World War II, the British voters replaced Prime Minister Winston Churchill and his conservative government with a Labor regime less wedded to imperialism. In the years which followed, the new Prime Minister, Clement Attlee, presided over the disman-tling of the British Empire and the withdrawal of the British presence from the Eastern Med-iterranean. The latter gesture left longtime rivals Greece and Turkey vulnerable to a possible Soviet takeover. President Harry Truman attempted to fill the power vacuum in the Eastern Mediterranean by calling for the U.S. to support both countries, in a message to Congress on March 12, 1947. This quickly became known as the Truman Doctrine. To implement his policy, Truman asked Congress for $400 million in economic and military aid, which Congress approved, following two months of debate, by a 67 to 23 vote in the Senate and a 287 to 107 vote in the House.

SOURCE: U.S. Department of State, *Bulletin*, March 23, 1947. See pp. 534–35.

DOCUMENT:

Mr. President, Mr. Speaker, Members of the Congress of the United States:

The gravity of the situation which confronts the world today necessitates my appearance before a joint session of the Congress.

The foreign policy and the national security of this country are involved.

One aspect of the present situation, which I wish to present to you at this time for your consideration and decision, concerns Greece and Turkey.

The United States has received from the Greek Government an urgent appeal for financial and economic assistance. Preliminary reports from the American Economic Mission now in Greece and reports from the American Ambassador in Greece corroborate the statement of the Greek Government that assistance is imperative if Greece is to survive as a free nation.

I do not believe that the American people and the Congress wish to turn a deaf ear to the appeal of the Greek Government.

Greece is not a rich country. Lack of sufficient natural resources has always forced the Greek people to work hard to make both ends meet. Since 1940 this industrious and peace-loving country has suffered invasion, four years of cruel enemy occupation, and bitter internal strife.

When forces of liberation entered Greece they found that the retreating Germans had destroyed virtually all the railways, roads, port facilities, communications, and merchant marine. More than a thousand villages had been burned. Eighty-five percent of the children were tubercular. Livestock, poultry, and draft animals had almost disappeared. Inflation had wiped out practically all savings.

The very existence of the Greek state is today threatened by the terrorist activities of several thousand armed men, led by Communists, who defy the Government's authority at a number of points, particularly along the northern boundaries. A commission appointed by the United Nations Security Council is at present investigating disturbed conditions in northern Greece and alleged border violations along the frontier between Greece on the one hand and Albania, Bulgaria, and Yugoslavia on the other.

Meanwhile, the Greek Government is unable to cope with the situation. The Greek Army is small and poorly equipped. It needs supplies and equipment if it is to restore authority to the Government throughout Greek territory.

Greece must have assistance if it is to become a self-supporting and self-respecting democracy.

The United States must supply that assistance. We have already extended to Greece certain types of relief and economic aid, but these are inadequate.

There is no other country to which democratic Greece can turn.

No other nation is willing and able to provide the necessary support for a democratic Greek Government.

The British Government, which has been helping Greece, can give no further financial or economic aid after March 31. Great Britain finds itself under the necessity of reducing or liquidating its commitments in several parts of the world, including Greece.

We have considered how the United Nations might assist in this crisis. But the situation is an urgent one requiring immediate action, and the United Nations and its related organizations are not in a position to extend help of the kind that is required.

Greece's neighbor, Turkey, also deserves our attention.

The future of Turkey as an independent and economically sound state is clearly no less important to the freedom-loving peoples of the world than the future of Greece. The circumstances in which Turkey finds itself today are considerably different from those of Greece. Turkey has been spared the disasters that have beset Greece. And during the war the United States and Great Britain furnished Turkey with material aid.

Nevertheless, Turkey now needs our support.

Since the war Turkey has sought additional financial assistance from Great Britain and the United States for the purpose of effecting that modernization necessary for the maintenance of its national integrity.

That integrity is essential to the preservation of order in the Middle East.

The British Government has informed us that, owing to its own difficulties, it can no longer extend financial or economic aid to Turkey.

As in the case of Greece, if Turkey is to have the assistance it needs, the United States must supply it. We are the only country able to provide that help.

1947 The Chicago *Tribune* and the Truman Doctrine

Not every member of Congress was enchanted with the Truman Doctrine. Republicans cast sixteen of the twenty-three votes against this measure, an indication that bipartisanship had its limits. They were joined in opposition by that group of liberal soft-liners whose leading spokesman was Henry Wallace, and by the hard-core isolationists whose major journalistic voice was the Chicago Tribune. *In one of its lead editorials, the* Tribune *went so far as to claim that the Truman Doctrine might lead to an eventual war between the United States and the Soviet Union. It also drew a parallel between the 1947 message and F.D.R.'s Quarantine Speech a decade earlier.*

SOURCE: "Here We Go Again," in Chicago *Tribune*, March 13, 1947. See p. 18.

DOCUMENT:

Mr. Truman made as cold a war speech yesterday against Russia as any President has ever made except on the occasion of going before congress to ask for a declaration of war. He gave notice that Russian communism is regarded as an enemy force which will be resisted wherever it is encountered, and that, if he has his way, the United States will go out of its way to seek the encounters.

If Mr. Truman's program of supporting the Greek and Turkish regimes is accepted by congress, America will be unable to refrain from adopting the same measure wherever soviet pressures are exerted. A vast expenditure of American money is in prospect. Wherever the money goes, there, too, will go American military missions, such as are proposed to whip the Greek and Turkish armies into fighting organizations.

The outcome will inevitably be war. It probably will not come this year or next year, but the issue is already drawn. The declaration of implacable hostility between this country and Russia is one which cannot be tempered or withdrawn. It has been read into the permanent record, to stand for all time. Two worlds and two systems are in opposition. In the nature of things, as Mr. Truman has shaped that nature, they must in the end come to grips.

The United States stands now where it stood after Franklin D. Roosevelt's speech dedicating the Outer Drive bridge in Chicago on October 8, 1937. If there is a difference, it is that we are now further advanced toward World War III by Mr. Truman than Mr. Roosevelt in 1937 carried us toward World War II. Mr. Roosevelt talked in generalities about the necessity of quarantining aggressors in general. Mr. Truman talked specifically about quarantining a specific aggressor. When Mr. Truman talked about totalitarianism there was no mistaking what nation he meant.

Mr. Truman did not even indulge the same rhetorical devotion to peace that Mr. Roosevelt affected. Yet in content and spirit the two speeches were strikingly parallel as a promise of war. Mr. Roosevelt talked of nations which invade and violate "the territory of other nations that have done them no real harm and are too weak to protect themselves adequately." Mr. Truman spoke of Greece and Turkey as being too poor and weak to resist soviet infiltration. He also spoke of Poland, Romania, and Bulgaria as having had "totalitarian regimes forced upon them against their will." Mr. Truman, like Mr. Roosevelt, proposes to make these matters America's business, and the end result is as certain in the one situation as it was in the other. We are to have the "commander in chief" back with us again.

Mr. Truman's statement constituted a complete confession of the bankruptcy of American policy as formulated by Mr. Roosevelt and pursued by himself. We have just emerged from a great war which was dedicated to the extinction of the three nations which were as vocally opposed to Russia as Mr. Truman proclaims himself to be now. If communism was the real danger all along, why did Mr. Roosevelt and Mr. Truman adopt Russia as an ally, and why, at Tehran, Yalta, and Potsdam, did they build up Russia's power by making her one concession after another?

The Truman speech also leaves the United Nations as a meaningless relic of mistaken intentions. The world league to insure a lasting peace is a fraud and a sham, so impotent that Mr. Truman proposes that the United States ignore it and seek peace by force and threat of force—the very means which U.N. was intended to exclude in international dealings.

1947 Under Secretary of State Will Clayton Analyzes the Marshall Plan

Following World War II, Western Europe made a slow economic recovery from the devastation inflicted by that conflict. There was a real possibility that the Communists might take over in such countries as France and Italy. To prevent this from happening Secretary of State George Marshall announced an economic recovery program for that area in a speech at Harvard University on June 5, 1947. This was to become known unofficially as the Marshall Plan, officially as the European Recovery Program (ERP). The Soviet Union and the East European bloc were invited to a general conference at Paris which lasted from July to September, but they refused to attend and instead directed their energies to sabotaging the Marshall Plan by means of the new Communist Information Bureau. Back in the United States, President Harry Truman signed the ERP bill on April 3, 1948, after it had passed the House by a vote of 329 to 74 and the Senate by a vote of 69 to 19. (There was some Republican opposition, although Senator Robert Taft voted for it.) Rather than quote from Marshall's Harvard address, we instead cite material from a speech that Under Secretary of State Will Clayton delivered in New York City on December 18, 1947, since this offers a more detailed analysis of the economic factors involved.

SOURCE: Frederick J. Dobney, Editor, *Selected Papers of Will Clayton* (Baltimore: Johns Hopkins Press, 1971). See pp. 225–27.

DOCUMENT:

The Marshall Plan is not a relief program; it is a recovery program for Western Europe. Hence our interests rather than our humanitarian instincts should be mainly considered, although the problem is certainly not lacking in humanitarian aspects.

The purpose of the Marshall Plan is to help these people help themselves to restore and strengthen their economy to the point where Western Europe can stand on its own feet by 1952 without special outside assistance.

All of you know why we are dealing with Western Europe instead of Europe as a whole.

That decision was made in Europe and not in the United States.

It has been reinforced by recent events in London.

Now, will the Marshall Plan work?

Europe is a very sick Continent. Facts and figures to prove this, or the why of it are unnecessary. All informed and intelligent persons know that it is so and why.

Production is still lagging; in some countries confidence in money has been destroyed; the area to a great extent is still separated into small, tight economic compartments just as if the world had stood still these past hundred years.

And still restoration of production in Europe has made remarkable progress, everything considered.

Coal and food are the principal laggards.

In recent weeks there has been a significant increase in coal output in England and the Ruhr, which proves that it can be done.

The Paris Conference for European Recovery organized itself into a Committee of European Economic Cooperation.

The report of this Committee presents an economic recovery program for Western Europe based on these major points:

A strong production effort by each of the participating countries, with stated goals for food, coal, steel and other essentials.

Creation of internal financial stability.

Lowering of trade barriers between the participating countries and with the rest of the world.

Development in partnership of common resources.

The participating countries are dependent on heavy imports of food and raw materials. Normally these were paid for by exports, mostly manufactured goods, by services or by income from investments abroad. The war dealt this system a heavy blow, and despite postwar progress this complicated economic machine still limps along. Without adequate outside help it will soon break down.

In Secretary Marshall's Harvard speech, he said: "The truth of the matter is that Europe's requirements for the next three or four years of foreign food and other essential products—principally from America—are so much greater than her present ability to pay that she must have substantial additional help, or face economic, social and political deterioration of a very grave character."

To put it very simply, the Marshall Plan proposes to make it possible for Western Europe to continue to eat and work until she can get her economic machine going again.

We are not planning to send only food and coal. There will be no recovery in Europe if there are no raw materials for the factories, even though the people do not starve or freeze. People out of work, walking the streets, with factories closed, cannot reconstruct their shattered economies.

We must not only render adequate material assistance, but we must hold out a helping hand in other ways; we must give spiritual and moral help and encouragement; we must make technical and administrative assistance available; we must understand Europe's problems and help solve them. Europe does not want our sympathy, but she does crave understanding and a helping hand.

1948–49 Ambassador to the Soviet Union Walter Bedell Smith Discusses the Berlin Blockade

Soviet harassment of the free world nations reached one of its major post-World War II climaxes on June 24, 1948, when the Russians blocked access by land into Berlin. The Soviets were upset at the cooperation among the American, British, and French zones of West Germany, as well as by Allied currency reform. They hoped that their bold action would force the Americans, British, and French to abandon their sectors of Berlin, but this did not happen. Instead, President Harry Truman implemented the Berlin airlift between that date and May 12, 1949, which brought 4,500 tons of supplies daily to 2,500,000 people. The Allies also counterblockaded shipments from West Germany to East Germany. Walter B. Smith, who was the American Ambassador to the Soviet Union from 1946 to 1949, wrote his account of the events surrounding the Berlin blockade in his diplomatic memoirs.

SOURCE: Walter Bedell Smith, *My Three Years in Moscow 1946–1949* (Philadelphia: J.B. Lippincott Company, 1950). See pp. 230–31, 253, and 257.

DOCUMENT:

Allied relations deteriorated during the first half of 1948 over the festering problem of Germany, which had not yielded to solution at the Moscow and London meetings of the Council of Foreign Ministers.

The Soviet Government persistently refused to carry out the Potsdam commitment signed by Premier Stalin, Prime Minister Attlee and President Truman for economic unification of Germany. It demanded as the price of keeping its promise rich additional concessions, including fulfillment from current production of its demand for overall reparations totaling ten billion dollars.

The governments of the United States, Great Britain and France, which had not always seen eye to eye on German policy, drew closer together in the face of Soviet recalcitrance based on an obvious "rule or ruin" program. Agreement had already been reached to fuse the Anglo–American occupation zones economically, and, in the spring, the French agreed to add their zone.

To the men in the Kremlin, on whose horizon Germany historically had always loomed large, either as the greatest potential threat or most valuable potential associate of the Soviet Union, this was a direct challenge—and they set out by every diplomatic maneuver to defeat the Western program for Trizonia to reduce the political popularity of Western methods and policies among the German people.

On June 24, 1948, despairing of achieving success by diplomatic methods, the Soviet Government attempted a solution by force—the imposition of a complete blockade on all land and water traffic from the Western zones into Berlin, a tiny international enclave completely surrounded by the Soviet zone. This was only the last (and most serious) of a series of restrictions and impediments successively applied from April, 1948, onwards. The Kremlin was willing to gamble on the hunger and privation of 2,250,000 Berliners to halt the Western program of economic and monetary reform, and perhaps force the Western powers out of Berlin itself.

Three hundred and twenty-one days later—on May 12, 1949—without achieving a single stated Soviet objective, the Russians ended the blockade and normal traffic flowed again to a city whose Western areas had been supplied entirely by air for nearly eleven months. Operation Vittles had seen the Americans and British mobilize their air forces for an airlift without parallel in world history—a combined operation that up to the day the blockade ended had moved a total of 1,592,787 tons of food, coal and other supplies to prevent starvation, disease and economic stagnation in Western Berlin.

Neither Stalin nor Molotov believed that the airlift could supply Berlin. They must have felt sure that cold and hunger, and the depressingly short, gloomy days of the Berlin winter, would destroy the morale of the Berlin population and create such a completely unmanageable situation that the Western Allies would have to capitulate and evacuate the city.

From the Soviet view, there was nothing to gain from an agreement that did not postpone the German constitutional convention. It is characteristic of Kremlin tactics that this—the main issue—was never approached directly or made an outright condition for the lifting of the blockade. Instead, the question of currency, actually unimportant as subsequent events have proved, was treated as the main issue. We all realized this in Moscow, and during our discussions with

Stalin and Molotov, I felt quite sure that we could have produced an agreement in fifteen minutes at any time by an offer to abandon the London decisions. This, of course, was impossible from our side.

But the Kremlin made the same mistake the Germans made in the past—they underestimated their opponents. I don't wonder at this, because I had my own doubts. Certainly I had far greater knowledge of our capabilities for action than did Mr. Molotov and his associates.

When, in December, 1948, at their city elections, the people of Berlin re-pudiated the Communist Party, the Kremlin certainly knew that their offensive in Berlin had failed. Our "counterblockade," preventing shipments from Western Germany to Eastern Germany, was hurting the economy of the Soviet zone and, indirectly, that of the Soviet Union, more than the direct blockade of Berlin was hurting its people or us.

It remained for the Kremlin only to pick the best tactical moment to re-open the discussions, and those results are too recent to require repetition.

The blockade was lifted; but we did not give up our plans for a Western German government or abandon the currency reform. The attempt to "starve out" Berlin gained the Russians nothing. Indeed, they lost a great deal.

1949 The Point IV Program: Technical Assistance to the Underdeveloped Nations

One of the most important Presidential inaugural addresses was that which President Harry Truman delivered on January 20, 1949. Point Four of this was the famous proposal to offer technical assistance to the underdeveloped nations of the world. Significantly, a number of Southern Senators opposed to helping such agriculturally competitive nations as Egypt and India voted against the scheme, which only passed the Senate by a vote of 37 to 36 on May 5, 1950. Republicans opposed the measure by a three-to-one margin. This long-term program hopefully would provide new markets overseas for American goods, and stimulate Third World prosperity to the detriment of Communism. The money which was appropriated under Point Four went for the eradication of disease, irrigation projects, hydroelectric installations, improved agriculture, and vocational education.

SOURCE: U.S. Department of State *Bulletin,* January 30, 1949. See p. 125.

DOCUMENT:

Fourth, we must embark on a bold new program for making the benefits of our scientific advances and industrial progress available for the improvement and growth of underdeveloped areas.

More than half the people of the world are living in conditions approaching misery. Their food is inadequate. They are victims of disease. Their economic life is primitive and stagnant. Their poverty is a handicap and a threat both to them and to more prosperous areas.

For the first time in history, humanity possesses the knowledge and the skill to relieve the suffering of these people.

The United States is pre-eminent among nations in the development of industrial and scientific techniques. The material resources which we can afford to use for the assistance of other peoples are limited. But our imponderable resources in technical knowledge are constantly growing and are inexhaustible.

I believe that we should make available to peace-loving peoples the benefits of our store of technical knowledge in order to help them realize their aspirations for a better life. And, in cooperation with other nations, we should foster capital investment in areas needing development.

Our aim should be to help the free peoples of the world, through their own efforts, to produce more food, more clothing, more materials for housing, and more mechanical power to lighten their burdens.

We invite other countries to pool their technological resources in this undertaking. Their contributions will be warmly welcomed. This should be a cooperative enterprise in which all nations work together through the United Nations and its specialized agencies wherever practicable. It must be a world-wide effort for the achievement of peace, plenty, and freedom.

With the cooperation of business, private capital, agriculture, and labor in this country, this program can greatly increase the industrial activity in other nations and can raise substantially their standards of living.

Such new economic developments must be devised and controlled to benefit the peoples of the areas in which they are established. Guarantees to the investor must be balanced by guarantees in the interest of the people whose resources and whose labor go into these developments.

The old imperialism—exploitation for foreign profit—has no place in our plans. What we envisage is a program of development based on the concepts of democratic fair-dealing.

All countries, including our own, will greatly benefit from a constructive program for the better use of the world's human and natural resources. Experience shows that our commerce with other countries expands as they progress industrially and economically.

Greater production is the key to prosperity and peace. And the key to greater production is a wider and more vigorous application of modern scientific and technical knowledge.

Only by helping the least fortunate of its members to help themselves can the human family achieve the decent, satisfying life that is the right of all people.

Democracy alone can supply the vitalizing force to stir the peoples of the world into triumphant action, not only against their human oppressors, but also against their ancient enemies—hunger, misery, and despair.

1949 Senator Robert A. Taft Opposes American Entry into NATO

The growing Soviet threat to Western Europe led the nations there to join with the United States in the twelve-member North Atlantic Pact. The dozen signatories were America, Canada, Great Britain, France, Italy, Belgium, the Netherlands, Luxembourg, Norway, Denmark, Iceland, and Portugal. Should one of the members be attacked, the others pledged to take "such action as it deems necessary," including the use of armed forces. Clearly, this was as much of a departure from traditional American foreign policy as was the U.S. entry into the United Nations. Nevertheless, the North Atlantic Pact passed the Senate by an overwhelming 82 to 13 vote in July, 1949, with the partisan Republican opposition focusing in the North Central States. Sharply critical was neo-isolationist Senator Robert Taft of Ohio, who regarded the pact as implementing a war program. Eleven of the nay votes came from Republicans.

SOURCE: *Congressional Record,* July 21, 1949. See pp. 9886–88.

DOCUMENT:

Mr. Taft. Mr. President, I have already stated at length and in detail the reasons why I intend to vote against the North Atlantic Pact. In substance, those reasons consist of the fact that, in my opinion, the North Atlantic Pact is part of a larger project including the arms program. The State Department in some places says it is incidental to the arms program. I think we close our eyes to realities unless we realize that this is one thing, and that in going into this pact we are committing ourselves to an arms program. Therefore I shall vote against the North Atlantic Pact, unless it is made clear that these two things are separate.

The declaration proposed by the Senator from Nebraska [Mr. Wherry] says:

> The United States of America ratifies this treaty with the understanding that article 3 commits none of the parties thereto, morally or legally, to furnish or supply arms, armaments, military, naval or air equipment or any other party or parties to this treaty.

If the reservation is adopted, I shall vote for the treaty. But with the reservation, this whole program in my opinion is not a peace program; it is a war program. Mr. President, I do not wish to make so didactic a statement as that, so I shall say that with the arms factor the whole tendency of this program is toward a third world war, instead of away from a third world war; because we are in the first place committing ourselves to a vast program of foreign aid.

In the second place, we are committing ourselves to a policy of war, not a policy of peace. We are building up armaments. We are undertaking to arm half the world against the other half. We are inevitably starting an armament race. The more the pact signatories arm, the more the Russians are going to arm. It is said they are armed too much already. Perhaps that is true. But that makes no difference. The more we arm, the more they will arm, the more they will devote their whole attention to the building up of arms. The general history of armament races in the world is that they have led to war, not to peace.

In the third place, we are going back to the old balance-of-power theory. Every American has denounced that theory. Every man who has thoroughly thought out the question of international organization has said the only ultimate hope of peace depends upon the establishment of law and justice among nations, with international action by joint force against an aggressor. We abandon that theory under the treaty and arms program; and we go back to the old balance-of-power theory, which England followed for years. We are following exactly the theory she practiced—"Keep Europe divided more or less equally so that neither can afford to attack safely and, ultimately, England has the balance of power." That is the effect of this program to turn back to the balance of power, which never prevented war, except for brief periods of time. It always led to a series of wars in Europe, and it will lead to a series of wars in the world, if that is all we develop.

So, Mr. President, I believe that if we simply want to take a purely defensive action, if we want to warn Russia, we ought to adopt this reservation and then ratify the treaty. But I feel as strongly as I can that if we go ahead with the arms program, in which I think the treaty now involves us, we are adopting a policy far more likely to lead to a third war, and the real tragedy of a third world war, than to peace.

Other Episodes in Truman Diplomacy 42

1946 U.S. Oil Policy in the Postwar Era

Ever since the years between the two world wars, the United States government has encouraged the activities of American petroleum firms in such nations as the Netherlands East Indies and Mesopotamia (now Iraq), and has protested the expropriation of their oil properties in such countries as Bolivia and Mexico. During World War II, the United States government sought to reach an understanding on a global oil policy with its British counterpart. Following World War II, however, as colonialism gave way to independence, the American petroleum firms had to operate under a new set of conditions. In 1946, just as this transition was beginning, John Loftus, Chief of the Petroleum Division of the Department of State, assessed the role of oil in United States foreign policy up to that time. Significantly, the key principles of American foreign policy resembled those of U.S. foreign commercial policy, rather than being different in character.

SOURCE: U.S. Department of State *Bulletin*, October 1, 1946. See pp. 755–56.

DOCUMENT:

About 1910 an overwhelmingly important development took place. It simultaneously occurred to many military strategists and planners that techniques of warfare would need to be modified to reflect the superiority of oil as fuel. The British Admiralty shifted from coal to oil. Plans were laid for the employment of gasoline-fired land and air vehicles. At the outbreak of World War I in 1914 a major shift had taken place in mechanical methods of waging war. As the war progressed it became more and more evident that oil was a determining factor; and the outcome of the war led to such statements by Allied statesmen as that "The Allies floated to victory upon a sea of oil," and "A drop of oil was worth a drop of blood."

Thus petroleum was precipitated onto the center of the stage of world politics. During the period between World War I and World War II a continuing struggle went on among nations for control of strategically located oil resources. As World War II approached it became evident that planning of both offensive and defensive warfare would take cognizance of the location of oil resources, of the possibilities for quick seizure or neutralization of oil producing potentialities, and of what reliance could be placed upon synthetics and substitutes. As World War II moved on to its conclusion oil played a role of supreme importance. It could only provoke controversy to assert that petroleum supplies were the main determining factor of the eventual outcome. It is beyond controversy, however, that a critical element in the defeat of Germany and Japan was the throttling of the precarious access to oil supplies which those nations enjoyed.

Until about 1920 the petroleum industry did not enter significantly into the foreign relations of the United States. Abundant supplies of oil were available domestically and indeed a substantial export business was developed. The Government from time to time intervened in protection of the right of American oil companies to do this export business in foreign countries on nondiscriminatory terms. Beyond this, however, the oil industry went its own way and had little to do with the Government and the Government had little to do with it.

After 1920, for a short while the apparent imminence of a decline in domestic reserves engendered keen interest on the part of American oil men and the American public in the acquisition of foreign oil reserves by American companies. To further this end, American oil operators sought concessions in various parts of the world, principally in Latin America, the Middle East, and the Dutch East Indies. Whenever in this process they encountered obstacles arising out of the apparent intention of other governments to award rights and privileges to develop oil on a basis that would discriminate against American capital, the Government, through the Department of State, intervened vigorously and effectively to insist on recognition and application of the "open door" principle of equal commercial opportunity. The two most conspicuous and well-known instances of this kind arose in the case of Mesopotamia (now Iraq) and the Dutch East Indies. There were others.

In instances such as arose in Mexico and Bolivia, when foreign governments decided to nationalize their oil resources and the development thereof, our Government when called in at a late stage insisted upon the principles of just and adequate compensation and facilitated negotiations looking toward that end in so far as it could be attained under the then existing political circumstances.

In summary we find that the activities of the United States Government with respect to foreign oil operations prior to World War II fall under one or another of these four heads:

1. Insistence upon nondiscriminatory commercial treatment of American oil marketers operating in foreign countries.
2. Insistence upon the "open door" principle of equal commercial opportunity (most-favored-nation treatment) with respect to the granting of rights to explore for and develop oil reserves.
3. Insistence on the principle of just and adequate compensation in circumstances where a foreign government exercises its sovereign right to nationalize the oil industry.

4. Diplomatic assistance to and support of American oil companies in their various dealings with foreign governments, when requested, such assistance and support being more or less routine, depending upon the circumstances.

All four of these points, however, are basic concepts in the foreign commercial policy of the United States. There is nothing in them peculiar to oil. With respect to any industry or any American commercial operation abroad we insist upon nondiscriminatory most-favored-nation treatment (the "open door") and just and adequate compensation, and the Government, upon request, renders to American commercial interests without discrimination or favoritism whatever measure of diplomatic assistance or support is necessary or appropriate under the particular circumstances.

In this sense then, we have not had until now a foreign oil policy in any way significantly different from, larger than, or more concrete than our foreign commercial policy generally. If there was at certain times greater emphasis upon the application of these principles to oil than upon their application to other commodities, it was attributable primarily to the large importance of oil in the total volume of United States foreign investments and, in some slight degree, to a recognition of the strategic importance of oil. This latter recognition, however, was tempered by a soothing awareness of apparently unlimited oil resources available within the United States.

1946 Assessing the Perón Era: The Argentine Blue Book

During World War II, the American government was offended by the continuing neutrality of Argentina, as well as by the presence of a pro-German faction there. In 1943, a "colonel's clique" came to power in a military coup, and its policies proved so offensive to the United States that the American government eventually decided to freeze Argentine gold stocks and to tighten shipping regulations. At the end of the war, Colonel Juan Perón became the leader of Argentina, much to the displeasure of American Ambassador Spruille Braden, who returned to Washington to become Assistant Secretary of State. In February, 1946, the Department of State issued a strongly anti-Peron Blue Book, but if anything this added to Perón's margin of victory in the upcoming Argentine Presidential election.

SOURCE: U.S. Department of State *Bulletin*, February 24, 1946. See p. 285.

DOCUMENT:

On October 3, 1945 the Department of State initiated consultation among the American republics with respect to the Argentine situation. All of the other American republics agreed to participate in this consultation.

During the intervening period, this Government has made a careful study and evaluation of all the information in its possession with regard to Argentina. An enormous volume of documents of the defeated enemy, in many cases found only with much difficulty and after prolonged search, have now been studied and verified. German and Italian officials charged with responsibility for activities in and with Argentina have been interrogated. Although this work of investigation continues, the Government of the United States at present has information which establishes that:

1. Members of the military government collaborated with enemy agents for important espionage and other purposes damaging to the war effort of the United Nations.
2. Nazi leaders, groups and organizations have combined with Argentine totalitarian groups to create a Nazi–Fascist state.
3. Members of the military regime who have controlled the government since June, 1943 conspired with the enemy to undermine governments in neighboring countries in order to destroy their collaboration with the Allies and in an effort to align them in a pro-Axis bloc.
4. Successive Argentine governments protected the enemy in economic matters in order to preserve Axis industrial and commercial power in Argentina.
5. Successive Argentine governments conspired with the enemy to obtain arms from Germany.

This information warrants the following conclusions:

1. The Castillo Government and still more the present military regime pursued a policy of positive aid to the enemy.
2. Solemn pledges to cooperate with the other American republics were completely breached and are proved to have been designed to protect and maintain Axis interests in Argentina.
3. The policies and actions of the recent regimes in Argentina were aimed at undermining the Inter-American System.
4. The totalitarian individuals and groups, both military and civilian, who control the present government in Argentina, have, with their Nazi collaborators, pursued a common aim: The creation in this Hemisphere of a totalitarian state. This aim has already been partly accomplished.
5. Increasingly since the invasion of Normandy, and most obviously since the failure of the last German counteroffensive in January, 1945, the military regime has had to resort to a defensive strategy of camouflage. The assumption of the obligations of the Inter-American Conference on Problems of War and Peace to wipe out Nazi influence and the repeated avowals of pro-democratic intentions proceeded from this strategy of deception.
6. By its brutal use of force and terrorist methods to strike down all opposition from the Argentine people the military regime has made a mockery of its pledge to the United Nations "to reaffirm faith in human rights, in the dignity and worth of the human person."

1947 General Douglas MacArthur on the Reconstruction of Japan

After World War II, General Douglas MacArthur presided over occupied Japan as the Supreme Commander of the Allied Powers. MacArthur completely disarmed Japan, abolished the privileged status of Shinto as a state religion, and subordinated Emperor Hirohito to himself. Among the other key reforms implemented under him were the downgrading of the business monopolies, land redistribution, a revamped educational system, more labor unions, the emancipation of women, and more political democracy. Collectively, these represented a highly original synthesis of conservative ideology and the New Deal. By the late 1940s, Japanese industrial activity and overseas trade had begun to revive. As for MacArthur, in his 1947 assessment of the occupation he stressed moral values and Christian principles, as well as the avoidance of vengeance and injustice. Four years later, in 1951, the United States finally signed a peace treaty with Japan.

SOURCE: Douglas MacArthur, *A Soldier Speaks* (New York: Frederick A. Praeger, 1965). See pp. 191–93.

DOCUMENT:

During those two years, both sides—Allies and Japanese—have by adherence to the letter and spirit of their respective undertakings acquitted themselves honorably and well—and both have benefited from the relationship. History records no other instance wherein the military occupation of a conquered people has been conducted with the emphasis placed, as it has been here, upon the moral values involved between victor and vanquished. Right rather than might has been the criterion.

Avoiding vengeance, intolerance, and injustice, Allied policy apart from its rigidly destructive phase designed to eliminate from Japanese life both the will and the capacity to wage war, has rested squarely upon the fundamental concept which finds immortal exposition in the Sermon on the Mount. And by bringing into clear focus the commanding influence moral values thus have played in this relationship between nations and men, the results here attained invoke standards which might well be recognized and carried forward if the grave international issues which perplex mankind are to be resolved dispassionately in harmony and peace. There is no novelty in this simple concept, but too often it is ignored in the international sphere—betrayed through the misuse of power over the lives and destinies of others, with war the price the world inevitably has paid for this, man's greatest folly.

A peace treaty is shortly to be discussed. It is essential that it be approached in that same tolerant and just atmosphere to insure that this defeated country has the opportunity to become self-sustaining, rather than reduced to a condition of mendicancy. A post-treaty Japan should not become a burden upon the economy of any other country.

There need be no concern over fears recently expressed of imminent economic collapse. It must be understood that the actual collapse of the Japanese economy, which was a major Allied war aim, occurred prior to the surrender as a result of attrition caused by the crushing force of Allied arms, the severance of Japan's lifelines abroad, the wresting from Japan of Manchuria, Korea, Formosa and the island groups mandated to her following the First World War, and the destruction of Japan's shipping afloat and her centers of industry and commerce at home. The economic prostration of the country was complete at the beginning of the occupation, industry then being at a practical standstill. In reality, since the surrender, under the guidance of the occupation and with American help, Japan has been gradually restoring her shattered economy and the curve is up not down. The industrial output has now risen to over 45 per cent of pre-war normal, and the improvement can be expected to continue. This relative stability, especially by comparison with more fortunately favored countries, and even under the blighting effects of practical blockade, has been one of the most amazing and encouraging features of the occupation period. To become self-supporting, however, it is essential that the economic isolation imposed by the Allies be modified so that trade with the outside world can be resumed.

If Japan in the post-treaty era is given a just opportunity to live in freedom and peace with her neighbors in the community of nations, there will be no threat to the survival and strengthening of the democratic processes here inaugurated under the occupation. For democracy, once firmly rooted in the human heart, has never voluntarily yielded before any other conflicting ideology known to man. If liberty and public morality do not bring national stability, nothing can.

1948 President Harry Truman Recognizes the Independent State of Israel (1956)

In 1896, the Austrian writer Theodor Herzl proposed the establishment of a Jewish state in Palestine. Zionism now became an important force in a number of countries. During 1917, Arthur James Balfour, the British Foreign Secretary, openly came out in favor of a Jewish "National Home" in Palestine. But it was not for another generation that this dream became a reality, after the Jews had suffered through the Holocaust under the Nazis. A stumbling block to an independent Israel was the presence in Palestine of a large number of Arabs, whose cause the British felt obligated to support. As for the United States, the presence of a large number of Jews in New York and elsewhere doubtless influenced the American government to side with their brethren in the Middle East. President Harry Truman, who originally had favored the partition of the Holy Land between the Arabs and the Jews under the auspices of the United Nations, officially recognized the new state of Israel on May 14, 1948, a mere eleven minutes after it proclaimed its independence.

SOURCE: Harry Truman, *Years of Trial and Hope* (Garden City: Doubleday and Company, 1956). See pp. 163–64.

DOCUMENT:

It seemed difficult, if not impossible, to find any basis for reconciliation between the parties: The Jews fervently wanted partition; the Arabs opposed it hotly; and the British were determined to free themselves of the entire entanglement.

Under these conditions, and faced with the evidence of mounting violence inside Palestine, the Security Council was to decide whether or not it would accept the General Assembly resolution of November 29, 1947, as the basis for a Palestine solution. That is the reason that our State Department proposed, on March 19, 1948, that unless a peaceful transition to the partitioned status could be found the former British mandate should be placed under the United Nations Trusteeship Council. This was not a rejection of partition but rather an effort to postpone its effective date until proper conditions for the establishment of self-government in the two parts might be established.

My policy with regard to Palestine was not a commitment to any set of dates or circumstances; it was dedication to the twin deal of international obligations and the relieving of human misery. In this sense, the State Department's trusteeship proposal was not contrary to my policy.

On the other hand, anybody in the State Department should have known—and I am sure that some individual officials actually expected—that the Jews would read this proposal as a complete abandonment of the partition plan on which they so heavily counted and that the Arabs would also believe that, like them, we had come to oppose the solution approved by the General Assembly. In this sense, the trusteeship idea was at odds with my attitude and the policy I had laid down.

The suggestion that the mandate be continued as a trusteeship under the U.N. was not a bad idea at the time. However, there were strong suspicions voiced by many that the diplomats thought of it as a way to prevent partition and the establishment of the Jewish homeland.

There were some men in the State Department who held the view that the Balfour Declaration could not be carried out without offense to the Arabs. Like most of the British diplomats, some of our diplomats also thought that the Arabs, on account of their numbers and because of the fact that they controlled such immense oil resources, should be appeased. I am sorry to say that there were some among them who were also inclined to be anti-Semitic.

Secretary Marshall and Under Secretary Lovett saw eye to eye with me, as did Ambassador Austin at the United Nations.

On May 14 I was informed that the Provisional Government of Israel was planning to proclaim a Jewish state at midnight that day, Palestine time, which was when the British mandate came to an end. I had often talked with my advisers about the course of action we would take once partition had come about, and it was always understood that eventually we would recognize any responsible government the Jews might set up. Partition was not taking place in exactly the peaceful manner I had hoped, to be sure, but the fact was that the Jews were controlling the area in which their people lived and that they were ready to administer and to defend it. On the other hand, I was well aware that some of the State Department "experts" would want to block recognition of a Jewish state.

Now that the Jews were ready to proclaim the State of Israel, however, I decided to move at once and give American recognition to the new nation. I instructed a member of my staff to communicate my decision to the State Department and prepare it for transmission to Ambassador Austin at the United

Nations in New York. About thirty minutes later, exactly eleven minutes after Israel had been proclaimed a state, Charlie Ross, my press secretary, handed the press the announcement of the *de facto* recognition by the United States of the provisional government of Israel.

I was told that to some of the career men of the State Department this announcement came as a surprise. It should not have been if these men had faithfully supported my policy.

1945–46 General Marshall's Mission to Civil War-torn China (1956)

Late in 1945, the Truman administration sent General George C. Marshall on a mission to China, with the basic objective of helping to end the civil war there between the Communists and Nationalists. According to Truman's memoirs, Marshall advised Generalissimo Chiang Kai–shek that he should avoid fighting a war with the Communists, and that his nation was in a precarious economic condition. The President and Marshall were under no delusion that Chou En–lai and Mao Tse–tung and their compatriots were mere "agrarian reformers," but Chiang Kai–shek was apparently oblivious to the necessity of instituting certain reforms which might have pacified the restless Chinese masses.

SOURCE: Truman, *Years of Trial and Hope,* See pp. 88–91.

DOCUMENT:

Marshall reminded the Generalissimo that, if Russian aid were given to the Communists, their supply line would be much shorter than his own and much more immune from attack. By every means at his command he sought to convince Chiang Kai–shek that in a purely military conflict, however much the odds appeared in his favor at the moment, he would not be able to secure lasting control of the country.

Despite this warning, the Generalissimo remained unconvinced. He was certain that the Communists had never had any intention of cooperating and that only their military defeat would settle the issue. Nor did he take other important matters into consideration. For example, he dismissed Marshall's references to China's precarious economic condition by saying, in effect, that China was accustomed to that.

In spite of these open disagreements over the prospects in view, the Generalissimo asked General Marshall to remain in China as adviser to the government, an offer Marshall declined because he thought the strong anti-American sentiment whipped up by the extremists in the Kuomintang and their predominant position in the government would make the position of any American adviser difficult.

I had sent General Marshall to China to try to end the fighting and to help put into effect the agreement between the Nationalists and the Communists to form a coalition government. He set up an executive headquarters, and the fighting stopped, temporarily. The Chinese began these endless, oriental negotiations between themselves, and only an expert chess player can follow them. This is the way it goes. Someone makes a proposal which is accepted by the other side, with three qualifications. They are then accepted by the other side with three qualifications to each of the first three qualifications. It was an old Chinese way to be sure nothing would happen. Well, fighting broke out again in 1946, and Chiang Kai–shek then decided he was going to occupy North China and Manchuria. General Marshall argued against it, and General Wedemeyer argued against it, but he went ahead. We furnished him equipment, money, and a water-lift to Manchuria, and he sent the best divisions he had, well trained and well armed, to Mukden. They stayed there until finally the whole thing disintegrated, and they surrendered. They would make a series of extended movements into the country in North China and take up a position in a walled city. Chiang's commanders were very poor. They had a walled-city complex. They thought the open country was dangerous. Open country was the one place in which they should have been. But they thought a walled city was fine; they could see people coming. Of course no one came, and they stayed in the city. The Communists cut their communication lines and broke up their single-track railroad so it was no good to them. At the beginning of 1947 General Marshall threw in the towel. He said that both parties were unwilling to carry out their agreements. Chiang Kai–shek would not heed the advice of one of the greatest military strategists in history and lost to the Communists.

There is no question that Marshall's mission failed to yield the results he and I had hoped for. Fighting soon enveloped all of China, and it did not end until the Communists were masters of the land and Chiang Kai–shek, with the remnants of his army, sought refuge on Formosa.

Neither Marshall nor I was ever taken in by the talk about the Chinese Communists being just "agrarian reformers." The general knew he was dealing with Communists, and he knew what their aims were. When he was back in Washington in March, he told me that their chief negotiator, Chou En–lai, had very frankly declared that, as a Communist, he believed firmly in the teachings of Marx and Lenin and the eventual victory of the proletariat. Marshall's messages from China show, also, that he fully assumed that the Chinese Communists would, in the end, be able to count on Russian support.

Neither had I been taken in by Stalin's declaration at Potsdam that the Chinese Communists were not really "proper" Communists, nor by his later statement to Harriman that he thought the civil war in China would be foolish. I realized that the Communists had been engaged in a struggle for the power in China for nearly twenty years. What I hoped to achieve was to see China made into a country in which Communism would lose its appeal to the masses because the needs of the people and the voice of the people would have been answered.

1950 President Harry Truman's Statement on the Status of Taiwan

On January 5, 1950, shortly after Generalissimo Chiang Kai–shek had withdrawn with his Nationalist troops to the island of Taiwan (formerly Formosa) one hundred miles off the Chinese coast, President Harry Truman made an important statement on the status of Taiwan. Unquestionably the most significant aspect of this document was the affirmation that while the American government would maintain the current program of economic sanctions, it would provide neither military aid nor advice to the Chinese forces on Taiwan. This stands in marked contrast to a House Joint Resolution adopted five years later, which authorized the President (Dwight Eisenhower) to use American forces to protect the island.

SOURCE: U.S. Department of State, *American Foreign Policy: Basic Documents,* 4 Volumes (Washington: Government Printing Office, 1957). See III, 2448–49.

DOCUMENT:

The United States Government has always stood for good faith in international relations. Traditional United States policy toward China, as exemplified in the open-door policy, called for international respect for the territorial integrity of China. This principle was recently reaffirmed in the United Nations General Assembly resolution of December 8, 1949, which, in part, calls on all states—

To refrain from (a) seeking to acquire spheres of influence or to create foreign controlled regimes within the territory of China; (b) seeking to obtain special rights or privileges within the territory of China.

A special application of the foregoing principles is seen in the present situation with respect to Formosa. In the joint declaration at Cairo on December 1, 1943, the President of the United States, the British Prime Minister, and the President of China stated that it was their purpose that territories Japan had stolen from China, such as Formosa, should be restored to the Republic of China. The United States was a signatory to the Potsdam declaration of July 26, 1945, which declared that the terms of the Cairo declaration should be carried out. The provisions of this declaration were accepted by Japan at the time of its surrender. In keeping with these declarations, Formosa was surrendered to Generalissimo Chiang Kai–shek, and for the past 4 years, the United States and the other Allied Powers have accepted the exercise of Chinese authority over the Island.

The United States has no predatory designs on Formosa or on any other Chinese territory. The United States has no desire to obtain special rights or privileges or to establish military bases on Formosa at this time. Nor does it have any intention of utilizing its armed forces to interfere in the present situation. The United States Government will not pursue a course which will lead to involvement in the civil conflict in China.

Similarly, the United States Government will not provide military aid or advice to Chinese forces on Formosa. In the view of the United States Government, the resources on Formosa are adequate to enable them to obtain the items which they might consider necessary for the defense of the Island. the United States Government proposes to continue under existing legislative authority the present ECA program of economic assistance.

1950 Secretary of State Dean Acheson's Far Eastern Policy Excludes South Korea from the American Defense Perimeter

One week after President Harry Truman had issued a statement defining American policy toward Taiwan, Secretary of State Dean Acheson gave a speech on Asia before the National Press Club in Washington. In this January 12, 1950 address Acheson defined the U.S. defense perimeter in the Pacific as running from the Aleutians to Japan to the Ryukyu Islands to the Philippines. Not included was Taiwan; not included was South Korea. That summer, North Korea invaded South Korea, and as the Korean War moved to its stalmated conclusion, Republican critics of the Truman administration increasingly blamed North Korea's decision to precipitate the conflict on Acheson's National Press Club speech.

SOURCE: U.S. Department of State *Bulletin*, January 23, 1950. See pp. 115–16.

DOCUMENT:

What is the situation in regard to the military security of the Pacific area, and what is our policy in regard to it?

In the first place, the defeat and the disarmament of Japan has placed upon the United States the necessity of assuming the military defense of Japan so long as that is required, both in the interest of our security and in the interests of the security of the entire Pacific area and, in all honor, in the interest of Japanese security. We have American—and there are Australian—troops in Japan. I am not in a position to speak for the Australians, but I can assure you that there is no intention of any sort of abandoning or weakening the defenses of Japan and that whatever arrangements are to be made either through permanent settlement or otherwise, that defense must and shall be maintained.

This defensive perimeter runs along the Aleutians to Japan and then goes to the Ryukyus. We hold important defense positions in the Ryukyu Islands, and those we will continue to hold. In the interest of the population of the Ryukyu Islands, we will at an appropriate time offer to hold these islands under trusteeship of the United Nations. But they are essential parts of the defensive perimeter of the Pacific, and they must and will be held.

The defensive perimeter runs from the Ryukyus to the Philippine Islands. Our relations, our defensive relations with the Philippines are contained in agreements between us. Those agreements are being loyally carried out and will be loyally carried out. Both peoples have learned by bitter experience the vital connections between our mutual defense requirements. We are in no doubt about that, and it is hardly necessary for me to say an attack on the Philippines could not and would not be tolerated by the United States. But I hasten to add that no one perceives the imminence of any such attack.

So far as the military security of other areas in the Pacific is concerned, it must be clear that no person can guarantee these areas against military attack. But it must also be clear that such a guarantee is hardly sensible or necessary within the realm of practical relationship.

The Korean War, 1950–53 43

1950 First Secretary Harold Noble Describes the
Outbreak of the Korean War (1975)

During the summer of 1950, Harold J. Noble was the First Secretary of the American Embassy in Korea, the third-ranking political officer there. John J. Muccio was the American Ambassador to South Korea. According to Noble, the military and economic aid which the U.S. government was extending to South Korea was not sufficient to halt a large-scale invasion by the North Koreans. In addition, he and Muccio were in disagreement as to priorities, with Noble emphasizing military strength first of all, and Muccio focusing on the democratization of South Korea. Muccio wrote a firsthand account of the war as seen from the American Embassy.

SOURCE: Harold J. Noble, *Embassy at War*, edited by Frank Baldwin (Seattle: University of Washington Press, 1975). See pp. 224–25.

DOCUMENT:

With the constant military threat of a hostile army thirty miles away and with continuous fighting in the mountains, we at the embassy gave much thought to the security problems of the Republic of Korea. South Korean officials were sometimes impatient with us, thinking we didn't pay enough attention to these problems. But they never once knew how often we sent urgent recommendations to Washington on this very subject.

United States policy regarding Korea was decided in Washington, not at the embassy. We only executed our government's policies. We were kept informed of decisions but often were not consulted in advance. Still, there was always some latitude in the interpretation of general decisions, and we always had the privilege of proposing changes.

American policy was essentially to assist the South Korean government and people for a short period of time, economically through ECA and militarily through KMAG, in developing a viable economy which eventually they could protect through their own efforts and at their own expense. ECA assistance was to end in 1952, and KMAG was strictly a training mission to assist the ROK government to develop sufficient strength to maintain domestic order and protect the border against minor attacks. Quite specifically the KMAG and arms assistance program was not aimed at assisting the Republic of Korea to defend itself against full-scale invasion from the north.

At Embassy Seoul we were not happy about this policy, and we did our best to get it changed. The leader in this attempt, naturally, was Ambassador Muccio. Like all the political officers, he believed it was not enough to help the South Koreans to maintain domestic order. They had to be given a reasonable chance to protect themselves against the one enemy likely to attack them: the northern Communist regime directed by the Soviet Union.

Not that Muccio thought strictly in military terms. Far from it. I sometimes thought his insistence that there was no point in having an independent Korea unless it was also a democratic Korea was unrealistic. I believe that with independence it was possible for the South Koreans to develop a truly democratic society, but if their independence were crushed by the Communists, all hope of a democratic Korea would disappear. Probably this was chiefly a difference of emphasis, but a difference of emphasis when put into words often sounds contradictory. Muccio saw the major problem in South Korea to be developing a society of free men, with the military problem secondary. Knowing the Communists' intention to invade and conquer, I saw the major problem to be keeping South Korea free by military means, with the question of the exact status of democracy secondary. On this question the senior staff saw the problem much as I did.

1950 The Authority of the President to Repel the North Korean Attack

Unlike World War II—and unlike all other major wars in which it was involved—the United States did not formally declare war on North Korea. Thus there was no Congressional vote. Instead, the United States acted under Article 39 of the Charter of the United Nations. According to a Department of State memorandum dated July 31, 1950, moreover, the President enjoys various Constitutional powers with respect to the Armed Forces as Commander-in-Chief of the Army and Navy of the United States. This document discusses these powers at considerable length.

SOURCE: U.S. Department of State *Bulletin,* July 31, 1950. See pp. 173–74.

DOCUMENT:

The President's control over the Armed Forces of the United States is based on article 2, section 2 of the Constitution which provides that he "shall be Commander in Chief of the Army and Navy of the United States."

In *United States v. Sweeny,* the Supreme Court said that the object of this provision was "evidently to vest in the President the supreme command over all the military forces,—such as supreme and undivided command as would be necessary to the prosecution of a successful war."

That the President's power to send the Armed Forces outside the country is not dependent on Congressional authority has been repeatedly emphasized by numerous writers.

For example, ex-President William Howard Taft wrote:

> The President is made Commander in Chief of the Army and Navy by the Constitution evidently for the purpose of enabling him to defend the country against invasion, to suppress insurrection and to take care that the laws be faithfully executed. If Congress were to attempt to prevent his use of the Army for any of these purposes, the action would be void....Again, in the carrying on of war as Commander in Chief, it is he who is to determine the movements of the Army and of the Navy. Congress could not take away from him that discretion and place it beyond his control in any of his subordinates, nor could they themselves, as the people of Athens attempted to carry on campaigns by votes in the marketplace.

In an address delivered before the American Bar Association in 1917 on the war powers under the Constitution, Mr. Hughes stated that "There is no limitation upon the authority of Congress to create an army and it is for the President as Commander-in-Chief to direct the campaigns of that Army wherever he may think they should be carried on." He referred to a statement by Chief Justice Taney in *Fleming v. Page* (9 How.615) in which the Chief Justice said that as Commander in Chief the President "is authorized to direct the movements of the naval and military forces placed by law at his command."

Not only is the President Commander in Chief of the Army and Navy, but he is also charged with the duty of conducting the foreign relations of the United States and in this field he "alone has the power to speak or listen as a representative of the Nation."

Obviously, there are situations in which the powers of the President as Commander in Chief and his power to conduct the foreign relations of this country complement each other.

The basic interest of the United States is international peace and security. The United States has, throughout its history, upon orders of the Commander in Chief to the Armed Forces and without congressional authorization, acted to prevent violent and unlawful acts in other states from depriving the United States and its nationals of the benefits of such peace and security. It has taken such action both unilaterally and in concert with others. A tabulation of 85 instances of the use of American Armed Forces without a declaration of war was incorporated in the *Congressional Record* for July 10, 1941.

1950 General Douglas MacArthur's Letter to Representative Joseph Martin: "There Is No Substitute for Victory"

As the Korean War bogged down in an inconclusive outcome, relations between the commander of the international force there, General Douglas MacArthur, and President Harry Truman continued to deteriorate. Republican attacks on Truman's policy toward Korea increased the significance of the fact that MacArthur himself was a member of that party. The Truman administration's containment doctrine did not require an outright United Nations triumph in Korea, since merely repulsing the attack from the North would be enough to teach the Communists a lesson. On the other hand, to General MacArthur Asia was just as significant as Europe, Communist China just as important as the Soviet Union, and there was no substitute for victory. He made these views known in a highly controversial letter which he wrote on March 20, 1951 to Representative Joseph Martin of Massachusetts, which this Republican leader publicly read on the floor of the House on April 5.

SOURCE: *Congressional Record*, April 5, 1951. See p. 3380.

DOCUMENT:

I am most grateful for your note of the eighth forwarding me a copy of your address of February 12. The latter I have read with much interest, and find that with the passage of years you have certainly lost none of your old-time punch.

My views and recommendations with respect to the situation created by Red China's entry into war against us in Korea have been submitted to Washington in most complete detail. Generally these views are well known and clearly understood, as they follow the conventional pattern of meeting force with maximum counter-force, as we have never failed to do in the past. Your view with respect to the utilization of the Chinese forces on Formosa is in conflict with neither logic nor this tradition.

It seems strangely difficult for some to realize that here in Asia is where the Communist conspirators have elected to make their play for global conquest, and that we have joined the issue thus raised on the battlefield; that here we fight Europe's war with arms while the diplomats there still fight it with words; that if we lose the war to Communism in Asia the fall of Europe is inevitable; win it, and Europe most probably would avoid war and yet preserve freedom.

As you point out, we must win. There is no substitute for victory.

1951 Harry Truman Recalls Douglas MacArthur (1956)

It was only a matter of time before President Truman would remove General MacArthur from his Korean command. The public reading of MacArthur's letter to Representative Martin in the House precipitated his final decision, which he reached after conferring with various high-level advisors. Significantly, the President observed that he fired MacArthur not because the General wished to broaden the Korean War, but rather because he was challenging the long-established tradition in the United States of the civilian ascendance over the military. To Truman, the democratic mentality was at odds with the military one, with its emphasis on command and obedience.

SOURCE: Truman, *Years of Trial and Hope.* See pp. 444–45.

DOCUMENT:

If there is one basic element in our Constitution, it is civilian control of the military. Policies are to be made by the elected political officials, not by generals or admirals. Yet time and again General MacArthur had shown that he was unwilling to accept the policies of the administration. By his repeated public statements he was not only confusing our allies as to the true course of our policies but, in fact, was also setting his policy against the President's.

I have always had, and I have to this day, the greatest respect for General MacArthur, the soldier. Nothing I could do, I knew, could change his stature as one of the outstanding military figures of our time—and I had no desire to diminish his stature. I had hoped, and I had tried to convince him, that the policy he was asked to follow was right. He had disagreed. He had been openly critical. Now, at last, his actions had frustrated a political course decided upon, in conjunction with its allies, by the government he was sworn to serve. If I allowed him to defy the civil authorities in this manner, I myself would be violating my oath to uphold and defend the Constitution.

I have always believed that civilian control of the military is one of the strongest foundations of our system of free government. Many of our people are descended from men and women who fled their native countries to escape the oppression of militarism. We in America have sometimes failed to give the soldier and the sailor their due, and it has hurt us. But we have always jealously guarded the constitutional provision that prevents the military from taking over the government from the authorities, elected by the people, in whom the power resides.

It has often been pointed out that the American people have a tendency to choose military heroes for the highest office in the land, but I think the statement is misleading. True, we have chosen men like George Washington and Andrew Jackson, and even Ulysses S. Grant, as our Chief Executives. But only Grant among these three had been raised to be a professional soldier, and he had abandoned that career and been brought back into service, like thousands of other civilians, when war broke out. We have chosen men who, in time of war, had made their mark, but until 1952 we had never elevated to the White House any man whose entire life had been dedicated to the military.

One reason that we have been so careful to keep the military within its own preserve is that the very nature of the service hierarchy gives military commanders little if any opportunity to learn the humility that is needed for good public service. The elected official will never forget—unless he is a fool—that others as well or better qualified might have been chosen and that millions remained unconvinced that the last choice made was the best one possible. Any man who has come up through the process of political selection, as it functions in our country, knows that success is a mixture of principles steadfastly maintained and adjustments made at the proper time and place—adjustments to conditions, not adjustment of principles.

These are things a military officer is not likely to learn in the course of his profession. The words that dominate his thinking are "command" and "obedience," and the military definitions of these words are not definitions for use in a republic.

That is why our Constitution embodies the principles of civilian control of the military. This was the principle that General MacArthur threatened. I do not believe that he purposefully decided to challenge civilian control of the military, but the result of his behavior was that this fundamental principle of free government was in danger.

It was my duty to act.

1950–53 Secretary of State Dean Acheson Views the Korean War Retrospectively (1969)

In his memoirs, Secretary of State Dean Acheson notes that MacArthur's successor, General Matthew Ridgway, understood what the Truman administration wanted him to do, and unlike MacArthur achieved the desired results. MacArthur was willing to risk a war with Communist China to obtain his objectives, an option which Harry Truman found totally unacceptable. To Acheson, MacArthur's reckless behavior had also eroded the confidence of our allies in the United States.

SOURCE: Dean Acheson, *Present at the Creation: My Years in the State Department* (New York: W.W. Norton and Company, 1969). See pp. 526–27.

DOCUMENT:

As one looks back in calmness, it seems impossible to overestimate the damage that General MacArthur's willful insubordination and incredibly bad judgment did to the United States in the world and to the Truman Administration in the United States. During the Senate hearings a good deal of discussion revolved about whether the General had disobeyed orders in a court-martial sense of the phrase. I believe that he probably did not and that the debate is beside the point. The General was surely bright enough to understand what his Government wanted him to do. General Ridgway, who succeeded him, understood perfectly and achieved the desired ends. MacArthur disagreed with the desired ends, and wished instead to unify Korea by force of arms even though this plan would involve general war with China and, quite possibly, with the Soviet Union as well. Indeed, far from being dismayed by this prospect, he seemed, as his letter to Congressman Martin strongly suggests, to welcome the wider war, for it was in Asia, as he saw it, that "the Communist conspirators [i.e., the Soviet Union and China] have elected to make their play for global conquest, and that we [i.e., he] have joined the issue thus raised on the battlefield." Having joined the issue thus raised on the Asian battlefield, he was willing, not to say eager, to fight it out there. This was exactly what his Government had told him, beginning with the directive of September 27 and continuing until his relief, that it would not do, even if to avoid it involved withdrawal from Korea. Nevertheless he pressed his will and his luck to a shattering defeat.

In appraising its consequences, two conclusions stand out: the defeat with its losses of men and national prestige was quite avoidable had he followed the agreed plan of campaign; the defeat and MacArthur's conduct in defeat profoundly changed both the national attitude toward the war and our allies' confidence in the judgment and leadership of the United States Government and, especially, in its control over General MacArthur. Regarding the first conclusion, we have already noted that when General Ridgway took over command of the Eighth Army and later the supreme command, he was able, starting much farther south, after a defeat and opposed by a strong enemy, to stabilize the front as MacArthur had been told to do and to hold it. Had General MacArthur, who faced no opposition after Inchon and the defeat of the North Koreans, occupied one of the strong positions in mid-Korea, fortified it, and kept his forces collected, he could have shattered a Chinese assault just as Ridgway did.

The effect of defeat and the General's ill-concealed disaffection upon domestic and foreign confidence were equally plain. The enthusiasm with which our people and allies received President Truman's bold leadership of the United Nations in military resistance to aggression survived even the hard fighting of the retreat to the Pusan perimeter and the surprising discovery of North Korean military competence and toughness. It was heightened by the September victories and the complete collapse of the invasion of South Korea. Opinion at home and abroad would have remained steady and united had the Army under the September 27 plan and directive sealed off the South from further attack until the war should peter out, as it eventually did, even though this would require, as it also did, some hard fighting to prove the strength of the line.

What lost the confidence of our allies were MacArthur's costly defeat, his open advocacy of widening the war at what they rightly regarded as unacceptable risks, and the hesitance of the Administration in asserting firm control over him. What disturbed and divided our people was the stream of propaganda flowing out of Tokyo that the cause of MacArthur's disasters was not his own stubborn folly, but conspiracy in Washington, probably inspired by concern for national interests other than our own.

1953 President Dwight Eisenhower's Plague-on-Both-Your-Houses Attitude Toward Korea

On January 20, 1953, newly inaugurated President Dwight Eisenhower inherited the Korean War from Harry Truman. A month earlier, "Ike" had visited the war-torn nation for several days. Early in February, Eisenhower ordered the U.S. Far Eastern fleet to halt its neutralization of Formosa, a move designed to threaten the Communists. But he was to discover that South Korean President Syngman Rhee could be just as much of a problem as the South Koreans. Committed to a unified nation, Rhee tried to disrupt the peace negotiations by freeing 27,000 North Korean and anti-Communist prisoners of war in June 1953, a month before the conclusion of an armistice on July 27 which divided Korea in half. Rhee only agreed to the latter after receiving promises of economic and military support from the United States. Eisenhower's disillusionment with Rhee is reflected in his diary entry for July 24.

SOURCE: Robert Ferrell, Editor, *The Eisenhower Diaries* (New York: W.W. Norton, 1981). See p. 248.

DOCUMENT:

It is almost hopeless to write about the Korea–Rhee situation. Both the communists and the South Korean government have raised so many difficulties in the prosecution of the negotiations intended to end the fighting that it raises in my mind a serious question as to whether or not the United Nations will ever again go into an area to protect the inhabitants against communist attack. It has been a long and bitter experience, and I am certain in my own mind that except for the fact that evacuation of South Korea would badly expose Japan, the majority of the United Nations now fighting there would have long since attempted to pull out.

It is impossible to attempt here to recite the long lists of items in which Rhee has been completely uncooperative, even recalcitrant. It is sufficient to say that the United Nations went into Korea only to repel aggression, not to reunite Korea by force. The armistice was intended to stop the fighting after the United Nations had proven its ability to stop such aggression and was intended also to mark the beginning of political discussion which would hope to reunite Korea and accomplish the evacuation of that country by both the Chinese and the Allied troops.

There has been so much backing and filling, indecision, doubt, and frustration engendered by both Rhee and the communists that I am doubtful that an armistice even if achieved will have any great meaning. Certainly we must be extremely wary and watchful of both sides. Of course the fact remains that the probable enemy is the communists, but Rhee has been such an unsatisfactory ally that it is difficult indeed to avoid excoriating him in the strongest of terms.

1950–53 Disunity among the Allies: General James Van Fleet Views the Korean War

A somewhat different perspective on the Korean War was offered by General James A. Van Fleet, who commanded United Nations forces in Korea for two years. His focus was not on the civilian rivalry with the military; all-out vs. limited war; or Europe first or Asia first. Van Fleet instead pointed out that America's minor partners in the Korean War were sometimes a hindrance rather than a help. The United States contributed ninety-five percent of the total United Nations effort in Korea. It nevertheless had to confer with diplomats from the other sixteen countries sending troops before it reached a decision, sometimes with unsatisfactory results. To Van Fleet the solution to this dilemma was reliance on regional security facts, whose members have more common interests than do those countries belonging to the United Nations.

SOURCE: James A. Van Fleet, "Catastrophe in Asia," in *U.S. News and World Report,* September 17, 1954. See p. 28.

DOCUMENT:

I believe in the United Nations. I applaud its successes in mediation, in relieving distress, and its efforts to improve world living standards. But it would be folly to rely on the United Nations as an instrument for collective security.

Fifty of these United Nations joined up in the summer of 1950, denouncing aggression and calling for armed resistance—in response to heavy American pressure. But when the chips were down, only sixteen were willing to send forces to Korea and, as Sir Winston Churchill has pointed out, America contributed ninety-five per cent of that total U.N. effort.

Just who really fought in Korea? The Republic of Korea itself has at all times supplied all the divisions our policy makers would let us arm and train—a limit of ten during the days of hardest fighting, and sixteen at the date of the armistice.

America supplied seven divisions, plus those required in Japan, and most of the naval and air support, as well as logistical support for all, except for certain items for the Commonwealth Division.

Now for the other United Nations. I have often expressed my gratitude and high praise for the fighting qualities of the men they sent. But here are the totals: a single division from the entire British Commonwealth of Nations; a brigade from Turkey; two battalions from Greece; and a battalion each from Colombia, Ethiopia, the Philippines, Thailand, France, Holland and Belgium.

The price we paid for them was the *loss of decisive military command.* No important move could be made on the battlefield without first securing, through Washington, the approval of a caucus of 16 diplomats halfway 'round the world. And, after Red China entered the war, the enthusiasm of most of these 16 cooled rapidly. They controlled not only over-all strategy, but small-scale tactical moves, and even the choice of bombing targets within Korea.

For months during my stay there, the commander of the magnificent Eighth Army was limited in his offensive moves to actions requiring not more than a single platoon. And often I feared the time might come when the caucus of diplomats might take over from us command even of the platoons! To paraphrase Sir Winston Churchill: Never in the history of combat has so much authority been bought by so small a contribution!

Our superb fighting men plus the equally superb divisions of the Korean Republic might have engaged and destroyed the enemy. Instead they became pawns of that diplomatic caucus. We had to appease our allies who feared offending Peiping. We had to appease "neutrals" who had piously joined in condemning aggression but who, when the call went out for fighting men, loftily sat on the fence. Above all, we appeased our enemies; if we offended them by fighting vigorously, they might not grant our plea for an armistice.

If we must again send our sons abroad to fight for freedom, I hope they go unshackled; that no appeaser's chains bind their arms behind their backs.

And I feel that the true road to collective security lies beyond the United Nations in regional pacts, like the Monroe Doctrine in the Americas, and others we have negotiated in the Pacific. In the frameworks of such smaller groupings, the nations involved can identify the aggressor, can appraise their rival interests, and can throw their whole united strength into their defense.

In such areas we can pick out brave allies anxious to defend themselves, and give them the aid they need.

Such pacts are tailor-made to fit the curious war which we, for eight years, have been losing to the Kremlin. If we can turn this tide, World War III may never come.

The Diplomatic Ideology of the Eisenhower Administration 44

1953 Secretary of State John Foster Dulles's Captive Peoples Speech

As Dwight Eisenhower's Secretary of State, the strongly anti-Communist John Foster Dulles periodically made controversial statements about the global scene. One was his Captive Peoples Speech, delivered over both radio and television on January 27, 1953. This address called for encouraging a desire for freedom among the captive peoples behind the Iron Curtain and the Bamboo Curtain. Dulles was less than specific as to how this was to be accomplished, but he did assert that both he and the President were opposed to the United States obtaining its objectives through war.

SOURCE: U.S. Department of State *Bulletin*, February 9, 1953. See pp. 215–16.

DOCUMENT:

We will not try to meet the Soviet strategy of encirclement by ourselves starting a war. Take that for certain. A few people here and there in private life have suggested that a war with Soviet Russia is inevitable and that we'd better have it soon rather than later because, they said, time is running against us. President Eisenhower is absolutely opposed to any such policy and so, of course, am I and all of my associates in the State Department and the Foreign Service. We shall never choose a war as the instrument of our policy.

It says in the *Bible*, you recall, that all they that take the sword perish with the sword. And even people who do not accept that as a doctrine of faith should at least remember that twice within our generation great and powerful despots have taken the sword. Germany and Japan, for example, have taken the sword with seemingly overwhelming power only in the end to perish miserably. Now, of course, we know that our enemies do not have moral scruples. In fact, they deny that there is such a thing as a moral law. They preach violence. Stalin has said, and it is taught to every one of his Communist followers, that the world transformation which they seek cannot, they say, be achieved without violence.

And Stalin went on to say that any who thought that their goals could be achieved peacefully have either gone out of their minds or are traitors to the Communist cause. We know that they've used violence, at least on a local scale, in several countries of the world, including Korea and Indochina. They're building up a vast military machine; they've rejected U.N. proposals for an armistice in Korea; and they've rejected U.N. proposals for effective limitation of armament. Therefore we ourselves must have a strong military establishment and we should encourage the creation of military strength among our friends; but the purpose is never to wage war but only to deter war.

Now the other purpose of our foreign policy, and this is the positive aspect, must be to create in other peoples such a love and respect for freedom that they can never really be absorbed by the despotism, the totalitarian dictatorship, of the Communist world. The Russian Communists, as I've pointed out, have swallowed a great many people to date, approximately 800 million, but you know there is such a thing as indigestion. People don't always get stronger by eating more; sometimes they eat more than they can digest and then they get weaker instead of getting stronger. Already there are signs of indigestion within the Russian Communist world. The purges and the trials that are going on in Eastern Europe, the wholesale executions that are going on in Communist China—all these things show the people are resistive and are unhappy. The fact that the Communist rulers feel that they have to resort to these tactics of terrorism in order to make the people do their will—that fact is a sign of weakness, not a sign of strength. And a great deal can be done to make these peoples, *these captive peoples*, retain such a love of freedom and independence, and to bring such a love and determination to keep independence on the part of these peoples that I've talked about, who are menaced, that they can't be swallowed and digested by Soviet communism. And perhaps in time the indigestion will become so acute that it might be fatal.

Now what's our job and our task in that respect? Our job is to serve our own enlightened self-interest by demonstrating by our own performance, by our own examples, how good freedom is and how much better it is than despotism is.

1954 An Unwelcome Proposal: The Bricker Amendment

Over a period of two decades, Republican members of Congress became increasingly disturbed by the decisive foreign policy initiatives of Democratic Presidents Franklin D. Roosevelt and Harry Truman. Shortly after the voters had installed Dwight Eisenhower in the White House, Republican Senator John Bricker of Ohio introduced a proposed Constitutional amendment which would require Congressional approval of executive agreements negotiated by the President with other countries, and would also invalidate those parts of a treaty which conflicted with the Constitution. Rather than support the amendment, Republican President Dwight Eisenhower made known his opposition to it. A modified version offered by Democratic Senator Walter George of Georgia failed by a single vote (60 to 31) to obtain the necessary two-thirds majority in the Senate on February 26, 1954. Fourteen Re-

publicans voted against it, along with maverick Wayne Morse. While Northern Democrats narrowly rejected the Bricker Amendment, their Southern counterparts overwhelmingly favored it.

SOURCE: U.S. Department of State *Bulletin*, February 8, 1954. See p. 195.

DOCUMENT:

Joint Resolution

Proposing an amendment to the Constitution of the United States, relating to the legal effect of certain treaties and executive agreements.

Resolved by the Senate and House of Representatives of the United States of America in Congress assembled (two-thirds of each House concurring therein), That the following article is proposed as an amendment to the Constitution of the United States, which shall be valid to all intents and purposes as part of the Constitution when ratified by the legislatures of three-fourths of the several States:

"Article—

SECTION 1. A provision of a treaty which conflicts with this Constitution shall not be of any force or effect.

SECTION 2. A treaty shall become effective as internal law in the United States only through legislation which would be valid in the absence of treaty.

SECTION 3. Congress shall have power to regulate all executive and other agreements with any foreign power or international organization. All such agreements shall be subject to the limitations imposed on treaties by this article.

SECTION 4. The Congress shall have power to enforce this article by appropriate legislation.

SECTION 5. This article shall be inoperative unless it shall have been ratified as an amendment to the Constitution by the legislatures of three-fourths of the several States within seven years from the date of its submission.

Following is the text of a letter dated January 25 from President Eisenhower to Senate Majority Leader William F. Knowland setting forth the President's views with respect to the treaty-making functions of the Federal Government.

In response to your inquiry, I give the following as my attitude toward the proposal for amending the treaty-making functions of the Federal Government.

I am unalterably opposed to the Bricker Amendment as reported by the Senate Judiciary Committee. It would so restrict the conduct of foreign affairs that our country could not negotiate the agreements necessary for the handling of our business with the rest of the world. Such an amendment would make it impossible for us to deal effectively with friendly nations for our mutual defense and common interests.

These matters are fundamental. We cannot hope to achieve and maintain peace if we shackle the Federal Government so that it is no longer sovereign in foreign affairs. The President must not be deprived of his historic position as the spokesman for the nation in its relations with other countries.

Adoption of the Bricker Amendment in its present form by the Senate would be notice to our friends as well as our enemies abroad that our country intends to withdraw from its leadership in world affairs. The inevitable reaction would be of major proportion. It would impair our hopes and plans for peace and for the successful matters now under discussion. This would include the diversion of atomic energy from warlike to peaceful purposes.

I fully subscribe to the proposition that no treaty or international agreement can contravene the Constitution. I am aware of the feeling of many of our citizens that a treaty may override the Constitution. So that there can be no question on this point, I will gladly support an appropriate amendment that will make this clear for all time.

1956 John Foster Dulles's Policy of Brinkmanship

On January 16, 1956, an article by James R. Shepley entitled "How Dulles Averted War" appeared in Life. *Among other things, it discussed John Foster Dulles's policy of brinkmanship. On occasion, the United States might be forced to go to the very brink of war to achieve its objectives. Few, if any, statements made by the Secretary of State caused such a furor. On the next day, Dulles commented on the article at a news conference, at which he further clarified his ideas on brinkmanship.*

SOURCE: U.S. Department of State *Bulletin*, January 30, 1956. See pp. 156–57.

DOCUMENT:

A. I said—perhaps I didn't make it as clear as I should—that most of the statements specifically attributed to me are quotations or close paraphrases of what I have already said publicly. That should be made clear.

Q. *You said, except for one ambiguous statement. What was that ambiguous statement?*

A. That was a phrase—I don't have the text here with me—which went on to say that, which implied that the getting to the brink of war might be our choice rather than a choice that was forced upon us. The whole paragraph I think is perfectly clear. But one phrase taken out of context could be ambiguous.

Q. *Could you state now what is the proper concept that you were trying to get across there?*

A. Yes. We have faced a situation where in many parts of the world, in Europe and more recently in the Far East, there has been a threat of armed attack against what I referred to here as basic moral values and vital interests. Now, we had the choice of retreating in the face of those threats or making it clear that, if they were pursued, it would involve a war. We believed that the best way to avoid a war was to make that clear. That meant that we stood firm at a point where there was a threat. But I have believed very strongly, as a result of my study of history, particularly the history of this century, that the greatest risk of war comes from not making it clear that you are prepared to defend the moral values and vital interests of the United States. We have had a history of wars which we got into despite the fact that we were always very eager for peace. I believe that it is not enough to want peace—which surely we all do—but that to get peace requires taking what Senator Vandenberg referred to as a calculated risk and making clear that certain things cannot be attacked with impunity.

Q. *Mr. Secretary, is this the sentence that you considered ambiguous: "The ability to get to the verge without getting into the war is the necessary art"?*

A. Will you read the preceding sentence, I think.

Q. *The preceding sentence is—it is two sentences: "You have to take chances for peace, just as you must take chances in war. Some say that we were brought to the verge of war. The ability to get to the verge without getting into the war is the necessary art."*

A. Yes, that second sentence if read out of context does, I think, give an incorrect impression. The important thing is that we were "brought" to the verge of war by threats which were uttered in relation to Korea, in relation to Indochina, and in relation to Formosa.

1954 President Dwight Eisenhower Promises Continuing Aid to South Vietnam After the French Depart

It is the exception rather than the rule when a native people defeat the colonial power in battle. The Zulus conquered the British at Ishandhlwana in 1879; the Ethiopians beat the Italians at Adowa in 1896; and the Vietnamese humiliated the French at Dienbienphu in 1954. On the latter occasion, the American and British governments refused to send military aid to the besieged French garrison. That summer at Geneva, the diplomatic negotiators discussing the fate of Indo China agreed to a partition of Vietnam, with the Communists retaining the North and the anti-Communists holding the South. A general election scheduled for the South in 1956 was never held. On October 25, 1954, President Dwight Eisenhower sent a letter to Prime Minister Ngo Dinh Diem of South Vietnam, in which he promised that country aid. Military hardware began arriving shortly thereafter, along with an increasing number of U.S. advisors. During the next decade lay American involvement in the seemingly endless Vietnam War.

SOURCE: *Public Papers by the Presidents of the United States: Dwight Eisenhower 1954* (Washington: Government Printing Office, 1960). See pp. 948–49.

DOCUMENT:

I have been following with great interest the course of developments in Viet-Nam, particularly since the conclusion of the conference at Geneva. The implications of the agreement concerning Viet-Nam have caused grave concern regarding the future of a country temporarily divided by an artificial military grouping, weakened by a long and exhausting war and faced with enemies without and by their subversive collaborators within.

Your recent requests for aid to assist in the formidable project of the movement of several hundred thousand loyal Vietnamese citizens away from areas which are passing under a *de facto* rule and political ideology which they abhor, are being fulfilled. I am glad that the United States is able to assist in this humanitarian effort.

We have been exploring ways and means to permit our aid to Viet-Nam to be more effective and to make a greater contribution to the welfare and stability of the Government of Viet-Nam. I am, accordingly, instructing the American Ambassador to Viet-Nam to examine with you in your capacity as Chief of Government, how an intelligent program of American aid given directly to your Government can serve to assist Viet-Nam in its present hour of trial, provided that your Government is prepared to give assurances as to the standards of performance it would be able to maintain in the event such aid were supplied.

The purpose of this offer is to assist the Government of Viet-Nam in developing and maintaining a strong, viable state, capable of resisting attempted subversion or aggression through military means. The Government of the United States expects that this aid will be met by performance on the part of the Government of Viet-Nam in undertaking needed reforms. It hopes that such aid, combined with your own continuing efforts, will contribute effectively toward an independent Viet-Nam endowed with a strong government. Such a government would, I hope, be so responsive to the nationalist aspirations of its people, so enlightened in purpose and effective in performance, that it will be respected both at home and abroad and discourage any who might wish to impose a foreign ideology on your free people.

1954 Repulsing the Communist Threat to Guatemala (1957)

As the Eisenhower administration progressed, the presence of a Communist sympathizing regime in Guatemala led by Jacobo Arbenz became an increasing concern to the United States. This red-tinged government not only seized the holdings of the United Fruit Company, it also embarked on a radical program of land redistribution. By the spring of 1954, however, Guatemala was purchasing arms from the Soviet sphere. It was at this time that an Inter-American Conference met at Caracas, Venezuela, and stated over Guatemalan objections that Communist infiltration of the Western Hemisphere was posing a threat to the region's security. The United States began to send munitions to the neighboring countries of Central America, and an army of Guatemalan exiles overthrew the Arbenz regime. Three years later, the obviously delighted State Department published a brief monograph on why the Communists lost in Guatemala.

SOURCE: U.S. Department of State, *Guatemala: A Case History of Communist Penetration* (Washington: Government Printing Office, 1957). Inter-American Series No. 52. See pp. 66–69.

DOCUMENT:

Because of the light it sheds on current Communist Party strategy, it is worth examining the Communists' own analysis of the reasons for their defeat in Guatemala and the lessons it taught them.

The primary lesson the Communists learned in Guatemala was that "the working class and not the bourgeoisie must be the class leading the struggle for national liberation." What they meant by this was that they had been unsuccessful in enslaving the masses of the people and had been able to convert only a small group of intellectuals, students, and professionals belonging chiefly to the middle or lower-middle class who, although they exercised a disproportionate influence on Government policy, did not represent the thinking of the Guatemalan people as a whole. The current strategy of the Communists in Guatemala is to work for a "revolution of the masses" and to reject the familiar Latin American tactic of the *coup d'etat*. Given the attitude of the Guatemalan people and the measures adopted by the Government to control Communist activities, there is no prospect that this strategy will prosper.

Another lesson which the Communists learned, as mentioned earlier, was that Guatemala should increase its commercial ties with the countries of the Soviet orbit. While the reason they give is to decrease Guatemala's economic dependence on the United States, the real reason is that they envisage commercial relations as a means of facilitating Communist penetration of Guatemala and of making Guatemala economically and politically dependent on the Soviet Union. That this policy is doomed to failure is evident in the fact that Guatemala has a complete embargo on trade with the Soviet and satellite countries and that the Guatemalan Government has categorically rejected the new Soviet policy of *rapprochement*.

Still another lesson which the Communists cite is that the state should allow the exercise of democratic rights only to its friends (i.e. the Communists) and should be empowered to use dictatorial measures against its enemies (i.e. the anti-Communists). This means, essentially, that under the Communist system there can be no opposition, no dissenters. Obviously the implementation of this objective is contingent upon the Communists again gaining control of the Government, an eventuality which will not come to pass as long as the Government itself remains as unalterably opposed to communism as it now is.

One of the reasons for the defeat of the Communists in Guatemala was that they were not able to subvert the army nor to arm a peasant militia as a counterforce to the army. The Communists themselves realize this perfectly well, admitting that they "committed a serious error in undertaking democratic [read Communist], revolutionary changes while leaving the old army intact.: They state that in the future it will be necessary to gain the adherence of army officers and enlisted men and "to rely on the very strength of the people in arms, organized in worker and peasant detachments...." Considering the fact that even when they were in the ascendancy in Guatemala the Communists were not successful in achieving these objectives, there is correspondingly less chance that they will be able to do so now that they are forced to operate clandestinely from a position of weakness.

A fourth lesson which the Communists cited was that "Guatemala can hope for nothing from the Organization of American States," which they claim "is used by the United States, with the complicity of all the servile and anti-democratic governments of the continent, to shore up reactionary regimes, to intervene in the internal affairs of other states, and to undermine the security and independence of our countries."

In spite of the way in which the Soviet Union and other Communist countries "defend peace and international security in the U.N.," the United Nations under present circumstances is "an ineffective instrument for impeding aggression...." The conclusion is, then that the Guatemalan Communists want no part of the OAS and have considerable reservations regarding the effectiveness of the United Nations in the political field in spite of the membership therein of friendly Communist countries. The present Guatemalan Government, in contrast, has cooperated effectively with both these organizations and has ratified the Rio nonaggression treaty, which its predecessor had refused to do.

These then are some of the principal reasons which the Communists give for their failure to convert Guatemala into a slave state and an advance guard of Soviet power in the Western Hemisphere. Their blueprint for the future should afford adequate warning to all those who would be inclined to relax their vigilance.

1955 House Joint Resolution Authorizing the President to Use American Forces to Protect Taiwan

On August 11, 1954, Communist Chinese leader Chou En–lai announced that the Nationalist government on Taiwan must be liquidated, only to have President Dwight Eisenhower announce six days later that any Chinese Communist invasion of the island would have to run over the American Seventh Fleet. The Chinese Communists began to bomb the Nationalist-held offshore island of Quemoy in September. By December, the United States had concluded a mutual defense treaty with the Taiwanese regime. Then on January 29, 1955, President Dwight Eisenhower asked Congress for authority to protect Taiwan and the neighboring Pescadores Islands militarily. This joint resolution easily passed both the House (410 to 3) and the Senate (85 to 3) shortly thereafter. The three Senatorial foes of this resolution were Herbert Lehman, Wayne Morse, and William Langer.

SOURCE: U.S. Department of State, *American Foreign Policy: Basic Documents 1950–1955*, Volume Three (Millwood: Kraus Reprint Corporation, 1974). See pp. 2486–87.

DOCUMENT:

Whereas the primary purpose of the United States, in its relations with all other nations, is to develop and sustain a just and enduring peace for all; and

Whereas certain territories in the West Pacific under the jurisdiction of the Republic of China are now under armed attack, and threats and declarations have been made by the Chinese Communists that such armed attack is in aid of and in preparation for armed attack on Formosa and the Pescadores,

Whereas such armed attack if continued would gravely endanger the peace and security of the West Pacific Area and particularly of Formosa and the Pescadores; and

Whereas the secure possession by friendly governments of the Western Pacific Island chain, of which Formosa is a part, is essential to the vital interests of the United States and all friendly nations in or bordering upon the Pacific Ocean, and;

Whereas the President of the United States on January 6, 1955, submitted to the Senate for its advice and consent to ratification a Mutual Defense Treaty between the United States of America and the Republic of China, which recognizes that an armed attack in the West Pacific area directed against territories, therein described, in the region of Formosa and the Pescadores, would be dangerous to the peace and safety of the parties to the treaty: Therefore be it Resolved by the Senate and House of Representatives of the United States of America in Congress assembled, That the President of the United States be and he hereby is authorized to employ the Armed Forces of the United States as he deems necessary for the specific purpose of securing and protecting Formosa and the Pescadores against armed attack, this authority to include the securing and protection of such related positions and territories of that area now in friendly hands and the taking of such other measures as he judges to be required or appropriate in assuring the defense of Formosa and the Pescadores.

This resolution shall expire when the President shall determine that the peace and security of the area is reasonably assured by international conditions created by action of the United Nations or otherwise, and shall so report to the Congress.

1956 Withdrawal of U.S. Support for the Aswan Dam in Egypt

During the 1950s, Egypt underwent a period of revolutions, policy change, and war. A military junta overthrew King Farouk in a 1951 coup d'etat, and by the fall of 1953 Colonel Gamal Nasser had taken over the leadership of the nation. One of Nasser's favorite projects was a high dam at Aswan on the Nile. At the same time that he was obtaining arms from the Communists, Nasser sought financial aid from Great Britain and the United States to construct the dam. By the summer of 1956, Secretary of State John Foster Dulles had tired of Nasser's international maneuverings, and he publicly withdrew American support from the Aswan project on July 19. Dulles pointed to the inability of the riparian states to reach an agreement and the failure of Egypt to devote sufficient economic resources to the project. Southern Senators in particular were pleased by this development, since they feared Egyptian cotton rivalry.

SOURCE: U.S. Department of State *Bulletin,* July 30, 1956. See p. 188.

DOCUMENT:

At the request of the Government of Egypt, the United States joined in December 1955 with the United Kingdom and with the World Bank in an offer to assist Egypt in the construction of a high dam on the Nile at Aswan. This project is one of great magnitude. It would require an estimated 12 to 16 years to complete at a total cost estimated at some $1,300,000,000, of which over $900,000,000 represents local currency requirements. It involves not merely the rights and interests of Egypt but of other states whose waters are contributory, including Sudan, Ethiopia, and Uganda.

The December offer contemplated an extension by the United States and United Kingdom of grant aid to help finance certain early phases of the work, the effects of which would be confined solely to Egypt, with the understanding that accomplishment of the project as a whole would require a satisfactory resolution of the question of Nile water rights. Another important consideration bearing upon the feasibility of the undertaking, and thus the practicability of American aid, was Egyptian readiness and ability to concentrate its economic resources upon this vast construction program.

Developments within the succeeding 7 months have not been favorable to the success of the project, and the U.S. Government has concluded that it is not feasible in present circumstances to participate in the project. Agreement by the riparian states has not been achieved, and the ability of Egypt to devote adequate resources to assure the project's success has become more uncertain than at the time the offer was made.

This decision in no way reflects or involves any alteration in the friendly relations of the Government and people of the United States towards the Government and people of Egypt.

The United States remains deeply interested in the welfare of the Egyptian people and in the development of the Nile. It is prepared to consider at an appropriate time and at the request of the riparian states what steps might be taken toward a more effective utilization of the water resources of the Nile for the benefit of the peoples of the region. Furthermore, the United States remains ready to assist Egypt in its effort to improve the economic condition of its people and is prepared, through its appropriate agencies, to discuss these matters within the context of funds appropriated by the Congress.

1956 President Eisenhower Mediates on President Nasser's Seizure of the Suez Canal

Eight days after Secretary of State Dulles withdrew U.S. financial support for the Aswan Dam, President Gamal Nasser retaliated by seizing the Suez Canal, whose international character had been defined by an 1888 convention. Officially, the United States had less of an interest in the Suez Canal than it had in the Panama Canal, but President Dwight

Eisenhower was nevertheless quite disturbed about Nasser's bold move. In a diary entry made during the following month, on August 8, Eisenhower discussed the history of the Suez Canal. But this series of events had yet to reach its climax. On October 31, the British and French launched a joint attack on the Suez Canal area, two days after the Israelis had begun an all-out military campaign against Egypt. Both the United States and the Soviet Union criticized these actions, as did the United Nations, and the Anglo–French–Israeli forces eventually withdrew from Egypt. The Suez Canal, however, remained closed temporarily, because sunken ships were blocking the channel.

SOURCE: Ferrell, Editor, *The Eisenhower Diaries*. See pp. 329–30.

DOCUMENT:

August 8, 1956

The Suez affair has a long and intricate background, and at this moment the outcome of the quarrel is so undetermined that it would be difficult indeed to predict what will probably happen.

Unlike the Panama Canal, which was built as a national undertaking by the United States under the terms of a bilateral treaty with Panama, the Suez Canal was built by an international group. There seems to have been felt the need for clarifying rights and privileges of the several nations in the use of the canal, and so in 1888 a convention or treaty was signed, among a group of nations (about ten, I think), which was left open for the purpose of permitting other nations to sign later should they so choose. That treaty, among other things, made the waterway an international one forever, open to the shipping of all countries both in peace and war.

The canal was originally constructed under a concession from Egypt, which expires in 1968, but the 1888 convention specifically provided that the international character will continue no matter what the future ownership or concession arrangements might be.

Originally, I believe the stock was held largely by Egypt and by Frenchmen, but during the course of the years Egyptian rulers sold theirs. In any event a large block was acquired by the British government. I am not certain, but it is possible that the British government may have owned some of the original stock. In any event, as of today the British own about 400,000 shares.

On the morning of July 27, Gamal Abdel Nasser, the president of Egypt, made a very inflammatory speech, in which he announced the nationalizing of the canal company. This meant that the Egyptian government took over the entire resources of the Suez canal company wherever they might be located. He also issued an extraordinary order to the effect that all people working for the canal would be required to continue in their present employment under penalty of imprisonment. A further statement indicated that he expected to realize something on the order of $100 million profit a year out of the canal and this undoubtedly meant a steep increase in canal tolls, since today after the payment to Egypt of the normal ground rental of some $17 million there is only about $35 million profit.

Another point in this connection is that the volume of traffic and the size of vessels is increasing so rapidly that very soon an extra $750 million must be spent to deepen and widen the canal.

Nasser said he was doing these things because of the refusal of the United States to help him build the Aswan Dam.

1957 The Eisenhower Doctrine for the Middle East

The Suez crisis of 1956 had far-reaching implications for American foreign policy, and broadened Dwight Eisenhower's margin of victory over Adlai Stevenson in the Presidential election held that November. On January 5, 1957, President Eisenhower submitted a proposal to Congress, under which U.S. military and economic assistance would be made available to any Communist-threatened Middle Eastern nation that requested it. There was an obvious parallel with the Formosa Resolution two years earlier. The Chicago Tribune dismissed the Eisenhower Doctrine as a "goofy design for foreign meddling," but during March the Senate nevertheless approved the proposal 72 to 19; the House 350 to 60. Sixteen Democratic Senators voted nay, as did eleven Senators from the South.

SOURCE: U.S. Department of State *Bulletin*, January 21, 1957. See pp. 86–87.

DOCUMENT:

There have been several Executive declarations made by the United States in relation to the Middle East. There is the Tripartite Declaration of May 25, 1950, followed by the Presidential assurance of October 31, 1950, to the King of Saudi Arabia. There is the Presidential declaration of April 9, 1956, that the United States will within constitutional means oppose any aggression in the area. There is our Declaration of November 29, 1956, that a threat to the territorial integrity or political independence of Iran, Iraq, Pakistan or Turkey would be viewed by the United States with the utmost gravity.

Nevertheless, weaknesses in the present situation and the increased danger from International Communism, convince me that basic United States policy should now find expression in joint action by the Congress and the Executive. Furthermore, our joint resolve should be so couched as to make it apparent that if need be our words will be backed by action.

The action which I propose would have the following features.

It would, first of all, authorize the United States to cooperate with and assist any nation or group of nations in the general area of the Middle East in the development of economic strength dedicated to the maintenance of national independence.

It would, in the second place, authorize the Executive to undertake in the same region programs of military assistance and cooperation with any nation or group of nations which desires such aid.

It would, in the third place, authorize such assistance and cooperation to include the employment of the armed forces of the United States to secure and protect the territorial integrity and political independence of such nations, requesting such aid, against overt armed aggression from any nation controlled by International Communism.

These measures would have to be consonant with the treaty obligations of the United States, including the Charter of the United Nations and with any action or recommendations of the United Nations. They would also, if armed attack occurs, be subject to the overriding authority of the United Nations Security Council in accordance with the Charter.

The present proposal would, in the fourth place, authorize the President to employ, for economic and defensive military purposes, sums available under the Mutual Security Act of 1954, as amended, without regard to existing limitations.

The legislation now requested should not include the authorization or appropriation of funds because I believe that, under the conditions I suggest, presently appropriated funds will be adequate for the balance of the present fiscal year ending June 30. I shall, however, seek in subsequent legislation the authorization of $200,000,000 to be available during each of the fiscal years 1958 and 1959 for discretionary use in the area, in addition to the other mutual security programs for the area hereafter provided for by the Congress.

In the situation now existing, the greatest risk, as is often the case, is that ambitious despots may miscalculate. If power-hungry Communists should either falsely or correctly estimate that the Middle East is inadequately defended, they might be tempted to use open measures of armed attack. If so, that would almost surely involve the United States in military action. I am convinced that the best insurance against this dangerous contingency is to make clear now our readiness to cooperate fully and freely with our friends of the Middle East in ways consonant with the purposes and principles of the United Nations. I intend promptly to send a special mission to the Middle East to explain the cooperation we are prepared to give.

1958 The United States Sends Troops into Lebanon

The first major test under the Eisenhower Doctrine occurred during the summer of 1958. There was a coup in Iraq on July 14 in which the pro-U.S. King and other governmental officials were killed, as well as a yet unrealized plot to overthrow the government of Jordan. A danger also existed, moreover, that President Nasser of the newly formed United Arab Republic (Egypt and Syria) might attempt to take over Lebanon. President Chamoun of Lebanon accordingly requested U.S. assistance, and President Eisenhower honored his request by sending in 14,000 troops. In his statement following the landing on July 15, Eisenhower emphasized the threat posed to the Middle East by the Communists rather than Egyptian imperialist maneuverings.

SOURCE: *Public Papers of the Presidents of the United States: Dwight D. Eisenhower 1958* (Washington: Government Printing Office, 1959). See pp. 553 and 555.

DOCUMENT:

Yesterday was a day of grave developments in the Middle East. In Iraq a highly organized military blow struck down on the duly constituted government and attempted to put in its place a community of Army officers. The attack was conducted with great brutality. Many of the leading personalities were beaten to death or hanged and their bodies dragged through the streets.

At about the same time there was discovered a highly organized plot to overthrow the lawful government of Jordan.

Warned and alarmed by these developments, President Chamoun of Lebanon sent me an urgent plea that the United States station some military units in Lebanon to evidence our concern for the independence of Lebanon, that little country, which itself has for about two months been subjected to civil strife. This has been actively fomented by Soviet and Cairo broadcasts and abetted and aided by substantial amounts of arms, money and personnel infiltrated into Lebanon across the Syrian border.

President Chamoun stated that without an immediate show of United States support, the Government of Lebanon would be unable to survive against the forces which had been set loose in the area.

The plea of President Chamoun was supported by the unanimous action of the Lebanese Cabinet.

After giving this plea earnest thought and after taking advice from leaders of both the Executive and Congressional branches of the government, I decided to comply with the plea of the Government of Lebanon. A few hours ago a battalion of United States Marines landed and took up stations in and about the city of Beirut.

The mission of these forces is to protect American lives—there are about 2500 Americans in Lebanon—and by their presence to assist the Government of Lebanon to preserve its territorial integrity and political independence.

Some will ask, does the stationing of some United States troops in Lebanon involve any interference in the internal affairs of Lebanon? The clear answer is "no."

First of all we have acted at the urgent plea of the Government of Lebanon, a government which has been freely elected by the people only a little over a year ago. It is entitled, as are we, to join in measures of collective security for self-defense. Such action, the United Nations Charter recognizes, is an "inherent right."

In the second place what we now see in the Middle East is the same pattern of conquest with which we became familiar during the period of 1945 to 1950. This involves taking over a nation by means of indirect aggression; that is, under the cover of a fomented civil strife the purpose is to put into domestic control those whose real loyalty is to the aggressor.

It was by such means that the Communists attempted to take over Greece in 1947. That effort was thwarted by the Truman Doctrine.

It was by such means that the Communists took over Czechoslovakia in 1948.

It was by such means that the Communists took over the mainland of China in 1949.

It was by such means that the Communists attempted to take over Korea and Indo China, beginning in 1950.

Last year, the Congress of the United States joined with the President to declare that "the United States regards as vital to the national interest and world peace the preservation of the independence and integrity of the nations of the Middle East."

I believe that the presence of the United States forces now being sent to Lebanon will have a stabilizing effect which will preserve the independence and integrity of Lebanon. It will also afford an increased measure of security to the thousands of Americans who reside in Lebanon.

We know that stability and well-being cannot be achieved purely by military measures. The economy of Lebanon has been gravely strained by civil strife. Foreign trade and tourist traffic have almost come to a standstill. The United States stands ready, under its Mutual Security Program, to cooperate with the Government of Lebanon to find ways to restore its shattered economy. Thus we shall help to bring back to Lebanon a peace which is not merely the absence of fighting but the well-being of the people.

1958 A Mob Attacks Vice President Richard Nixon's Motorcade at Caracas, Venezuela (1962)

Latin Americans long have experienced a love–hate relationship with the United States. At times they have needed our protection or assistance, yet they have resented the fact that they were dependent on their powerful neighbor to the North. This phenomenon, moreover, predated the growing power of the Communist movement in Latin America since World War II, but the latter obviously aggravated it. Thus, when Vice President Richard Nixon visited Caracas in 1958, he had to contend not only with resentment at the sanctuary granted to deposed dictator Pérez Jiménez and his hated Chief of Secret Police in the United States, but also a Communist-sponsored assassination plot. As Nixon points out in Six Crises, *the American government knew in advance that there probably would be trouble.*

SOURCE: Richard M. Nixon, *Six Crises* (Garden City: Doubleday and Company, 1962). See pp. 210–11.

DOCUMENT:

The report of an assassination plot in Venezuela came with a whole sheaf of background intelligence messages. But it was backed up with a report from Frank M. Berry, a former Secret Service agent who had become a principal adviser on security matters for Nicaragua. He sent word that his private intelligence sources had reported that a huge anti-American demonstration was being organized by a Communist-led student group in Caracas with an assassination attempt as the highlight of the plan. The day before we took off from Bogota for Caracas, I questioned Sherwood in detail with regard to these reports. Were these the regular run of rumors and threats? Or were they more serious? Sherwood's answer was that in either event we should and would take every precaution, especially in view of what had already happened in Lima.

He arranged to have the advance Secret Service agents, who had preceded us to Ecuador and Colombia to check security there, go on to Caracas rather than return to Washington as was customary. Thus we would have a twelve-man detail of Secret Service agents in Caracas while I was there instead of the usual three or four. At the same time, the U.S. Embassy in Caracas was told to prod the Venezuelan authorities into double-checking their security arrangements and to keep us posted. We received periodic reports from the Embassy up to the time we landed in Caracas and each one stated that the Venezuelan Government foresaw no serious trouble and was prepared to deal with any incidents which might arise.

On the eve of my departure for Caracas, the reporters traveling with me learned of the assassination reports and asked me for comment. I told them that such rumors were "just one of those things" which had occurred many times in the past and that I would not be frightened away by such obvious threats.

Actually, I had sent word that the Venezuelan Government should clearly understand that they were free to withdraw their invitation if they felt at all unable to handle the security arrangements incumbent upon the host country. The night before our departure for Caracas, our Embassy there sent me this message: "Venezuelan government security agencies are confident of their ability to handle the situation but are increasing security measure to such an extent that the advance representatives feel the Vice President might believe he is being overguarded."

My decision to go to Caracas as scheduled was not an act of "bravery." Security arrangements there were outside my domain and I relied upon Security Service and intelligence estimates. It was far more significant to me that the State Department considered Venezuela potentially the most important stop of the entire South American tour. In January, only five months earlier, the ten-year-old dictatorship of Pérez Jiménez, second only to Perón in power and entrenchment, had been overthrown by revolution. Pérez Jiménez, who was probably the most hated dictator in all of Latin America, had fled with his despised Chief of Secret Police, Pedro Estrada, to exile in the United States.

There was plenty of evidence that the Communists intended to demonstrate vociferously during my visit. But Charles R. Burroughs, the Minister-Counselor of our Embassy in Venezuela, reported to me on our flight from Bogota to Caracas that there would be tremendous numbers of friendly people who also would demonstrate their warm regard for the United States. He showed me various newspaper reports about my impending visit. One which I remember was the *Tribune Popular*, the Communist Party daily. This paper contained a particularly vicious attack on the United States and a front-page photograph of me, doctored so that my teeth looked like fangs and my face like that of a war-mongering fiend. I was to see that retouched photograph on hundreds of placards during my two-day visit to Caracas.

Yet, at the time, neither our Embassy staff nor our intelligence people in Venezuela were able to discover that the Communist high command in South America had made a high-level decision to regain the ground they had lost in Lima by mounting a massive pay-off demonstration in Caracas. It was the scope of the effort which our people failed to assess properly.

Security arrangements in Caracas were checked and rechecked through the night prior to my arrival. At midnight, eleven hours before my plane was to put down at the Caracas airport, our Embassy advised that the government authority had "everything under control." A rumor of a plot to poison me had caused a switch in the caterer for the buffet reception in my honor. At 3 a.m. Sherwood got final word: the Caracas authorities had made still another check of security arrangements and they definitely wanted me to come.

1959 Vice President Nixon's Confrontation with Soviet Leader Nikita Khrushchev (1962)

A year after the incident at Caracas, Vice President Nixon was involved in another traumatic experience: his sharp verbal exchange with Soviet leader Nikita Khrushchev at the American Exhibition in Moscow. This culminated in the so-called kitchen conference, during which Nixon and Khrushchev debated the relative merits of Communism and capitalism. Their dialogue clearly demonstrates the serious problems involved in establishing common objectives for the United States and the Soviet Union.

SOURCE: Nixon, *Six Crises*, pp. 254–57.

DOCUMENT:

As at our previous conference, I decided this was not the time to take him on. I tried to change the subject to color television, and the other consumer items which were on display at the American Exhibition. I urged that we needed a free exchange of ideas between our two countries. "You must not be afraid of ideas," I said, "After all, you don't know everything..."

"If I don't know everything," he interrupted, "you don't know anything about Communism—except fear of it."

Still determined not to be provoked or goaded into saying anything which could be misinterpreted, I tried again to change the tone of the conversation, but he would have none of it. Constantly interrupting me, he insisted that I was a lawyer and he was a coal miner, but that he still could outargue me on Communism vs. capitalism.

Consequently, as we walked by a model American grocery store, I commented, "You may be interested to know that my father owned a small general store in California, and all the Nixon boys worked there while going to school." Khrushchev with a wave of his arms snorted, "Oh, all shopkeepers are thieves." But this one I did not let pass. "Thieving happens everywhere," I responded. "Even in the store I visited this morning, I saw people weighing food after they had bought it from the State." This time it was Khrushchev who changed the subject.

Then we came to the center attraction of the exhibition, a model American home, fully furnished and equipped with all our modern conveniences. The Soviet press had focused their ridicule on this model home during the past week, saying that it was no more typical of a worker's home in the United States than the Taj Mahal was typical in India or Buckingham Palace in Great Britain. Khrushchev and I walked up the center hall of the model home, looking into the exposed rooms, and we stopped at the kitchen.

And here we had our famous "kitchen conference" or, as some reporters put it, the "Sokolniki Summit." This conversation, incidentally, was not carried on television in the United States but was reported in the newspapers.

"On political differences, we will never agree," Khrushchev said, again cutting in on me. "If I follow you, I will be led astray from Mikoyan. He likes spicy soups and I don't. But that doesn't mean we differ."

I tried again to point up our belief in freedom of choice, and I put in a plea for more exchanges between our two countries to bring about a better understanding. But Khrushchev did not want to debate me on my grounds. He changed the subject back to washing machines, arguing that it was better to have one model than many. I listened to his long harangue on washing machines, realizing full well that he was not switching arguments by chance or accident; he was trying to throw me off balance.

"Isn't it better to be talking about the relative merits of our washing machines than the relative strength of our rockets?" I said at the end of his long speech. "Isn't this the kind of competition you want?"

At this he gave the appearance of turning angry and, jamming his thumb into my chest, he shouted: "Yes, that's the kind of competition we want, but your generals say we must compete in rockets. Your generals say they are so powerful they can destroy us. We can also show you something so that you will know the Russian spirit. We are strong, we can beat you."

I pointed my finger at him and said:

"To me, you are strong and we are strong. In some ways, you are stronger than we are. In others, we are stronger. But to me it seems that in this day and age to argue who is the stronger completely misses the point...No one should ever use his strength to put another in the position where he in effect has an ultimatum. For us to argue who is the stronger misses the point. If war comes we both lose."

"You raised the point," he went on. "We want peace and friendship with all nations, especially with America."

I could sense now that he wanted to call an end to the argument. And I certainly did not want to take the responsibility for continuing it publicly. We both had had enough. I said, "We want peace too."

He answered, "Yes, I believe that."

And so we ended our discussion on the underlying question of the whole debate—the possibility of easing Cold War tensions at the then current Four Power Conference in Geneva.

1960 The U-2 Incident: The Downing of an American Spy Plane over the Soviet Union

One of the more clandestine aspects of the Cold War between the United States and the Soviet Union was the intelligence gathering over flights of each other's territory in time of peace. Technically, this violated international law. On May 1, 1960, the Russians shot down an American plane approximately 1,200 miles inside the Soviet Union and captured its pilot, Francis Gary Powers, whom they later released. This gave the Russians an excuse to withdraw from a long-planned summit conference of world leaders. But the Soviet Union's hands were hardly clean, since their espionage network had bugged the American Embassy in Moscow, and the Security Council of the United Nations failed to condemn the United States. President Dwight Eisenhower could have blamed the episode on some subordinate, but he instead accepted full responsibility for it in a White House press release dated May 11.

SOURCE: U.S. Department of State *Bulletin*, May 30, 1960. See pp. 851–52.

DOCUMENT:

I have made some notes from which I want to talk to you about this U-2 incident.

A full statement about this matter has been made by the State Department, and there have been several statesmanlike remarks by leaders of both parties.

For my part, I supplement what the Secretary of State has had to say with the following four main points. After that, I shall have nothing further to say—for the simple reason I can think of nothing to add that might be useful at this time.

First point is this: the need for intelligence-gathering activities.

No one wants another Pearl Harbor. This means that we must have knowledge of military forces and preparations around the world, especially those capable of massive surprise attack.

Secrecy in the Soviet Union makes this essential. In most of the world no large-scale attack could be prepared in secret. But in the Soviet Union there is a fetish of secrecy and concealment. This is a major cause of international tension and uneasiness today. Our deterrent must never be placed in jeopardy. The safety of the whole free world demands this.

As the Secretary of State pointed out in his recent statement, ever since the beginning of my administration I have issued directives to gather, in very feasible ways, the information required to protect the United States and the free world against surprise attack and to enable them to make effective preparations for defense.

My second point: the nature of intelligence-gathering activities.

These have a special and secret character. They are, so to speak, "below the surface" activities.

They are secret because they must circumvent measures designed by other countries to protect secrecy of military preparations.

They are divorced from the regular, visible agencies of government, which stay clear of operational involvement in specific detailed activities.

These elements operate under broad directives to seek and gather intelligence short of the use of force, with operations supervised by responsible officials within this area of secret activities.

We do not use our Army, Navy, or Air Force for this purpose, first, to avoid any possibility of the use of force in connection with these activities and, second, because our military forces, for obvious reasons, cannot be given latitude under broad directives but must be kept under strict control in every detail.

These activities have their own rules and methods of concealment, which seek to mislead and obscure—just as in the Soviet allegations there are many discrepancies. For example, there is some reason to believe that the plane in question was not shot down at high altitude. The normal agencies of our Government are unaware of these specific activities or of the special efforts to conceal them.

Third point: How should we view all of this activity?

It is a distasteful but vital necessity.

We prefer and work for a different kind of world—and a different way of obtaining the information essential to confidence and effective deterrence. Open societies, in the day of present weapons, are the only answer.

This was the reason for my open-skies proposal in 1955, which I was ready instantly to put into effect, to permit aerial observation over the United States and the Soviet Union which would assure that no surprise attack was being prepared against anyone. I shall bring up the open-skies proposal again at Paris, since it is a means of ending concealment and suspicion.

My final point is that we must not be distracted from the real issues of the day by what is an incident or a symptom of the world situation today.

This incident has been given great propaganda exploitation. The emphasis given to a flight of an unarmed, nonmilitary plane can only reflect a fetish of secrecy.

1960 Dwight Eisenhower Offers a Program for Africa to the United Nations General Assembly

By 1960, Africa was rapidly making the transition from colonial status to independence. The United States had frequently sided with its NATO allies in Western Europe whenever a dispute arose between a European nation and its African colony. But this policy had become increasingly difficult for the American government. On September 22, 1960, President Dwight Eisenhower presented a five-point program for Africa to the General Assembly of the United Nations. In this address, he emphasized such points as non-interference in another country's internal affairs, the avoidance of an arms race, international assistance for long-term development programs, and aid to education.

SOURCE: U.S. Department of State *Bulletin*, October 10, 1960. See pp. 552–53.

DOCUMENT:

If the United Nations system is successfully subverted in Africa, the world will be on its way back to the traditional exercise of power politics, in which small countries will be used as pawns by aggressive major powers. Any nation, seduced by glittering promises into becoming a cat's-paw for an imperialistic power, thereby undermines the United Nations and places in jeopardy the independence of itself and all others. It is imperative that the international community protect the newly emerging nations of Africa from outside pressures that threaten their independence and their sovereign rights.

First: A pledge by all countries represented at this Assembly to respect the African peoples' right to choose their own way of life and to determine for themselves the course they choose to follow. And this pledge would involve three specific commitments:

To refrain from intervening in these new nations' internal affairs-by subversion, force, propaganda, or any other means;

To refrain from generating disputes between the states of this area or from encouraging them to wasteful and dangerous competition in armaments;

Second: The United Nations should be prepared to help the African countries maintain their security without wasteful and dangerous competition in armaments.

I hope that the African states will use existing or establish new regional machinery in order to avert an arms race in this area. In so doing they would help to spare their continent the ravages which the excesses of chauvinism have elsewhere inflicted in the past. If, through concerted effort, these nations can choke off competition in armaments, they can give the whole world a welcome lesson in international relations.

Third: We should all support the United Nations response to emergency needs in the Republic of the Congo which the Secretary-General has shown such skill in organizing. I hope that states represented here will pledge substantial resources to this international program and agree that it should be the preferred means of meeting the Congo's emergency needs. The United States supports the establishment of a United Nations fund for the Congo. We are prepared to join other countries by contributing substantially for immediate emergency needs to the $100-million program that the Secretary-General is proposing.

Fourth: The United Nations should help newly developing African countries shape their long-term modernization programs. To this end:

The United Nations Special Fund and Expanded Technical Assistance Program should be increased so that in combination they can reach their annual $100-million goal in 1961. The Special Fund's functions should be expanded so that it can assist countries in planning economic development.

The United Nations operational and executive personnel program for making available trained administrators to newly developing countries should be expanded and placed on a permanent basis. The United States is prepared to join other countries in contributing increased funds for this program, and for the Special Fund, and for the United Nations Technical Assistance Program.

The World Bank and International Monetary Fund should be encouraged increasingly to provide counsel to the developing countries of Africa through missions and resident advisers. We should also look forward to appropriate and timely financial assistance from these two multilateral financial sources as the emerging countries qualify for their aid.

Of course, many forms of aid will be needed: both public and private, and on a bilateral and multilateral basis. For this assistance to be most effective it must be related to the basic problems and changing needs of the African countries themselves.

Fifth: As the final element of this program I propose an all-out United Nations effort to help African countries launch such educational activities as they may wish to undertake.

If the African states should wish to send large numbers of their citizens for training abroad under this program, my country would be glad to set up a special commission to cooperate with the United Nations in arranging to accommodate many more of these students in our institutions of learning.

American Diplomacy under Kennedy, Johnson, and Dean Rusk

46

1960 Senator John Kennedy's Approach to Foreign Policy: A Twelve-point Agenda

In 1960, the Democrats nominated the youthful Senator John Kennedy of Massachusetts for President. His father Joseph had been Ambassador to Great Britain on the eve of World War II. Kennedy had served on the Senate Foreign Relations Committee while a member of the upper house, and in the mid-1950s he began championing the Algerian independence movement, which set him aside from those officials in Washington who usually sided with France and the other European colonial powers. On June 14, 1960, J.F.K. gave an important speech in the U.S. Senate, in which he set forth a twelve-point foreign policy agenda.

SOURCE: John F. Kennedy, *The Strategy of Peace* (New York: Harper and Brothers, 1960). See pp. 4–10.

DOCUMENT:

First, we must make invulnerable a nuclear retaliatory power second to none—by making possible now a stop-gap air alert and base dispersal program—and by stepping up development and production of the ultimate missiles that can close the gap and will not be wiped out in a surprise attack—Polaris, Minuteman and long-range air-to-ground missiles—meanwhile increasing our production of Atlas missiles, hardening our bases and improving our continental defense and warning systems.

Second—We must regain the ability to intervene effectively and swiftly in any limited war anywhere in the world—augmenting, modernizing and providing increased mobility and versatility for the conventional forces and weapons of the Army and Marine Corps.

Third—We must rebuild NATO into a viable and consolidated military force, capable of deterring any kind of attack, unified in weaponry and responsibility.

Fourth—We must, in collaboration with Western Europe and Japan, greatly increase the flow of capital to the under-developed areas of Asia, Africa, the Middle East and Latin America—frustrating the Communists hopes for chaos in those nations—enabling emerging nations to achieve economic as well as political independence—and closing the dangerous gap that is now widening between our living standards and theirs.

Fifth—We must reconstruct our relations with the Latin–American democracies—bringing them into full Western partnership—working through a strengthened Organization of American States—increasing the flow of technical assistance, development capital, private investment, exchange students and agricultural surpluses, perhaps through the large-scale "Operation Pan-America," which has been proposed by the President of Brazil—and pursuing practical agreements for stabilizing commodity prices, trade routes and currency convertibility.

Sixth—We must formulate, with both imagination and restraint, a new approach to the Middle East—not pressing our case so hard that the Arabs feel their neutrality and nationalism are threatened, but accepting those forces and seeking to help channel them along constructive lines, while at the same time trying to hasten the inevitable Arab acceptance of the permanence of Israel.

Seventh—We must greatly increase our efforts to encourage the newly emerging nations of the vast continent of Africa—to persuade them that they do not have to turn to Moscow for the guidance and friendship they so desperately need—to help them achieve the economic progress on which the welfare of their people and their ability to resist Communist subversion depend.

Eighth—We must plan a long-range solution to the problems of Berlin. We must show no uncertainty over our determination to defend Berlin—but we must realize that a solution to the problems of the beleaguered city is only possible in the context of a solution of the problems of Germany, and indeed, the problems of all Europe.

Ninth—We must prepare and hold in readiness more flexible and realistic tools for use in Eastern Europe. The policy of "liberation," proudly proclaimed eight years ago, has proved to be a snare and a delusion.

Tenth—We must reassess a China policy which has failed dismally to move toward its principal objective of weakening Communist rule in the mainland—a policy which has failed to prevent a steady growth in Communist strength—and a policy which offers no real solution to the problems of a militant China.

Eleventh—We must begin to develop new, workable programs for peace and the control of arms. We have been unwilling to plan for disarmament, and unable to offer creative proposals of our own, always leaving the initiative in the hands of the Russians.

Twelfth and finally—We must work to build the stronger America on which our ultimate ability to defend the free world depends.

1961 J.F.K. Establishes the Peace Corps

During the 1960 Presidential campaign, Democratic nominee John F. Kennedy proposed that Americans be sent abroad to help the underdeveloped nations of the world in a number of areas: agriculture, education, sanitation, irrigation, and so forth. On March 1, 1961, J.F.K. issued an executive order establishing a Peace Corps program on a temporary pilot basis and justified his action in a separate message to Congress, excerpts from which follow. A hard-to-convince Congress made the program permanent in September, and one might well argue that in the long run it proved more successful than the more elaborate Alliance for Progress. There were no roll-calls on the two key Senate votes, but the two House votes revealed only marginal Republican support.

SOURCE: U.S. Department of State *Bulletin,* March 20, 1961. See pp. 401–3.

DOCUMENT:

Throughout the world the people of the newly developing nations are struggling for economic and social progress which reflects their deepest desires. Our own freedom, and the future of freedom around the world, depend, in a very real sense, on their ability to build growing and independent nations where men can live in dignity, liberated from the bonds of hunger, ignorance, and poverty.

One of the greatest obstacles to the achievement of this goal is the lack of trained men and women with the skill to teach the young and assist in the operation of development projects—men and women with the capacity to cope with the demands of swiftly evolving economies, and with the dedication to put that capacity to work in the villages, the mountains, the towns, and the factories of dozens of struggling nations.

The vast tasks of economic development urgently requires skilled people to do the work of the society—to help teach in the schools, construct development projects, demonstrate modern methods of sanitation in the villages, and perform a hundred other tasks calling for training and advanced knowledge.

To meet this urgent need for skilled manpower we are proposing the establishment of a Peace Corps—an organization which will recruit and train American volunteers, sending them abroad to work with the people of other nations.

This organization will differ from existing assistance programs in that its members will supplement technical advisers by offering the specific skills needed by developing nations if they are to put technical advice to work. They will help provide the skilled manpower necessary to carry out the development projects planned by the host governments, acting at a working level and serving at great personal sacrifice. There is little doubt that the number of those who wish to serve will be far greater than our capacity to absorb them.

Among the specific programs to which Peace Corps members can contribute are teaching in primary and secondary schools, especially as part of national English language teaching programs; participation in the worldwide program of malaria eradication; instruction and operation of public health and sanitation projects; aiding in village development through school construction and other programs; increasing rural agricultural productivity by assisting local farmers to use modern implements and techniques. The initial emphasis of these programs will be on teaching. Thus the Peace Corps members will be an effective means of implementing the development programs of the host countries—programs which our technical assistance operations have helped to formulate.

The Peace Corps will not be limited to the young, or to college graduates. All Americans who are qualified will be welcome to join this effort. But undoubtedly the corps will be made up primarily of young people as they complete their formal education.

Peace Corps personnel will be made available to developing nations in the following ways:

1. Through private voluntary agencies carrying on international assistance programs.
2. Through overseas programs of colleges and universities.
3. Through assistance programs of international agencies.
4. Through assistance programs of the U.S. Government.
5. Through new programs which the Peace Corps directly administers.

In all instances the men and women of the Peace Corps will go only to those countries where their services and skills are genuinely needed and desired. U.S. operations missions, supplemented where necessary by special Peace Corps teams, will consult with leaders in foreign countries in order to determine where Peace Corpsmen are needed, the types of job they can best fill, and the number of people who can be usefully employed. The Peace Corps will not supply personnel for marginal undertakings without a sound economic or social justification. In furnishing assistance through the Peace Corps careful regard will be given to the particular country's developmental priorities.

The benefits of the Peace Corps will not be limited to the countries in which it serves. Our own young men and women will be enriched by the experience of living and working in foreign lands. They will have acquired new skills and experience which will aid them in their future careers and add to our own country's supply of trained personnel and teachers. They will return better able to assume the responsibilities of American citizenship and with greater understanding of our global responsibilities.

1961 John Kennedy Proposes an Alliance for Progress for Latin America

Although Latin America largely had thrown off its European colonial yoke by the end of the Monroe Administration (1825), over the years its economic, social, and educational progress had been inadequate. With the Communist threat manifesting itself in such New

World countries as Guatemala and Cuba during the 1950s, clearly the time was at hand for a large-scale anti-Communist program to transform Latin America. President John Kennedy accordingly made public a ten-point scheme early in his administration. This was essentially a Marshall Plan for Latin America, and it would cost $20 billion over a ten-year period, most of it coming from the United States. Congress approved the initial $500 million appropriation in May, 1961; the House by a 329 to 83 vote and the Senate by a 41 to 26 one, with no less than thirty-three abstentions in the upper house. Twenty Republican Senators voted nay.

SOURCE: U.S. Department of State *Bulletin*, April 3, 1961. See pp. 472–73.

DOCUMENT:

Throughout Latin America—a continent rich in resources and in the spiritual and cultural achievements of its people—millions of men and women suffer the daily degradations of hunger and poverty. They lack decent shelter or protection from disease. Their children are deprived of the education or the jobs which are the gateway to a better life. And each day the problems grow more urgent. Population growth is outpacing economic growth, low living standards are even further endangered, and discontent—the discontent of a people who know that abundance and the tools of progress are at last within their reach—that discontent is growing. In the words of Jose Figueres, "once dormant peoples are struggling upward toward the sun, toward a better life."

If we are to meet a problem so staggering in its dimensions, our approach must itself be equally bold, an approach consistent with the majestic concept of Operation Pan America. Therefore I have called on all the people of the hemisphere to join in a new Alliance for Progress—*Alianza para Progreso*—a vast cooperative effort, unparalleled in magnitude and nobility of purpose, to satisfy the basic needs of the American people for homes, work and land, health and schools—*techo, trabajo y tierra, salud y escuela.*

First, I propose that the American Republics begin on a vast new 10-year plan for the Americas, a plan to transform the 1960's into an historic decade of democratic progress. These 10 years will be the years of maximum progress, maximum effort—the years when the greatest obstacles must be overcome, the years when the need for assistance will be the greatest.

Secondly, I will shortly request a ministerial meeting of the Inter-American Economic and Social Council, a meeting at which we can begin the massive planning effort which will be at the heart of the Alliance for Progress.

Third, I have this evening signed a request to the Congress for $500 million as a first step in fulfilling the Act of Bogota. This is the first large-scale inter-American effort—instituted by my predecessor President Eisenhower—to attack the social barriers which block economic progress. The money will be used to combat illiteracy, improve the productivity and use of their land, wipe out disease, attack archaic tax and land-tenure structures, provide educational opportunities, and offer a broad range of projects designed to make the benefits of increasing abundance available to all. We will begin to commit these funds as soon as they are appropriated.

Fourth, we must support all economic integration which is a genuine step toward larger markets and greater competitive opportunity. The fragmentation of Latin American economics is a serious barrier to industrial growth. Projects such as the Central American common market and free-trade areas in South America can help to remove these obstacles.

Fifth, the United States is ready to cooperate in serious, case-by-case examinations of commodity market problems. Frequent violent changes in commodity prices seriously injure the economies of many Latin American countries, draining their resources and stultifying their growth. Together we must find practical methods of bringing an end to this pattern.

Sixth, we will immediately step up our food-for-peace emergency program, help to establish food reserves in areas of recurrent drought, and help provide school lunches for children and offer feed grains for use in rural development. For hungry men and women cannot wait for economic discussions or diplomatic meetings; their need is urgent, and their hunger rests heavily on the conscience of their fellow men.

Seventh, all the people of the hemisphere must be allowed to share in the expanding wonders of science—wonders which have captured man's imagination, challenged the powers of his mind, and given him the tools for rapid progress. I invite Latin American scientists to work with us in new projects in fields such as medicine and agriculture, physics and astronomy, and desalinization, and to help plan for regional research laboratories in these and other fields, and to strengthen cooperation between American universities and laboratories.

Eighth, we must rapidly expand the training of those needed to man the economies of rapidly developing countries. This means expanded technical training programs, for which the Peace Corps, for example, will be available when needed. It also means assistance to Latin American universities, graduate schools, and research institutes.

Ninth, we reaffirm our pledge to come to the defense of any American nation whose independence is endangered. As confidence in the collective security system of the OAS [Organization of American States] spreads, it will be possible to devote to constructive use a major share of those resources now spent on the instruments of war. Even now, as the Government of Chile has said, the time has come to take the first steps toward sensible limitations of arms. And the new generation of military leaders has shown an increasing awareness that armies can not only defend their countries—they can, as we have learned through our own Corps of Engineers, help to build them.

Tenth, we invite our friends in Latin America to contribute to the enrichment of life and culture in the United States. We need teachers of your literature and history and tradition, opportunities for our young people to study in your universities, access to your music, your art, and the thought of your great philosophers. For we know we have much to learn.

With steps such as these we propose to complete the revolution of the Americas, to build a hemisphere where all men can hope for a suitable standard of living and all can live out their lives in dignity and in freedom.

1961 The New York *Times* Attacks Kennedy for Lying About the Bay of Pigs Invasion

At the beginning of 1959, a group of Cuban revolutionaries led by Fidel Castro overthrew the long-entrenched but now disintegrating Batista regime. Fulgencio Batista had been strongly pro-U.S., but the left-leaning Castro eventually proclaimed himself to be a Marxist– Leninist. Even before John Kennedy took office, Dwight Eisenhower had approved a scheme under which a group of Cuban exiles would attempt to take back their homeland with the assistance of the Central Intelligence Agency. John Kennedy made the mistake of implementing the plan, and then not supporting the Cuban landings with American air cover. The result was a fiasco for the invaders. The New York Times *was scathing in its denunciation of Kennedy, whom it accused of lying.*

SOURCE: "The Right Not to Be Lied To," in New York *Times*, May 10, 1961. See p. 44.

DOCUMENT:

The Cuban tragedy has raised a domestic question that is likely to come up again and again until it is solved. The cause may be something that is happening in Laos, in Central Africa or in Latin America, but the question remains the same: is a democratic government in an open society such as ours ever justified in deceiving its own people?

In this period of cold war, with its nightmares of hot war just around the corner, there must be secrets kept from the American public in order to preserve them from our adversaries. The Central Intelligence Agency is specifically authorized to "correlate and evaluate intelligence relating to the national security and provide for the appropriate dissemination of such intelligence within the Government." The existence of the cold war implies secret operations on our side in self-defense against the normal subversive operations of the other side that cannot be revealed, nor would the responsible American press want to reveal them.

But the Government has a duty also. Neither prudence nor ethics can justify any administration in telling the public things that are not so. A year ago this month, when an American plane was shot down over Russia, the State Department said that "there was no deliberate attempt to violate Soviet space and there never has been." This wasn't true. It was not even usefully untrue, for the Russians already held the pilot, Francis Gary Powers, and had secured a confession from him.

The recent Cuban episode has not been so clear. As has been reported in this and other newspapers, there is no doubt that men were recruited in this country for the projected attack on Cuba. The fact was well known in and around Miami prior to the attack and could not be kept secret from Castro's own spies.

What some leaders of our Government stated in this regard did not square with the facts, they would have done better to remain silent. A democracy—our democracy—cannot be lied to. This is one of the factors that make it more precious, more delicate, more difficult and yet essentially stronger than any other form of government in the world.

The basic principle involved is that of confidence. A dictatorship can get along without an informed public opinion. A democracy cannot. Not only is it unethical to deceive one's own public as part of a system of deceiving an adversary government; it is also foolish. Our executive officers and our national legislators are elected on stated days, but actually they must be re-elected day by day by popular understanding and support.

This is what is signified by a government of consent.

1962 John Kennedy Demands the Withdrawal of Soviet Offensive Missiles from Cuba

After the Bay of Pigs invasion, Fidel Castro became increasingly concerned about another U.S. attack on his island, and accordingly sought additional military hardware from the Soviet Union to supplement Cuba's army, currently the second largest in the Western Hemisphere. In mid-October, the American government denounced the presence in Cuba of a number of missile launching pads, which obviously posed a threat to the cities of the United States. John Kennedy reacted strongly to this menace. He made a televised address to the nation on October 22, 1962 about the deteriorating Cuban situation, and then imposed a quarantine on all vessels attempting to transfer offensive weapons to Cuba. J.F.K. received the unanimous support of the Organization of American States, but there followed several days of great international tension. Fortunately for world peace, the Soviet Union did not attempt to challenge the U.S. blockade, and Nikita Khrushchev eventually removed the Russian missiles from Cuba.

SOURCE: U.S. Department of State *Bulletin*, November 12, 1962. See pp. 715–16 and 718.

DOCUMENT:

This Government, as promised, has maintained the closest surveillance of the Soviet military buildup on the island of Cuba. Within the past week unmistakable evidence has established the fact that a series of offensive missile sites is now in preparation on that imprisoned island. The purpose of these bases can be none other than to provide a nuclear strike capability against the Western Hemisphere.

Upon receiving the first preliminary hard information of this nature last Tuesday morning [October 16] at 9:00 a.m., I directed that our surveillance be stepped up. And having now confirmed and completed our evaluation of the evidence and our decision on a course of action, this Government feels obliged to report this new crisis to you in fullest detail.

The characteristics of these new missile sites indicate two distinct types of installations. Several of them include medium-range ballistic missiles capable of carrying a nuclear warhead for a distance of more than 1,000 nautical miles. Each of these missiles, in short, is capable of striking Washington, D.C., the Panama Canal, Cape Canaveral, Mexico City, or any other city in the southeastern part of the United States, in Central America, or in the Caribbean area.

Additional sites not yet completed appear to be designed for intermediate-range ballistic missiles capable of traveling more than twice as far—and thus capable of striking most of the major cities in the Western Hemisphere, ranging as far north as Hudson Bay, Canada, and as far south as Lima, Peru. In addition, jet bombers, capable of carrying nuclear weapons, are now being uncrated and assembled in Cuba, while the necessary air bases are being prepared.

This urgent transformation of Cuba into an important strategic base—by the presence of these large, long-range, and clearly offensive weapons of sudden mass destruction—constitutes an explicit threat to the peace and security of all the Americas, in flagrant and deliberate defiance of the Rio Pact of 1949, the traditions of this nation and hemisphere, the Joint Resolution of the 87th Congress, the Charter of the United Nations, and my own public warnings to the Soviets on September 4 and 13.

This action also contradicts the repeated assurances of Soviet spokesmen, both publicly and privately delivered, that the arms buildup in Cuba would retain its original defensive character and that the Soviet Union had no need or desire to station strategic missiles on the territory of any other nation.

Acting, therefore, in the defense of our own security and of the entire Western Hemisphere, and under the authority entrusted to me by the Constitution as endorsed by the resolution of the Congress, I have directed that the following *initial* steps be taken immediately:

First: To halt this offensive buildup, a strict quarantine on all offensive military equipment under shipment to Cuba is being initiated. All ships of any kind bound for Cuba from whatever nation or port will, if found to contain cargoes of offensive weapons, be turned back. This quarantine will be extended, if needed, to other types of cargo and carriers. We are not at this time, however, denying the necessities of life as the Soviets attempted to do in their Berlin blockade of 1948.

Second: I have directed the continued and increased close surveillance of Cuba and its military buildup. The Foreign Ministers of the OAS [Organization of American States] in their communique of October 3 rejected secrecy on such matters in this hemisphere. Should these offensive military preparations continue, thus increasing the threat to the hemisphere, further action will be justified. I have directed the Armed Forces to prepare for any eventualities; and I trust that, in the interest of both the Cuban people and the Soviet technicians at the sites, the hazards to all concerned of continuing this threat will be recognized.

Third: It shall be the policy of this nation to regard any nuclear missile launched from Cuba against any nation in the Western Hemisphere as an attack by the Soviet Union on the United States, requiring a full retaliatory response upon the Soviet Union.

Fourth: As a necessary military precaution I have reinforced our base at Guantanamo, evacuated today the dependents of our personnel there, and ordered additional military units to be on a standby alert basis.

Fifth: We are calling tonight for an immediate meeting of the Organ of Consultation, under the Organization of American States, to consider this threat to hemispheric security and to invoke articles 6 and 8 of the Rio Treaty in support of all necessary action. The United States Charter allows for regional security arrangements—and the nations of this hemisphere decided long ago against the military presence of outside powers. Our other allies around the world have also been alerted.

Sixth: Under the Charter of the United Nations, we are asking tonight that an emergency meeting of the Security Council be convoked without delay to take action against this latest Soviet threat to world peace. Our resolution will call for the prompt dismantling and withdrawal of all offensive weapons in Cuba, under the supervision of U.N. observers, before the quarantine can be lifted.

Seventh and finally: I call upon Chairman Khrushchev to halt and eliminate this clandestine, reckless, and provocative threat to world peace and to stable relations between our two nations. I call upon him further to abandon this course of world domination and to join in an historic effort to end the perilous arms race and transform the history of man.

1962 Attorney General Robert Kennedy on the Cuban Missile Crisis (1969)

Despite J.F.K.'s bold public statements and actions with respect to the presence of Soviet missiles in Cuba, there was an absence of unanimity behind the scenes at the White House as to the proper course of action. An invasion of the island was a possibility, but a poll published on the same day as Kennedy's speech revealed that 90 percent of the American people opposed this drastic step. One reason why J.F.K. opted for a naval blockade instead of an air attack was that the latter would not necessarily destroy all of the missile sites and nuclear weapons. The dovish Adlai Stevenson unsuccessfully proposed that the United States give up its naval base at Guantanamo Bay in southeastern Cuba, in return for the Soviets withdrawing their missiles. These deliberations were discussed at length in Attorney General Robert Kennedy's memoirs of the event.

SOURCE: Robert Kennedy, *Thirteen Days: A Memoir of the Cuban Missile Crisis* (New York: W.W. Norton and Company, 1969). See pp. 47–50.

DOCUMENT:

We met all day Friday and Friday night. Then again early Saturday morning we were back at the State Department. I talked to the President several times on Friday. He was hoping to be able to meet with us early enough to decide on a course of action and then broadcast it to the nation Sunday night.

The meeting went on until ten minutes after five. Convened as a formal meeting of the National Security Council, it was a larger group of people who met, some of whom had not participated in the deliberations up to that time. Bob McNamara presented the arguments for the blockade; others presented the arguments for the military attack.

The discussion, for the most part, was able and organized, although, like all meetings of this kind, certain statements were made as accepted truisms, which I, at least, thought were of questionable validity. One member of the Joint Chiefs of Staff, for example, argued that we could use nuclear weapons, on the basis that our adversaries would use theirs against us in an attack. I thought, as I listened, of the many times that I had heard the military take positions which, if wrong, had the advantage that no one would be around at the end to know.

The President made his decision that afternoon in favor of the blockade. There was one final meeting the next morning, with General Walter C. Sweeney, Jr., Commander in Chief of the Tactical Air Command, who told the President that even a major surprise air attack could not be certain of destroying all the missile sites and nuclear weapons in Cuba. That ended the small, lingering doubt that might still have remained in his mind. It had worried him that a blockade would not remove the missiles—now it was clear that an attack could not accomplish that task completely, either.

The strongest argument against the all-out military attack, and one no one could answer to his satisfaction, was that a surprise attack would erode if not destroy the moral position of the United States throughout the world.

Adlai Stevenson had come from New York to attend the meeting Saturday afternoon, as he had attended several of the Ex Comm meetings. He had always been dubious about the air strike, but at the Saturday meeting he strongly advocated what he had only tentatively suggested to me a few days before—namely, that we make it clear to the Soviet Union that if it withdrew its missiles from Cuba, we would be willing to withdraw our missiles from Turkey and Italy and give up our naval base at Guantanamo Bay.

There was an extremely strong reaction from some of the participants to his suggestion, and several sharp exchanges followed. The President, although he rejected Stevenson's suggestion, pointed out that he had for a long period held reservations about the value of Jupiter missiles in Turkey and Italy and some time ago had asked the State Department to conduct negotiations for their removal; but now, he said, was not the appropriate time to suggest this action, and we could not abandon Guantanamo Bay under threat from the Russians.

Stevenson has since been criticized publicly for the position he took at this meeting. I think it should be emphasized that he was presenting a point of view from a different perspective than the others, one which was therefore important for the President to consider. Although I disagreed strongly with his recommendations, I thought he was courageous to make them, and I might add they made as much sense as some others considered during that period of time.

1962 Under Secretary of State George Ball on American Policy in the Revolution-torn Congo

On June 30, 1960, Belgium granted independence to the Republic of the Congo, its sole African possession. Unfortunately, the Belgians had not trained a group of Congolese leaders capable of running the country after independence. Within a brief period of time, some of the native troops revolted against their white officers, the mineral-rich southern province of Katanga seceded under the anti-Communist Moise Tshombé, and the pro-Communist Prime Minister of the Congo, Patrice Lumumba, met his death. It became necessary for the United Nations to send in a police force to keep order. As for the American government, it favored the reabsorption of Katanga Province into the Congo, and agreed to buy as much as $100 million in UN bonds to keep that organization solvent after it had spent heavily on the Congolese operation. The Congressional votes on this appropriation revealed heavy Northern Democratic support. Right-wing groups in the United States, however, backed Moise Tshombé, who eventually went down to defeat in January, 1962. Among the defenders of American Congo policy was Under Secretary of State George Ball.

SOURCE: George W. Ball, "American Policy in the Congo," in Helen Kitchen, Editor, *Footnotes to the Congo Story* (New York: Walker and Company, 1967). See pp. 61 and 66–68.

DOCUMENT:

The Congo is the centerpiece of Africa. It is one third the geographical size of the United States. It has a population of almost 14,000,000 people. What happens in this former Belgian colony will obviously play a decisive role in what happens in the areas around it.

What in the longer run do we seek to achieve in the Congo? Much the same thing that we seek to achieve elsewhere in Africa. What we wish for the Congo and for other African countries is a stable society, under a stable and progressive government. That government may be "nonaligned" in its international policies. That is for it to decide. But it must be strong enough and determined enough to safeguard its real independence. And it is important that it maintain with us, and with the European states who are contributing to its development, the kind of friendly and constructive relations that will serve our mutual purposes. Equally important, we wish to avoid the creation in Africa of a new Korea or a new Laos. We wish to insulate the African continent from the kind of military intervention by the Soviet bloc that has created such problems in other parts of the world.

Let me sum up the main points of the US policy in relation to the Congo:

First, our objective in the Congo, as elsewhere in Africa, is a free, stable non-Communist government for the Congo as a whole, dedicated to the maintenance of genuine independence, and willing and able to cooperate with us and with other free nations in meeting the tremendous internal challenges it must face.

Second, the United Nations is in the Congo with objectives that by and large parallel our own to help the Adoula government create a stable and unified Congo, and to ward off the dangers of civil war and great-power intervention. So far the United Nations has been remarkably successful in its efforts toward this end; had it not been available for this purpose we should have had to invent it—or the situation would already be lost. The United Nations effort deserves our support. We have given it. We should continue to do so.

Third, the Adoula government, the only legitimate government of the Congo, is a broadly based coalition under the leadership of an outstanding non-Communist African nationalist. This government's objectives are fully consistent with ours. It too deserves our support and will have it. Before it can buckle down to its true task of pursuing the national development of the Congo, this government must cope successfully with the threat of armed secession in the Katanga and deal effectively with political dissidence in Stanleyville. We shall continue to support both of these efforts.

Fourth, the issue in the Katanga is not self-determination. It is the threat of armed secession by a tribal area that happens to contain a disproportionate part of the wealth of the entire country. There is no legal, political, or moral basis for these secessionist efforts. To allow them to be pursued by provincial leaders with outside support can only place in jeopardy the success of our efforts in the Congo as a whole, threaten the entire Congo with chaos and civil war, and lead to the establishment of a Communist base in the heart of Central Africa. The armed secession in the Katanga plays into the hands of the Communists. This is a fact that all Americans should ponder.

Fifth, the only way out of the present situation in the Katanga is to bring an end to secession by negotiations between Prime Minister Adoula and Mr. Tshombe' designed to secure agreement on any necessary changes in the existing constitution of the Congo. Our efforts will continue to be devoted to this end.

Sixth, the difficulties and dangers in this complex situation are extraordinary, and only enormous effort and a certain amount of good luck have brought us as far as we have come since the dark days of August and September of 1960. Even now, the chances for success are precarious. No matter what we do we have no assurance that the situation will turn out to our liking.

1963 John Kennedy's *Ich Bin Ein Berliner* Speech

The wall which the Communists erected during August, 1961 to separate West Berlin from East Berlin was tangible evidence, as well as a symbol, of the Soviet Iron Curtain. When John Kennedy was in West Berlin on June 26, 1963, he used the opportunity to update the proud boast "I am a Roman citizen" to the catchy slogan "I am a Berliner." Elsewhere in the speech, there was a comment which also is of importance, since it anticipated Ronald Reagan's "evil empire" remark of the 1980s with respect to the Soviet Union. Today, the Berlin wall still stands, although West Berlin remains free, while the American and Russian governments are in the process of working out a less hostile relationship. The following account of the Ich Bin Ein Berliner *Speech is that of J.F.K.'s special counsel, Theodore Sorenson.*

SOURCE: Theodore C. Sorenson, *Kennedy* (New York: Harper & Row, 1965). See pp. 600–1.

DOCUMENT:

In 1963 the Wall was still there, but the East Germans had initiated proposals for openings in exchange for trade. West Berlin was still a city in danger, an island of freedom and prosperity deep within imprisoned East Germany. And incidents still occurred—including an unseemly squabble in the fall of 1963 over whether Western troops at the Autobahn checkpoints needed to dismount or lower their truck tailgates to be counted. But access to West Berlin remained free—West Berlin remained free—and neither a devastating nuclear war, nor a collapse of the Western Alliance, nor a one-sided treaty of peace had taken place as once feared. "I think [the Communists] realize," said President Kennedy, "that West Berlin is a vital interest to us…and that we are going to stay there."

The West Berliners also realized it. They gave John Kennedy the most overwhelming reception of his career on the twenty-sixth of June, 1963. The size of the crowd, their shouts and the look of hope and gratitude in their eyes moved some in our party to tears—even before we surveyed the Wall. The President—who would later remark that his trip had given him a far deeper understanding of the necessity of ultimate reunification—was moved to extemporaneous eloquence. "When I leave tonight," he told a trade union conference, "the United States stays." "You are now their hostages," he said to the American troops stationed in the city, "you are…the arrowhead." And at a luncheon given by Mayor Brandt at Berlin City Hall, he offered a toast, "to the German people on both sides of the Wall [and] to the cause of freedom on both sides of the Wall."

It was on the platform outside the City Hall—from where I could see only a sea of human faces chanting "Kenne–dy," "Kenne–dy" as far as my vision could reach—that he delivered one of his most inspired and inspiring talks:

> Two thousand years ago the proudest boast was "Civis Romanus sum." Today in the world of freedom, the proudest boast is: "Ich bin ein Berliner."
> There are many people in the world who really don't understand, or say they

don't, what is the great issue between the free world and the Communist world. Let them come to Berlin. There are some who say that Communism is the wave of the future. Let them come to Berlin....And there are even a few who say that it is true that Communism is an evil system, but it permits us to make economic progress. "Lasst sie nach Berlin kommen."

Freedom has many difficulties and democracy is not perfect, but we have never had to put a wall up to keep our people in...

We...look forward to that day when this city will be joined as one—and this country, and this great continent of Europe—in a peaceful and hopeful globe. When that day finally comes, as it will, the people of West Berlin can take sober satisfaction in the fact that they were in the front lines for almost two decades.

All free men, wherever they may live, are citizens of Berlin, and, therefore, as a free man, I take pride in the words "Ich bin ein Berliner."

1963 The Nuclear Test Ban Treaty with the Soviet Union

On July 25, 1963, representatives of the United States and the Soviet Union initiated a treaty banning modern weapon tests in the atmosphere, in outer space, and under water. On the following day, President John Kennedy delivered a televised address in which he explained what this treaty covered—and did not cover. When the treaty came before the Senate for ratification on September 24, 1963, it received a 80 to 19 favorable vote, with twenty-five Republicans and forty-one Northern Democrats voting for it. Ten Southern Democrats led the opposition.

SOURCE: U.S. Department of State *Bulletin*, August 12, 1963. See pp. 234–35.

DOCUMENT:

Eighteen years ago the advent of nuclear weapons changed the course of the world as well as the war. Since that time, all mankind has been struggling to escape from the darkening prospect of mass destruction on earth. In an age when both sides have come to possess enough nuclear power to destroy the human race several times over, the world of communism and the world of free choice have been caught up in a vicious circle of conflicting ideology and interest. Each increase of tension has produced an increase of arms; each increase of arms has produced an increase of tension.

In these years the United States and the Soviet Union have frequently communicated suspicion and warnings to each other, but very rarely hope. Our representatives have met at the summit and at the brink; they have met in Washington and in Moscow, in Geneva and at the United Nations. But too often these meetings have produced only darkness, discord, or disillusion.

Yesterday a shaft of light cut into the darkness. Negotiations were concluded in Moscow on a treaty to ban all nuclear tests in the atmosphere, in outer space, and under water. For the first time, an agreement has been reached on bringing the forces of nuclear destruction under international control—a goal first sought in 1946, when Bernard Baruch presented a comprehensive control plan to the United Nations.

That plan and many subsequent disarmament plans, large and small, have all been blocked by those opposed to international inspection. A ban on nuclear tests, however, requires on-the-spot inspection only for underground tests. This nation now possesses a variety of techniques to detect the nuclear tests of other nations which are conducted in the air or under water. For such tests produce unmistakable signs which our modern instruments can pick up.

The treaty initialed yesterday, therefore, is a limited treaty which permits continued underground testing and prohibits only those tests that we ourselves can police. It requires no control posts, no on-site inspection, no international body.

We should also understand that it has other limits as well. Any nation which signs the treaty will have an opportunity to withdraw if it finds that extraordinary events related to the subject matter of the treaty have jeopardized its supreme interests; and no nation's right of self-defense will in any way be impaired. Nor does this treaty mean an end to the threat of nuclear war. It will not reduce nuclear stockpiles; it will not halt the production of nuclear weapons; it will not restrict their use in time of war.

Nevertheless, this limited treaty will radically reduce the nuclear testing which would otherwise be conducted on both sides; it will prohibit the United States, the United Kingdom, the Soviet Union, and all others who sign it from engaging in the atmospheric tests which have so alarmed mankind; and it offers to all the world a welcome sign of hope.

For this is not a unilateral moratorium, but a specific and solemn obligation. While it will not prevent this nation from testing underground, or from being ready to conduct atmospheric tests if the acts of others so require, it gives us a concrete opportunity to extend its coverage to other nations and later to other forms of nuclear tests.

But the achievement of this goal is not a victory for one side—it is a victory for mankind. It reflects no concessions either to or by the Soviet Union. It reflects simply our common recognition of the dangers in further testing.

This treaty is not the millennium. It will not resolve all conflicts, or cause the Communists to forgo their ambitions, or eliminate the dangers of war. It will not reduce our need for arms or allies or programs of assistance to others. But it is an important first step—a step toward peace—a step toward reason—a step away from war.

1964 Anti-American Riots in Panama and the Future of the Canal (1971)

While the United States was still concerned with relations with its troublesome neighbor just to the South, Cuba, there were some riots in Panama during January, 1964. Here the issue at stake was the practice of flying the Panamanian flag beside the American flag in the Canal Zone, which some Americans living there resented bitterly and refused to honor. The ensuing disturbances left twenty-five persons dead, four of them U.S. soldiers. After Panama had broken off diplomatic relations with the United States, President Lyndon Johnson announced in December of that year that he favored both the renegotiation of the 1903 treaty and the construction of a new sea-level canal. The eventual result was the two treaties which the Senate ratified during the Carter Presidency. L.B.J. wrote his version of the Panamanian riots which precipitated this chain of events in his Presidential memoirs.

SOURCE: Lyndon B. Johnson, *The Vantage Point: Perspectives on the Presidency 1963–1969* (New York: Holt, Rinehart and Winston, 1971). See pp. 180–84.

DOCUMENT:

The first foreign crisis of my administration began only six weeks after I had taken office. On January 7, 1964, a group of American students at Balboa High School in the Panama Canal Zone set into motion events that soon threatened our relations with Panama and endangered operation of the Panama Canal. It was, on the surface, an inoffensive act: The students raised the American flag in front of the school.

The flag-raising violated an agreement President Kennedy had made in 1962 with Panamanian President Roberto Chiari. Our two governments had been trying to reach an understanding regarding changes in the sixty-year-old treaty governing U.S. control over the canal and the surrounding zone. No break-through had been made in those talks, but the Presidents had agreed that the flags of their two countries would fly side by side at designated sites in the zone.

The reaction came quickly. On June 9, two days after the incident, Panamanian students organized a protest march. They entered the Canal Zone and went to Balboa High School. A scuffle with Canal Zone police followed. As they marched out of the zone, the students broke windows, burned automobiles, and caused extensive property damage. Several students and policemen were injured.

More serious trouble followed. Large crowds of Panamanians gathered along the Canal Zone boundary, shouting, jeering, and throwing rocks and anything else that came to hand. Rioting broke out and continued for several days in Panama City and Colon, the major cities at each end of the canal. Panamanian students and civilians threw Molotov cocktails at buildings and automobiles. Cars with Canal Zone license plates were attacked and their occupants were pulled out and savagely beaten.

Panamanian authorities made little effort to maintain law and order. The Panamanian police stood aside, and the National Guard stayed in its barracks to ride out the storm. The Canal Zone police force, consisting of about eighty men, was too small to control the rioters and was in danger of being overwhelmed. The only remaining instruments of security were the U.S. Army troops stationed in the Canal Zone, and they were called out.

At first we ordered our troops to hold their fire, even though they were being shot at. Finally, with our troops suffering casualties, we had no choice but to order our men to return the fire of rooftop snipers. When the rioting finally ended on January 12, four American soldiers had been killed and dozens wounded. Twenty Panamanian rioters were also dead.

Despite the restraint we used from the outset of the crisis, President Chiari's government decided very quickly—on January 9—to break diplomatic relations with the United States. We were advised formally of this move the next afternoon. The Panamanian government accused our country of aggression, though we were only defending our nationals and protecting territory legally under our control.

My advisers recommended that I talk directly with President Chiari. I agreed and asked Pierre Salinger to phone Panama and find out if the President was available to talk to me. Salinger went to check.

Chiari ignored what I said about restoring order and calm. He seemed to want to take advantage of the situation to win larger objectives. "I feel, Mr. President," he said, "that what we need is a complete revision of all treaties which affect Panama–U.S. relations because that which we have at the present time is nothing but a source of dissatisfaction which has recently, or just now, exploded into violence which we are witnessing."

Chiari remarked that he had come to Washington in 1961 and had talked with President Kennedy about treaty revisions, but that since those conversations "not a thing has been done to alleviate the situation." I told the Panamanian President that we had to look forward, not backward, and that violence was no way to settle grievances. First, I said, let us end the violence; then we can begin to talk over our differences and find solutions.

Chiari claimed the United States had shown "indifference" to Panama's problems. I promised that our delegation would be on a plane "in thirty minutes" and would be in Panama in five hours. I could not act much faster than that. Chiari said he was grateful for this cooperation. He said he was glad I was "a man of action and of few words." He expressed confidence that the difficulties could be ironed out.

1965 American Intervention in the Dominican Republic

In 1961, assassins ended the thirty-one year long dictatorship of the Dominican tyrant Rafael Leonidas Trujillo Molina. Unused to democracy, the Dominicans struggled to maintain their fragile new freedom. When a revolt broke out in the Dominican Republic in April, 1965, during which 2,000 individuals died, President Lyndon Johnson revived the long-abandoned U.S. policy of intervening military in Latin America, and sent in about 25,000 American troops to prevent a Communist takeover or Cuban invasion. Like his predecessor, John F. Kennedy, L.B.J. also dispatched John Bartlow Martin on a fact-finding expedition to the Dominican Republic, and Martin summarized his experiences in Overtaken by Events *(1966). Back in the United States, the leading critics of this military incursion were liberal Democrats, the strongest backers military-minded Southerners. When the House of*

Representatives voted by a 6 to 1 margin on September 20, 1965 to endorse the unilateral use of force to prevent a Communist coup anywhere in the Western Hemisphere, Northern Democrats cast forty-nine of the fifty-two nay votes.

SOURCE: John Bartlow Martin, *Overtaken by Events: The Dominican Crisis from the Fall of Trujillo to the Civil War* (Garden City: Doubleday and Company, 1966). See pp. 704–7.

DOCUMENT:

As I write, it is more than four years since I left Upper Michigan to go to the Dominican Republic on a fact-finding mission for President Kennedy. During those years I lived through the death throes of Trujillo's old order and the birth agony of Dominican democracy, the strangulation of that democracy and the assassination of President Kennedy, the Dominican Civil War that swept away everything we had built; and I undertook missions for two Presidents, President Kennedy and President Johnson. Four years—what can we conclude from all this?

Let us deal first with the Civil War of 1965.

Our policy in the Dominican Republic that Spring has been severely criticized by much of the influential United States press, by Senator Fulbright and other political leaders, by students and government officials around the world.

Critics asked five main questions about our Dominican policy:

- Was there really danger of a Communist takeover?
- Should we have intervened militarily and unilaterally?
- Hadn't we overreacted?
- Having intervened, why didn't we espouse the rebel cause or at least maintain strict neutrality between the rebels and loyalists?
- Wasn't our policy erratic, uncertain, and contradictory? Weren't we less than candid in explaining it?

On the first point, I have no doubt whatsoever that there was a real danger of a Communist takeover of the Dominican Republic. Again I wish to emphasize that this is not primarily a question of names and numbers. It is a question of the process, of the bloodbath that fuses men and women of all ideologies into a fanatic mass and erases the fine distinctions that are possible in ordinary times.

On the second point, given the circumstances that existed at the time, in my opinion President Johnson had no choice but to send the troops. There can be no question that, with the police and military demoralized and all but defeated, with thousands of arms and embittered civilians roaming the streets, U.S. lives were endangered. Had the President not sent the troops, the rebels probably would have defeated the San Isidro troops, spread the rebellion throughout the Republic, killed some Americans and many Dominicans, and in the end established a Communist-dominated government.

On the third point, whether we "overreacted" and sent too many troops—"more than twenty thousand troops to catch fifty Communists," as critics have put it—I would point out that in such a situation a few leaders can exert great leverage on large numbers of uniformed people. The situation in the capital was chaotic and that in the interior virtually unknown. If, as the troop buildup increased, our purpose became to prevent a Communist takeover, then prudence argued for a large force. From a purely military point of view, how many is too many? I am not competent to judge but certainly would have hesitated to send only four hundred Marines to rescue several thousand civilians in the face of several thousand armed rebels. The Marines might have been thrown out.

On the fourth point, we did not espouse the rebel cause because it had fallen under Communist domination. As we have seen, we did everything possible to support President Bosch before he was overthrown in 1963. It would have been logical to support him in 1965 had he returned to lead the rebellion at its very outset. But although his men started the rebellion, and although Molina Urena and other PRD leaders apparently expected him to return immediately, Bosch did not return. Why he did not has never been satisfactorily explained, even by Bosch himself in all his writings on the rebellion that I have seen.

On the fifth point, I believe our policy seemed more erratic than it was. During the first few days, in a situation so chaotic and confused, it would be surprising if we had been able to lay out a policy neatly. (But in fact, on two fundamental points, our policy did set early and never changed: To protect United States lives, and to prevent a Castro/Communist takeover.) Most critics, however, complained that at various times we seemed to be collaborating first with San Isidro, then with Caamaño, then with Imbert, then with Guzmán. This can be called erratic; it can also be called exploring all possibilities.

1967 Lyndon Johnson Meets with Aleksei Kosygin at Glassboro, New Jersey (1971)

On October 14, 1964, Nikita Khrushchev fell from power in the Soviet Union. His successor, Aleksei Kosygin, proved less strident than Khrushchev had been at times, but the widening Vietnamese conflict acted as a barrier to closer relations between the United States and the Soviet Union. In the summer of 1967, Kosygin attended a United Nations session in New York City. He used this occasion to meet with President Lyndon Johnson on June 23 at the unlikely locale of Glassboro State College in New Jersey, approximately half way between Washington and New York City. Their conference dealt with a wide variety of topics in addition to the Vietnam War, as L.B.J. revealed in his memoirs.

SOURCE: Johnson, *The Vantage Point*. See pp. 483–85.

DOCUMENT:

For the most part, Kosygin was reserved but friendly during our long talks. We spoke of our grandchildren and of our hopes that they would grow up in a world of peace. He described his experiences in Leningrad through the long German siege of that great city during World War II. The memory of war's horror was always with the Soviet people, he said, and they wanted nothing but peace.

I picked up his point and reviewed all the steps I had taken as President to lessen Cold War tensions. Now, I said, it was time to take new steps. I told him that I had been waiting for three months for his answer on starting talks on ABMs and ICBMs. As soon as I brought up strategic arms talks, he changed the subject to the Middle East. This became a pattern during both days of our talks. Each time I mentioned missiles, Kosygin talked about Arabs and Israelis.

At only one point in our first session did Kosygin seem close to becoming really heated. He said we had talked about territorial integrity before the Middle East war, but we had ended by protecting aggression. He insisted that Israeli troops go back to the original armistice lines, and that the question of opening the Gulf of Aqaba be referred to the International Court of Justice. Then, he said, and the implication was "only then," could we discuss other problems. At that point, he came close to issuing a threat. Unless we agreed to his formula, he declared, there would be a war—"a very great war." He said the Arabs would fight with arms if they had them and, if not, with bare hands.

"All troops must be withdrawn at once," he said.

If they fight with weapons, I replied, we would know where they got them. Then I leaned forward and said slowly and quietly: "Let us understand one another. I hope there will be no war. If there is a war, I hope it will not be a big war. If they fight, I hope they fight with fists and not with guns." I told him that I hoped both our countries could keep out of any Middle East explosion because "if we do get into it, it will be a most serious matter."

I tried repeatedly to bring the talks back to limiting the missile race. I invited McNamara to join this discussion. At lunch, he and I made the strongest case we could for opening strategic arms talks immediately, but Kosygin apparently had come to Glassboro with a block against this subject. Time and time again, he implied that we only wanted to talk about limiting ABMs, while the Soviets felt that ABMs and offensive nuclear weapons should be linked. I reassured him repeatedly that we wanted to limit both offensive and defensive weapons, and McNamara said the same. But the point did not get across clearly—or Kosygin chose not to understand.

That Friday, and when we met again on Sunday, I tried several times to persuade Kosygin to agree to a time and a place for missile limitation talks. "Name the place," I said. "Give us a date—next week, next month. We will be there. Secretary McNamara is ready now." But it seemed obvious that Kosygin had come without the authority needed from the Soviet Presidium to make a firm commitment. We did promise to continue our search for agreement through talks between Rusk and Gromyko in New York.

I left Glassboro on Sunday evening, June 25, with mixed feelings—disappointment that we had not solved any major problem but hope that we had moved to a better understanding of our differences.

The Interminable
Vietnamese Conflict 47

1961 President John Kennedy and the Neutralization of Laos

Despite the basic focus on Vietnam, the war in Southeast Asia also involved Cambodia and Laos. American-financed aid to Laos did not prevent Communist guerillas from attempting to seize power there. Rather than escalate U.S. support for the threatened nation, President John Kennedy instead made the proposal on March 23 that Laos be neutralized. A fourteen-nation conference agreed to this scheme at Geneva on July 23. The new Laotian government was to include Communist as well as neutralist and pro-Western elements, much to the displeasure of hard-lining cold warriors in the United States, who regarded this plan as appeasement. But the President viewed his proposal quite differently. In his March 23 message, J.F.K. invoked the so-called domino theory: Should one Southeast Asia nation fall to the Communists, then the other countries there also would be in danger of a Marxist takeover.

SOURCE: U.S. Department of State *Bulletin*, April 17, 1961. See pp. 543–44.

DOCUMENT:

Our special concern with the problem in Laos goes back to 1954. That year, at Geneva, a large group of powers agreed to a settlement of the struggle for Indochina. Laos was one of the new states which had recently emerged from the French Union, and it was the clear premise of the 1954 settlement that this new country would be neutral, free of external domination by anyone. The new country contained contending factions, but in its first years real progress was made toward a unified and neutral status. But the efforts of a Communist-dominated group to destroy this neutrality never ceased, and in the last half of 1960 a series of sudden maneuvers occurred and the Communists and their supporters turned to a new and greatly intensified military effort to take over.

       The position of this administration has been carefully considered, and we have sought to make it just as clear as we know how to the governments concerned. First: We strongly and unreservedly support the goal of a neutral and independent Laos, tied to no outside power or group of powers, threatening no one, and free from any domination. Our support for the present duly constituted Government is aimed entirely and exclusively at that result, and if in the past there has been any possible ground for misunderstanding of our support for a truly neutral Laos, there should be none now.

Secondly, if there is to be a peaceful solution, there must be a cessation of the present armed attacks by externally supported Communists. If these attacks do not stop, those who support a genuinely neutral Laos will have to consider their response.

No one should doubt our own resolution on this point. We are faced with a clear threat of a change in the internationally agreed position of Laos. This threat runs counter to the will of the Laotian people, who wish only to be independent and neutral. It is posed rather by the military operations of internal dissident elements directed from outside the country. This is what must end if peace is to be kept in southeast Asia.

Third, we are earnestly in favor of constructive negotiation—among the nations concerned and among the leaders of Laos—which can help Laos back to the pathway of independence and genuine neutrality. We strongly support the present British proposal of a prompt end of hostilities and prompt negotiation. We are always conscious of the obligation which rests upon all members of the United Nations to seek peaceful solutions to problems of this sort. We hope that others may be equally aware of this responsibility.

My fellow Americans, Laos is far away from America, but the world is small. Its 2 million peaceful people live in a country three times the size of Austria. The security of all of southeast Asia will be endangered if Laos loses its neutral independence. Its own safety runs with the safety of us all—in real neutrality observed by all.

I want to make it clear to the American people, and to all the world, that all we want in Laos is peace, not war—a truly neutral government, not a cold-war pawn—a settlement concluded at the conference table, not on the battlefield.

1964 The Gulf of Tonkin Resolution Authorizing American Military Action in Southeast Asia

On August 2 and 4, 1964, Vietnamese torpedo boats supposedly attacked two U.S. destroyers in the Gulf of Tonkin outside of the territorial limits in international waters. L.B.J. retaliated with a bombing raid up and down the coast of North Vietnam. Then he asked Congress for a blank check to take all necessary measures to protect Southeast Asia rather than request a declaration of war against North Vietnam. Excerpts from his August 5 address follow. The vote in Congress two days later was almost unanimous: 416 to 0 in the House, 88 to 2 in the Senate; it was as overwhelming as that in favor of American entry into World War II. The two nay votes were cast by Democratic Senators Wayne Morse of Oregon and Ernest Gruening of Alaska. The 1972 Democratic Presidential candidate,

George McGovern, later stated in his memoirs that his vote for the Gulf of Tonkin Resolution was the one Congressional vote which he in retrospect most regretted. Many other Senators and Representatives of both parties came to feel the same way.

SOURCE: U.S. Department of State *Bulletin,* August 24, 1964. See pp. 261–62, 268.

DOCUMENT:

To the Congress of the United States:

Last night I announced to the American people that the North Vietnamese regime had conducted further deliberate attacks against U.S. naval vessels operating in international waters, and that I had therefore directed air action against gunboats and supporting facilities used in these hostile operations. This air action has now been carried out with substantial damage to the boats and facilities. Two U.S. aircraft were lost in the action.

After consultation with the leaders of both parties in the Congress, I further announced a decision to ask the Congress for a resolution expressing the unity and determination of the United States in supporting freedom and in protecting peace in southeast Asia.

These latest actions of the North Vietnamese regime have given a new and grave turn to the already serious situation in southeast Asia. Our commitments in that area are well known to the Congress. They were first made in 1954 by President Eisenhower. They were further defined in the Southeast Asia Collective Defense Treaty approved by the Senate in February 1955.

This treaty with its accompanying protocol obligates the United States and other members to act in accordance with their constitutional processes to meet Communist aggression against any of the parties or protocol states.

The threat to the free nations of southeast Asia has long been clear. The North Vietnamese regime has constantly sought to take over South Vietnam and Laos. This Communist regime has violated the Geneva accords for Vietnam. It has systematically conducted a campaign of subversion, which includes the direction, training, and supply of personnel and arms for the conduct of guerrilla warfare in South Vietnamese territory. In Laos, the North Vietnamese regime has maintained military forces, used Laotian territory for infiltration into South Vietnam, and most recently carried out combat operations—all in direct violation of the Geneva agreements of 1962.

In recent months, the actions of the North Vietnamese regime have become steadily more threatening. In May, following new acts of Communist aggression in Laos, the United States undertook reconnaissance flights over Laotian territory, at the request of the Government of Laos. These flights had the essential mission of determining the situation in territory where Communist forces were preventing inspection by the International Control Commission. When the Communists attacked these aircraft, I responded by furnishing escort fighters with instructions to fire when fired upon. Thus, these latest North Vietnamese attacks on our naval vessels are not the first direct attack on armed forces of the United States.

As President of the United States I have concluded that I should now ask Congress, on its part, to join in affirming the national determination that all such attacks will be met, and that the United States will continue in its basic policy of assisting the free nations of the area to defend their freedom.

As I have repeatedly made clear, the United States intends no rashness, and seeks no wider war. We must make it clear to all that the United States is united in its determination to bring about the end of Communist subversion and aggression in the area. We seek the full and effective restoration of the international agreements signed in Geneva in 1954, with respect to South Vietnam, and again in Geneva in 1962, with respect to Laos.

I recommend a resolution expressing the support of the Congress for all necessary action to protect our Armed Forces and to assist nations covered by the SEATO Treaty. At the same time, I assure the Congress that we shall continue readily to explore any avenues of political solution that will effectively guarantee the removal of Communist subversion and the preservation of the independence of the nations of the area.

TEXT OF JOINT RESOLUTION, AUGUST 7

Joint Resolution

To promote the maintenance of international peace and security in southeast Asia.

Whereas naval units of the Communist regime in Vietnam, in violation of the principles of the Charter of the United Nations and of international law, have deliberately and repeatedly attacked United States naval vessels lawfully present in international waters, and have thereby created a serious threat to international peace; and

Whereas these attacks are part of a deliberate and systematic campaign of aggression that the Communist regime in North Vietnam has been waging against its neighbors and the nations joined with them in the collective defense of their freedom; and

Whereas the United States is assisting the peoples of southeast Asia to protect their freedom and has no territorial, military or political ambitions in that area, but desires only that these peoples should be left in peace to work out their own destinies in their own way: Now, therefore, be it

Resolved by the Senate and House of Representatives of the United States of America in Congress assembled, That the Congress approves and supports the determination of the President, as Commander in Chief, to take all necessary measures to repel any armed attack against the forces of the United States and to prevent further aggression.

SECTION 2. The United States regards as vital to its national interest and to world peace the maintenance of international peace and security in southeast Asia.

Consonant with the Constitution of the United States and the Charter of the United Nations and in accordance with its obligations under the Southeast Asia Collective Defense Treaty, the United States is, therefore; prepared, as the President determines, to take all necessary steps, including the use of armed force, to assist any member or protocol state of the Southeast Asia Collective Defense Treaty requesting assistance in defense of its freedom.

SECTION 3. This resolution shall expire when the President shall determine that the peace and security of the area is reasonably assured by international conditions created by action of the United Nations or otherwise, except that it may be terminated earlier by concurrent resolution of the Congress.

1964 L.B.J.'s Campaign Rhetoric on the Vietnam War

In 1964, the Democrats portrayed Republican Presidential nominee Barry Goldwater as a trigger-happy right-wing extremist who would defoliate the jungles of North Vietnam. At the same time, L.B.J. was secretly accelerating U.S. involvement in Southeast Asia, while telling the American people that he was not going to have American soldiers fight a war that the South Vietnamese soldiers should be fighting. There is an eerie parallel between some of his campaign utterances and F.D.R.'s "again and again and again" speech of 1940 reassuring the American people that he was not going to send U.S. troops into combat abroad.

SOURCE: Arthur Schlesinger, Jr., *The Bitter Heritage: Vietnam and American Democracy 1941–1966* (Boston: Houghton Mifflin Company, 1967). See pp. 28–29.

DOCUMENT:

Some others are eager to enlarge the conflict. They call upon us to supply American boys to do the job that Asian boys should do. They ask us to take reckless actions which might risk the lives of millions and engulf much of Asia.

(August 12)

I have had advice to load our planes with bombs and to drop them on certain areas that I think would enlarge the war and result in committing a good many American boys to fighting a war that I think ought to be fought by the boys of Asia to help protect their own land. And for that reason I haven't chosen to enlarge the war.

(August 29)

There are those that say you ought to go north and drop bombs, to try to wipe out the supply lines, and they think that would escalate the war. We don't want our American boys to do the fighting for Asian boys. We don't want to get involved in a nation with 700 million people and get tied down in a land war in Asia.

(September 25)

We are not going north and we are not going south; we are going to continue to try to get them to save their own freedom with their own men, with our leadership and our officer direction, and such equipment as we can furnish them.

(September 28)

We are not going to send American boys nine or ten thousand miles away from home to do what Asian boys ought to be doing for themselves.

(October 21)

1967 The Knight Newspapers Criticize American Involvement in Vietnam

One of the most powerful newspaper publishers in the United States during the 1960s was John S. Knight of the Knight newspapers. Ever since the fall of Dienbienphu, he had been leery of the increasing American involvement in Southeast Asia, and ten of his columns on Vietnam won him the Pulitzer Prize for journalism in 1968. We quote here from "Our 'Commitments' Open to Question" (May 7, 1967), in which Knight discussed in turn the 1954 Dwight Eisenhower letter to Ngo Dinh Diem, the Southeast Asia Treaty Organization of the same year, and the 1964 Gulf of Tonkin Resolution.

SOURCE: Sloan, *Pulitzer Prize Editorials.* See pp. 146–48.

DOCUMENT:

Three so-called "commitments" are involved. The first was the October 25, 1954, Eisenhower letter to Ngo Dinh Diem, then head of the Saigon government, promising American aid "provided your government is prepared to give assurances as to the standard of performance it would be able to maintain in the event such aid is supplied."

The second "commitment" turned on the SEATO treaty, a collective defense pact signed by the United States, Britain, France, Australia, New Zealand, the Philippines, Pakistan and Thailand.

Our third "commitment" was the Tonkin Gulf resolution as passed by Congress in 1964.

1—As seen in retrospect, the Eisenhower letter was not a commitment but a proposal to give economic aid to South Vietnam if certain conditions for self-help and reform were accepted. Incidentally, these terms were not met.

At no time did President Eisenhower intend to send U.S. military forces to Vietnam, a fact which he readily admits today. And as historian Henry Steele Commager has written, "even had President Eisenhower intended his letter to be a kind of commitment, it would have had not binding force; the President cannot, by private letter, commit the United States to war or quasi-war."

2—The SEATO "commitment" is vague and legalistic, depending upon whether the parties thereto were dealing with "aggression" or "subversion."

The section dealing with aggression provides that whatever measures are taken "shall be immediately reported to the Security Council" of the United Nations.

This step was never taken, although a gesture was made in January of 1966—well after the fact.

The second section under which our "commitment" is defended provides for "collective consultation" in instances of subversion. The late John Foster Dulles, architect of SEATO, so interpreted this provision.

As Senator Walter George of the Foreign Relations Committee said at the time, "the treaty does not call for automatic action, it calls for consultation. All that we are obligated to do is to consult together."

Yet there was no consultation. Although Secretary Rusk talks about "the sanctity of our Pacific alliances," only SEATO members Australia, New Zealand, Thailand and the Philippines have made any contributions to the cause of South Vietnam. France openly opposes U.S. policy, Britain offers only sympathy, Pakistan is disenchanted. So as Commager says, "If our 'honor' is involved, why is not the honor of the other SEATO nations equally involved?"

The American Bar Association upholds our "commitment" in Vietnam on the ground that Article 52 of the United Nations Charter provides for regional agreements for the maintenance of international peace.

It does indeed, but such activities must be "consistent with the purposes and principles of the United Nations" and no enforcement "shall be taken...without authorization of the Security Council."

So the question remains: Is the United States committed to unilateral action in Vietnam under the SEATO treaty?

It is my opinion, based upon extensive study of the subject, that we are not committed either legally or morally to our present course of action.

3—The Tonkin Gulf resolution was passed without debate after the North Vietnamese had fired torpedoes at two American destroyers. The resolution pledged support to the President of the United States, as commander-in-chief, to "take all necessary measures to repel any armed attack against the forces of the United States and to prevent further aggression."

The question is now raised as to whether the North Vietnamese committed an act of aggression, since our destroyers were only 11 miles from shore in violation of the "international waters" understanding which is honored by most nations.

When North Vietnam asserted that we had violated her waters, Senator Gaylord Nelson asked on the floor of the Senate: "The patrolling (American destroyers) was for the purpose of demonstrating to the North Vietnamese that we did not recognize a 12-mile limit?" Senator J.W. Fulbright replied: "That was one reason given."

As Mr. Commager has written: "If the Tonkin Gulf affair was a clear case of aggression, why is it that the other members of SEATO have not rallied to our support, as is required by the treaty? If it was a clear case of aggression, why is it that we did not choose to follow the procedure laid down by the charter and submit it to the United Nations?"

It is not the dissent at home which is prolonging the war.

Rather, it is the determination of the man in the White House—entrapped by pride and circumstances—to bring about a victory or at least an accommodation with honor prior to the 1968 elections.

1968 Senator Ernest Gruening Attacks South Vietnam as a Dictatorship

A number of Americans exposed to the spread of Communism across the world nevertheless realized that simply because a government was anti-Communist, it was not necessarily democratic. A case in point was South Vietnam, which Gulf of Tonkin Resolution foe Ernest Gruening harshly characterized as a "cruel, corrupt military dictatorship." Was it not time, observed Gruening, that the United States demanded a free, democratic South Vietnam? Should it continue its present course of action, the tragic result might well be a global holocaust.

SOURCE: Ernest Gruening and Herbert Wilton Beaser, *Vietnam Folly* (Washington: National Press, 1968). See pp. 382–84.

DOCUMENT:

It should be clear that all the United States so-called peace offenses, staged with much fanfare, have failed and were bound to fail because:

First, they were based on a refusal to concede that the United States was not fighting aggression, but was itself the aggressor;

Second, the proposal tentatively advanced as United States' objectives for the return to the Geneva Accords—which were predicated on a united Vietnam—while the United States insisting on an independent South Vietnam were incompatible and hence just double talk;

Third, the real adversaries were the Viet Cong or National Liberation Front with whom the United States has persistently refused to deal.

Until the present approach is changed to conform with reality there is little prospect of bringing the adversaries to the conference table.

The United States today is the richest and most powerful nation in the world. No one, anywhere, could doubt but that the United States—if it desires to do so—could raze all of South Vietnam as it is now doing to considerable parts of it. The withdrawal of the United States from its military involvement in South Vietnam would not be interpreted as an act of weakness but rather as an act of great moral strength.

When Great Britain made the decision that it could not crush, at the point of a Hessian bayonet, the great yearning for freedom of the American colonists, and decided not to continue further its military efforts to put down the rebellion, it became the greater for it.

When France decided that the spirit of freedom of the Algerian people could not be crushed by bullet and bomb, and gave them their freedom, France, too, became the greater for it.

Neither country "lost face."

So, too, with the United States' involvement in South Vietnam.

In a nation—as in an individual—it takes great moral fortitude to confess error. Has the United States the moral fortitude—on a scale with its great strength and wealth—to confess that it has acted in error in Vietnam?

The United States stands today at the crossroads of a great moral decision and must ask itself: "What shall it profit" a nation if it "gain the whole world but loses" its own soul?

The time has come for the United States to institute in South Vietnam its own style of War of National Liberation. Let the United States show the world that its strength lies not in its wealth and military might but rather in the ideals for which it stands.

Let the United States stop raining death and destruction over the people in the countryside of North and South Vietnam.

Let the United States turn aside from its support of cruel, corrupt military dictatorship in South Vietnam and embrace there instead a government that will recognize, support, and defend the worth, the dignity, and the fundamental freedom of each individual in South Vietnam.

The course the United States now pursues in Vietnam is fraught with the gravest dangers for all mankind. It is a collision course destined—unless changed—to bring about a world holocaust.

1968 L.B.J. Halts the Bombing of North Vietnam (1971)

On March 31, 1968, President Lyndon Johnson announced over television that he would not seek reelection, but instead would concentrate his energies on ending the war in Vietnam. Frustration over the war had a major impact on the Presidential campaign during that year, and doubtless contributed to the rioting outside the Democratic convention in Chicago. With Republican Richard Nixon locked in a tight contest for the White House with Democrat Hubert Humphrey, L.B.J. announced on October 31 that he was halting the bombing of North Vietnam so as to facilitate peace talks. (Nixon still won.) In his memoirs, Johnson pointed out that it was just as difficult for the American government to deal with South Vietnam as with North Vietnam, despite the aid which the United States was furnishing to the Thieu regime.

SOURCE: Johnson, *The Vantage Point.* See pp. 522–24.

DOCUMENT:

The sixty-five plus hours between that early morning meeting of October 29, when General Abrams came from Saigon, and the evening of October 31, when I announced my decision, were a period of hectic diplomatic and political activity. Those three days were a blur of meetings and phone calls, of cables and conferences. I seemed to be listening, reading, or talking right around the clock. The same was true for all my principal advisers and assistants. In Saigon Bunker and his top aides and Thieu and his lieutenants suffered the same tension and sleepless activity. Similarly, in Paris Harriman and Vance were busy explaining the delay to the North Vietnamese delegates and working out the final details of our agreement.

The report we had been waiting for finally arrived from Bunker. I read his account of the National Security Council session in Saigon with deep disappointment. There was still no agreement to move with us. The South Vietnamese had raised several objections to an immediate decision. First, they told Bunker, there was a constitutional question. Under Vietnam's national charter, the President had to have the approval of the National Assembly on major foreign policy questions. That would take time, and perhaps even a plenary session of the assembly.

Second, the South Vietnamese felt they had been given different interpretations of U.S. policy by Bunker in Saigon and Harriman in Paris. This concerned the role of the Liberation Front in the expanded talks. We had said all along that we would regard the coming meetings as "two-sided" and would consider the Liberation Front part of Hanoi's delegation on the "other side." However, we had explained to our Vietnamese allies that we could not control what the Communist side said or claimed on this matter. We knew the Communists would argue that the Liberation Front representatives were a separate delegation.

Third, the South Vietnamese wanted all procedural arrangements for the expanded Paris meetings worked out before they agreed to attend. We knew that was impossible; Hanoi would never accept this condition. Finally, the South Vietnamese told Bunker they could not be ready for a meeting by November 2.

"This may mean that everything we have done is in vain," I said. "There is no basic change—no breakthrough." I asked my advisers to study Bunker's report carefully and consider what we could or should do next. I said we would meet again later in the day.

At 6:30 p.m. I met again in the Cabinet Room with my advisers. By then we had received Bunker's recommendation that we hold off any announcement of a bombing halt for twenty-four hours and that we tell the South Vietnamese we were willing to hold the first enlarged Paris meeting on November 4 instead of November 2, which would give them more time to organize their delegation. We discussed this suggestion at length and finally agreed to allow our allies the additional time. "I would be willing to postpone things a day or two before I broke up the alliance," I said.

Meanwhile, our delegates in Paris were in an embarrassing position. The North Vietnamese were pressing for word on what they thought was a firm agreement. Harriman and Vance had to say that they were still waiting for final instructions from Washington.

I had sent President Thieu a personal message on October 29 urging him to join us in Paris under the arrangements already worked out. On the 30th, just before noon, I received his answer.

It was friendly and expressed deep appreciation for everything the United States had done to help his country survive, but it was clear that Thieu would not accept our proposal unless certain conditions were met. First, he wanted firm assurance that Hanoi would join in deescalating the war. Second, he wanted Hanoi's pledge to negotiate directly with his government. Finally, he wanted Hanoi to agree that the Liberation Front would not attend the conference as a separate delegation. My advisers and I recognized that these conditions were impossible. Moreover, we had been explaining for months to the South Vietnamese in Saigon and in Paris why they could not be met.

I decided then, with genuine regret, that we had to go forward with our plans. Perhaps Bunker could work things out in the next twenty-four hours, but that seemed doubtful. Perhaps our Vietnamese allies would have a change of heart. That seemed equally doubtful. I asked Bunker to do his best, but I knew he was working against long odds.

It was one of the rare occasions, in my years of dealing with them, that I felt Thieu, Ky, and their advisers had let me down. More important, I felt that their action put in peril everything both governments had worked so long and sacrificed so much to achieve. They were, however, Vietnamese and the legally elected authorities of their country. It was their decision to make, right or wrong.

1970 President Richard Nixon's Incursion into Cambodia

Once he had been installed in the White House, it took Richard Nixon another four years to disengage the United States from the Vietnamese conflict. At one time, of course, what today is North Vietnam, South Vietnam, Cambodia, and Laos were all part of French Indo China, and boundary lines now run through jungle areas where there is no logical place to divide the adjacent countries. There were occasions, moreover, when the North Vietnamese operated out of eastern Cambodia, and Richard Nixon accordingly sent U.S. troops into the latter area during late April, 1970. He justified this bold maneuver in an address to the American people on April 30 as a defensive action, but the U.S. troops failed to discover the Communist sanctuary there, and the broadening of the Vietnamese conflict into Cambodia intensified the antiwar agitation back in the United States.

SOURCE: U.S. Department of State *Bulletin*, May 18, 1970. See pp. 617–19.

DOCUMENT:

Tonight I shall describe the actions of the enemy, the actions I have ordered to deal with that situation, and the reasons for my decision.

Cambodia, a small country of 7 million people, has been a neutral nation since the Geneva agreement of 1954—an agreement, incidentally, which was signed by the Government of North Vietnam.

American policy since then has been to scrupulously respect the neutrality of the Cambodian people. We have maintained a skeleton diplomatic mission of fewer than 15 in Cambodia's capital, and that only since last August. For the previous 4 years, from 1965 to 1969, we did not have any diplomatic mission whatever in Cambodia. And for the past 5 years, we have provided no military assistance whatever and no economic assistance to Cambodia.

North Vietnam, however, has not respected that neutrality.

For the past 5 years, as indicated on this map that you see here, North Vietnam has occupied military sanctuaries all along the Cambodian frontier with South Vietnam. Some of these extend up to 20 miles into Cambodia. The sanctuaries are in red, and as you note, they are on both sides of the border. They are used for hit-and-run attacks on American and South Vietnamese forces in South Vietnam.

These Communist-occupied territories contain major base camps, training sites, logistics facilities, weapons and ammunition factories, airstrips, and prisoner of war compounds.

For 5 years neither the United States nor South Vietnam has moved against these enemy sanctuaries, because we did not wish to violate the territory of a neutral nation. Even after the Vietnamese Communists began to expand these sanctuaries 4 weeks ago, we counseled patience to our South Vietnamese allies and imposed restraints on our own commanders.

In contrast to our policy, the enemy in the past 2 weeks has stepped up his guerrilla actions, and he is concentrating his main forces in these sanctuaries that you see on this map, where they are building up to launch massive attacks on our forces and those of South Vietnam.

North Vietnam in the last 2 weeks has stripped away all pretense of respecting the sovereignty or the neutrality of Cambodia. Thousands of their soldiers are invading the country from the sanctuaries; they are encircling the Capital of Phnom Penh. Coming from these sanctuaries, as you see here, they have moved into Cambodia and are encircling the Capital.

Cambodia, as a result of this, has sent out a call to the United States, to a number of other nations, for assistance. Because if this enemy effort succeeds, Cambodia would become a vast enemy staging area and a springboard for attacks on South Vietnam along 600 miles of frontier, a refuge where enemy troops could return from combat without fear of retaliation.

North Vietnamese men and supplies could then be poured into that country, jeopardizing not only the lives of our own men but the people of South Vietnam as well.

Now, confronted with this situation, we have three options.

First, we can do nothing. Well, the ultimate result of that course of action is clear. Unless we indulge in wishful thinking, the lives of Americans remaining in Vietnam after our next withdrawal of 150,000 would be gravely threatened.

Our second choice is to provide massive military assistance to Cambodia itself. Now, unfortunately, while we deeply sympathize with the plight of 7 million Cambodians, whose country is being invaded, massive amounts of military assistance could not be rapidly and effectively utilized by the small Cambodian Army against the immediate threat.

Our third choice is to go to the heart of the trouble. That means cleaning out major North Vietnamese and Viet Cong occupied territories—these sanctuaries which serve as bases for attacks on both Cambodia and American and South Vietnamese forces in South Vietnam. Some of these, incidentally, are so close to Saigon as Baltimore is to Washington. This one, for example [indicating], is called the Parrot's Beak. It is only 33 miles from Saigon.

Now, faced with these three options, this is the decision I have made.

In cooperation with the armed forces of South Vietnam, attacks are being launched this week to clean out major enemy sanctuaries on the Cambodian–Vietnam border.

A major responsibility for the ground operations is being assumed by South Vietnamese forces. For example, the attacks in several areas, including the Parrot's Beak that I referred to a moment ago, are exclusively South Vietnamese ground operations under South Vietnamese command, with the United States providing air and logistical support.

There is one area, however, immediately above Parrot's Beak, where I have concluded that a combined American and South Vietnamese operation is necessary.

Tonight American and South Vietnamese units will attack the headquarters for the entire Communist military operation in South Vietnam. This key control center has been occupied by the North Vietnamese and Viet Cong for 5 years in blatant violation of Cambodia's neutrality.

This is not an invasion of Cambodia. The areas in which these attacks will be launched are completely occupied and controlled by North Vietnamese forces. Our purpose is not to occupy the areas. Once enemy forces are driven out of these sanctuaries and once their military supplies are destroyed, we will withdraw.

1970 The McGovern–Hatfield Amendment and U.S. Withdrawal from Vietnam

One day before Richard Nixon announced the U.S. incursion into Cambodia, Democrat George McGovern of South Dakota and Republican Mark Hatfield introduced the Mc-Govern–Hatfield Amendment into the Senate. This set a December 31, 1971 deadline for the complete withdrawal of American troops from Vietnam. It soon became the focal point of the antiwar effort, and McGovern attempted to sway Senators to vote for it in a speech in which he lamented those American soldiers killed and injured in the Vietnamese conflict, placed the blame for the war on his colleagues, and complained that "this Chamber reeks of blood." When the McGovern–Hatfield Amendment came up for a final vote on September 1, 1970, it went down to defeat, 39 to 55. Strong Northern Democratic backing (29 to 6) proved insufficient to offset equally strong Republican and Southern Democratic (15 to 3) hostility.

SOURCE: George McGovern, *Grassroots: The Autobiography of George McGovern* (New York: Random House, 1977). See pp. 167–68.

DOCUMENT:

Presently the McGovern–Hatfield Amendment became the rallying point against the war. All during the summer of 1970 a steady procession of antiwar delegations poured into Washington lobbying their senators and congressmen to support our Amendment to End the War. These delegations, representing every stratum of American society, had an unmistakable impact on many senators. Their efforts reached a climax on the morning of Tuesday, September 1, 1970, when I rose in the Senate to give the concluding speech in support of the amendment. It was the hardest-hitting speech I had ever delivered to my colleagues. Nearly the entire Senate was there to hear it.

> Mr. President, the vote we are about to cast could be one of the most significant votes Senators will ever cast.
>
> I have lived with this vote night and day since last April 30—the day before the Cambodia invasion—the day this amendment was first submitted....
>
> What is the choice it presents us? It presents us with an opportunity to end a war we never should have entered. It presents us with an opportunity to revitalize constitutional government in America by restoring the war powers the Founding Fathers obliged the Congress to carry.
>
> Every Senator in this Chamber is partly responsible for sending 50,000 young Americans to an early grave. This Chamber reeks of blood.
>
> Every Senator here is partly responsible for that human wreckage at Walter Reed and Bethesda Naval and all across our land—young men without legs, or arms, or genitals, or faces, or hopes.
>
> There are not very many of these blasted and broken boys who think this war is a glorious venture.
>
> Do not talk to them about bugging out, or national honor, or courage.
>
> It does not take any courage at all for a Congressman, or a Senator, or a President to wrap himself up in the flag and say we are staying in Vietnam, because it is not our blood that is being shed.
>
> But we are responsible for those young men and their lives and their hopes.
>
> And if we do not end this damnable war, those young men will some day curse us for our pitiful willingness to let the Executive carry the burden that the Constitution places on us.

These words angered some senators, but they also put the entire Senate on trial. The vote was 39 in favor of the amendment and 55 against. To some, that seemed like a defeat; to me, it was a victory. For the first time in American history, more than a third of the Senate had publicly voted to terminate a war which the Commander in Chief was most anxious to continue. (Ironically, the 39 percent of the Senate that stood with me on this issue was the same percentage of the national electorate that was to support me for the presidency against Richard Nixon two years later.)

1971 The Senator Mike Gravel Edition of the Pentagon Papers

The national government in the United States has become more large and more complex in recent years, but in certain respects it also has become more clandestine. Evidence of this is found in The Pentagon Papers. *These came to light with the unauthorized release by the New York* Times, *beginning in June, 1971, of excerpts from a full-length Department of Defense study of American decision-making in Vietnam. The Department of Justice obtained an injunction shortly thereafter to stop the further publication of this material. When Democratic Senator Mike Gravel of Alaska tried to read from a collection of these papers on the floor of the Senate on June 29, a parliamentary maneuver threatened his efforts. The Beacon Press of Boston nevertheless released four volumes of these documents later in the year, thus guaranteeing even wider circulation for them. As Senator Gravel points out in his introduction, there had been a "purposeful withholding and distortion of facts" with regard to Vietnam, which was compounded by a government-imposed secrecy incompatible with the democratic tradition in the United States.*

SOURCE: The Senator Gravel Edition, *The Pentagon Papers* (Boston: Beacon Press, 1971). See xi–xii.

DOCUMENT:

The Pentagon Papers tell of the purposeful withholding and distortion of facts. There are no military secrets to be found here, only an appalling litany of faulty premises and questionable objectives, built one upon the other over the course of four administrations, and perpetuated today by a fifth administration.

The Pentagon Papers show that we have created, in the last century, a new culture, a national security culture, protected from the influences of American life by the shield of secrecy. As New York *Times* reporter Neil Sheehan has written, "To read the Pentagon Papers in their vast detail is to step through the looking glass into a new and different world. This world has a set of values, a dynamic, a language, and a perspective quite distinct from the public world of the ordinary citizen and of the other two branches of the republic—Congress and the judiciary."

The Pentagon Papers reveal the inner workings of a government bureaucracy set up to defend this country, but now out of control, managing an international empire by garrisoning American troops around the world. It created an artificial client state in South Vietnam, lamented its unpopularity among its own people, eventually encouraged the overthrow of that government, and then supported a series of military dictators who served their own ends, and at times our government's ends, but never the cause of their own people.

The Pentagon Papers show that our leaders never understood the human commitments which underlay the nationalist movement in Vietnam, or the degree to which the Vietnamese were willing to sacrifice in what they considered to be a century-long struggle to eliminate colonialism from their land. Like the empires that have gone before us, our government has viewed as legitimate only those regimes which it had established, regardless of the views of those governed. It has viewed the Viet Minh and their successors, the Viet Cong, as insurgents rebelling against a legitimate government, failing to see that their success demonstrated the people's disaffection from the regime we supported. Our leaders lived in an isolated, dehumanized world of "surgical air strikes" and "Viet Cong infrastructure," when the reality was the maiming of women and children and the rise of a popular movement.

The Papers show that there was no concern in the decision making process for the impact of our actions upon the Vietnamese people. American objectives were always to preserve the power and prestige of this country. In the light of the devastation we have brought to that unhappy land, it is hard to believe that any consideration was given to the costs of our policies that would be borne by the very people we claimed to be helping.

But the American people too were treated with contempt. The Pentagon Papers show that the public statements of optimism, used to sustain public support for an increasingly unpopular policy, were contrary to the intelligence estimates being given our leaders at the time. While we were led to believe that just a few more soldiers or a few more bombing runs would turn the tide, the estimates were quite clear in warning that escalation would bring no significant change in the war.

The Pentagon Papers show that the enemy knew what we were not permitted to know. Our leaders sought to keep their plans from the American people, even as they telegraphed their intentions to the enemy, as part of a deliberate strategy to cause him to back down. The elaborate secrecy precautions, the carefully contrived subterfuges, the precisely orchestrated press leaks, were intended not to deceive "the other side," but to keep the American public in the dark. Both we and the enemy were viewed as "audiences" before whom various postures of determination, conciliation, inflexibility, and strength were portrayed. The American public, which once thought of itself as a central participant in the democratic process, found itself reduced to the status of an interested, but passive, observer.

The people do not want, nor should they any longer be subjected to, the paternalistic protection of an Executive which believes that it alone has the right answers. For too long both the people and Congress have been denied access to the needed data with which they can judge national policy. For too long they have been spoon-fed information designed to sustain predetermined decisions and denied information which questioned those decisions. For too long they have been forced to subsist on a diet of half-truths or deliberate deceit, by executives who consider the people and the Congress as adversaries.

1972 National Security Advisor Henry Kissinger's Peace Negotiations with Pham Van Dong (1982)

During the course of the Vietnam peace negotiations, National Security Advisor Henry Kissinger visited Hanoi, where he talked with Prime Minister Pham Van Dong and other top officials. Although both mainland China and North Vietnam were Communist states, Kissinger contrasted rather than compared the two, and also declared that he found Chou En-lai quite different from Pham Van Dong from the standpoint of negotiating. These talks were to end in an official halt to the Vietnamese conflict in late January, 1973, just as Richard Nixon was beginning his second term as President.

SOURCE: Henry Kissinger, *Years of Upheaval* (Boston: Little, Brown and Company, 1982). See pp. 28–30.

DOCUMENT:

As we turned to serious talks, we soon found ourselves in the position of survivors of an ancient vendetta who have reluctantly concluded that their inability to destroy each other compels an effort at coexistence—though without conviction or real hope. We were both aware of the dictates of prudence, but neither side could shake off its memories, nor could Hanoi abandon its passions. The attempts to behave in a friendly manner were so studied and took so much exertion that they created their own tension; the slightest disagreement tended to bring to the fore the underlying suspicion and resentment.

Hanoi's leaders soon showed that they had lost none of the insolence that for years had set our teeth on edge. My opposite number in these talks was Pham Van Dong, Prime Minister of the Democratic Republic of Vietnam for nearly twenty years. But the change of personality brought no alteration in the familiar style of condescending superiority or of deception masquerading as moral homily.

Pham Van Dong had come to my attention in January 1967, when he had given a brilliant interview to Harrison Salisbury of the New York *Times*, explaining why Hanoi was confident of winning against the mightiest power in the world. Dong had argued that the disparity in strength was illusory; the North Vietnamese were prepared to fight for generations; American's material superiority could operate only in a more limited time span. They would simply outlast us. Pham Van Dong turned out to be right-aided not a little by an American military strategy massive enough to hazard our international position yet sufficiently inhibited to guarantee an inconclusive outcome....

Pham Van Dong was wiry, short, wary, his piercing eyes watchful for the expected trickery and at the same time implying that the burden of proof of any statement by an arch-capitalist would be on the speaker. He greeted me on the steps of the elaborate structure now called the President's House. From here French colonial administrators had ruled all of Indochina and established in the minds of their all-too-receptive Vietnamese subjects the conviction that the boundaries of Indochina should forever coincide with those of the French colonial empire. Vietnamese expansionism, which had already proved the nightmare of its neighbors even before the arrival of the French, was thus given new impetus and legitimacy by colonial rule. We entered a large reception hall and seated ourselves in a semicircle for the introductory informal conversation—as in China. Also as in China, this was an occasion for subtle hints to establish the mood....

Pham Van Dong...did not take long to dash my dim hope that he might prove to be another Zhou Enlai and become a partner in transforming old enmity into new cooperation. He was not—indeed, could not be—a partner, any more than Vietnam was China. Pham Van Dong represented a people who had prevailed by unremitting tenacity; Zhou Enlai was the leader of a country that had made its mark through cultural preeminence and majesty of conduct. Pham Van Dong's strength was monomaniacal absorption with the ambitions of one country; Zhou was quintessentially Chinese in his conviction that China's performance was morally relevant to the rest of the world. Pham Van Dong was of the stuff of which revolutionary heroes are made. Zhou, while a revolutionary himself, was of the stuff of which great leaders are made.

Pham Van Dong, it is now clear, sought to tranquilize us so that Hanoi could complete its conquest of Indochina without American opposition. Zhou Enlai acted on the conviction that China's security—at least in the face of imminent Soviet threat—depended on America's strong commitment to the global balance of power. To Pham Van Dong the encounter with me was a tactic in a revolutionary struggle. He was prepared to improve relations with America if, as he had implied in our banter, this gained him a free hand in Indochina; otherwise the struggle would resume. In no case did Hanoi see any benefit in heightened American strength and self-confidence. Zhou Enlai's aims were strategically compatible with ours at least in the foreseeable future; his strategy presupposed shared interests that we would consider worth defending. Far from desiring to undermine America's international position and national self-assurance, as time went on Zhou attempted discreetly to strengthen both....

1975 Henry Kissinger on the Fall of the Saigon Government

Much happened in the United States in the two years between the signing of the Vietnamese peace accord in January, 1973 and the final fall of the Saigon regime in April, 1975. Later in 1973, Congress passed the War Powers Resolution—which placed certain limitations on the President in the area of foreign affairs—over Richard Nixon's veto. Then, in the autumn of 1974, Nixon resigned in the wake of the Watergate scandal, with Vice Presi-

dent Gerald Ford taking his place. Congress sharply reduced U.S. aid to South Vietnam. As a result of these developments, it is perhaps not surprising that South Vietnam collapsed rather quickly in the wake of the final North Vietnamese offensive during the spring of 1975. Secretary of State Henry Kissinger offered an assessment of the defeat in an interview with Barbara Walters on May 5.

SOURCE: U.S. Department of State *Bulletin*, May 26, 1975. See pp. 665–68.

DOCUMENT:

MISS WALTERS Mr. Secretary, we are about to celebrate our Bicentennial. Is Vietnam our first defeat in 200 years?

SECRETARY KISSINGER When a nation is engaged in a major effort for 10 years and then doesn't achieve its basic objectives, you have to say it is a significant setback, yes.

MISS WALTERS Is Vietnam our first defeat in 200 years?

SECRETARY KISSINGER Well, it depends how you assess the War of 1812 and other events. It is a significant setback.

MISS WALTERS Let me make a suggestion—not to run your foreign policy. But for example, one alternative is, after Congress had the arms cutoff, we might have gone to President Thieu and told him, "Look, it is a new world, and you had better negotiate unless you want defeat."

SECRETARY KISSINGER Let me first go back to where we were in January 1973 and where we wound up in April of '75. In January '73 we did not foresee that Watergate would sap the executive authority of the United States to such a degree that flexibility of executive action inherently would be circumscribed. We did not foresee that the Congress would pass a law which prohibited us from enforcing the Paris agreement; and while we probably might have done nothing anyway, it makes a lot of difference for Hanoi whether it thinks the United States probably will not or whether it thinks that we certainly can not.

I do not believe that Hanoi would have sent 19 of its 20 divisions south if these two things hadn't happened. Nor did we foresee that aid to Vietnam would be cut in successive years by 50 percent each year at a time when inflation quadrupled the oil prices and inflation increased the cost of everything—so that after May 1974 no new equipment of any kind was sent to Vietnam and not even spare parts in any substantial quantities reached Vietnam, so that ammunition had to be rationed for the Vietnamese forces. Maybe the South Vietnamese Army was not ever one of the better armies in the world, but even a good army would have been demoralized by these successive cuts.

None of this was predictable. After it became clearer that a gradual erosion of morale was occurring, we tried very hard to get negotiations started; and President Thieu, whatever you may think of him, on a number of occasions made proposals to get these talks started unconditionally.

But once the North Vietnamese realized what the trends were, they blocked all negotiations and went for a military solution.

MISS WALTERS	So that you feel there was no other possibility?
SECRETARY KISSINGER	There was no other possibility.
MISS WALTERS	It is now known that President Nixon wrote a letter to President Thieu in January of 1973 promising that the United States would move "full force" to punish any violations of the Paris peace agreement. You obviously knew of the content of this letter.
SECRETARY KISSINGER	Of course.
MISS WALTERS	Mr. Secretary, do you see our government recognizing the North Vietnamese Government?
SECRETARY KISSINGER	Well, we now have to see what the conduct of this Government is internationally and partially domestically. For example, we know that in Cambodia very tragic and inhuman and barbarous things are going on. We don't regret not having recognized Cambodia immediately.

We want to observe the conduct of the Vietnamese Government for a while before we make this decision.

MISS WALTERS	Can you tell us what part the Soviet Union played diplomatically, militarily, during the waning days of the South Vietnam collapse?
SECRETARY KISSINGER	The Soviet Union played, in the last two weeks, a moderately constructive role in enabling us to understand the possibilities there were for evacuation, both of Americans and South Vietnamese, and for the possibilities that might exist for a political evolution.

On the other hand, I do not want to give the Soviet Union excessive credit for moderating the consequences that its arms brought about. Therefore we have to see it in perspective.

The Foreign Policy of Nixon, Ford, and Henry Kissinger

48

1969 President Richard Nixon's Guam Doctrine and the Future of Asia

Four days before the first American astronauts landed on the moon, President Richard Nixon stopped off at Guam during the course of a nine-day, eight-nation tour. On July 25, Nixon set forth his Guam Doctrine in a conference with reporters, excerpts from which follow. The key point expressed in this highly important statement was that Asians would have to fight their own wars, although the United States would honor its treaty commitments and also provide military and economic assistance where and when it was needed. As applied to the Southeast Asia conflict, this meant the Vietnamization of the war. Despite the activities of a vocal minority in the United States who demanded an immediate pullout from Southeast Asia, Nixon held his ground and slowly began to withdraw American troops from Vietnam while at the same time pursuing a negotiated settlement of the conflict.

SOURCE: *Public Papers of the Presidents of the United States: Richard Nixon 1969* (Washington: Government Printing Office, 1971). See pp. 546–48.

DOCUMENT:

When I talked to Prime Minister Gorton [of Australia], he indicated, in the conversations he had had with a number of Asian leaders, they all wondered whether the United States, because of its frustration over the war in Vietnam, because of its earlier frustration over the war in Korea—whether the United States would continue to play a significant role in Asia, or whether the United States, like the French before, and then the British, and, of course, the Dutch—whether we would withdraw from the Pacific and play a minor role.

As I see it, even though the war in Vietnam has been, as we know, a terribly frustrating one, and, as a result of that frustration, even though there would be a tendency for many Americans to say, "After we are through with that, let's not become involved in Asia," I am convinced that the way to avoid becoming involved in another war in Asia is for the United States to continue to play a significant role.

I think the way that we could become involved would be to attempt withdrawal, because, whether we like it or not, geography makes us a Pacific power. And when we consider, for example, that Indonesia at its closest point is only 14 miles from the Philippines, when we consider that Guam, where we are presently standing, of course, is in the heart of Asia, when we consider the interests of the whole Pacific as they relate to Alaska and Hawaii, we can all realize this.

As we look at Asia today, we see that the major world power which adopts a very aggressive attitude and a belligerent attitude in its foreign policy, Communist China, of course, is in Asia, and we find that the two minor world powers—minor, although they do have significant strength as we have learned—that most greatly threaten the peace of the world, that adopt the most belligerent foreign policy, are in Asia, North Korea and, of course, North Vietnam.

When we consider those factors we, I think, realize that if we are thinking down the road, down the long road—not just 4 years, 5 years, but 10, 15, or 20—that if we are going to have peace in the world, that potentially the greatest threat to that peace will be in the Pacific.

Now, one other point I would make very briefly is that in terms of this situation as far as the role we should play, we must recognize that there are two great, new factors which you will see, incidentally, particularly when you arrive in the Philippines—something you will see there that we didn't see in 1953, to show you how quickly it has changed; a very great growth of nationalism, nationalism even in the Philippines, vis-a-vis the United States, as well as other countries in the world. And, also, at the same time that national pride is becoming a major factor, regional pride is becoming a major factor.

The second factor is one that is going to, I believe, have a major impact on the future of Asia, and it is something that we must take into account. Asians will say in every country that we visit that they do not want to be dictated to from the outside, Asia for the Asians. And that is what we want, and that is the role we should play. We should assist, but we should not dictate.

At this time, the political and economic plans that they are gradually developing are very hopeful. We will give assistance to those plans. We, of course, will keep the treaty commitments that we have.

But as far as our role is concerned, we must avoid that kind of policy that will make countries in Asia so dependent upon us that we are dragged into conflicts such as the one that we have in Vietnam.

This is going to be a difficult line to follow. It is one, however, that I think, with proper planning, we can develop.

1971 The Nixon Administration Tilts Toward Pakistan in Its War with India (1979)

By 1971, India had established a number of ties to the Soviet Union, while neighboring Pakistan had done the same thing with Communist China. During that year, Pakistan and India went to war, creating a dilemma for the United States, which needed Pakistan to

open up a channel of communications with the Chinese Communists. The Nixon adminis-
tration therefore made the rather controversial decision to tilt in the direction of Pakistan,
which also was its ally in SEATO. Unfortunately, West Pakistan had hurt its international
image by brutally putting down a revolt in East Pakistan in March. That December, India in-
vaded East Pakistan and set it free as the independent state of Bangladesh. Chou En-lai
was of the opinion that the United States had saved West Pakistan, as Henry Kissinger
points out in his memoirs.

SOURCE: Henry Kissinger, *White House Years* (Boston: Little, Brown and Company, 1979). See pp. 913–14.

DOCUMENT:

The India–Pakistan war of 1971 was perhaps the most complex issue of Nixon's first term. Not that emotions ran as high as on Vietnam, or that its effects were very long-lasting, though the "tilt toward Pakistan" entered the polemic folklore as a case history of political misjudgment. What made the crisis so difficult was that the stakes were so much greater than the common perception of them. The issue burst upon us while Pakistan was our only channel to China; we had no other means of communication with Peking. A major American initiative of fundamental importance to the global balance of power could not have survived if we colluded with the Soviet Union in the public humiliation of China's friend—and our ally. The naked recourse to force by a partner of the Soviet Union backed by Soviet arms and buttressed by Soviet assurances threatened the very structure of international order just when our whole Middle East strategy depended on proving the inefficacy of such tactics and when America's weight as a factor in the world was already being undercut by our divisions over Indochina. The assault on Pakistan was in our view a most dangerous precedent for Soviet behavior, which had to be resisted if we were not to tempt escalating upheavals. Had we acquiesced in such a power play, we would have sent a wrong signal to Moscow and unnerved all our allies, China, and the forces for restraint in other volatile areas of the world. This was, indeed, why the Soviets had made the Indian assault on Pakistan possible in the first place.

But an essentially geopolitical point of view found no understanding among those who conducted the public discourse on foreign policy in our country. (By "geopolitical" I mean an approach that pays attention to the requirements of equilibrium.) This dramatized one of the root dilemmas of the foreign policy of the Nixon Administration. Nixon and I wanted to found American foreign policy on a sober perception of permanent national interest, rather than on fluctuating emotions that in the past had led us to excesses of both intervention and abdication. We judged India by the impact of its actions, not by its pretensions or by the legacy of twenty years of sentiment. But our assessments depended on conjecture about the wider consequences of India's assault. To shape events one must act on the basis of assessments that cannot be proved correct when they are made. All the judgments we reached about the implications of an assault on Pakistan were undemonstrable. By the time the implications were clear it would be too late; indeed, there might then be another dispute as to what had actually produced them.

The majority of informed opinion sought to judge the confrontation on the subcontinent on the merits of the issues that had produced the crisis. Pakistan had unquestionably acted unwisely, brutally, and even immorally, though on a matter which under international law was clearly under its domestic jurisdiction. But even here, I would have to say we had an assessment of the facts different from that of our critics. I remain convinced to this day that Mrs. Gandhi was not motivated primarily by conditions in East Pakistan; many solutions to its inevitable autonomy existed, several suggested by us. Rather, encouraged by the isolation of Pakistan, the diplomatic and military support of the Soviet Union, the domestic strains in China, and the divisions in the United States, the Indian Prime Minister decided in the spring or summer of 1971 to use the opportunity to settle accounts with Pakistan once and for all and assert India's preeminence on the subcontinent....

1971 Secretary of State William Rogers Endorses the Two Chinas Policy

By the time that Richard Nixon took office as President, pressure was mounting in the United Nations to admit Communist China, which the United States refused to recognize diplomatically between 1949 and 1978. As a result, Secretary of State William Rogers announced a Two Chinas policy. The United States affirmed its willingness to allow the seating of Communist China in the General Assembly of the United Nations, but at the same time it opposed the expulsion from that body of the Taiwanese government, which had provided technical assistance to a number of less developed countries.

SOURCE: U.S. Department of State *Bulletin*, August 23, 1971. See pp. 193–94.

DOCUMENT:

In October 1969 President Nixon said with regard to Latin America that "we must deal realistically with governments...as they are." Both in Asia and elsewhere in the world we are seeking to accommodate our role to the realities of the world today. Our objective is to contribute in practical terms to the building of a framework for a stable peace.

No question of Asian policy has so perplexed the world in the last 20 years as the China question—and the related question of representation in the United Nations. Basic to that question is the fact that each of two governments claims to be the sole government of China and representative of all of the people of China.

Representation in an international organization need not prejudice the claims or views of either government. Participation of both in the United Nations need not require that result.

Rather, it would provide governments with increased opportunities for contact and communication. It would also help promote cooperation on common problems which affect all of the member nations regardless of political differences.

The United States accordingly will support action at the General Assembly this fall calling for seating the People's Republic of China. At the same time the United States will oppose any action to expel the Republic of China or otherwise deprive it of representation in the United Nations.

Our consultations, which began several months ago, have indicated that the question of China's seat in the Security Council is a matter which many nations will wish to address. In the final analysis, of course, under the charter provision, the Security Council will make this decision. We, for our part, are prepared to have this question resolved on the basis of a decision of members of the United Nations.

Our consultations have also shown that any action to deprive the Republic of China of its representation would meet with strong opposition in the General Assembly. Certainly, as I have said, the United States will oppose it.

The Republic of China has played a loyal and conscientious role in the U.N. since the organization was founded. It has lived up to all of its charter obligations. Having made remarkable progress in developing its own economy, it has cooperated internationally by providing valuable technical assistance to a number of less developed countries, particularly in Africa.

The position of the United States is that if the United Nations is to succeed in its peace-keeping role, it must deal with the realities of the world in which we live. Thus, the United States will cooperate with those who, whatever their views on the status of the relationship of the two governments, wish to continue to have the Republic of China represented in the United Nations.

The outcome, of course, will be decided by 127 members of the United Nations. For our part we believe that the decision we have taken is fully in accord with President Nixon's desire to normalize relations with the People's Republic of China in the interests of world peace and in accord with our conviction that the continued representation in the United Nations of the Republic of China will contribute to peace and stability in the world.

1972 Richard Nixon's Visit to Mainland China (1978)

It is ironic that hardlining anti-Communist Richard Nixon would be the first American President to visit mainland China. The American composer John Adams recently immortalized this significant event in a full-length opera. Nixon's conversations with both Chou En-lai and Mao Tse-tung during February, 1972 were often fascinating, a case in point being Nixon's visit to Mao's home in Peking. As one might expect, his China trip occupies a central position in Nixon's memoirs.

SOURCE: Richard Nixon, *RN: The Memoirs* (New York: Warner Books, 1978). See pp. 561–63.

DOCUMENT:

Although Mao spoke with some difficulty, it was clear that his mind was moving like lightning. "Our common old friend Generalissimo Chiang Kai-shek doesn't approve of this," he said, with a sweeping gesture that might have meant our meeting or that might have taken in all China. "He calls us Communist bandits. He recently made a speech. Have you seen it?"

"Chiang Kai-shek calls the Chairman a bandit," I replied. "What does the Chairman call Chiang Kai-shek?"

Mao chuckled when my question was translated, but it was Chou who answered, "Generally speaking, we call them 'Chiang Kai-shek's clique,' " he said. "In the newspapers sometimes we call him a bandit; he calls us bandits in turn. Anyway, we abuse each other."

"I voted for you during your last election," Mao said with a broad smile.

"When the Chairman says he voted for me," I replied, "he voted for the lesser of two evils."

"I like rightists," Mao responded, obviously enjoying himself. "People say that you are rightists—that the Republican Party is on the right—that Prime Minister Heath is also to the right."

"And General de Gaulle," I added.

Without dropping a beat, Mao said, "De Gaulle is a different question." Then he continued, "They also say the Christian Democratic Party of West Germany is to the right. I am comparatively happy when these people on the right come into power."

"I think the most important thing to note is that in America, at least at this time, those on the right can do what those on the left can only talk about," I said.

Although the meeting with Mao dealt mainly with what he called the "philosophy" of our new and potential relationship, I raised in general terms the major substantive questions we would be discussing. I said that we should examine our policies and determine how they should develop in order to deal with the entire world as well as the immediate problems of Korea, Vietnam, and Taiwan.

I went on, "We, for example, must ask ourselves—again in the confines of this room—why the Soviets have more forces on the border facing you than they do on the border facing Western Europe? We must ask ourselves, What is the future of Japan? Is it better—and here I know we have disagreements—from China's standpoint for Japan to be neutral and totally defenseless, or is it better for Japan to have some mutual defense relations with the United States? One thing is sure—we can leave no vacuums, because they can be filled. The Prime Minister, for example, has pointed out that the United States 'reaches out its hands' and that the Soviet Union 'reaches out its hands.' The question is, which danger does the People's Republic of China face? Is it the danger of American aggression—or of Soviet aggression? These are hard questions, but we have to discuss them."

1972 The SALT I Treaty with the Soviet Union

Several months after visiting mainland China for the first time, Richard Nixon made his fifth trip to the Soviet Union, accompanied by Secretary of State William Rogers, National Security Advisor Henry Kissinger, and a huge press corps. The occasion for Nixon's May, 1972 visit was the signing of the Treaty on Anti-Ballistic Systems, the product of two and one-half years of strategic arms limitation talks. This treaty in essence made it illegal for either nation to defend its cities other than Washington or Moscow against nuclear attack, a policy which Ronald Reagan challenged in the 1980s with his endorsement of the Strategic Defense Initiative. On August 2, the Senate approved the SALT I treaty by an overwhelming 88 to 2 vote. Nixon, moreover, also reached an agreement with the Soviet Union at Moscow on quite a few other topics, as he pointed out in his address to Congress on June 1 reviewing the accomplishments of the Moscow summit.

SOURCE: U.S. Department of State *Bulletin*, June 26, 1972. See pp. 856–57.

DOCUMENT:

This was a working summit. We sought to establish not a superficial "Spirit of Moscow," but a solid record of progress on solving the difficult issues which for so long have divided our two nations and also have divided the world. Reviewing the number and the scope of the agreements that emerged, I think we have accomplished that goal.

Recognizing the responsibility of the advanced industrial nations to set an example in combating mankind's common enemies, the United States and the Soviet Union have agreed to cooperate in efforts to reduce pollution and enhance environmental quality. We have agreed to work together in the field of medical science and public health, particularly in the conquest of cancer and heart disease.

Recognizing that the quest for useful knowledge transcends differences between ideologies and social systems, we have agreed to expand United States–Soviet cooperation in many areas of science and technology.

We have joined in plans for an exciting new adventure, a new adventure in the cooperative exploration of space, which will begin—subject to congressional approval of funding—with a joint orbital mission of an Apollo vehicle and a Soviet spacecraft in 1975.

By forming habits of cooperation and strengthening institutional ties in areas of peaceful enterprise, these four agreements to which I have referred will create on both sides a steadily growing vested interest in the maintenance of good relations between our two countries.

Expanded United States–Soviet trade will also yield advantages to both of our nations. When the two largest economies in the world start trading with each other on a much larger scale, living standards in both nations will rise and the stake which both have in peace will increase.

Progress in this area is proceeding on schedule. At the summit, we established a Joint Commercial Commission which will complete the negotiations for a comprehensive trade agreement between the United States and the U.S.S.R. And we expect the final terms of such an agreement to be settled, later this year.

Two further accords which were reached last week have a much more direct bearing on the search for peace and security in the world.

One is the agreement between the American and Soviet navies aimed at significantly reducing the chances of dangerous incidents between our ships and aircraft at sea.

And second, and most important, there is the treaty and the related executive agreement which will limit, for the first time, both offensive and defensive strategic nuclear weapons in the arsenals of the United States and the Soviet Union.

Three-fifths of all the people alive in the world today have spent their whole lifetimes under the shadow of a nuclear war which could be touched off by the arms race among the great powers. Last Friday in Moscow we witnessed the beginning of the end of that era which began in 1945. We took the first step toward a new era of mutually agreed restraint and arms limitation between the two principal nuclear powers.

With this step we have enhanced the security of both nations. We have begun to check the wasteful and dangerous spiral of nuclear arms which has dominated relations between our two countries for a generation. We have begun to reduce the level of fear by reducing the causes of fear for our two peoples and for all peoples in the world.

The ABM [antiballistic missile] Treaty will be submitted promptly for the Senate's advice and consent to ratification, and the interim agreement limiting certain offensive weapons will be submitted to both Houses for concurrence—because we can undertake agreements as important as these only on a basis of full partnership between the executive and legislative branches of our government.

From the standpoint of the United States, when we consider what the strategic balance would have looked like later in the seventies if there had been no arms limitation, it is clear that the agreements forestall a major spiraling of the arms race—one which would have worked to our disadvantage, since we have no current building programs for the categories of weapons which have been frozen and since no new building program could have produced any new weapons in those categories during the period of the freeze.

No power on earth is stronger than the United States of America today. And none will be stronger than the United States of America in the future.

This is the only national defense posture which can ever be acceptable to the United States. This is the posture I ask the Senate and the Congress to protect by approving the arms limitation agreements to which I have referred. This is the posture which, with the responsible cooperation of the Congress, I will take all necessary steps to maintain in our future defense programs.

1973 Henry Kissinger on the Meaning of *Détente* (1982)

Few foreign policy concepts of the post-World War II era have been misunderstood or misinterpreted more than détente. *The implementation of this policy toward the Soviet Union was one of the major objectives of the Nixon Administration.* Détente *did not mean being soft on Communism, or appeasing the Russians, but rather a relaxation of tensions, and increased contacts between the United States and the Soviet Union. (The numerous understandings which Nixon agreed to at Moscow in 1972 reflect the latter goal.) The more involved the Russians became with the free world, the easier it would be for the free world to apply various nonmilitary pressures on the Russians, such as economic restraints, should they behave improperly. How successful was* détente? *Its critics have declared that it was far less than a complete triumph, but Henry Kissinger strongly defended it in his memoirs as the best way of dealing with the Soviet Union.*

SOURCE: Kissinger, *Years of Upheaval.* See pp. 236–37.

DOCUMENT:

It is therefore important to recall what *détente* was and what it was not.

Richard Nixon came into office with the well-deserved reputation of a lifetime of anti-Communism. He despised liberal intellectuals who blamed the Cold War on the United States and who seemed to believe the Soviet system might be transformed through the strenuous exercise of goodwill. Nixon profoundly distrusted Soviet motives; he was a firm believer in negotiations from positions of strength; he was, in short, the classic Cold Warrior. Yet after four tumultuous years in office, it was this man, so unlike the conventional intellectual's notion of a peacemaker, who paradoxically was negotiating with the Soviets on the broadest agenda of East–West relations in twenty-five years. And not long afterward he found himself accused of what had been a staple of his own early campaign rhetoric: of being "soft on Communism."

The paradox was more apparent than real. We did not consider a relaxation of tensions a concession to the Soviets. We had our own reasons for it. We were not abandoning the ideological struggle, but simply trying—tall order as it was—to discipline it by precepts of national interest. Nor was *détente* without its successes. There is no doubt that our better relations with the Soviet Union (and China) isolated Hanoi. In 1972 Moscow acquiesced in the mining of North Vietnamese harbors and the bombing of Hanoi and Haiphong; by the end of the year Hanoi settled for terms it had contemptuously rejected for years. In Europe the knowledge that the Americans, too, could talk to the Russians reined in the temptation to blame all tensions on the United States and to seek safety in quasi-neutralism. And later on it helped us to bring about a diplomatic revolution in the Middle East.

I also believe that the evidence proves exactly the opposite of what our critics charged: *Détente* helped rather than hurt the American defense effort. Before the word *détente* was even known in America the Congress cut $40 billion from the defense budgets of Nixon's first term; even so dedicated a supporter of American strength as Senator Henry M. Jackson publicly advocated small defense cuts and a "prudent defense posture." After the signature of SALT I, our defense budget increased and the Nixon and Ford administrations put through the strategic weapons (the MX missile, B-1 bomber, cruise missiles, Trident submarines, and more advanced warheads) that even a decade later are the backbone of our defense program and that had been stymied in the Congress prior to the easing of our relations with Moscow.

Détente did not prevent resistance to Soviet expansion; on the contrary, it fostered the only possible psychological framework for such resistance. Nixon knew where to draw the line against Soviet adventure whether it occurred directly or through proxy, as in Cienfuegos, Jordan, along the Suez Canal, and during the India–Pakistan war. He drew it with cool fortitude, and all the more credibly because there was national understanding that we were not being truculent for its own sake. If the Vietnam war had taught us anything, it was that a military confrontation could be sustained only if the American people were convinced there was no other choice.

Any American President soon learns that he has a narrow margin for maneuver. The United States and the Soviet Union are ideological rivals. *Détente* cannot change that. The nuclear age compels us to coexist. Rhetorical crusades cannot change that, either....

1973 Richard Nixon's Veto of the War Powers Resolution

The Senate failed to approve the Bricker Amendment in 1954 restricting the authority of the President to enter into executive agreements with foreign nations, but it did pass the War Powers Resolution (House Joint Resolution 542) over President Richard Nixon's veto in the fall of 1973. Under this, the President was allowed to send troops abroad for sixty days, but then had to obtain the authorization of Congress to extend the operation. To Nixon, this measure not only interfered with certain powers which the President Constitutionally enjoys in the area of foreign affairs, but also might cripple the ability of the United States to act decisively at the time of an international crisis. These concerns are emphasized in Nixon's October 24 veto message. The President, though, was not able to keep his own party united behind the successful veto override attempt, which passed the Senate 75 to 18 on November 7 and the House 284 to 135 on the same day. Twenty-two Southern Democrats voted to sustain the veto, but no less than eighty-six Republicans voted to override it.

SOURCE: U.S. Department of State *Bulletin*, November 26, 1973. See pp. 662–64.

DOCUMENT:

House Joint Resolution 542 would attempt to take away, by a mere legislative act, authorities which the President has properly exercised under the Constitution for almost 200 years. One of its provisions would automatically cut off certain authorities after sixty days unless the Congress extended them. Another would allow the Congress to eliminate certain authorities merely by the passage of a concurrent resolution—an action which does not normally have the force of law, since it denies the President his constitutional role in approving legislation.

I believe that both these provisions are unconstitutional. The only way in which the constitutional powers of a branch of the Government can be altered is by amending the Constitution—and any attempt to make such alterations by legislation alone is clearly without force.

While I firmly believe that a veto of House Joint Resolution 542 is warranted solely on constitutional grounds, I am also deeply disturbed by the practical consequences of this resolution. For it would seriously undermine this Nation's ability to act decisively and convincingly in times of international crisis. As a result, the confidence of our allies in our ability to assist them could be diminished and the respect of our adversaries for our deterrent posture could decline. A permanent and substantial element of unpredictability would be injected into the world's assessment of American behavior, further increasing the likelihood of miscalculation and war.

If this resolution had been in operation, America's effective response to a variety of challenges in recent years would have been vastly complicated or even made impossible. We may well have been unable to respond in the way we did during the Berlin crisis of 1961, the Cuban missile crisis of 1962, the Congo rescue operation in 1964, and the Jordanian crisis of 1970—to mention just a few examples. In addition, our recent actions to bring about a peaceful settlement of the hostilities in the Middle East would have been seriously impaired if this resolution had been in force.

I am particularly disturbed by the fact that certain of the President's constitutional powers as Commander in Chief of the Armed Forces would terminate automatically under this resolution 60 days after they were invoked. No overt Congressional action would be required to cut off these powers—they would disappear automatically unless the Congress extended them. In effect, the Congress is here attempting to increase its policy-making role through a provision which requires it to take absolutely no action at all.

In my view, the proper way for the Congress to make known its will on such foreign policy questions is through a positive action, with full debate on the merits of the issue and with each member taking the responsibility of casting a yes or no vote after considering those merits. The authorization and appropriations process represents one of the ways in which such influence can be exercised. I do not, however, believe that the Congress can responsibly contribute its considered, collective judgment on such grave questions without full debate and without a yes or no vote. Yet this is precisely what the joint resolution would allow. It would give every future Congress the ability to handcuff every future President merely by doing nothing and sitting still. In my view, one cannot become a responsible partner unless one is prepared to take responsible action.

I believe that full and cooperative participation in foreign policy matters by both the executive and the legislative branches could be enhanced by a careful and dispassionate study of their constitutional roles. Helpful proposals for such a study have already been made in the Congress. I would welcome the establishment of a non-partisan commission on the constitutional roles of the Congress and the President in the conduct of foreign affairs. This commission could make a thorough review of the principal constitutional issues in Executive–Congressional relations, including the war powers, the international agreement powers, and the question of Executive privilege, and then submit its recommendations to the President and the Congress. The members of such a commission could be drawn from both parties—and could represent many perspectives including those of the Congress, the executive branch, the legal profession, and the academic community.

1975 President Gerald Ford, Cambodia, and the *Mayaguez* Crisis (1979)

Shortly after the fall of South Vietnam, during the spring of 1975, an incident occurred which provided a serious challenge to the Ford administration. The Cambodians seized the S.S. Mayaguez *off the coast of Cambodia in international waters. In the hours which followed, Gerald Ford unsuccessfully sought the assistance of the Chinese Communists, the Thais, and the United Nations. Thwarted in his diplomatic initiatives, he finally resorted to military force, which led to the rescue of the* Mayaguez *crew, but at a heavy cost in American lives. The President discussed this episode in his memoirs.*

SOURCE: Gerald Ford, *A Time to Heal: The Autobiography* (New York: Harper and Row, 1979). See pp. 275–80.

DOCUMENT:

In the wake of our humiliating retreat from Cambodia and South Vietnam in the spring of 1975, our allies around the world began to question our resolve. "America—A Helpless Giant," ran the headline over a page-one editorial in the respected *Frankfurter Allgemeine Zeitung*. The British were concerned. So, too, were the French. Our friends in Asia were equally upset. In the Middle East the Israelis began to wonder whether the U.S. would stand by them in the event of a war.

At 7:40 on the morning of May 12, Brent Scowcroft stepped into the Oval Office to tell me that an American merchant ship, S.S. *Mayaguez,* had been seized in international waters off the coast of Cambodia. First reports from the scene were very sketchy, but there were indications that the Cambodians were towing the ship toward the port of Kompong Som. Shortly after noon that day, I convened a meeting of the National Security Council in the Cabinet Room.

Kissinger leaned forward over the table and with emotion stressed the broad ramifications of the incident. The issues at stake went far beyond the seizure of the ship, he said; they extended to international perceptions of U.S. resolve and will. If we failed to respond to the challenge, it would be a serious blow to our prestige around the world. "At some point," he continued, "the United States must draw the line. This is not our idea of the best such situation. It is not our choice. But we must act upon it now, and act firmly."

At the conclusion of that meeting, I decided to move forward on two fronts simultaneously. I told Kissinger to have the State Department demand the immediate release of the ship and her crew. The problem there, of course, was that State didn't know upon whom to serve the demand. We had no diplomatic relations with the new Khmer Rouge regime. Perhaps the Chinese would act as intermediaries. It was unlikely but still worth a try. At the same time, I ordered *Coral Sea* and other ships to speed toward the site of the incident. Additionally, I directed aircraft based in the Philippines to locate *Mayaguez* and keep her in view.

The diplomatic approach didn't seem promising. Summoned to the State Department, the Chinese representative in Washington refused to accept our message for the Cambodians.

At 10:22 that morning, I convened a second meeting of the NSC. In Bangkok, Thai Premier Kukrit Pramoj had just issued a statement warning that he would not permit us to use Thai bases for operations against Cambodia. I sensed that this was more political rhetoric than anything else; the Thais knew we had no alternative but to use the base at Utapao.

Our efforts to solve the crisis diplomatically had failed. The Chinese in Peking had returned the second message we had asked them to give the Cambodians. Significantly, however, a Chinese official in Paris had said that his country wouldn't do anything should we decide to use military force.

During that third meeting of the NSC—which didn't break up until 12:30 Wednesday morning—we decided to make one final approach diplomatically. Our ambassador to the United Nations, John Scali, would give U.N. Secretary General Kurt Waldheim a letter requesting his help in securing the release of the ship and her crew. I didn't really expect any results from that, so I determined that we would probably have to move militarily. But first we would wait and see.

At 3:52 on Wednesday afternoon, I convened the fourth and final meeting of the NSC.

Slightly more than an hour after the meeting began, I started issuing the orders. *Holt* was to seize and secure *Mayaguez*. Marines were to land on Koh Tang, rescue crew members there and destroy any Cambodian units that got in the way. *Coral Sea* was to launch four air strikes against military installations near Kompong Som, including an oil depot, railroad marshaling yards and the airfield at Ream. The first of these attacks was to occur at 8:45 p.m. EDT to coincide with the estimated time of our capture of the ship.

New Diplomatic Initiatives under Jimmy Carter 49

1976 Eastern Europe and the Ford–Carter Presidential Debates

Following World War II, a Soviet Iron Curtain descended over all of Eastern Europe, with the exception of Greece and Turkey, which were protected by the Truman Doctrine. Members of various Eastern European nationality groups in the United States—especially Polish–Americans—were highly sensitive to Russian control over that area. Therefore, when President Gerald Ford claimed in one of his debates with Democratic challenger Jimmy Carter during the 1976 election that there was no Soviet domination of Eastern Europe, he may have cost himself votes in a close Presidential contest, which he lost.

SOURCE: Sidney Kraus, Editor, *The Great Debates: Carter vs. Ford 1976* (Bloomington: Indiana University Press, 1979). See pp. 481–82.

DOCUMENT:

PRES. FORD   If we turn to Helsinki—I'm glad you raised it, Mr. Frankel. In the case of Helsinki, thirty-five nations signed an agreement, including the secretary of state for the Vatican—I can't under any circumstances believe that His Holiness, the Pope would agree by signing that agreement that the thirty-five nations have turned over to the Warsaw Pact nations the domination of—Eastern Europe. It just isn't true. And if Mr. Carter alleges that His Holiness by signing that has done it, he is totally inaccurate. Now, what has been accomplished by the Helsinki agreement? Number one, we have an agreement where they notify us and we notify them of any military maneuvers that are to be undertaken. They have done it. In both cases where they've done so, there is no Soviet domination of Eastern Europe and there never will be under a Ford administration.

MS. FREDERICK   Governor Carter?

MR. FRANKEL   I'm sorry. Did I understand you to say, sir, that the Russians are not using Eastern Europe as their own sphere of influence in occupying most of the countries there and in making sure with their troops that it's a Communist zone, whereas on our side of the line the Italians and the French are still flirting with the possibility of Communism?

PRES. FORD   I don't believe, Mr. Frankel, that the Yugoslavs consider themselves dominated by the Soviet Union. I don't believe that the Rumanians consider themselves dominated by the Soviet Union. Each of those countries is independent, autonomous; it has its own territorial integrity and the United States does not concede that those countries are under the domination of the Soviet Union. As a matter of fact, I visited Poland, Yugoslavia and Rumania to make certain that the people of those countries understood that the president of the United States and the people of the United States are dedicated to their independence, their autonomy and their freedom.

MS. FREDERICK   Governor Carter, may I have your response?

GOV. CARTER   Well, in the first place, I'm not criticizing His Holiness the Pope. I was talking about Mr. Ford. The fact is that secrecy has surrounded the decisions made by the Ford administration. In the case of the Helsinki agreement—it may have been a good agreement at the beginning, but we have failed to enforce the so-called basket three part, which insures the right of people to migrate, to join their families, to be free, to speak out. The Soviet Union is still jamming Radio Free Europe—Radio Free Europe is being jammed. We've also seen a very serious problem with the so-called Sonnenfeldt document, which apparently Mr. Ford has just endorsed, which said that there's an organic linkage between the Eastern European countries and the Soviet Union. And I would like to see Mr. Ford convince the Polish–Americans and the Czech–Americans and the Hungarian–Americans in this country that those countries don't live under the domination and supervision of the Soviet Union behind the Iron Curtain.

1977 Jimmy Carter's Notre Dame Address on Foreign Policy

On May 22, 1977, President Jimmy Carter delivered an address on foreign policy at Notre Dame University. Carter regarded this speech as being of great importance, and continued to alter the text up to the very last moment. The orientation of this message—with its heavy emphasis on human rights—is at sharp variance with the national interest philosophy of

Henry Kissinger. Like Woodrow Wilson, Carter emphasized the moral element in diplomacy. Subsequent events during his Presidency, though, highlighted the problems involved in trying to attain idealistic objectives in the global arena.

SOURCE: *Weekly Compilation of Presidential Documents,* Vol 13, No. 22. See pp. 774–79.

DOCUMENT:

Democracy's great recent successes—in India, Portugal, Spain, Greece—show that our confidence in this system is not misplaced. Being confident of our own future, we are now free of that inordinate fear of communism which once led us to embrace any dictator who joined us in that fear. I'm glad that that's being changed.

For too many years, we've been willing to adopt the flawed and erroneous principles and tactics of our adversaries, sometimes abandoning our own values for theirs. We've fought fire with fire, never thinking that fire is better quenched with water. This approach failed, with Vietnam the best example of its intellectual and moral poverty. But through failure, we have now found our way back to our own principles and values, and we have regained our lost confidence.

The world is still divided by ideological disputes, dominated by regional conflicts, and threatened by danger that we will not resolve the differences of race and wealth without violence or without drawing into combat the major military powers. We can no longer separate the traditional issues of war and peace from the new global questions of justice, equity, and human rights.

It is a new world—but America should not fear it. It is a new world—and we should help to shape it. It is a new world that calls for a new American foreign policy—a policy based on constant decency in its values and on optimism in our historical vision.

We can no longer have a policy solely for the industrial nations as the foundation of global stability, but we must respond to the new reality of a politically awakening world.

We can no longer expect that the other 150 nations will follow the dictates of the powerful, but we must continue—confidently—our efforts to inspire, to persuade, and to lead.

Let me review what we have been doing and discuss what we intend to do.

First, we have reaffirmed America's commitment to human rights as a fundamental tenet of our foreign policy. In ancestry, religion, color, place of origin, and cultural background, we Americans are as diverse a nation as the world has ever seen. No common mystique of blood or soil unites us. What draws us together, perhaps more than anything else, is a belief in human freedom.

Second, we've moved deliberately to reinforce the bonds among our democracies. In our recent meetings in London, we agreed to widen our economic cooperation, to promote free trade, to strengthen the world's monetary system, to seek ways of avoiding nuclear proliferation. We prepared constructive proposals for the forthcoming meetings on North–South problems of poverty, development, and global well-being, and we agreed on joint efforts to reinforce and to modernize our common defense.

Third, we've moved to engage the Soviet Union in a joint effort to halt the strategic arms race. This race is not only dangerous, it's morally deplorable. We must put an end to it.

Fourth, we are taking deliberate steps to improve the chances of lasting peace in the Middle East. Through wide-ranging consultation with leaders of the countries involved—Israel, Syria, Jordan, and Egypt—we have found some areas of agreement and some movement toward consensus. The negotiations must continue.

And fifth, we are attempting, even at the risk of some friction with our friends, to reduce the danger of nuclear proliferation and the worldwide spread of conventional weapons.

Finally, let me say that we are committed to a peaceful resolution of the crisis in southern Africa. The time has come for the principle of majority rule to be the basis for political order, recognizing that in a democratic system the rights of the minority must also be protected.

Let me conclude by summarizing: Our policy is based on an historical vision of America's role. Our policy is derived from a larger view of global change. Our policy is rooted in our moral values, which never change. Our policy is reinforced by our material wealth and by our military power. Our policy is designed to serve mankind. And it is a policy that I hope will make you proud to be Americans.

1977 The Two Panama Canal Treaties (1982)

Ever since the Panamanian riots of 1964, there had been increasing pressure in the United States for a new Panama Canal treaty. The fact that this would involve the eventual termination of American control over this strategic waterway caused a problem, however, since many Americans did not want to surrender it. During 1974, with Richard Nixon in the White House, the United States signed an agreement with Panama establishing the principles which would underlie a new treaty. Two years later, in 1976, Democratic Presidential candidate Jimmy Carter promised not to surrender the canal, only to throw his support behind the two new treaties as President.

SOURCE: Jimmy Carter, *Keeping Faith: Memoirs of a President* (Toronto: Bantam Books, 1982). See pp. 155–56.

DOCUMENT:

As I conferred with my foreign policy advisers after the election, it seemed clear that if we were going to negotiate seriously with Panama, two facts would have to be faced: we would have to begin immediately; and the eventual agreement would have to include a phasing out of our absolute control of the Canal, as well as the acknowledgment of Panamanian sovereignty.

These were not easy decisions for me to make. I knew that we were sure to face a terrible political fight in Congress. During the fall of 1975, a Senate resolution had been introduced that directly contravened the terms our country would be offering at the negotiating table. It opposed any new treaty and expressed strong opposition to any termination of United States sovereignty over the Canal Zone. The resolution had been sponsored by thirty-eight senators, four more than the one-third needed to prevent ratification of a treaty! Furthermore, public-opinion polls showed that the American public strongly opposed relinquishing control of the Canal.

Nevertheless, I believed that a new treaty was absolutely necessary. I was convinced that we needed to correct an injustice. Our failure to take action after years of promises under five previous Presidents had created something of a diplomatic cancer, which was poisoning our relations with Panama.

In addition, though we could not talk about it much in public, the Canal was in serious danger from direct attack and sabotage unless a new and fair treaty arrangement could be forged. This concern was an important consideration for me and the Joint Chiefs of Staff. Our military leaders came to tell me—and also testified to Congress—that the Canal could not be defended permanently unless we were able to maintain a working partnership and good relations with Panama. Secretary of Defense Harold Brown expressed it well when he said that the Canal could best be kept in operation "by a cooperative effort with a friendly Panama," rather than by an "American garrison amid hostile surroundings." The commanding Army officer in the Canal Zone estimated that it would require a force of at least a hundred thousand armed men to mount a reasonable defense of the Canal within a hostile environment. Even then a successful defense would be doubtful, especially if other Latin American nations became antagonistic to us.

Both we and the Panamanian leaders had to be careful not to present this crucial argument in the form of a threat, because there would, understandably, be a negative reaction from Congress and the American public. In fact, opponents of a new treaty were the ones who would raise this issue often, claiming that we were negotiating only as a response to "blackmail."

Of course, the security of the Canal was also of crucial importance to Panama. More than anything else, the Panamanians wanted to guarantee its continued operation. The stability of their government and the strength of their economy depended on a successful resolution of the treaty dispute. Dissident groups, some known to be subject to strong communist influences, were using the old treaty terms to support their vituperative charges against the United States as an "imperialistic colonial power." These persistent attacks were not only damaging to us, but comprised a serious threat to the political and business leaders of Panama. It was certainly to our advantage to have a strong, stable, and prosperous Panama, and it was important that we prevent the strengthening of communists and terrorist groups by proving we could be fair.

I was additionally concerned because our failure to act on the treaty was driving a wedge between us and some of our best friends and allies among the other American nations. They were being forced to take sides between us and Panama, and they were not supporting us. In a way not of our choosing, this issue had become a litmus test throughout the world, indicating how the United States, as a superpower, would treat a small and relatively defenseless nation that had always been a close partner and supporter.

Despite the opposition of Congress and the public, I decided to plow ahead, believing that if the facts could be presented clearly, my advisers and I could complete action while my political popularity was still high and before we had to face the additional complication of the congressional election campaigns of 1978.

1977 A Leading Critic of the Canal Treaties: Representative Daniel Flood

The American people were less than enamored by the Carter administration's two Panama Canal treaties, the first of which surrendered the Canal at the end of 1999, the second of which jointly maintained the neutrality of the Canal in perpetuity. Conservative political leaders like Republican Senator Jesse Helms of North Carolina were skeptical about any agreement reached with the left-leaning Panamanian strongman, General Omar Torrijos, but opposition to the treaties was by no means restricted to the right wing of the political spectrum. A case in point was Democratic Representative Daniel Flood of Pennsylvania, who testified against them before a Senatorial subcommittee. When the second Panama Canal treaty came up for a vote on March 16, 1978, the margin of approval was narrow: 68 to 32; an important amendment permitted the United States to intervene militarily to guarantee the right of transit during an emergency situation. The assembled Senators then approved the first treaty by the same margin. Fifty-two Democrats and sixteen Republicans voted in the affirmative, while ten Democrats and twenty-two Republicans cast nay ballots.

SOURCE: U.S. Senate, Committee on the Judiciary, Subcommittee on the Separation of Powers, *Panama Canal Treaty (Disposition of United States Territory), Hearings Part 3*, Ninety-Fifth Congress, First Session, 1977. See pp. 33–36.

DOCUMENT:

One of the most flagrant examples of fallacious prosurrender propaganda so often stressed is that, if we do not surrender the Canal Zone to Panama, the relations of the United States with all of Latin America will be seriously impaired. There could be no greater deception, for major Latin American countries, especially those on the west coast, know Panama well.

Their leaders from Presidents down know what the consequences of such surrender would be for their own economy in the way of increased transit tolls. Attention is invited to the perceptive 1976 article by Dr. Mario Lazo on "Panama

Canal Giveaway: A Latin American's View," which I request be included with my remarks.

Soviet power, understanding the vacuum that would be created by the projected relinquishment by the United States of its sovereignty over the Canal Zone, has already moved toward establishing a beachhead in Panama by means of a July 19, 1977, U.S.S.R.–Panama economic pact. This matter was discussed at length in the *American Legion National Security–Foreign Relations Bulletin,* July–August 1977, major excerpts of which I ask be included in my remarks.

Mr. Chairman, the pact, I believe, is most significant for it includes provisions for the Soviet Union to utilize the Panama free zone in Colon, which in turn now includes Old France Field in the Canal Zone, a World War II airfield located within the zone territory and is thus within our defense perimeter.

Surrender of the U.S. Canal Zone would undoubtedly have serious far-away consequences, which would include the loss of U.S. naval bases at Guantanamo in Cuba and in Puerto Rico. These two bases, with the Panama Canal, form the defense triangle for protecting the strategic Caribbean, which Admiral Mahan and other eminent strategists long ago described as the Mediterranean of the Americas. Upon the outcome of the projected giveaway will depend whether the advantageously located Caribbean Sea and Gulf of Mexico shall be transformed from peaceful avenues for ocean commerce into red lakes, thereby bisecting the Americas with enormous potentials for evil for the United States, Latin America, and the entire Free World.

In the past, the responsible leaders of the United States always safeguarded and defended the territories over which it had sovereign control. They and the Congress never surrendered U.S. sovereign territory under threats of foreign military or mob assaults, however large the country, but stood up for American rights under international law.

Yet, since World War II, through a succession of administrations, certain leaders have sought to surrender our sovereign control over the U.S. owned Canal Zone and, eventually, the Panama Canal itself to the Republic of Panama.

A small, weak and industrially primitive tropical country, it simply does not possess the resources, the manpower, or technical skills required for the efficient maintenance, operation, sanitation, and protection of the most vital waterway of the Americas. The satisfactory performance of these crucial functions requires the combined technological, industrial, military, and naval might of the United States, or that of some other great power—if you know what I mean.

1978 Egypt and Israel: The Camp David Negotiations
(1982)

During the Carter administration, there was an improvement in relations between longtime foes Egypt and Israel. The precipitating incident in this gradual thaw was a visit by President Anwar el-Sadat to Jerusalem in 1977. Sadat and Prime Minister Menachem Begin of

Israel then consulted privately in Washington with President Jimmy Carter, who invited them to a summit conference at Camp David, Maryland in September, 1978. Despite widespread advanced skepticism about the prospects for a convergence of views, the Egyptians and Israelis reached agreement on a number of points after thirteen days of negotiations, including a peace treaty between the two countries. In his memoirs, Jimmy Carter describes the climax of these often frustrating yet eventually successful talks.

SOURCE: Carter, *Keeping Faith*. See pp. 398–401.

DOCUMENT:

A serious problem has erupted with the Israelis. Vance had just shown them a copy of our draft letter that would go to Sadat, restating the United States' position on Jerusalem, which had been spelled out officially in United Nations debates over the years. There was an absolute furor, and Begin announced that Israel would not sign any document if we wrote any letter to Egypt about Jerusalem.

Earlier, my secretary, Susan Clough, had brought me some photographs of Begin, Sadat, and me. They had already been signed by President Sadat, and Prime Minister Begin had requested that I autograph them for his grandchildren. Knowing the trouble we were in with the Israelis, Susan suggested that she go and get the actual names of the grandchildren, so that I could personalize each picture. I did this, and walked over to Begin's cabin with them. He was sitting on the front porch, very distraught and nervous because the talks had finally broken down at the last minute.

I handed him the photographs. He took them and thanked me. Then he happened to look down and saw that his granddaughter's name was on the top one. He spoke it aloud, and then looked at each photograph individually, repeating the name of the grandchild I had written on it. His lips trembled, and tears welled up in his eyes. He told me a little about each child, and especially about the one who seemed to be his favorite. We were both emotional as we talked quietly for a few minutes about grandchildren and about war.

Then he asked me to step into his cabin, requesting that everyone else in the room leave. He was quiet, sober, surprisingly friendly. There were no histrionics. He said that the Jerusalem matter was fatal, that he was very sorry but he could not accept our letter to Egypt. I told him I had drafted a new version and submitted it to Dayan and Barak. He had not yet seen it. I suggested he read it over and let me know his decision, but that there was no way that I could go back on my commitment to Sadat to exchange letters. The success of any future peace talks might depend on his and Sadat's assessment of my integrity, and I could not violate a promise once it was made.

I walked back to Aspen, very dejected. Sadat was there with el-Baz, both dressed to go back to Washington. I asked everyone else to leave and told Sadat what was happening. We realized that all of us had done our best, but that prospects were dim indeed.

Then Begin called. He said, "I will accept the letter you have drafted on Jerusalem." I breathed a sigh of relief, because it now seemed that the last obstacle had been removed.

Then Barak came in with Begin's draft of the language about the West Bank settlements and on the Knesset vote. Both were unsatisfactory and contrary to what we had earlier agreed. I read to Barak from my detailed notes what we had mutually decided, and told him to take the letters back to the Prime Minister. Barak confirmed that my language was correct.

In a few minutes, Begin called to say that he could not accept my language on the Knesset vote, because he interpreted it as a threat to the independence of the parliament. This point was difficult to understand, but it was essential. Sadat's willingness to negotiate was contingent on the Knesset's approval of Israeli withdrawal of the settlers. Begin wanted it stated that the peace negotiations would commence after the Knesset voted, but I insisted that it say that the peace negotiations would not commence until after the Knesset had voted. After some argument, Barak finally agreed to my formulation.

I ran toward Sadat's cabin, and saw that Begin was just leaving in a golf cart with Barak. He was quite happy as he told me that they had had a love feast and that Sadat had agreed to Begin's language on the Knesset vote. I knew this could not be true, and I asked Barak to tell me exactly what Sadat had said. Each time he tried to answer, Begin would have something else to say. I finally asked the Prime Minister point-blank to let Barak answer my question.

Barak described the conversation to me. What Begin had asked was, "Do you think the Knesset should be under pressure when it votes?" Predictably, Sadat had replied, "No, the Knesset should not be under pressure." That was all. Begin had interpreted this to mean that he could draft any language he preferred to insure that the Knesset would be free of any implied adverse consequences if its decision should be negative.

I asked Barak to come with me. Begin excused him, and we went to my cabin just a few steps away. I checked the Israeli language most carefully. It was a very confusing point, and all of us were dead tired. Momentarily, my mind seemed to clear and I thought of a way to phrase all three final letters that would be satisfactory to both Begin and Sadat.

Only then did I fully realize we had succeeded.

1978 The Carter Administration Recognizes Mainland China

Although it was President Richard Nixon who first visited mainland China in 1972, it was President Jimmy Carter who officially recognized the Communist regime on December 15, 1978, twenty-nine years after it had come to power. That evening, Carter spoke to the nation on television and explained the reasons why the United States had agreed to a joint communiqué on the establishment of diplomatic relations between the United States and the Peoples Republic of China, starting January 1, 1979. As one would have expected, right-wing elements in the United States and the derecognized Taiwanese greeted the announcement with disapproval, since mainland China gave no pledge that it would refrain from attacking Taiwan in the future.

SOURCE: U.S. Department of State *Bulletin*, January, 1979. See p. 25.

DOCUMENT:

PRESIDENT'S ADDRESS

Yesterday, our country and the People's Republic of China reached this final historic agreement. On January 1, 1979, a little more than 2 weeks from now, our two governments will implement full normalization of diplomatic relations.

As a nation of gifted people who comprise about one-fourth of the total population of the Earth, China plays, already, an important role in world affairs, a role that can only grow more important in the years ahead.

We do not undertake this important step for transient tactical or expedient reasons. In recognizing the People's Republic of China, that it is the single Government of China, we are recognizing simple reality. But far more is involved in this decision than just the recognition of a fact.

Before the estrangement of recent decades, the American and the Chinese people had a long history of friendship. We've already begun to rebuild some of those previous ties. Now our rapidly expanding relationship requires the kind of structure that only full diplomatic relations will make possible.

The change that I'm announcing tonight will be of great benefit to the peoples of both our country and China—and, I believe, to all the peoples of the world. Normalization—and the expanded commercial and cultural relations that it will bring—will contribute to the well-being of our own nation, to our own national interest, and it will also enhance the stability of Asia. These more positive relations with China can beneficially affect the world in which we live and the world in which our children will live.

We have already begun to inform our allies and other nations and the Members of the Congress of the details of our intended action. But I wish also tonight to convey a special message to the people of Taiwan—I have already communicated with the leaders in Taiwan—with whom the American people have had and will have extensive, close, and friendly relations. This is important between our two peoples.

As the United States asserted in the Shanghai communique of 1972, issued on President Nixon's historic visit, we will continue to have an interest in the peaceful resolution of the Taiwan issue. I have paid special attention to insuring that normalization of relations between our country and the People's Republic will not jeopardize the well-being of the people of Taiwan. The people of our country will maintain our current commercial, cultural, trade, and other relations with Taiwan through nongovernmental means. Many other countries in the world are already successfully doing this.

These decisions and these actions open a new and important chapter in our country's history and also in world affairs.

To strengthen and to expedite the benefits of this new relationship between China and the United States, I am pleased to announce that Vice Premier Teng has accepted my invitation and will visit Washington at the end of January. His visit will give our governments the opportunity to consult with each other on global issues and to begin working together to enhance the cause of world peace.

These events are the final result of long and serious negotiations begun by President Nixon in 1972 and continued under the leadership of President Ford. The results bear witness to the steady, determined, bipartisan effort of our own country to build a world in which peace will be the goal and the responsibility of all nations.

The normalization of relations between the United States and China has no other purpose than this: the advancement of peace. It is in this spirit, at this season of peace, that I take special pride in sharing this good news with you tonight.

PRESIDENT'S REMARKS

Joint Communique, December 15

JOINT COMMUNIQUE ON THE ESTABLISHMENT OF DIPLOMATIC RELATIONS BETWEEN THE UNITED STATES OF AMERICA AND THE PEOPLE'S REPUBLIC OF CHINA JANUARY 1, 1979

The United States of America and the People's Republic of China have agreed to recognize each other and to establish diplomatic relations as of January 1, 1979.

The United States of America recognizes this Government of the People's Republic of China as the sole legal Government of China. Within this context, the people of the United States will maintain cultural, commercial, and other unofficial relations with the people of Taiwan.

The United States of America and the People's Republic of China reaffirm the principles agreed on by the two sides in the Shanghai Communique and emphasize once again that:

- Both wish to reduce the danger of international military conflict.
- Neither should seek hegemony in the Asia–Pacific region or in any other region of the world and each is opposed to efforts by any other country or group of countries to establish such hegemony.
- Neither is prepared to negotiate on behalf of any third party or to enter into agreements or understandings with the other directed at other states.
- The Government of the United States of America acknowledges the Chinese position that there is but one China and Taiwan is part of China.

- Both believe that normalization of Sino–American relations is not only in the interest of the Chinese and American peoples but also contributes to the cause of peace in Asia and the world.

The United States of America and the People's Republic of China will exchange Ambassadors and establish Embassies on March 1, 1979.

1979 Secretary of State Cyrus Vance and the Fall of the Somoza Regime in Nicaragua

For over forty years, the Somoza family controlled Nicaragua. The last member of the dynasty, Anastasio Somoza, attended the U.S. Military Academy at West Point. By the 1970s, though, the Somozas' grip on the Central American nation had begun to weaken. An earthquake devastated Managua in 1972; there was widespread resentment at the Somoza family's wealth; and the Sandinista rebels were winning increased support throughout the country. The Carter administration gave the pro-American Somoza less than all-out support, as did the Organization of American States, and on July 16, 1979, Somoza was forced to resign the Presidency and to flee into exile. A month earlier, on June 21, Secretary of State Cyrus Vance commented on the deteriorating situation in Nicaragua before the Ministers of Foreign Affairs of the Organization of American States.

SOURCE: U.S. Department of State *Bulletin,* August, 1979. See pp. 56–57.

DOCUMENT:

We are faced with the inescapable fact that the situation in Nicaragua continues to deteriorate and at an accelerating pace. The conflict in that country is becoming a war of national destruction.

The Organization of American States has, over the past 9 months, made a concerted effort to help resolve the crisis in Nicaragua peacefully.

Yet, despite these efforts, the situation today is far graver than it was 9 months ago.

It is, first and foremost, a mounting human tragedy. The fighting in Nicaragua and on its borders is now incessant, limited only by the means of destruction available to the combatants. Thousands are dying. The economy of the country is in shambles. The dimensions of the human suffering grow each day.

- Humanitarian assistance is virtually impossible in the midst of all-out war.
- The persistent and widespread pattern of serious human rights abuses by the government, reported in November by the Inter-American Human Rights Commission, has become even worse. Thousands of Nicaraguans have been the victims of these wholesale abuses. This terror was brought home vividly to the

American people yesterday with the cold-blooded murder by a National Guardsman of an American newsman who was simply carrying out his journalistic mission.

· Foreign support for both sides has steadily increased. There is mounting evidence of involvement by Cuba and others in the internal problems of Nicaragua. This involvement may transform these internal problems into international and ideological issues, making it increasingly difficult to arrive at a peaceful solution.

· The Civilian Observer Mission, which for a time was able to perform effectively, is now unable to function.

The efforts of individual nations, and groups of nations, have not succeeded. We believe that the time has come to bring the full strength of our hemispheric organization to bear directly on the root cause of the crisis in Central America. We must act now, in unison, as a united hemisphere.

The heart of the problem in Nicaragua is the breakdown of trust between government and people. Any effort to deal with this crisis which ignores the breakdown of the internal political process will fail. We must, then, seek a political solution which will take into account the interests of all significant groups in Nicaragua.

Such a solution must begin with the replacement of the present government with a transitional government of national reconciliation, which would be a clear break with the past. It would consist of individuals who enjoy the support and confidence of the widest possible spectrum of Nicaraguans. Such a government would bring about a cease-fire and proceed to build the base for a free and representative political system—one which inspires the trust and confidence of the Nicaraguan people. We must call upon all Nicaraguan leaders to recognize this avenue to a lasting peace and to take the steps necessary to carry it out.

We are fully conscious of the difficulty of accomplishing these steps in the present circumstances in Nicaragua. It is clear that the people of this devastated country will require all of the assistance which this organization can place at their disposal.

These then are the elements the United States sees as essential to an enduring solution to the crisis that has brought us here today:

· Formation of an interim government of national reconciliation acceptable to all major elements of the society;

· The dispatch by this meeting of a special delegation to Nicaragua;

· A cessation of arms shipments;

· A cease-fire;

· An OAS peacekeeping presence to help establish a climate of peace and security and to assist the interim government in establishing its authority and beginning the task of reconstruction; and

· A major international relief and reconstruction effort.

1979–81 Deputy Secretary of State Warren Christopher Discusses the Iranian Hostage Crisis (1985)

Another pro-U.S. head of state to fall from power in 1979 was the Shah of Iran, whose nation possessed vast petroleum reserves. A quarter of a century earlier, the American government had used its influence to help maintain the Shah in power when he was in danger of being toppled, and the anti-Shah forces never forgave the United States for this. After the departure of the Shah from Iran in January, 1979, power soon passed into the hands of the Ayatollah Rutollah Khomeini, an aged Moslem fanatic who proved just as dictatorial as the Shah had been. On November 4, a group of Iranians seized the U.S. Embassy in Teheran, and they did not release the American hostages until the day that Ronald Reagan took office as President (January 20, 1981). Deputy Secretary of State Warren Christopher reflected on the agonizing series of events which unquestionably damaged the Carter administration politically in his retrospective account of the Iranian hostage crisis.

SOURCE: Warren Christopher, *American Hostages in Iran: The Conduct of a Crisis* (New York: Yale University Press, 1985). See pp. 2–4.

DOCUMENT:

Phases.   Viewed in retrospect, the crisis can be seen to divide itself into a number of distinct phases:

The Pre-Crisis.   For months before the hostage taking, the United States had been reassessing its relationship with Iran. The revolution there did not make Iran a less significant country to the United States. Its location on the Persian Gulf and the Arabian Sea, its status as a land bridge between the Middle East and Asia, and its energy reserves still defined it as a strategically important country and no less so because of its internal turmoil. On the contrary, now U.S. policymakers also had to concern themselves with the reality that Iran's internal divisions made it weaker and therefore more vulnerable to Soviet opportunism. All things considered, American interests argued strongly against hastily giving up on Iran. Thus, although the official American presence in that country had been drastically reduced after the Iranian revolution, nevertheless a decision also had been taken to maintain a diplomatic presence in order to continue communications and to promote a mature and correct, if considerably cooler, relationship with the revolutionary government. We were not prepared to walk away from the situation, and we should not have been. At the same time, businesses and banks with commercial contacts in Iran had begun to reassess their operations and prospects there and to adjust to the new environment.

The Immediate Aftermath of the November 4, 1979, Hostage Taking. This period began with an expectation, which survived for only a matter of days, that the Iranian authorities would rescue our embassy personnel in line with their assurances and with their behavior in a similar incident the prior February. When that hope proved vain, and it appeared that the Iranian government was condoning the actions of those who took the embassy, the Carter Administration rather quickly reviewed its options and imposed economic sanctions, including the freeze of Iranian assets. In addition, our case was taken to the International Court of Justice, to the U.N. Security Council, and to other countries around the world.

The Failed Negotiations. This phase lasted from late November into March 1980 and involved working out, through Paris lawyers and with the cooperation of United Nations Secretary-General Kurt Waldheim, a "scenario" under which the hostages would be released at the end of a series of reciprocal steps. In Iran this effort was backed by a Europe-oriented group—principally the President Abolhassan Bani-Sadr and Foreign Minister Sadegh Ghotbzadeh. The process led to the creation and dispatch to Iran of a U.N. Commission of Inquiry that was to investigate Iranian grievances against the Shah. The phase ended when the Ayatollah Khomeini and religious elements in Iran began adding new and unacceptable conditions and when it became apparent that Bani-Sadr and Ghotbzadeh could not control the situation, even to the extent of arranging the agreed meetings with all the hostages by members of the U.N. Commission.

The Nadir. In late March, as the Commission of Inquiry scenario collapsed, it became clear that the hostages' fate had become entangled in the internal political maneuvering of various factions in Iran. At least until the situation sorted itself out—until a new government was solidly in place—none of the competing groups could afford to take the political risk of appearing to yield to the United States by supporting the release of our people. It was under these circumstances that the ill-fated hostage rescue attempt was authorized and initiated. Later in the same period, Iranian officials with economic responsibilities, working through Iran's ambassador to Germany, began to explore with U.S. banks the possibilities for an economic settlement. It is quite possible that the Iranians involved in those talks hoped to settle economic matters separately from the hostage issue. However, under firm instructions from us, those representing the private sector on the U.S. side made clear from the beginning that any economic settlement would have to include release of the hostages as well.

Real Bargaining. By September 1980, the Iranian parliament, or Majlis, had been formed, a new government was in place, and the Iranians appeared ready to proceed. At this point the Iranians initiated contact with the United States through the Germans. At the outset of this phase, the Ayatollah Khomeini announced his four conditions for a settlement. Shortly thereafter, in mid-September, I had direct discussion with an Iranian emissary outside Bonn. That channel was severed after the outbreak of the Iraq–Iran war later in September. Then the negotiations opened up in earnest in November, with the Algerians serving as highly skilled intermediaries and facilitators.

The End Game. The closing days of the crisis were distinguished by the fact that the Iranians at last came to terms on the most disruptive issues. They plainly wanted to resolve the crisis prior to the change in administrations in the United States, and they gradually came to realize, with the help of the Algerians, that execution of the settlement, and especially of the intricate financial provisions, also would take considerable time. Therefore, while they remained deeply suspicious and often obstinate, the Iranians also made a number of far-reaching decisions rather quickly in the closing hours, permitting the release of the hostages before the day was out on January 20, 1981.

1977–81 The Carter Foreign Policy in Retrospect: Zbigniew Brzezinski (1983)

Like Henry Kissinger, Jimmy Carter's National Security Advisor Zbigniew Brzezinski was a prolific author with impressive academic credentials. According to Brzezinski, there were five major turning points in foreign relations during the Carter administration. Brzezinski also was of the opinion that the Carter years witnessed at least a dozen major foreign policy accomplishments. Many of these stand up today when subjected to careful scrutiny, but Brzezinski obviously claims too much with respect to Afghanistan, where the Soviets enjoyed a prolonged stay during the 1980s. The next President, Ronald Reagan, also modified some of Carter's policies, as when he endorsed "constructive engagement" towards South Africa: to encourage U.S. investment there, provided that the American corporations employ blacks.

SOURCE: Zbigniew Brzezinski, *Power and Principle: Memoirs of the National Security Advisor 1977–1981* (New York: Farrar, Straus, Giroux, 1983). See pp. 81, 193, and 528–29.

DOCUMENT:

When Jimmy Carter assumed office, U.S. foreign policy appeared to him and to his team to be stalemated on the level of power and excessively cynical on the level of principle. The new Administration therefore decided to move on a broad front and to tackle several key issues at once while the President's prestige was at its highest. We were determined to demonstrate also the primacy of the moral dimension in foreign policy.

During Carter's Presidency, there were five major foreign policy turning points—each requiring either a basic shift in strategy or generating consequences of great significance to the national security of the United States. The effort to achieve SALT without linkage to other issues or events was refuted by "history," or, more specifically, by excessively assertive Soviet behavior. But that, in turn, led to the President's decision to send me to Beijing in mid-1978 to accelerate normalization of relations with China—which then became one of Carter's principal and lasting accomplishments. The goal of a comprehensive peace in the Middle

East proved elusive—but Sadat's reactive initiative became the catalyst for Carter's greatest personal accomplishment: the Camp David agreement. Yet almost at the same time, our efforts to invigorate the Western alliance were partially set back—and Carter's personal credibility was unfairly damaged—by the President's decision in May 1978 not to proceed with the deployment of the neutron bomb and not to blame that decision (for the sake of allied unity) on the hesitations and conditions imposed by German Chancellor Helmut Schmidt.

In the meantime, the road to SALT proved longer and more difficult and by the time the agreement was finally signed in Vienna in July 1979, the deterioration in U.S.–Soviet relations made ratification increasingly uncertain. Soon after, the combined political impact of the "discovery" of the Soviet brigade in Cuba in September and the Soviet invasion of Afghanistan in late December made ratification unthinkable. U.S.–Soviet relations became frozen—a far cry from our early hopes. Finally, the internal upheaval in Iran, culminating by the end of 1978 in the overthrow of the Shah, destroyed the strategic pivot of the U.S.-sponsored shield for the Persian Gulf region and set in motion events that later proved politically most costly to the President himself.

To conclude, President Carter was innovative and activist in the area of foreign policy, enhancing America's power and recommitting America to principle. Foremost among his accomplishments were:

The reidentification of America with certain basic ideals; justice, equity, majority rule, self-determination, dignity of the individual—and here our human-rights policy was essential.

The Camp David Accords, promoting the first peace treaty ever between an Arab state and Israel, and the creation of a process for dealing with the Palestinian problem.

The normalization of relations with China and the growth of a more comprehensive political and even an incipient strategic relationship.

The Panama Canal Treaties, ushering in a more equitable relationship with our Latin American neighbors and avoiding a nasty confrontation in a strategically sensitive area.

Commitment to majority rule in Africa and the revival of constructive relationships with key African countries.

A policy of differentiation in Eastern Europe, developing U.S. relations not only with those Eastern European countries that defied Soviet foreign policy but also with those that engaged in quiet domestic liberalization, as well as the deterrence in 1980 of a Soviet military move against Poland.

The revitalization and modernization of American strategic doctrine and military posture, including PD-59, the RDF, and the MX.

The reinjection of American military presence into the Persian Gulf and the Indian Ocean and the initiation of a regional security framework for the area, including the Carter Doctrine.

The negotiation of a comprehensive international trade agreement, averting a relapse into destructive protectionism.

International energy agreements designed to give the West increased capacity for dealing with future energy crises through conservation and increased production.

Partially effective restraints on nuclear proliferation and worldwide sales of arms.

Lifting of the Turkish arms embargo and the reintegration of both Greece and Turkey into a more positive relationship with NATO.

Firm, even if politically costly, sanctions against the Soviet Union after the Soviet invasion of Afghanistan.

A SALT II agreement (not ratified but mutually honored), involving a considerable improvement on the asymmetrical arrangements negotiated by Nixon and Kissinger in SALT I.

This list speaks for itself. And it guarantees that President Carter will be appraised more generously by posterity than he was by the electorate in 1980.

Ronald Reagan and the Cold War 50

1983 Ronald Reagan on the Soviet Union as an "Evil Empire"

Unquestionably the ultimate verbal expression of Ronald Reagan's hardlining cold war stance toward the Soviet Union was his characterization of the latter as an "evil empire." The President elaborated on this point in an address which he delivered before the National Association of Evangelicals at Orlando, Florida, on March 8, 1983. Surprisingly, though, by the end of the Reagan administration relations between the United States and the new, seemingly reform-minded Mikhail Gorbachev regime in the Soviet Union had improved to the point that the two nations signed a missile limitation pact.

SOURCE: "Excerpts from President's Speech to National Association of Evangelicals," in New York *Times,* May 9, 1983. See Section I, p. 18.

DOCUMENT:

During my first press conference as President, in answer to a direct question, I pointed out that as good Marxists–Leninists the Soviet leaders have openly and publicly declared that the only morality they recognize is that which will further their cause, which is world revolution.

I think I should point out I was only quoting Lenin, their guiding spirit who said in 1920 that they repudiate all morality that proceeds from supernatural ideas or ideas that are outside class conceptions, morality is entirely subordinate to the interests of class war; and everything is moral that is necessary for the annihilation of the old exploiting social order and for uniting the proletariat.

I think the refusal of many influential people to accept this elementary fact of Soviet doctrine illustrates an historical reluctance to see totalitarian powers for what they are. We saw this phenomenon in the 1930's, we see it too often today. This does not mean we should isolate ourselves and refuse to seek an understanding with them.

I intend to do everything I can to persuade them of our peaceful intent to remind them that it was the West that refused to use its nuclear monopoly in the

40's and 50's for territorial gain and which now proposes 50 percent cuts in strategic ballistic missiles and the elimination of an entire class of land-based, intermediate-range nuclear missiles.

At the same time, however, they must be made to understand we will never compromise our principles and standards. We will never give away our freedom. We will never abandon our belief in God.

And we will never stop searching for a genuine peace. But we can assure none of these things America stands for through the so-called nuclear freeze solutions proposed by some. The truth is that a freeze now would be a very dangerous fraud, for that is merely the illusion of peace. The reality is that we must find peace through strength.

I would agree to a freeze if only we could freeze the Soviets' global desires. A freeze at current levels of weapons would remove any incentive for the Soviets to negotiate seriously in Geneva, and virtually end our chances to achieve the major arms reductions which we have proposed. Instead, they would achieve their objectives through the freeze.

A freeze would reward the Soviet Union for its enormous and unparalleled military buildup. It would prevent the essential and long-overdue modernization of United States and allied defenses and would leave our aging forces increasingly vulnerable. And an honest freeze would require extensive prior negotiations on the systems and numbers to be limited and on the measures to insure effective verification and compliance.

And the kind of freeze that has been suggested would be virtually impossible to verify. Such a major effort would divert us completely from our current negotiations on achieving substantial reductions.

Let us pray for the salvation of all those who live in totalitarian darkness, pray they will discover the joy of knowing God.

But until they do, let us be aware that while they preach the supremacy of the state, declare its omnipotence over individual man, and predict its eventual domination of all peoples of the earth—they are the force of evil in the modern world.

1983 The American Liberation of Marxist Grenada

During the fall of 1983, there was a revolt in Marxist Grenada, during which a Leninist faction overthrew the regime of Prime Minister Maurice Bishop, whom it regarded as a "bourgeois deviationist." Feeling that the lives of American citizens there were in danger, the Reagan administration militarily liberated the island at the request of the Organization of Eastern Caribbean States. Most Americans praised this bold maneuver, as did many members of Congress. Assistant Secretary of State Kenneth Dam gave the legal justification for this action in a speech which he delivered on November 4, 1983. This, it should be noted, was the first time that the tiny island had figured prominently in American foreign policy.

SOURCE: U.S. Department of State *Bulletin,* December 1983, pp. 80–81.

DOCUMENT:

Order began to disintegrate in Grenada the evening of October 12 with an attempt by Deputy Prime Minister Bernard Coard to force out Prime Minister Maurice Bishop. According to minutes of the party Central Committee, although Bishop had established close relations with Cuba and the Soviet Union, the Coard faction considered him a "bourgeois deviationist" for moving too slowly to consolidate a "Leninist" restructuring of Grenadian society.

Bishop was put under house arrest in the middle of the night October 14, then freed by his supporters on October 19. Troops opened fire on the crowd. Bishop and several Cabinet ministers and union leaders were taken away, then executed. Education Minister Jacqueline Creft was apparently beaten to death.

In the wake of these murders, the People's Revolutionary Army announced the government was dissolved and a 24-hour curfew imposed: anyone found outside would be shot on sight. Army General Hudson Austin was head of a 16-member Revolutionary Military Council (RMC). But it was never clear that Austin or any coherent group was in fact in charge. No one knew when—or how—a new government would be formed.

The disintegration of political authority in Grenada had created a dynamic that spread uncertainty and fear and that made further violence likely. The actions of Bishop's murderers made clear that they would have either driven the island into further chaos or turned it into an armed fortress. In either event, the threat to U.S. citizens and to the peace of the eastern Caribbean would have increased. Inaction would have made a hostage situation more likely and increased the costs in lives of any subsequent rescue operation.

The OECS decided to help its member state of Grenada and to ask Barbados, Jamaica, and the United States for assistance. In its formal request for U.S. assistance, the OECS cited:

> ...the current anarchic conditions, the serious violations of human rights and bloodshed that have occurred and the consequent unprecedented threat to the peace and security of the region created by the vacuum of authority in Grenada.

The OECS request also noted:

> ...that military forces and supplies are likely to be shortly introduced to consolidate the position of the regime and that the country can be used as a staging post for acts of aggression against its members; and
> ...that the capability of the Grenada armed forces is already at a level of sophistication and size far beyond the internal needs of that country.

We had, of course, also been following events with increasing concern. As is well known, Grenada's ties to Cuba and the Soviet Union and its abandonment of democracy and poor human rights record had led the United States to have serious disagreements with the Bishop regime.

What became our overriding concern as events unfolded, however, was not Grenada's political system. Rather, it was the safety of U.S. citizens in the midst of a growing anarchy which the countries of the Caribbean also saw as a direct threat.

Some 1,000 U.S. citizens, mainly students, retirees, and missionaries, made up the largest community of foreigners on Grenada. Our concern for their welfare was heightened by the murders, the shoot-on-sight curfew, and the difficulty of getting accurate information. And in the absence of a functioning government, there could be no credible assurances of their well-being and future prospects. I don't think that I need remind you that today is the fourth anniversary of the seizure of the U.S. Embassy in Tehran.

U.S. action to secure and evacuate endangered U.S. citizens on the island was undertaken in accordance with well-established principles of international law regarding the protection of one's nationals. That the circumstances warranted this action has been amply documented by the returning students themselves. There is absolutely no requirement of international law that compelled the United States to await further deterioration of the situation that would have jeopardized a successful operation. Nor was the United States required to await actual violence against U.S. citizens before rescuing them from the anarchic and threatening conditions the students themselves have described.

1985 The Kissinger Commission Report on Nicaragua

After the fall of the Somoza regime in Nicaragua in 1979, the Sandinistas finally came to power there. Rather than maintain a broad, democratic national consensus, they established a Marxist government under the leadership of Daniel Ortega which bore an uncomfortable resemblance to Fidel Castro's regime in Cuba. The Sandinistas quickly adopted an anti-U.S. stance, and the Reagan administration reciprocated. In the report of Henry Kissinger's Bipartisan Commission on Central America, there is a critical assessment of the Sandinistas which, among other things, stresses the threat which they pose to the remainder of Central America.

SOURCE: Peter Rosset and John Vandermeer, Editors, *Nicaragua: Unfinished Revolution* (New York: Grove Press, 1986). See pp. 14–17.

DOCUMENT:

In Nicaragua the revolution that overthrew the hated Somoza regime has been captured by self-proclaimed Marxist-Leninists. In July of 1979 the Sandinistas promised the OAS that they would organize "a truly democratic government" and hold free elections, but that promise has not been redeemed. Rather, the government has been brought fully under the control of the Sandinista National Directorate. Only two months after giving their pledge to the OAS and while successfully negotiating loans in Washington, the Sandinistas issued Decree No. 67, which converted their movement into the country's official political party and laid the foundation for the monopoly of political power they now enjoy. The

Sandinista Directorate has progressively put in place a Cuban-style regime, complete with mass organizations under its political direction, an internal security system to keep watch on the entire population, and a massive military establishment. This comprehensive police and military establishment not only ensures the monopoly on power within Nicaragua, it also produces an acute sense of insecurity among Nicaragua's neighbors.

From the outset, the Sandinistas have maintained close ties with Cuba and the Soviet Union. There are some 8,000 Cuban advisers now in Nicaragua, including at least 2,000 military advisers, as well as several hundred Soviet, East European, Libyan, and PLO advisers. Cuban construction teams have helped build military roads, bases, and airfields. According to intelligence sources, an estimated 15,000 tons of Soviet-bloc arms and equipment reached the Sandinista army in 1983. This military connection with Cuba, the Soviet Union, and its satellites internationalizes Central America's security problems and adds a menacing new dimension.

The Sandinista military forces are potentially larger than those of all the rest of Central America combined. The government in Managua volunteered to this Commission an intelligence briefing which left no reasonable doubt that Nicaragua is tied into the Cuban, and thereby the Soviet, intelligence network. The Commission encountered no leader in Central America, including democratic and unarmed Costa Rica, who did not express deep foreboding about the impact of a militarized, totalitarian Nicaragua on the peace and security of the region. Several expressed the view that should the Sandinista regime now be consolidated as a totalitarian state, their own freedom, and even their independence, would be jeopardized. In several countries, especially those with democratic traditions, we met leaders who expressed regret and outrage that the revolution against Somoza—which their own governments had supported—had been betrayed by the Sandinistas.

For all of these reasons, the consolidation of a Marxist–Leninist regime in Managua would be seen by its neighbors as constituting a permanent security threat. Because of its secretive nature, the existence of a political order on the Cuban model in Nicaragua would pose major difficulties in negotiating, implementing, and verifying any Sandinista commitment to refrain from supporting insurgency and subversion in other countries. In this sense, the development of an open political system in Nicaragua, with a free press and an active opposition, would provide an important security guarantee for the other countries of the region and would be a key element in any negotiated settlement.

Theoretically, the United States and its friends could abandon any hope of such a settlement and simply try to contain a Nicaragua which continued to receive military supplies on the present scale. In practical terms, however, such a course would present major difficulties. In the absence of a political settlement, there would be little incentive for the Sandinistas to act responsibly, even over a period of time, and much inducement to escalate their efforts to subvert Nicaragua's neighbors. To contain the export of revolution would require a level of vigilance and sustained effort that would be difficult for Nicaragua's neighbors and even for the United States. A fully militarized and equipped Nicaragua, with excellent intelligence and command and control organizations, would weigh heavily on the neighboring countries of the region. This threat would be particularly acute for democratic, unarmed Costa Rica. It would have especially serious implications for vital interests in the Panama Canal. We would then face the prospect, over time, of the collapse of the other countries of Central America, bringing with it the specter of Marxist domination of the entire region and thus the danger of a larger war.

Therefore, though the Commission believes that the Sandinista regime will pose a continuing threat to stability in the region, we do not advocate a policy of static containment.

Instead, we recommend, first, an effort to arrange a comprehensive regional settlement. This would elaborate and build upon the twenty-one objectives of the Contadora Group. Within the framework of basic principles, it would:

- Recognize linkage between democratization and security in the region.
- Relate the incentives of increased development aid and trade concessions to acceptance of mutual security guarantees.
- Engage the United States and other developed nations in the regional peace system.
- Establish an institutional mechanism in the region to implement that system.

1986 The American Retaliatory Attack on Libya

In 1969, King Idris of oil-rich Libya fell from power in a coup, and the increasingly anti-American climate of opinion there led the United States to close Wheelus Field during the following year. The individual who became the dominant figure in the Libyan government during the 1970s and 1980s, Colonel Muammar al–Qaddafi, soon attained international notoriety, not only because of his ideological fanaticism and unstable behavior, but also because he apparently encouraged various terroristic episodes throughout the Middle East and elsewhere. When Libya attacked U.S. airplanes and ships in the international waters off Libya on March 24, 1986, the Reagan administration quickly retaliated with an attack of its own. Ambassador to the United Nations Vernon Walters justified this action in a letter to the U.N. Security Council issued two days later, which emphasized both freedom of the seas (a traditional American diplomatic principle) and freedom of the skies.

SOURCE: U.S. Department of State *Bulletin*, May, 1986. See p. 80.

DOCUMENT:

We are here today because the Government of Libya has flouted international law and the Charter of the United Nations by using lethal force to assert its claim in the Gulf of Sidra. U.S. forces, engaged in a peaceful freedom of navigation exercise in international waters, have been subjected to an unprovoked and unjustified attack by Libyan forces. The Government of Libya notified the Secretary General on March 24, 1986, that it intended to disregard the role of this Council "to resort to its own strengths." One day later, Libyan forces launched six surface-to-air missiles against U.S. vessels and aircraft exercising, after proper notification to Libya and all other concerned parties, our rights to navigate in international waters and fly over them. I should add that advance notice had been posted in accordance with international practice and that the exercise was publicly and widely recorded.

On Monday, March 24, in daylight hours, U.S. Naval vessels proceeded south of 32°30'. They were, of course, in international waters. At 1252 Greenwich Mean Time (GMT), Libyan facilities launched two SA-5 missiles aimed at U.S. tactical naval aircraft conducting routine operations over international waters. No U.S. aircraft were hit. We did not respond.

Two additional SA-5 missiles and an SA-2 missile were launched at 1745 GMT. We still did not respond. Another SA-5 was launched at 1845 GMT. At this point, Libyan forces had fired a total of six SA missiles at U.S. forces operating properly in international waters. The United States responded to this unjustified attack by a proportionate exercise of its right of self-defense.

We reject Libya's efforts to subvert—by force—the international legal right of freedom of navigation and the responsibility of this Council under the charter. It is simply intolerable to allow states to subvert international law by threatening and using force against those peacefully exercising their legal rights. The Libyan claim to control navigation through international waters, as well as flight through international airspace, is inconsistent with traditional freedoms recognized in contemporary state practice. It has no basis in international law, and everyone in this chamber knows it.

The United States of America has been committed to ensuring the freedom of the seas ever since our birth as a nation. Freedom of the seas is essential to maintaining international security and the flow of commerce. All nations share a fundamental interest in maintaining and defending the principles of freedom of navigation and overflight. As a matter of longstanding policy, my government conducts naval and air exercises in waters and airspace in every part of the globe. So, too, do several members of this Council. As part of our regular program of operations around the world, we have been in the area of the Gulf of Sidra 16 times since 1981. We have been below the line claimed as a boundary by Libya seven times before this current operation.

Libya's claim to control navigation and overflight in a vast area of the Mediterranean Sea has no basis in customary practice or international law. The Government of Libya knows full well that its indefensible claim in the Gulf of Sidra and attacks on those exercising their rights to navigate in, and fly over, the international waters of the gulf have caused this conflict. These flagrant Libyan attacks against naval units of the United States, operating in international waters of the Gulf of Sidra, were entirely unjustified and unprovoked. In self-defense, under Article 51 of the Charter of the United Nations, U.S. forces responded to these attacks. I want to make clear that any further attacks will also be resisted with force, if required.

1987 The Inouye Committee and the Iran–Contra Affair

No episode which occurred during the second Reagan administration did more to undermine its credibility than the Iran–Contra affair. In November, 1986, a Lebanese weekly revealed that the United States privately had sold arms to Iran in hopes that this might encourage Lebanese terrorists to release American hostages. (There apparently also was an attempt to court favor with a moderate faction in Iran.) Shortly thereafter, the Attorney General stated that in another clandestine maneuver some of the proceeds from these arms sales had gone to the Nicaraguan contras for use in their fight against the Sandinista regime there. The obvious illegality of this bizarre scheme led President Reagan to appoint a three-man commission headed by former Republican Senator John Tower of Texas to investigate the matter. Its report was highly critical of the Reagan administration, as was the report of the Select Committee on Secret Military Assistance to Iran and the Nicaraguan Opposition, chaired by Democratic Senator Daniel Inouye of Hawaii. We quote here from the preface and recommendations of the latter document, which officially came out on November 17, 1987.

SOURCE: U.S. Congress, *Report of the Congressional Committees Investigating the Iran-Contra Affair*, Senate Report No. 100–216, 100th Congress, 1st Session, 1987. See pp. xv and 423.

DOCUMENT:

On November 3, 1986, *Al–Shiraa*, a Lebanese weekly, reported that the United States had secretly sold arms to Iran. Subsequent reports claimed that the purpose of the sales was to win the release of American hostages in Lebanon. These reports seemed unbelievable: Few principles of U.S. policy were stated more forcefully by the Reagan Administration than refusing to traffic with terrorists or sell arms to the Government of the Ayatollah Khomeini of Iran.

Although the Administration initially denied the reports, by mid-November it was clear that the accounts were true. The United States had sold arms to Iran and had hoped thereby to gain the release of American hostages in Lebanon. However, even though the Iranians received the arms, just as many Americans remained hostage as before. Three had been freed, but three more had been taken during the period of the sales.

There was still another revelation to come: on November 25 the Attorney General announced that proceeds from the Iran arms sales had been "diverted" to the Nicaraguan resistance at a time when U.S. military aid to the Contras was prohibited.

Iran and Nicaragua—twin thorns of U.S. foreign policy in the 1980s—were thus linked in a credibility crisis that raised serious questions about the adherence of the Administration to the Constitutional processes of Government.

* *

It is the conclusion of these Committees that the Iran–Contra Affair resulted from the failure of individuals to observe the law, not from deficiencies in existing law or in our system of governance. This is an important lesson to be learned from these investigations because it points to the fundamental soundness of our constitutional processes.

Thus, the principal recommendations emerging from the investigation are not for new laws but for a renewal of the commitment to constitutional government and sound processes of decisionmaking.

The President must "take care" that the laws be faithfully executed. This is both a moral and legal responsibility.

Government officials must observe the law, even when they disagree with it.

Decisionmaking processes in foreign policy matters, including covert action, must provide for careful considerations of all options and their consequences. Opposing views must be weighed, not ignored. Unsound processes, in which participants cannot even agree on what was decided (as in the case of the initial Iranian arms sale) produce unsound decisions.

Congress' role in foreign policy must be recognized, not dismissed, if the benefit of its counsel is to be realized and if public support is to be secured and maintained.

The Administration must not lie to Congress about what it is doing. Congress is the partner, not the adversary of the executive branch, in the formulation of policy.

Excessive secrecy in the making of important policy decisions is profoundly antidemocratic and rarely promotes sound policy decisions.

These recommendations are not remarkable. They embody the principles on which this country's success has been based for 200 years. What is remarkable is that they were violated so freely and so repeatedly in the Iran–Contra Affair.

Congress cannot legislate good judgment, honesty, or fidelity to law. But there are some changes in law, particularly relating to oversight of covert operations, that would make our processes function better in the future.

1987 Reagan and Gorbachev Thaw the Cold War

That cold warrior Richard Nixon would visit mainland China in 1972 came as a shock to many students of his career. A decade and a half later, in an equally astonishing development, Ronald Reagan and Mikhail Gorbachev signed the INF treaty on the elimination of

U.S. and Soviet intermediate and shorter range nuclear missiles—only four years after the President had delivered his "evil empire" speech attacking the Communists. The INF treaty won Senatorial approval easily in 1988, 93 to 5. Did its ratification indeed usher in a new, more harmonious era in Soviet–American relations? Is Gorbachev sincere, or is he attempting to give the United States a false sense of security, while Russia pursues world domination? Will he be able to maintain power in the Soviet Union, and to implement his policies of glasnost (openness) and perestroika (the domestic restructuring of Russian society)? As we enter the decade of the 1990s, only time will tell. The following were General Secretary Gorbachev's arrival remarks, delivered in Washington, December 8, 1987.

SOURCE: "Visit of Secretary Gorbachev of the Soviet Union," in Department of State *Bulletin*, February 1988, pp. 2–3.

DOCUMENT:

History has charged the governments of our countries and the two of us, Mr. President, with a solemn duty to justify the hopes of Americans and Soviet people, and of people the world over to undo the logic of the arms race by working together in good faith.

In the world's development much will depend upon the choice that we are to make—upon what is to triumph—fears and prejudice inherited from the cold war and leading to confrontation, or common sense which calls for action to ensure the survival of civilization.

We, in the Soviet Union, have made our choice. We realize that we are divided not only by the oceans, but also by profound historical ideological, socio-economic, and cultural differences. But the wisdom of politics today lies in not using those differences as a pretext for confrontation, enmity, and the arms race.

We are beginning our visit forty-six years after the days when the United States entered the Second World War, and it was in the same days in 1941 that the rout of Nazi forces began near Moscow—that is symbolic. Those days mark the beginning of our common path to victory over the forces of evil, in a war which we fought as allies.

History is thus reminding us both of our opportunities, and of our responsibility. Indeed, the very fact that we are about to sign a treaty eliminating Soviet and U.S. intermediate and shorter range nuclear missiles, which are now going to be scrapped, shows that, at crucial phases in history, our two nations are capable of shouldering their high responsibility.

This will, of course, be the first step down the road leading to a nuclear-free world whose construction you, Mr. President, and I discussed at Reykjavik. Yet it is a great step into the future—the future to which our two peoples and the peoples of all countries aspire.

I have come to Washington with the intention of advancing the next and more important goal of reaching agreement to reduce, by half, strategic offensive arms in the context of a firm guarantee of strategic stability. We are also looking forward to a most serious and frank dialogue on other issues of Soviet–American relations.

Soviet foreign policy today is most intimately linked with *perestroika*—the domestic restructuring of Soviet society. The Soviet people have boldly taken the path of radical reform and development in all spheres—economic, social, political, and intellectual.

Democratization and *glasnost* are the decisive prerequisites for the success of those reforms. They also provide the guarantee that we shall go a long way, and that the course we are pursuing is irreversible. Such is the will of our people.

In charting these ambitious plans, the Soviet people have a vital stake in preserving and strengthening peace everywhere on earth.

May I express the hope that the Soviet Union and the United States, working together with all nations, will take their place in the history of the outgoing twentieth century, not only as allies in the battle against Naziism, but also as nations that have paved mankind's way to a safe world, free from the threat of nuclear annihilation.

On behalf of the Soviet people, I declare that we are prepared to go all the way along our part of the road with the sincerity and responsibility that befit a great and peaceful power.

Proper Name
and Topical Index

Abrams, General, 461
Abd-el-Krim, 292
Acheson, Dean, 372–373, 396–397, 403–405
Act of Bogota (1948), 435
Adams, Brooks, 227
Adams, John, 476
Adoula government, 443
"Again and Again" Speech, 326–327, 456
Algeciras Conference (1906), 234–235
Alliance for Progress, 433, 435
Allies, 258, 263, 331, 348–350, 352, 356, 359, 362, 380–381, 389–390, 395, 405
Al Shiraa, 510
America First, 327, 333
American Bar Association, 400, 458
American Board, 257
American Legion, 328, 491
AMERICA'S RETREAT FROM VICTORY, 372
Anglo-Japanese Alliance (1902), 287
Anti-Ballistic Systems Treaty, 478–479
Arabs, 391–392, 451
Arbenz, Jacobo, 414
arms embargo, 322
Article 10 (X), 277
Article 231, 277
Aswan Dam, 417–418
Atherton, Ray, 306
Atlantic Charter, 333–334, 356
Attlee, Clement, 375, 381
atomic bomb, 373, 411
Austin, Warren, 392
AUTOBIOGRAPHY OF THEODORE ROOSEVELT, 237

Avezerra, Ambassador, 259
aviation gasoline, 334–335
Axis, 307, 336, 347, 366, 389

Baker, Newton, 266
balance of power, 385
Balfour, Arthur, 288
Balfour Declaration, 391–392
Ball, George, 442
Ballantine, Joseph W., 337
Bamboo Curtain, 408
bananas, 222
Bani-Sadr, Abdolhassan, 499
Bankhead, William, 314
Barclay, Arthur J., 297
Baruch, Bernard, 446
Batista, Fulgencio, 437
Battle of the Bulge, 361
Beacon Press, 466
Beaverbrook, Lord, 333
Begin, Menachem, 491–493
Berlin airlift (1948–9), 380–382
Berlin blockade (1948–9), 380–382, 439
Berlin Wall, 444
Bernstorff, Count, 265
Berry, Frank M., 423
Big Four, 277
"Big Stick," 247
bipartisanship, 369–370, 377
Bishop, Maurice, 504–505
Bliss, Tasker J., 278
Blue Book, Argentine, 388
Bonesteel, General, 344
Borah, William E., 282–283, 287, 298, 354

Boisson, General Pierre, 350
Bosch, Juan, 450
Boston *Transcript*, 224–225
Bowers, Claude, 317
Braden, Spruille, 388
Brandt, Willy, 444
Briand, Aristide, 264, 294
Bricker Amendment, 409–410, 481
Bricker, John, 409
Bridges, Styles, 364
brinkmanship, 411–412
Brown, Harold, 489
Bryan, William Jennings, 269
Brzezinski, Zbigniew, 500–502
Buchanan, James, 260
Bullitt, William, 304
Bunker, Ellsworth, 461–462
Burleson, Albert S., 266
Burroughs, Charles R., 424
Butler, Nicholas Murray, 327
Byrnes, James, 360, 362–363

Cabinet, 237–238, 266–267
Cairo Conference (1943), 352, 395
Cambon, Jules, 264
Camp David Accords (1978), 491–493, 501
Canadian election of 1911, 244
Canadian election of 1988, 244
"Captive Peoples" Speech, 408–409
Cárdenas, Lázaro, 341
Carranza, Venustiano, 252–253
Carter Doctrine, 501
Carter, Jimmy, 485–496, 499–502
Casablanca Conference (1943), 356
Castillo government, 389
Castillo Nájera, Don Francisco, 341
Castro, Cipriano, 220
Castro, Fidel, 437–438, 450, 506
Central Intelligence Agency, 437
Central Powers, 269
Chadborn, Daniel J., 253
Chamberlain, Neville, 319–320
Chambers, Whittaker, 362
Chamoun, Camille, 421–422
Chester, Colby M., 240
Chester concession, 240, 244
Chiang Kai-shek, 338, 351–353, 393–395, 477
Chiari, Roberto, 447–448

Chicago *Tribune*, 315, 321, 331, 377, 420
Chinese Exclusion Act (1882), 228
Ching-wei, Wang, 338
Christian Century, 294
Christian Science Monitor, 316
Christopher, Warren, 498–500
Churchill, Winston, 323, 333–334, 356, 358–60, 375, 406–407
Clark, Champ, 244
Clark-Darlan agreement, 350
Clark, J. Reuben, 295–296
Clark Memorandum (1928), 295
Clayton, Will, 378–380
Clemenceau, Georges, 282
coal, 386
Colby, Bainbridge, 259
Cold War, 365, 427, 437, 451–452, 480, 503, 512
Commager, Henry Steele, 457–458
Committee to Defend America by Aiding the Allies, 327–328
Communism, 259, 303, 318, 351, 362, 366–369, 371–372, 376, 378, 382, 393–394, 399, 401, 404–405, 408–409, 413–417, 420–426, 432, 434–435, 442–446, 448–450, 452–455, 459, 461–462, 464, 473–477, 480, 483, 486–487, 489–490, 493, 512
Congress, U.S., 216, 219–220, 223, 247, 253–254, 266, 268–269, 273, 306, 309, 313–314, 316, 322–323, 325–326, 330–332, 335, 339–340, 355, 358, 370, 375–377, 399–400, 409–410, 416–418, 420–423, 433, 435, 439, 442, 453–56, 468–470, 478, 480–483, 489–491, 494, 504, 511
Congressional Record, 400
Constitution, Liberian, 298
Constitution, Mexican, 341
Constitution, U.S., 254, 313–314, 325–326, 330, 363–364, 399–400, 402–403, 409–411, 439, 456, 465, 481–482, 511
Contador Group, 508
containment, 366–369, 375–385, 401
contras, Nicaraguan, 510
Cooke-Zevada Agreement (1942), 341
Coolidge, Calvin, 287, 295
Coral Sea, 484
Costa Carniero, Dr., 346

cotton, 417
Covenant of the League of Nations, 277, 315
Cuban missile crisis (1962), 438–442, 482
Curzon, Lord, 284

Daladier government, 319
Dam, Kenneth, 504–506
Daniels, Josephus, 251, 266
Darlan, Admiral Jean François, 349–351, 357
"A Date Which Will Live in Infamy" Speech, 339–340
Davies, Joseph, 318–320
Davis, Admiral C. H., 235–237
De Gaulle, Charles, 477
Democratic Party, 219, 223–224, 264, 286–287, 313, 355–356, 362, 369–370, 409–410, 420, 431, 442, 445, 448–449, 453, 456, 460, 465, 481, 490
Destroyers-for-bases deal (1940), 323–326
détente, 480–481
Dewey, Admiral George, 220–221
Diaz, Porforio, 249
Diem, Ngo Dinh, 413, 457
Dodd, William E., 317
Dollar Diplomacy, 247
Dolphin, 251
domino theory, 452
Dong, Pham Van, 468–469
Dulles, John Foster, 408–409, 411–412, 417, 458
Dumbarton Oaks, 362

Ebert, President, 279
Economic Cooperation Administration, 396, 398–399
Eden, Sir Anthony, 362
Ehrman, Felix, 217, 218
Eisenhower Doctrine, 420–421
Eisenhower, Dwight, 395, 405–406, 408–410, 413–414, 416, 418–421, 427, 429–430, 435, 437, 454, 457
Election of 1896, 256
Election of 1916, 264
Election of 1920, 283
Election of 1928, 279
Election of 1940, 326, 354, 456
Election of 1944, 354
Election of 1952, 370, 409

Election of 1956, 420
Election of 1960, 431, 433
Election of 1964, 456–457
Election of 1968, 460
Election of 1976, 485–486, 488
Embargo, 322
En-lai, Chou, 393–394, 416, 468–469, 474, 476–477
Entente, 286
Equal commercial opportunity, 387
Estrada, Pedro, 424
European Recovery Program, 378–380
"Evil Empire" Speech, 444, 503–504, 512
executive agreements, 409–410, 481
expropriation, 341–342, 386

Falkner, Roland, 242
Fall, Albert, 264
Farouk, King, 417
Fascists, 357
Feis, Herbert, 301, 303
Figueres, Jose, 435
Fish, Bert, 346–347
Fleming v. Page, 400
Fletcher, Admiral Frank, 251
Flood, Daniel, 490
Ford, Gerald, 470, 481, 483–486, 495
Foreign Affairs, 366–367
A FOREIGN POLICY FOR AMERICANS, 370
Formosa Resolution (1955), 416–417, 420
Fort San Carlos, 220
Four Freedoms, 330, 333
Four Power Treaty (1922), 287
Fourteen Points, 273–274, 282, 333, 357
Franco, Francisco, 347–349
Frankfurter Allgemeine Zeitung, 483
freedom of the seas, 284–285, 508–509
freedom of the skies, 508–509
Fulbright, J. William, 449, 458

Gandhi, Indira, 475
Garner, John Nance, 253
Garrett, Garet, 302
General Act of Algeciras, 234
General Assembly, 360, 392, 395, 429, 475–476
Geneva accords, 452, 454–455, 459, 463
Gentlemen's Agreement (1907), 228–229

George, Walter, 409, 458
Gerard, James, 317
Ghotbzadeh, Sadegh, 499
glasnost, 512–513
Glassboro Conference (1967), 450–451
gold standard, 301–303
Goldwater, Barry, 456
Good Neighbor Policy (1933), 300–301.
    311
Gorbachev, Mikhail, 503, 511–513
Gorton, Prime Minister, 472
Gravel, Mike, 466–468
Great Depression, 303
Great Red Scare, 259
Gregory, Thomas, 266
Grew, Joseph, 335–337
Grey, Edward, 263
Gromyko, Andrei, 451
Gruening, Ernest, 453, 459–460
Guam Doctrine (1969), 472–473
Guantanamo naval base, 440–441, 491
Gulf of Tonkin Resolution (1964), 453–459
Gummeré, 232–234

Hague Court, 220, 338
Hague Covenant of 1907, 325
Hapsburgs, 269, 271
Harding, Warren G., 282, 287
Harriman, Averell, 372, 394, 461–462
Hatfield, Mark, 464
Hay, John, 217–218, 232–234, 256, 299
Hay-Bunau Varilla Treaty (1903), 219
Hay-Pauncefote Treaty (1900), 254
Hayes, Carlton J. H., 317, 347
"He kept us out of war," 264
Hearst, William Randolph, 237, 254, 285,
    315
Heath, Edward, 477
Helms, Jesse, 490
Helsinki Agreements (1975), 485–486
Herrick, Ambassador, 294
Herzl, Theodore, 391
Hirohito, Emperor, 389
Hiss, Alger, 362–363
Hitler, Adolf, 307–308, 318–319, 325, 333,
    347, 356–357, 367
Hohenzollerns, 269, 271
Holocaust, 391
Holt, 484

Hopkins, Harry, 362–363
Hoover, Herbert, 279, 287, 298, 300
House, Edward M., 263–264, 278
House-Grey Memorandum, 263–264
House of Representatives, U.S., 226, 243,
    254, 271, 313, 322, 331, 375, 378, 395,
    401–402, 410, 416–417, 420, 435, 448,
    453–455, 479, 481
Houston, David H., 266
Howard, Roy, 328
Howe, Louis, 302
Hudson proposals, 320
Huerta, Victoriano, 249, 251–252, 259
Hughes, Charles Evans, 264, 287, 289,
    299, 400
Hull, Cordell, 300, 302, 305, 324, 336–338,
    341, 360
human rights, 486–488, 505
Humphrey, Hubert, 460
Hurley, Patrick J., 351
hyphenated Americans, 280

"I Hate War" Speech, 311
"Ich Bin Ein Berliner" Speech, 444–445
Idris, King, 508
Immigration Act of 1907, 228
India-Pakistan War (1971), 473–474, 481
INF treaty, 511–512
Inouye Committee, 510–511
Inouye, Daniel, 510
International Court of Justice, 451, 499
International Monetary Fund, 430
Iran-Contra Affair, 510–511
Iranian hostage crisis, 498–500
Iran-Iraq War, 499
Iron Curtain, 408, 444, 485
"Irreconcilables," 282
Ishii, Viscount, 258
isolationism, 277, 283, 285, 311, 314–315,
    317, 322, 333, 355, 363, 369, 377
Italo-Ethiopian War (1935), 305–307

Jackson, Henry M., 481
Japanese and Korean Exclusion League,
    226
Japanese Exclusion Act (1924), 228
Japanese peace treaty (1951), 390
Japanese Red Cross, 227
Jefferson, Thomas, 325

Jersey Standard, 289
Jews, 317, 348, 391–392, 451
Johnson Act (1934), 328
Johnson, Charles, 297
Johnson, Hiram, 282–283, 354, 363
Johnson, Lyndon, 447–451, 453, 456–457, 460–462

Kellogg-Briand Pact (1928), 294–295, 298–299
Kellogg, Frank, 294–295, 315
Kennan, George, 366–369
Kennedy, John, 431–442, 444–449, 452–453
Kennedy, Joseph, 323, 328, 431
Kennedy, Robert, 440–442
Kerensky, Alexander, 303
Keynes, John Maynard, 279
Khmer Rouge, 484
Khomeini, Ayatollah Rutollah, 498–499, 510
Khrushchev, Nikita, 425–427, 438, 440, 450
Kissinger Commission, 506–508
Kissinger, Henry, 468–471, 474–475, 478, 480–481, 484, 487, 500, 502
Kitchen, Claude, 270
Kitchen Conference, 426
Knight, John S., 457–459
Knight newspapers, 457–459
Knowland, William, 410
Knox, Philander Chase, 240, 247
Konoye, Prince, 335–336
Korean War (1950–3), 372, 396, 398–407, 472
Korusu, Saburo, 337–338
Kosygin, Aleksei, 450–451

LaFollette, Robert Sr., 271
Lane, Franklin, 266
Langer, William, 309, 363, 416
Lansing, Robert, 256, 258–259, 266, 278
Lansing-Ishii Agreement, 258
Lattimore, Owen, 373
Lazo, Mario, 490
League of Nations, 277–278, 280, 282–283, 285–286, 297–298, 306–309, 311, 315–316, 319, 354, 356
Leahy, Admiral, 372
Lehman, Herbert, 416
lend lease, 305, 331–333, 352

Lenin, 367, 503–504
Life, 411
Literary Digest, 293
Litvinov, Maxim, 304–305, 319
Lloyd George, David, 280, 282
Lodge Corollary (1912), 246
Lodge, Henry Cabot, 226, 246, 281–282
Loftus, John, 386
London Economic Conference (1933), 301, 303, 355–356
Long, Breckenridge, 306
Loomis, William, 217–218
Los Angeles *Times*, 316
Louisiana Purchase, 324–325
Louisville *Courier Journal*, 269
Lovett, Robert, 392
Ludlow Amendment, 313–314
Ludlow, Louis, 313
Lumumba, Patrice, 442
Lusitania, 262, 264, 270

MacArthur, Douglas, 372, 389–391, 401–405
Madero, Francisco, 249–250
Madison, James, 268
Mahan, Alfred T., 281, 491
"Making the world safe for democracy," 282
mandates, 392
Marshall, George C., 327, 372–373, 378–380, 393–394
Marshall Plan (1947), 378–380, 435
Martin, John Bartlow, 448–450
Martin, Joseph, 401–402, 404
Marxism-Leninism, 365, 394, 437, 503, 506–508
Maxwell, Colonel R. L., 335
Mayaguez, 483–484
Mayo, Admiral Henry, 251–252
McAdoo, William G., 266
McCarthy, Joseph, 372
McCormick, Robert R., 315
McGovern, George, 454, 464–465
McGovern-Hatfield Amendment, 464–466
McNamara, Robert, 441, 451
Mexican War, 219
Mikoyan, 426
Millspaugh, Arthur, 290–291
Milwaukee *Journal*, 316

Molotov, Vyacheslav, 381–382
Monroe Doctrine (1823), 220, 223, 225, 246, 285–286, 295–296, 407
Moore, John Bassett, 222
Moral Diplomacy, 249
Morgan, John T., 219
Morgenthau, Jr., Henry, 302, 304, 334, 359
Morgenthau, Sr., Henry, 256–257
Morgenthau Plan, 359
Morse, Wayne, 410, 416, 453
most-favored nation treatment, 387–388
Muccio, John J., 398–399
munition makers, 309–310
Murphy, Robert, 349
Mussolini, Benito, 306–308, 325, 347–348
Mutual Defense Treaty with China (1955), 417
Mutual Security Act (1954), 421, 423

Napoleon Bonaparte, 325, 367
Napoleonic Wars, 322
Nashville, 216, 218
Nasser, Gamal, 417–421
National Association of Evangelicals, 503
national interest philosophy, 486
Nationalists, Chinese, 351, 362, 393–395, 416
Nazis, 317–318, 357, 389, 391, 512–513
Nelson, Gaylord, 458
neo-isolationism, 370, 384
neutrality legislation, 309, 311, 322–323, 328
New Deal, 279, 302, 331, 390
New York *Evening Journal*, 285
New York *Herald Tribune*, 294
New York *Sun*, 225, 293
New York *Times*, 219, 262, 324, 437, 466, 468
New York *Tribune*, 234
New York *World*, 225
Newsweek, 324
Nimitz, Admiral, 372
Nine Power Treaty (1922), 287, 298–299, 315
Nineteenth Century, 235
Nixon, Richard, 423–427, 460, 462–464, 466, 468–469, 472–483, 488, 493, 495, 502, 511
Noble, Harold J., 398–399

Nogues, 350
Nomuru, Kichisaburo, 337–338
Nonintercourse Acts, 322
North Atlantic Treaty Organization (NATO), 384–385, 429, 431, 502
Notre Dame address, 486
Nuclear Test Ban Treaty, 445–446
nuclear freeze, 504
Nye Committee, 309
Nye, Gerald, 309

"Old Soldiers Never Die" Speech
ONE WORLD, 354
Open Door Policy, 230, 258–259, 287–288, 299, 387–388, 395
open skies proposal, 428
Operation Vittles, 381
Organization of American States, 415–416, 432, 436, 438–440, 496–497, 506
Organization of Eastern Caribbean States, 504–505
Ortega, Daniel, 506
Outlook, 227
OVERTAKEN BY EVENTS, 448

Page, Walter Hines, 272
Panama Canal, 216, 219, 239, 244, 254, 256, 418–419, 439, 447, 491, 508
Panama Canal Treaties, 488–491, 501
Panamanian Riots (1964), 488
partition of Palestine, 391–392
Passos e Sousa, General, 346
Payne-Aldrich Tariff (1909), 243
Peace Corps, 433–434, 436
PENTAGON PAPERS, 466–468
Perdicaris, Ion, 232–233
perestroika, 512–513
Pérez Jiménez, Marcos, 423–424
Perkins, Frances, 357
Perón, Juan, 388, 424
Pershing, John J., 253
petroleum, 222–223, 240, 289–290, 306, 334, 338, 341, 357, 366, 386–388, 392, 498
Philadelphia *Press*, 224
Phillips, William, 289, 304, 307
"picture brides," 228
Pittsburgh *Post*, 293
Pittsburgh *Press*, 224

Point IV, 382–383
Polk, James K., 219
Potsdam Conference (1945), 371, 378, 381, 394–395
Powers, Francis Gary, 427, 437
Pramoj, Kukrit, 484

Qaddafi, Muammar al, 508
Quarantine Speech, 314–316, 377–378
Quebec Conference (1944), 359

Radio Free Europe, 486
Raisuli, 232–233
Rankin, Jeanette, 270, 339
Reagan, Ronald, 478, 498, 500, 503–504, 506, 508, 510–512
Redfield, William, 266
Reid, Whitelaw, 234
Republican Party, 279, 282, 303, 313, 328, 354–356, 362, 369–370, 377, 379, 382, 384, 396, 401, 409–410, 433, 435, 445, 456, 465, 481, 490
"Reservationists," 282
Rhee, Syngman, 405–406
Ridgway, General Matthew, 403–404
Riffs, 292–294
Rio nonaggression treaty, 416, 439–440
Rogers, William, 475–476, 478
Roosevelt Corollary (1904), 223, 295–296
Roosevelt, Eleanor, 302
Roosevelt, Franklin D., 300–307, 311–312, 314–317, 321–326, 329–336, 339–340, 349–352, 354, 356–362, 373, 378, 409, 456
Roosevelt, Theodore, 216–217, 219–220, 222–224, 226, 228, 233–234, 237, 242, 247, 255–256, 264, 274, 282, 295
Root, Elihu, 230, 327
Root-Takahira Agreement (1908), 230
Ross, Charles, 393
Rusk, Dean, 451, 458
Russo-Japanese War (1904–5), 226

Sadat, Anwar el, 491–493, 501
St. Louis *Globe-Democrat*, 225
St. Louis *Post-Dispatch*, 324
Sale, George, 242
Salinger, Pierre, 448
Salisbury, Harrison, 468

Salisbury, Lord, 296
SALT I, 478, 481, 502
SALT II, 500–502
San Francisco Board of Education, 227–228
San Francisco *Chronicle*, 316
Sandinistas, 496, 506–508
Scali, John, 484
Schmidt, Helmut, 501
Scott, Emmett, 242
Scowcroft, Brent, 483
Secret Service, 424
Security Council, 376, 391, 421, 427, 440, 458, 476, 499, 508–509
Selassie, Haile, 306
Selective Service, 327
Senate, U.S., 223, 226, 229–230, 234, 242–243, 246, 254–255, 271, 278, 280, 282–284, 287, 294, 322, 325, 331, 363–364, 369, 374–375, 378, 382, 384, 403, 409–410, 416–417, 420, 431, 433, 435, 445, 453–455, 458, 465–466, 478–481, 489–490, 512
Serrano Suner, 348
Shah of Iran, 290, 292, 498–499, 501
Shanghai Communique (1972), 494–495
Sheehan, Neil, 466
Shepley, James R., 411
Sherwood, Robert E., 356
Shinto, 389
Shipstead, Henrik, 363
Shuster, W. Morgan, 245–246, 290
SIX CRISES, 423
Smith, Walter Bedell, 380–382
Smuts, Jan C., 279–280
Somoza, Anastasio, 496, 506–507
Sonnenfeldt document, 486
Sorenson, Theodore, 444
South Manchurian railroad, 298
Southeast Asia Treaty Organization (SEATO), 454–458, 474
Soviet-German Alliance (1939), 318
Spanish-American War (1898), 237, 285
Spanish Civil War, 347
spheres of influence (interest), 287–288, 395
Springfield *Republican*, 225
Stalin, Joseph, 318, 320, 325, 357–361, 371, 381–382, 408–409

Sternberg, Speck von, 234
Stettinius, Edward, 360, 362–363
Stevenson, Adlai, 420, 440–442
Stilwell, Joseph W., 351–353
Stimson Doctrine (1932), 298, 338
Stimson, Henry, 295, 297–298, 327, 334
Strang mission, 319
Strategic Defense Initiative, 478
Straus, Oscar, 240
submarine warfare, 265, 268, 309
Suez Canal, 418–420, 481
sugar, 222
Supreme Court, 400
Swettenham, Sir Alexander, 235–237

Taft, Robert A., 370, 379, 384–385
Taft, William Howard, 240, 244, 247, 249,
    254, 400
Takahira, Ambassador, 230
Taney, Roger, 400
Teheran Conference (1943), 357, 371, 378
Teng, Vice Premier, 495
Teutonic Menace Hypothesis, 268, 309
Thayer, William R., 220
THE SENATE AND THE LEAGUE OF
    NATIONS, 282
Thieu, Nguyen Van, 460–462, 471
Third World, 382
"To Hell with the Hohenzollerns and the
    Hapsburgs," 269
Torrijos, Omar, 490
Tower, John, 510
Treaty of Versailles (1919), 277–282, 321,
    363
Tribune Popular, 425
Triple Alliance, 286
Trujillo, Rafael, 448–449
Truman Doctrine (1947), 368–369, 375,
    377, 422, 485
Truman, Harry, 360, 365, 368–370, 372,
    375, 377–378, 380–382, 386, 391–396,
    401–404, 406, 409
trusteeship principle, 392
Tse-tung, Mao, 393, 477
Tshombe, Moise, 442–443
Twenty-One Demands (1915), 258
Two Chinas policy, 475

U-2 incident, 427–428

unconditional surrender, 356–357
Union and Progress committee, 258
United Fruit Company, 414
United Nations, 360–361, 369–372, 376,
    378, 383–384, 389, 391–392, 395, 401,
    404–406, 409, 416–417, 419, 421, 427,
    429–430, 442, 446, 450, 453, 456, 458–
    459, 475–476, 483, 499
United Nations Charter (1945), 309, 363–
    364, 366, 399, 421–422, 439–440, 443,
    455–456, 458, 508, 510
United States v. Sweeney, 400

Van Fleet, James, 406–407
Vance, Cyrus, 461–462, 492, 496–497
Vandenberg, Sr., Arthur, 322, 369–370, 412
Venezuelan debt crisis (1902–3), 220–221,
    234
Versailles Conference (1919), 277–279, 284
Vichy regime, 349–351
Viet Cong, 459, 467
Viet Minh, 467
Vietnam War, 366, 413, 450, 452–471, 481,
    487
Vietnamization, 472
Villa, Pancho, 252–253
Vincent, John Carter, 373

Waldheim, Kurt, 484, 499
Wall Street Journal, 315–316
Wallace, Henry, 365, 377
Walters, Barbara, 470–471
Walters, Vernon, 508
war guilt clause, 277
War of 1812, 322
War Powers Resolution (1973), 469
Warren, Charles, 302
Warsaw Pact, 481–483, 485
Washington Disarmament Conference
    (1921–2), 287, 299, 311, 338
Watergate scandal, 469–470
Watterson, Henry, 269
Wedemeyer, General, 373, 394
Welles, Sumner, 300
West Bank settlements, 493
Wheeler, Burton K., 331, 363
Wheelus Field, 508
Wherry, Kenneth, 384
White, Henry, 234, 278

White, William Allen, 327–328
Wilhelm, Kaiser, 234–235
Willkie, Wendell, 328, 354
Wilson, Henry Lane, 249
Wilson, William, 266
Wilson, Woodrow, 249–251, 253–255, 259,
  263–264, 266, 268, 271–273, 278–283,
  285, 289, 303, 325, 330, 333, 354–355,
  357, 487
wolfram, 347–348
World Bank, 418, 430
World Court, 283
World War I, 256, 262–276, 278, 290, 309,
  317, 323, 330–332, 339, 345, 355, 386, 390

World War II, 277, 317–318, 326, 328, 330–
  331, 334, 343, 345, 347, 350–351, 354,
  369–371, 375, 378, 380, 386–389, 399,
  423, 431, 453, 480, 485, 491, 512

**Yalta Conference (1945), 360–363, 371–
  372, 378**

Zaragoza, Morelos, 251–252
Zimmerman, Arthur, 265
Zimmerman Telegram (1917), 265
Zionism, 391
Zulus, 413

Geographical
Index

Adowa, 305, 413
Afghanistan, 500–502
Africa, 242, 306, 321–322, 350, 354, 362, 429–430, 432, 437, 442–443, 476, 488, 501
Albania, 376
Aleutians, 396
Algeciras, 234–235
Algeria, 348–351, 431, 460, 499–500
Alsace-Lorraine, 263, 275
Antigua, 323
Arabian Sea, 498
Argentina, 225, 388–389
Armenia, 256–258, 260
Asia, 281, 321–322, 365, 371, 373, 396, 401, 404, 406, 432, 452–457, 472–473, 475, 483, 494–495, 498
Aswan, 417–418, 420
Australia, 396, 457–458, 472
Austria, 281, 359, 453
Austria-Hungary, 275, 331
Azerbaijan, 260
Azores, 345–347

Bahamas, 323
Baja California, 246
Balearic Islands, 348
Balkan States, 286, 319
Baltic States, 260, 275, 320
Bangkok, 484
Bangladesh, 474
Barbados, 505
Barcelona, 349
Beirut, 422

Belgium, 263–264, 268, 274–275, 294, 320, 384, 406, 442
Berlin, 270, 316–317, 380–382, 432, 444–445, 482
Bermuda, 323, 325
Bogota, 424
Bolivia, 386–387
Bonn, 499
Brazil, 225, 432
British Guiana, 323
Bulgaria, 281, 376, 378
Burma, 351–352

Cairo, 352, 395, 422
Cambodia, 452, 462–464, 471, 483–484
Canada, 243–244, 284, 384
Canal Zone, 219–220, 447–448, 489–491
Caracas, 414, 423–425
Caribbean Sea, 235–236, 326, 439, 491, 505–506
Casablanca, 356–357
Central America, 220, 300–301, 414, 436, 439, 496–497, 506–508
Chamizal, 250
Chile, 225, 317, 436
China, 226, 230–231, 258–259, 285, 287–288, 298–299, 314, 336–338, 351–354, 357, 360–362, 367, 369–371, 373, 393–395, 401, 403–404, 407, 409, 416–417, 423, 432, 468–469, 473–478, 480, 483–484, 493–496, 500–501, 511
Chunking, 352
Cienfuegos, 481

Colombia, 216–217, 219–220, 255–256, 301, 406, 424
Colon, 218, 447, 491
Congo, 429–430, 442–443, 482
Constantinople, 241, 257–258
Costa Rica, 507–508
Crimea, 360–362
Cuba, 213, 296, 300–301, 435, 437–442, 446, 448, 482, 497, 501, 505–507
Czechoslovakia, 295, 319, 423, 486

Dakar, 350
Danzig, 321
Dardanelles, 258, 275
Denmark, 320, 325, 343, 384
Dienbienphu, 305, 413, 457
Djambi, 290
Dominican Republic, 222–225, 296, 301, 448–450

Ecuador, 424
Egypt, 240, 284–285, 382, 417–419, 421, 488, 491–492
Eire, 345
Ethiopia, 305–307, 406, 413, 418
Europe, 220, 224–225, 235, 238, 262–263, 265, 268, 270, 278–279, 281, 283–286, 293–294, 296, 317–318, 320–322, 326, 328, 347–348, 355, 358, 360–361, 364–371, 373, 378–380, 384–385, 401, 406, 409, 411, 429, 432, 434, 442, 445, 477, 480, 485–486, 499, 501, 507

Far East, 230–231, 247, 258, 298–299, 334, 354, 360–361, 374, 396, 411
Fernando Po, 297
Formosa, 390, 394–396, 401, 405, 412, 417
France, 223, 234–235, 241–242, 250, 258, 263, 270–271, 275, 283, 285, 287, 292–294, 303, 307, 309, 311, 318, 320–322, 326, 348–350, 354–357, 361, 364–365, 378, 380–381, 384, 406, 413, 419, 452, 457–458, 460, 469, 472, 483, 486

Geneva, 292, 306, 311, 316, 318, 413, 427, 445, 452, 455, 504
Georgia (Soviet state), 260

Germany, 220–221, 223, 227, 234–235, 238, 240–242, 250, 258, 262–273, 277, 279–281, 294, 303, 305, 307–309, 314, 317–322, 325, 333, 339, 346–349, 354–357, 359–361, 371, 373, 376, 380–382, 387–389, 408, 432, 444–445, 477, 499, 501
Gibraltar, 348
Glassboro, 450–451
Great Britain, 220–221, 228, 234–238, 241–242, 244–245, 250, 255, 258, 262–268, 270–273, 279–280, 283–285, 287, 294–295, 303, 306–309, 311, 318, 320–323, 325–326, 328–329, 331–333, 341, 343–344, 350, 354, 356, 359–360, 362, 364–366, 369, 375–377, 380–381, 384–386, 391–392, 395, 406, 413, 418–419, 426, 446, 453, 457–459, 472, 483
Great Plains, 244
Greece, 368–370, 373, 375–378, 406, 422, 485, 487, 502
Greenland, 343
Grenada, 504–506
Guam, 339, 472–473
Guatemala, 414–416, 435
Gulf of Aqaba, 451
Gulf of Sidra, 508–509

Haipong, 480
Haiti, 296, 301
Hanoi, 461–462, 468–470, 480
Havana, 236
Hawaii, 229, 335, 339, 473
Helsinki, 485–486
Hong Kong, 339
Honolulu, 339
Hudson Bay, 439
Hungary, 281, 348, 486

Iceland, 292, 343–345, 384
Inchon, 404
India, 284–285, 295, 363, 382, 426, 473–475, 481, 487
Indian Ocean, 501
Indochina, French, 336–338, 409, 412–413, 423, 452, 462, 469, 473–474
Iran, 290, 357, 420, 498–501, 510–511
Iraq, 386–387, 420–422, 499

Ireland, 262, 264, 268, 280, 295
Ishandhlwana, 413
Israel, 391–393, 419, 432, 451, 483, 488, 491–493, 501
Italy, 220, 223, 238, 250, 258–259, 275, 295, 305–308, 321, 325, 339, 347–348, 356–357, 378, 384, 413, 441, 486

Jamaica, 235–237, 323, 505
Japan, 221–226, 237–238, 246–247, 258–259, 265, 287, 295, 298–299, 303, 305, 314, 321, 326, 333–340, 349, 351, 356–357, 360–361, 369, 371, 387, 389–391, 395–396, 405–406, 408, 432, 477
Java, 363
Jerusalem, 491–493
Jordan, 421–422, 481–482, 488

Katanga, 442–443
Kiaochow, 221
Kingston, 235–236
Korea, 363, 372–373, 390, 396, 398–408, 423, 443, 472–473, 477
Kuriles, 360

Laos, 437, 443, 452–454, 462
Latin America, 220, 225, 246–247, 295–296, 300, 348, 354, 366, 369, 387, 415, 423–424, 432, 434–437, 448, 475, 489–491, 501
Lebanon, 421–423, 510
Leningrad, 451
Liberia, 241–243, 297–298
Libya, 507–510
Lima, 424–425, 439
Lisbon, 345
Lithuania, 260
London, 264, 316, 379–380, 382, 487
Low Countries, 270, 348
Luxembourg, 384

Madrid, 349
Magdalena Bay, 246–247
Malaya, 339
Malta, 362
Managua, 496, 507

Manchuria, 230, 298–299, 361, 371, 373, 390, 394
Marrakech, 362
Mediterranean Sea, 232, 268, 308, 375, 491
Mesopotamia, 284, 386–387
Mexico, 220, 246–247, 249–253, 259, 264–265, 341–343, 386–387
Mexico City, 439
Middle East (Near East), 240, 244, 260, 308, 354, 366, 377, 387, 391, 420–423, 432, 451, 474, 481–483, 488, 498, 500–501, 508
Middle West, 244, 255, 271, 331
Midway Island, 340
Monrovia, 242
Montenegro, 275
Morocco, 232–235, 292–294, 348, 350, 356
Moscow, 305, 319, 373, 380, 425, 427, 432, 445, 478–481, 512
Moselle River, 270, 359
Mukden, 394
Munich, 319

Naples, 362
Netherlands, 289–290, 320, 334, 384, 406, 472
Netherlands East Indies, 289–290, 334, 386–387
New Granada, 219
New Zealand, 457–458
Newfoundland, 323, 325, 333, 356
Nicaragua, 219–220, 296, 423, 496–497, 506–508, 510–511
Nile River, 417–418
North Africa, 348–350
North Central States, 384
North Sea, 262, 271–272
Norway, 384

Oahu, 339
Ottoman Empire, 275

Pacific Coast, 226, 246, 271, 280
Pakistan, 420, 457–458, 473–475, 481
Palestine, 391–392
Panama, 216–220, 238, 243, 254–256, 301, 419, 446–448, 488–491

Panama City, 217, 447
Paris, 260, 264, 278–281, 316, 378–379, 428, 461–462, 470–471, 484, 499
Parrot's Beak, 464
Pearl Harbor, 326, 334–335, 339, 427
Peking, 407, 474, 477, 484
Persia, 244, 284–285, 290–292
Persian Gulf, 498, 501
Pescadores Islands, 416–417
Philippines, 243, 328, 339, 396–397, 406, 457–458, 473, 484
Phnom Penh, 463
Poland, 275, 277, 295, 318, 321–322, 327, 360, 363, 378, 485–486, 501
Ponta Delgada, 345–347
Portugal, 345, 384, 487
Potsdam, 371, 378, 394–395
Prussia, 275, 359
Puerto Rico, 221, 491
Pusan, 404
Pyrenees, 347–348

Quemoy, 416

Reykjavik, 344–345, 512
Rhine River, 270, 359
Rhineland, 314, 360, 369
Rocky Mountains, 280
Rome, 308, 316–317
Ruhr, 359–360, 379
Rumania, 275, 378, 486
Russia, 228, 244–246, 257–258, 260, 263, 266–267, 271, 274–275, 304–305, 318–320, 325, 357–358, 361, 365–368, 373–374, 377–378, 381, 384–385, 393, 408–409, 426–427, 432, 437–438, 441, 480–481, 485–486, 512
Ryukyu Islands, 396

Saar, 359
Saigon, 457, 461–462, 464, 469
St. Lucia, 323
Santa Maria, 345
Santo Domingo, 224, 243
São Miguel, 346–347
Saudi Arabia, 420
Scandinavia, 309
Scotland, 272
Seoul, 399

Serbia, 270, 275
Shanghai, 299
Shantung, 287
Siberia, 305
Sicily, 356
Silesia, 359
South, 228, 287, 331, 382, 417
South Africa, 279, 500
South America, 220–221, 225, 271, 300–301, 424–425, 436
Soviet Union, 259–261, 303–305, 318–320, 333, 354, 357, 360–361, 365, 367–371, 373–375, 377–378, 380–382, 384, 399, 401, 404, 408–409, 414–416, 419, 422, 425–428, 437–441, 443–446, 450–451, 469, 471, 473–475, 477–481, 485–488, 491, 500–505, 507, 511–513
Spain, 234, 246, 250, 252, 292–293, 297, 317, 345, 347–349, 373
Stanleyville, 443
Stuttgart, 349
Sudan, 418
Sweden, 345
Switzerland, 345, 349
Syria, 285, 421–422, 488

Taiwan, 395–396, 416, 475, 477, 494–495
Tampico, 251–252
Tangier, 232–234, 293, 348
Teheran, 245, 357–358, 371, 378, 498, 506
Thailand, 406, 457–458, 483–484
Tokyo, 317, 338, 405
Trinidad, 323
Turkey, 240–241, 256–258, 275, 281, 345, 368–370, 373, 375–378, 406, 420, 441, 485, 502

Uganda, 418

Venezuela, 220–221, 234, 301, 414, 423–425
Versailles, 277, 279
Vienna, 501
Vietnam, 366, 413–414, 450, 452–474, 477, 480–481, 483, 487
Virgin Islands, 325

Wake Island, 340
West, 228, 255, 313